THE RELIGIOUS PILGRIMAGE OF ISRAEL

The
Religious Pilgrimage
of Israel

I. G. MATTHEWS

*Professor Emeritus of Old Testament
Literature and Exegesis
Crozer Theological Seminary,
Chester, Pennsylvania*

HARPER & BROTHERS PUBLISHERS

NEW YORK AND LONDON

THE RELIGIOUS PILGRIMAGE OF ISRAEL

Contents

FOREWORD xi

I. INTRODUCTION: THE MEANING OF RELIGION ... 1–6

Religion in general. Definitions. Universal; an experimental, vital process.
Religion in Israel, in particular. A social phenomenon; obscured by interpretations and translations. To be understood in its Oriental background.

II. THE RELIGION OF THE SEMINOMADS ... 7–40

Ancestry and background.
Economic and social conditions.
Organization. Kinship and blood revenge.
Mental characteristics.
Primitive philosophy.
Religious ideas and practices.

III. THE RELIGION OF THE SINAI CONFEDERATES.
1250 B.C. ... 41–70

The shepherd clans in Goshen. Geography and history.
Moses the deliverer. Legends. Kenite and Egyptian influence. A Levite?
Sinai an ancient sanctuary. Tribes that joined the union.
The process of assimilation.
Yahweh and the covenant. The name and the essential features. Pledges and rites.
Yahweh: absolute, kindly, mobile, moral, and jealous.
A final episode.

IV. THE RELIGION OF THE CANAANITES. 1250 B.C. ... 71–80

The population of Canaan.
Racial origins mixed.
Culture complex, of a high order.

v

The religion of the Canaanites.
Ancient and complex.
Cult of the Dead fundamental.
Continuity of life basic.
Community welfare primary.
Fertility rites; worship of Baal and Baalat.
The legends and mythology.

V. THE RELIGION OF THE INVADERS. 1250–1030 B.C.   81–92

Kinship of the two people. Ancestry, customs, language, philosophy.
Cultural differences.
Adjustments over two centuries.
Warfare; alliances; intermarriages.
Yahweh becomes a war-God. Compensations.
Yahweh an agricultural God and a God of commerce. Baalism assimilated.
Yahwism preserved essential human rights, parental authority, loyalty to the covenant.

VI. THE RELIGION OF NATIONALISM. 1030–931 B.C.   93–108

The kingship established.
Desire for freedom produced leaders.
The kings and their achievements.
Pattern of the kingship. Deification? Priest-king the vicegerent of Yahweh.
The temple erected and dedicated.
A royal sanctuary. Rites developed.
Symbols borrowed from neighbors.
Religion of Yahweh greatly enriched.

VII. THE RELIGION OF THE REACTIONARIES.
931–830 B.C.   109–119

Revolution in the North. Jeroboam, Elijah, and Jehu. Nationalism and internationalism opposed.
Elijah attacks Tyrian Baalism.
Yahweh a rain-God, at Carmel; sanctions international intrigue at Horeb.
Jehu anointed, massacres the Omri-Ahab dynasty and the Baal priests.
Blood bath the proof of loyalty to Yahweh.
Reformation in the South.
Activities of Asa, Jehoshaphat, and Joash.
Literary propaganda. J. document, seminomadic. Claims to Palestine.
A ritual Code.

VIII. THE RELIGION OF THE LAYMEN. 763–700 B.C.   120–132

National prosperity and lavish ritual.

Laymen become preachers. Amos, 763, Hosea, 740, Micah, 720–700,
and Isaiah, 740–700 B.C.

Destructive critics of society, business, government, and religion. Ruin
certain because of sins of the ruling classes. The will of Yahweh is
equivalent to human rights.

Revelation comes through normal channels, rather than through
ecstasy, visions, oracles.

Written messages of these prophets a guide to their disciples. Abiding values.

IX. THE RELIGION OF CO-OPERATION. DEUTERONOMY.

621 B.C.   133–143

The Assyrian rule, 686–608 B.C.

Yahwism overshadowed.

Composition of Deuteronomy, the book of the law. Anti-Assyrians,
priests, and prophets unite under pressure. Co-operation and compromise. Isolation and education.

The nation pledged to keep all the words of the law. A blood purge.

Literary activity. Values and limitations.

X. THE RELIGION OF INDIVIDUALISM. JEREMIAH AND
     EZEKIEL, 626–570 B.C.   144–167

Jeremiah a disciple of the eighth-century prophets 626–621 B.C. Inner
struggle. Message.

Jeremiah joins the reform of 621 B.C.

Personal experiences.

He rethinks his message; denounces temple worship and the book of
the law, 608 B.C. Heresy trial. First edition of his book in 603 B.C.

Captivities 597, 586 B.C.

Jeremiah in Egypt. The new covenant.

The law written in the heart.

Ezekiel, disciple of Jeremiah, 593–570 B.C.

XI. THE RELIGION OF THE INTELLECTUALS.
     550–100 B.C.   168–181

Problem of a supreme Deity. Origins and implications. Isa. 40:1–55:13.

Job 3:1–42:6.

Problem of human suffering. Servant Songs. Job 1:1–2:13; 42:7–17.

Isa. 42:1–4; 49:1–6; 5:4–9; 52:13–53:12.

Problem, What is Wisdom? Four views.

Ben Sirach 24:1–34; Prov. 8:1–9:6; Job 28:1–27; Wisd. of Solomon 7:1–8:36.

XIII. THE RELIGION OF THE STATE-CHURCH.
    550–400 B.C.   182–205
Radically different from the prophets.
Program, language, and outlook.
Holiness Code (Lev. 17:1–26:46), 550 B.C.
Ceremonial practices and prosperity.
Temple vision (Ezek. 40–48), 500 B.C.
National reorganization to attain prosperity.
Priest Code. 400 B.C.
Cleansing required for everything.
Water, blood, incense, and fire offerings are effective.
The chosen people. Responsibilities.

XIII. THE RELIGION OF MANKIND. 500–100 B.C.   206–216
The homely virtues.
The Jew in business, and at home.
The Jew under the influence of Greek culture.
Universal brotherhood of man. Legalism, racialism, and sacerdotalism
rejected. Ruth; Jonah. Isa. 56:1–8; 66:21; 19:19–25.

XIV. THE RELIGION OF SUPERNATURALISM.
    350 B.C.–A.D. 135   217–232
Messianism. The hope of the kingdom.
Apocalypticism.
Origin and background, court prophets.
Armageddon. Day of Yahweh.
Literature. Isa. 13:1–14:32; 24:1–23; 25:6–8; 26:20–27; 1, 12, 13;
Zeph. Joel. Daniel.
Characteristics; anonymous, pseudepigraphic, pessimistic, catastrophic.
Meaning unfolded in symbols.
Values.

XV. THE RELIGION OF JUDAISM. 400 B.C.–A.D. 135   233–268
The Jew in the homeland. 400–141 B.C.
  Ruled by Persia, Greece, Egypt, Syria.
  Insurrections; deportations.
  City life the norm. Hellenism and reactions therefrom.
  Wealth accumulated by leaders.
  Literary activity. I and II Chronicles, Ezra, Nehemiah. Septuagint.
  Ben Sirach. Psalms.

Organization of Levitical order.

Music. Scribal activity. Ritual.

The Second Jewish Commonwealth. 141–63 B.C.

The Maccabean revolt.

Freedom of religion established.

National ambitions aroused.

Independence granted. Conflicts within and without. Sanhedrin.

The Jew under Rome. 63 B.C.–A.D. 135.

Struggle for self-government. Problems of taxes and images. Rebellions and tragedy. Jerusalem destroyed in A.D. 73, wiped out in A.D. 135.

The Jew among the nations. 500 B.C.–A.D. 135.

Dispersion. More than 300 colonies, with some 4,000,000 people within the Roman Empire. Isolated, yet adopting the customs of the Gentiles. United to Jewry and Jerusalem by synagogue, worship, education.

After A.D. 70 the Torah, interpreted by the rabbinic schools and the teachers, remained.

Judaism, by the forces of history liberated from nation, land, and temple, a religion that emphasized a way of life.

APPENDICES

Abbreviations   271

Selected Bibliography   273

Index of Subjects   281

Index of Scripture Passages   289

Foreword

The Hebrew Scriptures have preserved for us the religious experiences, struggles, and ideals of an otherwise insignificant people, over a period of a thousand years. In miniature, here are found striking parallels to the attitudes and reactions, the programs and conclusions, that prevail everywhere in religion. Hostile class interests each resting on ancestry, power, prestige, or need, each claiming divine sanctions, stood arrayed against one another. Rivalries bred hatreds, and smoldering feuds were ever undermining the peace of the community. Insistence on local rights, and intrigue for a place in the sun, let loose fire and sword, plague and famine that again and again swept the land and at last laid low in desolation and exile the long-cherished hopes of the kingdom. But out of the ruins of each epoch, phoenixlike arose new forms and ideals, purified, strengthened, and better adapted, in the changing environment, to meet the growing needs of humanity and to express the will of God.

The story of Israel's travail is heroic and human. On a small stage, her thinkers faced all the problems of man, in the name of religion. Small beginnings, conflicting ideals, life and death struggles, lost causes and high hopes fill up her pages of history. The hard way was her lot. Thereby she was taught the abiding values of life, and her wise men learned to distinguish between the transient and the permanent.

Each chapter in this book forms a link in the development of Israel's religion, and at the same time treats, briefly, a type of religious life or a movement that came to expression amid the complex and divergent theories and practices of the period. Each of these movements was clear cut, assertive, and often defiant of all contemporary life and thought. Yet only a few of them were "closed corporations." In religious growth conversion was not uncommon, alliances were subject to change, and affiliations contracted and expanded under the ever changing environment. The processes of religion were always vital.

To the end that the reader may enter into the purposes and the experiences of these pioneers of the past, share the insights of men of yore of like passions with ourselves, and be undergirded by the assurance that, as of old, out of the confusion of tongues and the conflict of ideas and programs there is slowly emerging a finer and broader ideal for humanity and a firmer and saner faith in the ultimate Power in the universe—to this end is this volume dedicated.

I. G. MATTHEWS

May 1, 1947

THE RELIGIOUS PILGRIMAGE OF ISRAEL

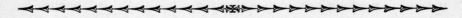

Chapter I

INTRODUCTION:

THE MEANING OF RELIGION

R ELIGION in the making" is a phrase that suggests that religion is a life process within the warp and woof of social consciousness. This being true, we should be able to find the origins, trace the growth, and understand, in part at least, the forces at play in and the values derived from the age-long interweaving of variant strands of culture. But a precise definition, one with sufficient flexibility to include the lowly origins and the ever emerging types, and that at the same time expresses the inherent vitality that gives adequate direction and ultimate authority to religion, is not easily phrased.

Many definitions are provincial to a degree, and are thus of local interest only. To conclude that religion—supported by the root meaning of *religo*, "to bind back"—is the sum of scruples that impede the free exercise of our faculties [1] lays all the emphasis on that phase prevalent among early people and not altogether absent in later days, in which taboos played a leading role. But this is no more the measure of religion, early or late, than are the games of childhood the motivating interests of the man. Likewise, to make either the sacerdotal or the rational the essential in religion, as is so often done, is altogether inadequate. The one rests on the fiction that the ritual when celebrated by the priest is the channel of magical power, while the other, by equating religion with dogma, places the primary emphasis on the intellectual processes. Nor should religion be limited to social activities and measured by good works. Externals are never the essentials. Nor is an experience, even an experience of the Holy,[2] the sum total of religion. In the interests of the inner life, the world of social relations has been largely neglected.

---

[1] S. Reinach, *Cultes, mythes, et religions*, I, 29.

[2] Mystics and many Protestants, in the interests of an emotional change, the response to the *Mysterium Tremendum*, or the "Wholly Other" (R. Otto, *The Idea of the Holy*, translated by J. W. Harvey, 13–41, 180, 181), have so defined it, and Wm. James, in *Varieties of Religious Experience*, gave an impetus to this emphasis. A well-guarded statement of this position is found in *Religion as I See It*, chap. 1, by H. E. Fosdick. Experience, indeed, to those emotionally and intellectually conditioned, has often been revolutionary and character forming, but at best such a definition omits much, and underscores the accidental rather than the normal. For an illuminating discussion of entangled religious expressions and mistaken notions see Vergilius Ferm, *First Chapters in Religious Philosophy*, 3–54. Like A. N. Whitehead's thought-provoking phrase, "Religion is what the individual does with his solitariness" (*Science and the Modern World*, 267, 268), experience only in part defines religion.

Students in recent years, working inductively, and conversant with the accumulating information from anthropology, sociology, and psychology, have sought a more comprehensive, even a more fundamental definition. The human personality, complex and mysterious though it be, like the world in which we live, is a unit, an interrelated and interacting whole; and religion is recognized as playing a part in the life of the whole man as he is related to his total environment. Behind rites, creeds, activities, and experiences lies the essential drive of which these are but the by-products, or the specific manifestations. Religion then must be defined in terms that are inclusive and basic, giving full value to both the subjective and the objective factors.

Definitions by the score have been attempted from this more comprehensive angle. A few of these that emphasize personal attitudes in relation to the social environment are here recorded for consideration. Religion has been characterized as man's whole bearing toward what seems to him best and greatest,[3] or as the co-operative quest for the ideally satisfying life, a quest of unrealized but approved values.[4] It has been spoken of as the pursuit on the part of the individual or the community of what are thought to be the highest values;[5] it has been called the expression of the shifting attitudes of man as he reacts to various stimuli;[6] or it has been identified with a general striving of humanity, rather than with the exclusive pretension of any one people or sect.[7] A high note has been struck by Professor Dewey, who considers a man to be religious when he acts in devotion to an ideal, especially if it be against obstacles and self-interest.[8] While Professor Ferm concludes that to be religious is to effect in some way and in some measure a vital adjustment (however tentative and incomplete) to whatever is reacted to and regarded implicitly or explicitly as worthy of serious and ulterior concern.[9] But for a simple and suggestive statement none is better than: "Religion at its best is the deepest response of the self to the highest we know."[10]

These definitions all differ greatly from those built on theological assumptions inherited from the prescientific era. But beneath the varying phrases they are in general agreement, and indicate a definite and growing trend toward an inclusive and profoundly realistic conception of religion. Analyzing religion on the basis of research in anthropology, archaeology, and psychology, we find that the following conclusions seem to be firmly established:

First, religion is universal, and from the earliest days has been a vital force in all branches of the human family. The disposal of his dead by early man, as

---

[3] G. W. Stratton, *Psychology of the Religious Life*, 343.
[4] A. E. Hayden, *Journal of Religion*, VIII, 126–129.
[5] E. A. Ames, *American Journal of Theology*, May, 1921, 265.
[6] E. W. Hopkins, *Origin and Evolution of Religion*, 108.
[7] R. R. Marett, *Anthropology*, 206.
[8] John Dewey, *A Common Faith*, 10, 17.
[9] Vergilius Ferm, *First Chapters in Religious Philosophy*, 61.
[10] G. W. Knox, the *Harvard Review*, 1908, 205.

recorded by the archaeologist, and his ideas of himself, and of the spirit world, and of their mutual relations, as reported by the anthropologist, furnish complete evidence that all mankind has sought to preserve and to improve *his* relation with the gods. *He* shared *his* food, gave gifts, performed rites, uttered petitions, experimented—wistfully anxious to know and, in extremity, eager to do what was pleasing to the gods. The attitude, to do the best possible, that is, the deepest response of the self to the highest he knew, was ever active. Behind and preceding all theories and beliefs were the acts and expressions; and behind these acts lay the urge, the desire, the attitude which is the unifying element in all religions, ancient and modern.

Second, all rites and ceremonies, innumerable and varied as they are, originated in the experimental effort of primitive man to gain and maintain the favor and friendship of the great, ever present, mysterious powers that continuously beset him behind and before.

Third, a class of experts, medicine men, oracle givers, priests, ecclesiasts, owing to temperament, training, and interest, gradually became the guardians and the promoters of all organized religious activities.

Fourth, changes in the forms, the concepts, and the interpretation of religion were always taking place, slowly, over long periods of time. Under the trial-and-error method, promoted by crises in history, the upward thrust of human idealism, and priestly decision, those customs and ideas that proved to be ineffective were sloughed off, while others that seemed to be more worthy were adopted. Many types, in both ritual and belief, passed out in adolescence. Others, probably the minority, owing to a better adaptation to the needs of human existence, and the growing intelligence of mankind, survived, took on new life, and contributed to the temporary, if not permanent, welfare of humanity.

Fifth, theology, or mythology, the product of those schools or guilds responsible for preserving, interpreting, and organizing all the inherited ceremonies and beliefs, of necessity ascribes all surviving customs and ideals to the revealed commands of the gods. Antiquity, emotional responses, and accepted values gave them divine sanctions.

Such conclusions are sobering. They shift support from an infallible revelation, complete and authoritative for all time, supernaturally communicated to man in the dim dawn of history, to the more understandable conviction that among all nations, and in all ages, knowledge of the good, the true, and the beautiful has been mediated through mental and moral discrimination, and that achievements in human welfare, and in religion, have ever rested on wise and adventuresome leadership that enlisted the energy of interested groups. Wherever there has been progress, and this has been the exception, not the rule, a static theology has been displaced by one that is vital, and authoritarianism has given way before *democracy*. Then the past is not the goal of life, and religion reaches out toward an ever enlarging vision.

The religion of Israel was marked by change and growth, in act, in thought, and in ideal, from the beginning of their history down to the final destruction of the temple. The various religious reactions, each one almost a religion in itself, like those of all the nations, were part of the social phenomena. They were group responses to the influences that, in the course of history, were ever at play in the life of the people. To appreciate fully each and all of these rival reactions is no easy task. We have a vast literature, and it is required that we understand sympathetically the meaning each message had to its own generation. To make these varied oracles, that were often the polemical expressions of hostile factions, conform one to the other, or to press them into the molds of our theology, is to lose the values of history and to become the slaves of personal prejudice. Nor should we approve or condemn them by our standards. Each message was definite, usually easily understood, addressed to a specific situation, and had but one meaning. To understand each we must know the problem and the outlook of the author, the history of his times, the customs, the ideals, and the world view of the people as a whole. These often differed as radically from ours as does the Arab costume. Their world was conceived to be small and flat, recently created by fiat, plague and famine ridden, infested by spirits, and ruled by inscrutable and arbitrary powers. Their customs, that is, their norms in ethics and religion, were primitive, Oriental, and strongly influenced by the ideals of the Arabian desert. To see through their eyes and to orient ourselves to their way of thinking is our first responsibility.

Three veils that often tend to obscure the meaning of the original messages must be lifted before we can fully enter into the hopes, the convictions, and the ideals of these pioneers of a turbulent past. Our translations, if we seek accurate conclusions in theology, are in sore need of careful interpretation, and often of drastic revision. The King James Version, the finest flower of British Protestant scholarship of the seventeenth century of our era, the mold that has fashioned all later versions, is far from perfect. It has an English, seventeenth-century, Protestant bias, and expresses ideas and doctrines that were no part of the original.[11] So familiar are we with these inaccuracies, and so agreeable are they to our way of thinking, that we are loath to accept the more correct. Yet we cannot build a permanent structure on a faulty foundation.

Further, the editorial work of the scribes must be segregated from the material which they interpreted before we can gain an accurate picture of men and movements in their own historical background. These additions give invaluable clues to the religious ideas of the various scribal schools, but

[11] Two texts will suffice to illustrate this fact. Job 19:25-27 in the Authorized Version is made to teach individual immortality, for which there is not the slightest evidence in the original. Isaiah 7:14 has been translated and interpreted in the interest of the Christian teaching of the virgin birth, which has no support in the text or in the context. In these and in innumerable other cases where current translations are inadequate modern standard commentaries provide valuable information.

like some modern sermons they often blur and distort the clear-cut message of earlier days by their apologetic interests. To understand the religious ideals and struggles of Israel during the twelfth and tenth centuries B.C. we must go behind the judgments of the seventh-century editors; and to know Amos, as his generation knew him, we must first excise all later accretions (esp. 9:8b–15).[12] During the slow process of determining the canon of Scripture which continued from 621 B.C. down to A.D. 119, the scribes in every generation exercised great care in selecting and harmonizing the literature of previous centuries and diverse schools of thought, and in bringing all into agreement with the practices and ideas of their own day. Through these centuries the theory that the religion of Judaism had been supernaturally revealed gradually gained assent, and at last became a dogma. Thus the Hebrew Scriptures, in all parts and in every word, were held to be a consistent, unchanging whole, and final. Hence, in reality, there could be no differences, no contradictions, no antagonisms between ideas expressed in various parts of the whole. The scribe continued to burn the midnight oil until he was so illumined that differences vanished, contradictions were resolved, antagonisms were co-ordinated, and he saw in the written and the unwritten word the glorious unity of the mind of the unchangeable God. By neglecting historical processes, yoking together phrases of quite different genre, adding explanatory and apologetic notes, and by the intensive use of the allegorical method of interpretation, he found in every oracle, early and late, the unity so greatly desired. The prophet was made to echo the priest, the skeptic linked arms with the pious, and the rapture of sex became a paean of adoration for the Most High. Illustrations of this harmonistic activity are legion, but none is more subtle than the scribal identification of the *law* in Ben Sirach 24:1–34 with *wisdom* in Proverbs 8:1–9:6.[13] While historical origins and development were totally ignored, the result was a syncretism of the various conflicting streams of thought, in which some of the values of each were brought together in a new unity. It was a solidification of those assets of the past that were congenial to the theological theories of the scribe, while all that were discordant or irritating were eliminated or by-passed. To appreciate at its true worth the religion of the people of the Old Testament we must, so far as possible, get behind the interpretations of the schools and learn the meaning each original writing had to its own generation. Often there was little unity; but there usually was a great sincerity, an eager inquiry, and a religious fervor that atones for at least some of the errors made by the seekers after truth.

Likewise, our third task is to see behind and beyond the Old Testament itself in order to understand clearly the genius of Israel amid ancient world

[12] R. E. Wolfe in a recently published volume has done this for the lay reader in clear and dramatic form for Amos and Hosea (*Meet Amos and Hosea*). This vividly illustrates how editors, by way of interpretation, generation after generation enlarged the material that passed through their hands.

[13] G. F. Moore treats the whole subject in *Judaism*, I, 235–280; see esp. 247–249, 263–290.

religions. All the neighboring nations, Arabia and Syria, Egypt and Hittite, Phoenicia and Canaan, Babylon, Persia, and Greece, were the tutors of Israel. Yet, strange as it may seem, the Hebrews, insignificant in numbers, lacking in social culture, and inferior in statecraft, were no whit behind any of these in moral passion and religious enthusiasm. Their leaders, by rejecting undesirable features and absorbing from each what seemed of value in thought and practice, by slow assimilation made it thoroughly their own. The result is an amazing literary heritage, a library of religious experiences, controversies, tragedies and triumphs, ideas and ideals, that both in quality and in variety ranks as one of the richest among all the nations. Thanks to the archaeologist and the student of comparative religion we are able, as in no earlier period, to mark the beginnings and the borrowings, follow the conflicts and the changes, and note the growing perfection in Israel's religion in her contacts with the nations. This will of necessity make some of the expressions and some of the emphases of a generation ago untenable, but in no wise does it dim the luster of Israel's message.

We acknowledge the difficulties of the task, and confess that we cannot always be certain that full justice is done the ancients. Yet the main lines of the development of the religion of the Old Testament people are beyond dispute. The crises in history with the divergent reactions are well marked. The achievements of the pioneers, the influences of alien neighbors, the main tenets of rival schools of thought, their clashes at times, their compromises when faced by common danger, and the editorial work with its propaganda of reconciliation, are all apparent to the student. Thus in the end we are able to appraise the contribution of each faction to the whole, the defeated as well as the victor, the primitive no less than the civilized, as religion rose to higher and still higher levels.

Each party in the long and constant struggle was convinced that its program was right and that it was divine; and each creative personality had the inner conviction, sometimes overwhelming, that his words were the words of his god. The democratic process of adjustment was slow, irritating, often painful and tragic. But a thousand years of trial and error brought to clear expression, for all who could read, the conclusions accredited by history, which, in very truth, were the Word of God.

Revelation was thus a vital process developing in history by means of that intelligence that in ever widening horizons contributed to the better solution of the problems of human existence. The principles of justice, mercy, humility, and reverence are permanent; but they are ever subject to new, broader, and more profound interpretations in human and divine relations. In the following chapters is presented, in brief form, the often devious but nevertheless upward pathway traveled by Israel for the better understanding of the way in which religion functions, and the greater appreciation of its dynamic qualities.

Chapter II

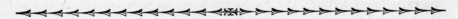

THE RELIGION OF THE SEMINOMADS

A KNOWLEDGE of pedigree, essential in all biological studies, is of like importance for the understanding of the religion of any people. Ancestry has set its stamp on both the tribe and the individual, and all bear the marks, physical, mental, social, and moral, of generations long forgotten. Tribal units such as the Basque in the western Pyrenees, or the Ainus, the aboriginal race of Japan, prove that every group reflects its paternity, even when memory of origins has long been lost in prehistory.

The progenitors of the Hebrews were no exception to the rule. Ancestry contributed to making them what they were. Like all others, when they first appeared on the scene they were of mixed blood.[1] The common practice of exogamy—marrying outside of one's own tribe—secured this intermingling of blood, while migratory movements from distant lands were always crossing frontiers, ever leaving behind them traces of their culture and their blood. The borders of Arabia, and Palestine in particular, were peculiarly susceptible to these influences.[2]

The Arabian desert was the early, if not the earliest, home of the basic group of the ancestors of the pre-Mosaic Hebrews, though no definite relation can be established with any single Arab tribe.[3] Here, as a natural response to climate, geography, and economic conditions, over a period of ten thousand years, a definite culture, called Semitic, with customs, traditions, and mythologies, fixed and all but final, had been developed. Here still is to be found the purest Semitic type, both biologically and linguistically. All the evidence goes to show that the early Semitic population in Palestine was directly or indirectly the result of periodic overflows from the desert in ancient times.

Beyond question there was as much diversity among the various Arabian tribes as in the physical geography of the land. Arabia, in size equal to all of the United States of America, east of the Mississippi, is blessed with almost every variety of climate and soil. Roughly speaking, one-third of it is uninhabitable desert, while two-thirds is more or less livable, with small areas that

---

[1] Franz Boas, in *Theory of Man*, clearly demonstrates that *race* in the old sense of the term is nonexistent; H. J. Seligmann, in *Race against Man*, 38–62, contends that *Homo sapiens* was the most hybrid of breeds.

[2] Sir Arthur Keith in an excellent study of the racial characteristics of the southern Arabs shows that Hamitic, Dravidian, Caucasian, and Semitic migratory waves swept over that country (Bertram Thomas, *Arabia Felix,* 301–333). Other parts of the country were subject to the same influences.

[3] D. S. Margoliouth, *The Relations between Arabs and Israelites Prior to the Rise of Islam,* 1–27.

are exceedingly fertile.[4] The border lands of the west are high and often moist toward the south. Yemen in the southwest, with its cities Aden, Saana, and Dhufar, bordered on Ethiopia, with which it shared in commerce, tradition, and peoples.[5] The southeast, facing Persia, had its mines of diorite, and was occupied by tribes whose history can only be conjectured. Northeast it faced the great river valley, and in the north reached up to the mountains, where were segregated tribes of hardy, rugged, mixed ancestry. Then there were the scorching, waterless deserts of the interior, in which wandered the Bedouin, the camel men. Here were thousands of square miles, reaching from centers a hundred miles or more toward merciless horizons, swept by driving sandstorms that cared not for man or beast. Concealed within these were five oases, rich in water, luxuriant with palm groves, and peopled by tribes that perpetuated the most distinctive forms of Arabic culture. Life was vastly varied in this peninsula. City civilization in the southeast had little resemblance to life in the northeast and north. Each of the oases nurtured its own tribe with its peculiar type of life, while in the desert wandered many clans, each one inured to hardship and poverty, but proud of its traditions, and satisfied with its lot. Then, in the nooks and the corners of the great spaces, smaller, poorer families clung most precariously to the ways of the fathers. Yet in the variety there was unity. Beneath the local color lay the broad bases of a common, Semitic heritage which in outlook and ideal was native to the genius of Israel.[6]

The nomadic or, better still, the seminomadic tribes, which were akin to the patriarchs and the Habiri,[7] belonged to those groups that geographically lived between the *desert* and the *sown,* and culturally were between the food gatherers and the food producers. In the pre-Mosaic times, these tribes though living in the middle and late bronze periods, that is, between 2000 and 1200 B.C., actually belonged to the neolithic culture and availed themselves of few, if any, of the contributions of the Bronze Age. They had a few domestic animals, the sheep, the goat, the ass, and the dog; they used fire, lived in tents, and were constantly on the move. Each tribe had its own centers, where water, either in springs or in wells, could be had; while tribal boundary lines were ever shifting, expanding or contracting. Pressure from the overflow of peoples from the oases was always on them, and resistance from those settled in the more fertile border lands ever held them in check.

---

[4] J. A. Montgomery, *Arabia and the Bible*, 76–113, presents an admirable sketch of the country.

[5] Bertram Thomas, *Arabia Felix*, 8, 47, 79, 122, 123.

[6] In spite of the minor differences among these people, there has persisted similarity of language, thought, and custom, and even of physical type, in all places and in all ages (S. A. Cook, *Cambridge Ancient History*, I, 189–191).

[7] The true nomad, or the Bedouin, despises agriculture; while the seminomad, or the Arab, depends on the sheep and the scant, uncertain returns from scattered patches of poorly tilled land (W. F. Albright, *The Archaeology of Palestine and the Bible*, 130–133).

Primitive agriculture was attempted as need and opportunity afforded, but it was wearisome, and climate and raiders were always a menace to such an adventure. At times, under stress, tribes wandered far for food for their flocks. In periods of severe drought, or owing to pressure from other tribes, migrations over hundreds or thousands of miles occurred. The story of Abraham leaving Harran, in Upper Mesopotamia, and sojourning in Shechem, Hebron, Gerar, and going down to Egypt (Gen. 12:4–10), or that of the Ephraimite clans moving from Goshen to Moab (Exod. 13: 17–22; 15:19–21; Num. 25:1–5), runs true to historic fact. Such tensions and migrations were always part of the tribal life, and reactions, favorable and unfavorable, were always in process. Gradual adjustment to pressures, and slow but continuous assimilation between tribes, belonged to the normal life of the seminomad.

In such a background it was natural that specific characteristics should be developed and become fixed in the habits and thinking of the pre-Mosaic tribes. Life to these people was one and indivisible, with no sharp lines of cleavage. But for convenience we may analyze the chief features under four heads, the economic, the sociopolitical, the intellectual, and the religious aspects of life.

Economic factors have always played an important, though not final, role in the culture of any people. The ancestors of Israel always had a meager food supply. The milk and curds from the sheep and goats were their chief stay. Not only was it monotonous but it was scant even when pasturage was abundant. In off seasons it was pitiful; often the tribe hovered on the verge of death. On festal occasions, when a guest arrived,[8] or on the occasion of a marriage or the celebration of some family or tribal sacred day (I Sam. 1:3–5; 13:9; 20:6, 29; 9:22–24), usually a sheep was sacrificed, and a few mouthfuls or a gorge of mutton fortified the body for long weeks of semifasting. In addition to milk and curds the diet was largely fortuitous. Bread, from cereals raised at haphazard, or obtained by barter, was often impossible. Dates and olives could be bought in certain places, while roots and small fruits were sparsely scattered throughout the desert. Grasses and tender shoots like sorrel were used in the springtime; locusts, a prime delicacy when dried, could be kept for the hour of need; honey might be found on rare occasions. There were fish for those who bordered certain streams, and birds' eggs in season. The sparrow, the curlew, the partridge, and the quail were hunted in the valleys by primitive methods. All such added variety and considerable

[8] Primitive customs naturally were often preserved to very late dates, as illustrated by Nathan's parable of the little ewe lamb (II Sam. 12:1–7). See St. John Philby, *Arabia of the Wahhabis*, 110, 112. W. B. Seabrook in *Adventures in Arabia*, 37, 68, 93–96, describes two great feasts, in one of which the platter was five feet in diameter and contained quantities of rice topped by two whole sheep; in the other the platter was nine feet across, and a camel was the *pièce de résistance*.

sustenance to the bill of fare. In times of dire distress all religious prohibitions were violated,[9] and the coney, the lizard, the dog, the fox, and even the vulture, the hyena, and the serpent become the victims of the never ending struggle for existence.

The tent was the shelter and the center of family life. The clothing was simple, much of it threadbare and all of it travel-stained and repaired. It sufficed for covering by day and comfort by night. Baggage they could not afford. The meager living, the wide search for pasture, and the too frequent raids kept all such at a minimum. A few cooking utensils, a club, possibly a spear, an ornament or two, the odds and ends essential for simple life—all could easily be bundled for the march on half an hour's notice.

Certain lands, with streams, springs, or wells, areas claimed by long occupancy or by recent conquest, belonged to individual tribes and their gods. Here their fathers had roamed, tented, had strange visitations, died, and been buried. This land thus became sacred to them and their posterity, and remained so as long as they had the power to protect it.

The immediate ancestors of the invading Hebrews, whosoever they may have been, were wandering migrants whose homeland from time immemorial had been this inhospitable desert. Some may have lived athwart the ancient caravan lines that ran from the lands rich in spices, cereals, precious stones, and metals to the great city centers.[10] Others may have been belated families of the Habiri, the main body of which entered Canaan during the fourteenth century. But beyond such various nondescript clans, the vigorous nucleus of the new nation was the restless band that preferred the ways of the desert to the greater abundance of Egypt. All the groups ultimately came from the desert, and bore the desert, with its bleakness, its freedom, and its far vision, in mind and heart.

It is no wonder, then, that the Hebrew Scriptures, both in passing phrase and in essential principle, bear constant witness to the stern, simple life in these ancient, illimitable wastes. Many of the phrases that have little meaning to Westerners were rooted in the common experience of the desert tribes and are even yet rich in emotional content to the peoples of the Bible lands. A great

9 C. M. Doughty, *Arabia Deserta,* is a treasury on the food customs of the desert tribes (I, 36, 179, 203, 214, 217, 218, 307, 472, 490, 498; II, 245, 246, 323). Unclean birds and animals were eaten when famine pressed hard: crows, kites, buzzards, owls, serpents, rats, lizards, etc. (I, 534). Carl Raswan, *The Black Tents of Arabia,* 88–94, depicts the desperate conditions in times of drought, and at the same time the lavish hospitality.

10 South Arabia was noted for spices; Sinai for lapis lazuli; northwest Arabia for cereals; Asia Minor, Cyprus, and the Caucasus for copper and iron; the oases for dates; while the great central markets were Bagdad, Palmyra, Damascus, Byblos, Gerar, and Memphis. Before 2000 B.C. well-established traffic lines ran from Egypt to Sinai, and to the north; from Yemen to Sinai, then to the markets of the north. Three or more caravan routes ran through Palestine and Syria, connecting them with the north and the east. The trade was plied from early days by groups organized for the purpose (cf. Ishmaelites, Gen. 37:25, 27; 39:1). Tribes along the way profited by tribute or toll, while the indigent at times were not averse to pillage (G. A. Smith, "Trade and Commerce," *Encyclopaedia Biblica,* esp. 4–16; 28–40).

rock in a weary land (Isa. 32:2) is the acme of comfort to the exhausted traveler on the desert sand. The water that means so little to the man in the Western city to the throat-parched Bedouin was the water of life, veritably a gift from the gods. "How much does water cost?" is quite likely to be the first question of a Palestinian peasant thinking of coming to America. Washing the feet was so essential to one who marched barefoot over the hard, gritty roadway that it easily acquired a religious significance (Gen. 18:4; 19:2; 24:32; 43:24; John 13: 2–10). Anointing with oil, the face, the head, and the beard, much needed as protection against the blistering heat, which stirs in our minds no pleasant anticipation, became a sacred act endowed with mystical meaning. Long hair, with us often a badge of eccentricity, but the best covering for the head and neck against the deadly actinic rays of the tropical sun, was adopted by some desert groups as an essential of their religion (Num. 6:5); while cutting off the beard, the honored symbol of maturity and dignity, was the greatest disgrace one could suffer (II Sam. 10:1–3).[11] The peace of God that passeth all understanding (Phil. 4:7), so foreign to the never ceasing, raucous roaring of our industrial life, was a gift of the great empty spaces to the contemporaries of Abraham. The time notations, evening and morning, the new moon, the springtime, so different from ours, were determined by the necessities of nomadic life in the tropics. The hour of sunset was the time to set out on a journey (Gen. 32:22; Exod. 12:24; II Sam. 2:29), to undertake a raid (Gen. 14:15; I Sam. 14:36), or to enter into converse with deity (Gen. 3:8). Evening and morning (Gen. 1:5, 8, 13, etc.), though the phrase of a late priestly writer, originated in primitive, desert life and still determines the beginning and the end of the official Jewish Sabbath. Rising early was no proof of moral earnestness on the part of those who were compelled to take a long siesta during the heat of the day. The new moon incited the tribe to pull up their tent pegs and move to new feeding grounds, while to every shepherd the springtime was the herald of promise, the beginning of a new year. Both the new moon and the springtime, in early days, won a place in the shepherd's religious calendar, and both are still honored in Judaism and Mohammedanism. These, and a multitude of other facts and phrases, all the product of preagricultural experiences, are freely interwoven in the Scriptures, and not a few of them have assumed significance in our religion.

Further, the barrenness of the desert, where life was reduced to the lowest common denominator, contributed much to later thought and practice. The petty tribes had little of this world's goods, and could accumulate nothing. Even the soil of their habitat was of little worth. Constantly on the move, often driven from their pre-empted water supply, the empty spaces and the

---

[11] Ibn Saud of Arabia, the Wahhabi, in A.D. 1831 sometimes punished the guilty by demanding the removal of the beard. This was most severe. A sheikh would rather forfeit his choicest possession than be shorn of this sign of manhood (J. L. Burckhardt, *Bedouins and Wahhabys*, II, 144).

heavens above were the only permanent realities. Thousands of years of desolating experiences had taught them that the heavens ruled, and that life in
the tribe alone was worthful. For them it was normal to think, Lay not up
for yourselves treasure, or What shall it profit a man if he gain the whole
world and lose his life? The law of the desert limited opportunity and ambi-
tion, but it established the simplest human values, and resignation to the
will of the gods.

The sociopolitical life of the nomad and seminomad was patriarchal. There
are evidences that in the far-off days of the hunter the matriarchate, or mother
rule, prevailed. But this had long since passed, leaving behind only faint, but
telltale, traces.[12] The tribe was an effective though somewhat loosely knit
unit, consisting of clans, which in turn were made up of families. The patriarch, or sheikh, was the provider for all, the judge in local disputes, the
director of the march, the leader in battle, and the officiating priest in the
hour of gratitude or distress. His leadership was by virtue of blood, and of
birth, rather than by oath of allegiance; and his rule, guided by ancient custom
and aided by conference with the elders, was absolute. His judgments in
due time carried divine sanctions for they were the way of the fathers and
the gods.[13] Occasionally, when with the weight of years his vitality was on
the wane, he delegated his duties to a subordinate, but still he was the power
behind the throne. At times a younger man rebelled and gained authority,
though the odds were that the rebel would become an outcast.[14] Such adven-
turers joined some other tribe, thereby accepting its customs and its god, or
if strong enough established families of their own. Not infrequently, following a period of increased food supply with the consequent growth of population, a tribe amicably split in two, for economic and personal reasons (Gen.
13:5–12).[15] The primacy of the patriarch, however, was so ingrained that it
always evoked emotional qualities that could not easily be disregarded. Honor
thy father and thy mother, so charming within the family circle, spread the

[12] In the early stages of family life, when among some groups promiscuity was practiced, the
mother was the permanent center of the home. She remained with her people while the husband
might visit her occasionally (Judg. 14:19; 15:1, 2; Gen. 2:24; cf. Gen. 24:5). Under these circumstances the tent, the home of the mother and the children, belonged to her and her tribe (Gen.
24:67; Judg. 4:17), and the mother's brother was usually the official guardian of this family.
Marriage with the father's daughter was allowable (Gen. 20:12; II Sam. 13:13), but not with the
mother's daughter, who had been brought up in the same tent. The oft-repeated statement in
the lineage of the kings in the Old Testament, *and his mother's name was*, is surely a remnant
of the matriarchal period (G. A. Barton, *Encyclopaedia of Religion and Ethics*, XI, 95–110; A.
Bertholet, *History of Hebrew Civilization*, 116–118).

[13] M. J. Lagrange, *Etudes sur les religions Sémitiques* (*deuxième édition*), 217–246.

[14] Jephthah (Judg. 11:3) and Abimelech (Judg. 9:4–6) illustrate the fact that the strong, or the
headstrong, were always asserting themselves. The story of Absalom shows the same spirit at work
in a more highly developed civilization (II Sam. 13:37–39).

[15] The area required for pasturage limited the size of the tribe. Beyond 350 was too unwieldy
for co-operation. The 318 trained men, reported in a very late tradition to have been under the
hand of Abraham (Gen. 14:14), would represent a large and prosperous alliance.

sanction of age-long tribal custom over every religious institution of Scripture. A bulwark against folly, at times it became a barrier to progress.

Kinship, that is, blood brotherhood, held the family, the clan, and the tribe together in an indissoluble religious bond. All the members thereof, whether by birth, by adoption, or by prolonged residence, had one father;[16] and it was one in all, and all—the living, the dead, and the unborn—in the one. Our language, rooted in a rampant individualism, has obscured the profound qualities, effective in social and religious life, native to Semitic kinship. Founder, family, tribe, and deity were felt to be as vitally related as the hand, the foot, and the eye are to the body. The tribe was permanent, the individual was incidental.

This tribal solidarity was the way of life to those people. As late as the time of Saul some families still held an annual family sacrifice (I Sam. 20:6, 27). Passages such as the children of *my clan* (Judg. 14:16); they have broken the *bond of kinship* (Amos 1:11); cut off from *his clan* (Lev. 17:10); and the proud claim of the woman of Shunem, I dwell among *mine own people* (II Kings 4:13), to the nomad expressed the essentials. It was in this soil that phrases such as *my people Israel* (II Sam. 7:11) flourished and in it the insistent vigor of modern Zionism is rooted.

It has long been recognized that in many pagan religions the deity of the tribe was believed to be its physical ancestor. Moreover, accumulated evidence points to a time in early Semitic prehistory when ancestors of the Babylonians, Phoenicians, and certain Arab tribes conceived that they and their tribal deity were blood relations;[17] in a very literal sense they were the sons and the daughters of their god. When in more enlightened days the crudities of this belief were rejected by the more thoughtful, much of it must have lingered long among the common people. At least echoes of it find expression in the Old Testament. Moabites were called the sons and daughters of Chemosh (Num. 21:29), while idolaters are accused of saying to a stock, Thou art my father, and to a stone, Thou hast brought me forth (Jer. 2:27). How much of this mythology may have persisted among some of the Hebrew tribes, and how deeply it may have functioned in the sacrificial use of blood in some of the Jewish ceremonies, it would be hard to say. That it had no influence is most unlikely. In fact, the kinship bond derived its greatest vitality from the belief that, in one way or another, the tribal deity was the senior member of the union. While kinship in the tribe was one of blood or alliance,

---

[16] Initiatory rites into a tribe were simple but binding. The mingling of blood with the pledge of loyalty (C. Raswan, *The Black Tents of Arabia*, 21–23); a simple oath as between Jonathan and David (I Sam. 18:3, 4); the gradual alliance of divergent elements under a strong man, who thus becomes the father of a new tribe (J. Pedersen, *Israel*, I, 6–18)—all such were sacred, and relationship thus acquired was more important in the desert than consanguinity (E. A. Westermarck, *Origin and Development of the Moral Ideas*, I, 107; W. R. Smith, *Lectures on the Religion of the Semites*, 3rd ed., 46, 47, 595; Ed. Meyer, *Geschichte des Altertums*, I, 1, 1–8, 72).

[17] W. R. Smith, *Rel. Sem.* (3), 39–47. D. Jacobson, *Social Background of the Old Testament*, 114–132. R. Kittel, *Religion of the People of Israel*, 93–122.

even more so was it one of spirit. Born of the flesh amid the hot sands of the desert, and in constant travail, each tribe was molded into a mystic brotherhood. Living in the same surroundings, partaking of the same dish, using a common vocabulary and a common accent, familiar with the same folklore and traditions, accepting the same friends, waging war against the same enemies, and devoted to the same deity, they grew into what has been called a *corporate personality*.[18]

Solidarity, however, without question was germane to kinship. The bond with family, clan, and tribe, the intensity increasing with proximity to the center, was paramount.[19] Group consciousness was primary in early Arabian life. In the struggle with the elements, with the animals, and with neighboring tribes, the tribe, not the individual, was always the vital interest. To raise the question, Am I my brother's keeper (Gen. 4:9) revealed at once the mind of a traitor. Likewise Achan by his theft (Josh. 7:24, 25) and Saul by violating his treaty with the Gibeonites (II Sam. 21:1-6) were each believed to have brought disaster on all Israel; hence Achan's household and Saul's grandchildren were accounted guilty and were executed. In primitive society the iniquity of the fathers was visited on the children to the third and fourth generation (Deut. 5:9).[20] Behind much of our religious literature lies this, to us, quite foreign method of thought, in which the deity, the tribe, and the individual are quite inseparable.

Individualism to a marked degree, paradoxical though it seems,[21] went hand in hand with solidarity. It is true that the individual, his interests, and his identity were submerged in the tribe; but the tribe was his, and was a part of himself. The boundary line between the *tribe* and the *I* was shadowy, and oscillated as interests changed. The tribe was patriarchal, but it was also com-

---

[18] Emile Durkheim, in *Les règles de la méthode sociologique*, 1895, suggested that man thinks in a group rather than as an individual, and thus emphasized *collective consciousness* (*The Rules of Sociological Method*, translation by Catlin, 1-13, 102-112). Ed. Meyer, *Gesch. Alt.*, I, 1, 9, emphasizes the fact that the tribe is *eine bestimmte Individualite*, while J. Pedersen has elaborated the same idea under the term *a corporate personality*, (*Israel* I, 6-18). The extreme form of the statement is opposed by C. C. J. Webb, *Group Theories of Religion and the Individual*.

[19] Clark Wissler, in *Man and Culture*, 273, interprets tribal loyalty as an inborn tribal response that will resist the invasion of its culture to the death. Herein lies the reason why so many rites persist long after they have lost all usefulness, and why so few religious groups are able adequately to adjust to the ever changing environment.

[20] At a higher level of civilization, when individualism had come to full expression, the old law was revised, so that the children should not be put to death for the fathers or vice versa (Deut. 24:16).

[21] Independence of the individual is one of the chief characteristics of the Arabs. Doughty asserts they are never of one assent, save in blind dogma and religion. The tent of the sheikh is as free as the desert (*Arabia Deserta*, II, 357-360). They love unfettered liberty more than life, so writes Bertram Thomas (*Arabia Felix*, 10, 11). They are always contentious (Lawrence in Doughty, *Arabia Deserta*, xxii), untamed and untamable (H. C. Armstrong, *The Lord of Arabia*, 14). It is this spirit bred in the desert that has made the equality of all believers a doctrine of Islam (W. H. Norton, *J. Rel.*, July, 1924, 383-396).

munal, and had all the give and take of an actual democracy. Responsibility in discussion and in the execution of plans was laid upon all. *All Israel stoned him with stones, and they burned them with fire* (Josh. 7:25, cf. Lev. 24:23; Deut. 13:10) was the tribal law that placed the responsibility squarely on the shoulders of every individual. *Let him that is without sin cast the first stone* (John 8:7) called for that individual judgment and participation that was second nature to the nomad.

The same desert that held the tribe together likewise contributed much to the spirit of independence. Here no goose-step system could ever be introduced. Tribal control there was, but dictatorship could not long prevail. Criticism of those in authority is customary among the free men of the desert, and all affairs of importance are settled in the coffee circle of the chief. True, the sheikh is absolute, his word is final; but that word, usually one of wisdom, is the crystallization of open discussion, assented to by those who were never slaves to any man. The leader, like Moses in the desert, is ever on trial (Exod. 32:1; Num. 11:1, 2; 12:1–3; 14:1–4; 16:1–3). Knowledge of customs, justice, good judgment, humaneness, and personal command are constantly required.

Blood revenge was the law of the tribes as the blood bond was the foundation of early Semitic society. This was the inescapable obligation of all the kin. *Whosoever sheds man's blood, by man shall his blood be shed* (Exod. 21:12) is the law of life and of justice.[22] Arising in prehuman reactions, it was inherent in the thinking and the emotions of primitive peoples everywhere. Axiomatic and universal, it was a divine imperative. Parallel to it, indeed a part of it, is the law *an eye for an eye, and a tooth for a tooth* (Exod. 21:24, 25). This is simple, is easily understood, and permits of little casuistry.[23] In many cases it appears crude, but at heart it is justice.

Kinship, that united the members of the clan and tribe in a protective pact, faced the alien world with deep-rooted prejudices. The primary laws, Thou shalt not steal, lie, commit adultery, or murder, were limited to the brotherhood; beyond the tribe their observance savored of treachery. The foreigner is always under suspicion. He is strange. His clothes, his face, his speech, even his interests are alien. As Rebekah wearied of the daughters of Heth (Gen. 27:46), so is humanity ever critical of peoples of strange customs. In no place is this so true as in the desert where, living severely alone, isolationism, intolerance, and arrogance are indigenous growths of long pedigree.[24]

[22] This principle was imperative both within the tribe and between the tribes. Both aspects were basic to tribal well-being. Blood revenge was a duty to the living, to the dead, and to deity, and as such was profoundly religious. That in its origin it was a type of human sacrifice to the god of the tribe seems well sustained (Westermarck, *Origin and Development of Moral Ideas*, I, 481–484).

[23] The man who shot another through the calf of the leg had a similar bullet drawn through his own leg, in approximately the same place (H. C. Armstrong, *Lord of Arabia*, 83). The man who stole had his right hand cut off (Bertram Thomas, *Arabia Felix*, 119).

[24] Bertram Thomas, *Arabia Felix*, xxiv.

The well-known Arabic proverb, "The stranger is for the wolf," is only the desert equivalent for the Scripture, one law for the homeborn and another for the stranger. To lie to a foreign potentate was in good form, and was fully approved by Yahweh (Gen. 12:13–13:2; 20:11–16). To double-cross an Aramaean in a sheep deal was blessed by Yahweh, and was a perpetual joy to posterity (Gen. 30:32–43). To slay a foreigner, even under a peace pact, was cited for heroism, and the culprit was blessed beyond women (Judg. 5:24–27). The men of Gibeah would not violate the daughter of a townsman, but the concubine from a different clan came under a different law (Judg. 19:14, 25), and Israel approved when the Benjamites raped four hundred virgins of Jabesh-gilead (Judg. 21:10–12). Even in late legislation such acts were legalized (Deut. 20:14; 21:10–13). In dealing with the foreigner, even at a late date, bad meat might be sold (Deut. 14:21), and usury might be charged (Deut. 15:3), acts that were considered dishonorable within the tribe. Such practices were born amid the enmities of the desert.

This attitude toward the stranger naturally led to the logical limits of blood revenge. While the law usually restrained the tribes from shedding blood, paradoxically it actually initiated a vicious circle, and perpetuated indefinitely the blood feud. Hence, today there exists no tribe in the desert, save the Solaiby,[25] that has not some blood score to settle with most of the tribes within striking distance. Logically the law leads to the *herem,* that is, the annihilation of the enemy, which may be regarded as the primitive law of self-preservation. The wiping out of a clan or a village has not been uncommon either in ancient or in modern times. The numerous cities reported to have been completely destroyed at the command of Yahweh at the time of the invasion of Canaan, though a late report, is not entirely void of foundation (Josh. 8:24; 10:28, 30, 32, 35), and in our own day families, even whole clans, have been wiped out in this strife.[26] Ancient custom, coupled with the desire for vengeance, approved these primitive reactions as divine. The flame of patriotism burned fiercely; the heroic had been achieved under the release of latent energies; it had thus been the will and the work of Allah. By all the tests it was the true religion. Hebrew writers were only restating the practice of the primitive tribes of Arabia when they asserted such wholesale slaughter to be the will of Yahweh (Num. 21:2, 3; Deut. 2:34; 3:6; 7:2). Whosoever disregarded the *herem,* as did Saul, was anathema to the religion of the fathers (I Sam. 15:14–23, 32, 33).

[25] The Solaiby, the people of the cross, are the wandering smiths of Arabia, who ply their trade throughout the length and breadth of the land. They never raid others and are never molested.

[26] A modern illustration, one of many, is the raid that 1,500 of the Ikhwan (Brethren) of the tribe of Harb, made in August, 1922, when they rode a thousand miles over the burning desert to the village of Turaib, belonging to a family of the Beni Shakir tribe, and wiped it out. The Beni Shakir retaliated, caught and slew all but eight of the raiders (H. C. Armstrong, *Lord of Arabia,* 153–155).

Blood revenge, however, when followed to the letter of the law, could not rest short of the annihilation of every potential enemy. This would ultimately mean the extinction of the desert population. Humanity quails before such a possibility, even should it be the law of the god. Even far back in nomadic days the custom must have been slowly undergoing changes for the general welfare of the tribes. The raid (*razzu* or *ghazzu*), the swift night dash against the enemy, became well organized, and was carried out under well-recognized rules, so that it has been called the gentleman's game, the only industry of the desert.[27] Honor and booty are the objectives; and the shedding of blood, save in the gravest cases, is carefully avoided. Preference is given to raids on distant tribes, even as remote as 500 or 1,000 miles,[28] rather than against those in the immediate neighborhood, who might easily retaliate. Immense booty, sometimes as many as 2,000 head of cattle, is reported to have been lifted in a single raid.[29] The need for seasonal explosion of tribal energies, as well as the demands of honor and the obligations of religion, is thereby satisfied. Further, though tribal memory of insults and raids sometimes extends over centuries (I Sam. 15:2, 3), blood revenge is usually outlawed in the third or fourth generation.[30] Even under these restrictive measures, it is inevitable that, in the never ceasing struggle against the forces of the desert and the reprisals of the enemy, the richest today may be the poorest tomorrow, and those dominant in one generation may be decimated or annihilated in the next. Indeed, it has been stated by one of the most competent historians that it is rare for a tribe to preserve its identity for more than a couple of hundred years.[31] The same tribal instability is found in Hebrew history. Dinah early disappeared from the records. Simeon and Reuben were soon scattered or assimilated, and the family of Saul was annihilated.

Binding as the law of blood revenge was in theory, in actual operation it was often faced by serious difficulties, both within the tribe and between the tribes. The slaying was sometimes accidental. Occasionally the guilty party, or even his family, could not be identified; and in no case did the death of the culprit bring back the victim. Often its execution must have been extremely dangerous, especially when the families or clans concerned were of equal strength. Thus it was that the growing complexities of civilization and the slow pressure of humane considerations conspired to moderate the extreme penalty among many tribes. Blood money, that is, a redemptive price for the life of the slayer, paid to the kin of the slain often tempered justice with mercy. In Oman, and among certain other tribes, ransom rang-

---

[27] Gertrude Bell, *Syria, the Desert and the Sown*, 65, 66.
[28] The camel breeders, the true Bedawi, rather than the sheep owners, enjoy these long-distance jaunts (C. Raswan, *The Black Tents of Arabia*, 15, 240; Albright, *Archaeology and Religion of Israel*, 97).
[29] Gertrude Bell, *Syria, the Desert and the Sown*, 65, 66.
[30] C. Raswan, *The Black Tents of Arabia*, 240.
[31] Ed. Meyer, *Gesch. Alt.*, I, 1, 72.

ing from $400 to $1,000 has become a standard compensation for a death.[32] This blood price, which also was incorporated in the religion of Israel, as it went to the tribe of the slain man, no doubt played an important role in changing the drastic ancient regulation. But such progress was never achieved without conflict, in which the layman frequently advocated the new, while the ecclesiast stood for the old.[33] (Cf. I Sam. 15:18–20.)

Slavery, in part, was the outcome of the same ameliorative movement. The *herem* that demanded the slaughter, not only of all the males but also of the women and children, gradually gave way to the captivity of the princes, slavery of the males, and concubinage of the women, especially the virgins. This not only was more humane, but was more satisfactory to both the victor and the vanquished (Judg. 5:30; Deut. 21:10–14; 20:14).[34] But slavery, or better, servitude also resulted from penury. The family on the verge of starvation could barter the son, or preferably the daughter, for a pittance of food to the traveling Ishmaelites, or in the slave market in Gaza, Mecca, or other emporia, and thus keep all alive.[35] Such arrangements, harsh though they seem to us, are definite marks of progress in human history. Furthermore, to the credit of humanity it is to be noted that changes for the betterment of the slave are constantly at work among even the most backward.[36]

Guest privileges to the stranger, probably a reaction against the ruthlessness of blood revenge amid the hardships of desert travel, were usually gladly granted and carefully safeguarded. It may well be that Westermarck, who collected a wealth of cogent material, is correct when he suggests that such hospitality was influenced by the wish to have the blessing of the stranger,[37] in the hope of having entertained an angel unawares. Whatever the origin, or however complex the motives, it is an expression of those finer, more humane qualities that lie deep within every human heart. To the nomad it is not only a privilege, it is an honor, and is accepted as a religious obligation. The assurance of C. M. Doughty that the hospitality of the worsted booths and the gentle entertainment of strangers is truly religious,[38] is amply attested by all visitors to Arabia. In the barren wilderness, where the life of every wanderer depended on hospitality, the tent was always open and its best was

32 Bertram Thomas, *Arabia Felix*, 27, 83, 272.
33 A woman smothered a child for its ornaments. The father held that the death of the murderess would not bring back to life his child, and would be of no value. But the emir insisted on a life for a life, otherwise some great evil would befall the tribe (Doughty, *Arabia Deserta*, II, 368).
34 Bertram Thomas, *Arabia Felix*, 11, 14, 19, 31–33, 67.
35 Traveling traders have passed along the caravan lines from the ancient past to the present (Gen. 37:28), and slave markets have been open for business until the most recent times (Eldon Rutter, *The Holy Cities of Arabia*, I, 133–136).
36 *Ibid.*, II, 90–94.
37 Westermarck, *The Origin and Development of Moral Ideas*, I, 580–587, esp. 583.
38 Doughty, *Arabia Deserta*, II, 237. Eldon Rutter, *The Holy Cities of Arabia*, I, 86; II, 13–15. Philby, *Arabia of the Wahhabis*, 112, 113.

at the disposal of the wayfarer. Where accessories could not be accumulated life itself stood supreme. Three days, the period needed to restore strength for the journey, was the well-understood limit of sojourn, but should one remain longer, even for life, the host proved his worth by asking no questions.[39] Even the law of blood revenge for the time being had to take second place. Should the slayer be able to touch the guy rope of a tent, even that of the avenger, or claim his protection by a single word, *dakhlek* ("your guest"), or in some cases even pronounce the peace greeting, or *eat salt* with his enemy, the right of sanctuary was his.[40] Rarely, as in the case of the notorious Jael (Judg. 4:17–22), was this right violated.[41] In such cases the primitive savage triumphed over the more civilized human. In times of war many people *see red,* and revert to the primitive.

The woman holds a vital, if secondary, place among the Arab nomads. In general, though great differences are found among different tribes, she is the caretaker of the tent, the weaver, the burden bearer, often the shepherdess, and always the drudge of the camp. But her chief function, and her glory, is to be fruitful and multiply (Gen. 1:28). On her depends the very existence of the tribe. The natives of Kerak put it crudely: "The woman is an ass by day and a wife by night." [42] She was considered a mysterious, even a dangerous, creature.[43] She was at once the attraction and the distraction of the male. She had ever-recurring periods, which owing to the general abhorrence of blood made her taboo.[44] She gave birth to children in great travail, surely a punishment for some waywardness. God's curse was on her, and on her was cast much of the blame for the evil that was in the world (Gen. 3:6–8).[45]

While the status of woman was that of an inferior, even a dangerous, member of society, by virtue of her personality at times she achieved a role of supreme importance. Some, like the wise woman of Tekoa (II Sam. 14:4–11), the deliverer of Abel-beth-Maacah (II Sam. 20:16), and Huldah, the prophetess, gained renown because of their wisdom, knowledge of customs, and good judgment. Others were believed to have occult powers through an alliance with evil spirits (Lev. 20:27; Deut. 18:10, 11; I Sam. 28:7–14). The witch and the sorceress, though found among the nomads, were probably quite uncommon. As the tribal system grew in complexity, the aged women performed many duties such as adorning the bride for the marriage ceremony

---

[39] W. B. Seabrook, *Adventures in Arabia,* 43, 44, 105–107, 170, 171, 280, 281. A. Bertholet, *History of Hebrew Civilization,* 119, 120.

[40] Père Jaussen, *Coutumes des Arabes au pays Moab,* 215–220. Bertram Thomas, *Arabia Felix,* 84.

[41] A modern parallel is reported by H. C. Armstrong, *The Lord of Arabia,* 108.

[42] A. Musil, *Arabia Petraea,* III, 211.

[43] R. R. Marett, *The Threshold of Religion,* 109–112.

[44] *Ibid.,* 29. J. Singer, *Taboo in Hebrew Scripture,* 15–40.

[45] Doughty, *Arabia Deserta,* I, 238. Woman is reputed to have seven lives, each one of them full of evil nature.

and acting as accoucheuse. Initiatory and purificatory rites, and many mourning customs, naturally devolved on them.

The right of every mature woman to bear children and to have a home was accepted by all the tribes. When women were more numerous than men plurality of wives, a head wife with her subordinate or subordinates, seemed the most natural solution to the problem. The morality of this was never questioned, or rather, it was a social and pious obligation. It was a religious requirement, especially among the well-to-do.[46] The patriarchal practice and the Moslem rule that a man should not have more than four wives at any one time were in keeping with the best ethics of the day. Intertribal and interracial marriages were constantly contracted by the desert nobility, so that on the plateaus of Arabia from time immemorial there has been the free intermingling of the blood of Abyssinia and Egypt, Mesopotamia and India, the far north and the islands of the sea.[47] The beena marriage, one in which the wife remains with her own tribe, while the husband visits her occasionally (Judg. 14:1, 5, 10; 15:1), an ancient custom, has not yet been entirely discredited.[48]

Divorce was no disgrace and among those in comfortable circumstances was common. When for any reason a man desired to be free from a wife, all that was required of him was to say to her *you go*. Explanations were not necessary; and the woman, with her few possessions, must return to her own family. The man, however, had lost some private property. Among the very poor, monogamy was the rule and divorce was extremely rare.[49] These marriage customs provided for tribal expansion and contraction in direct relation to the food supply and the sex ratio, and prevented a taboo on the creative functions of woman. Also, knowing no racial barriers, they added color, even virility, to family life, and contributed their quota to gradual social change.[50]

The young unmarried women were not without power and privilege. At nature festivals, and in tribal triumphs, they participated, often being the leaders in song and dance. The song of Miriam at the Red Sea (Exod. 15:20, 21), the dance of the daughters of Shiloh at the time of vintage (Judg. 21:21), and the procession of maidens to meet the home-coming warrior (Judg. 11:34; I Sam. 21:11) illustrate the activities of girls in still earlier days. Nor were they found wanting in the sterner phases of life. In the decisive hour of battle, the maid sometimes became the Joan of Arc among the warriors. When the armed men were facing defeat, a virgin with the gifts of leadership has at times taken command of the weary fighters. Riding in the forefront,

46 Paul du Chaillu, *Exploration and Adventures in Egyptian Africa*, 17, 18.

47 Doughty, *Arabia Deserta*, II, 25, 362.

48 Eldon Rutter, *Holy Cities of Arabia*, II, 246.

49 A. Musil, *Arabia Petraea*, III, 207, 208, 212–214. Doughty, *Arabia Deserta*, I, 230, 231.

50 H. C. Armstrong, *Lord of Arabia*, 137. An interesting comparison is made between Moslem and Christian customs, in which the Moslem is thoroughly shocked by our practices.

with slogan and song, she has led the men to victory or to death[51] (cf. Deborah, a married woman, Judg. 5:7). Acts such as these, which were carried out with religious rites, may be akin to, or an adaptation of, the widespread idea that the sacrifice of a maiden was peculiarly pleasing to deity.[52]

Chastity was the unalterable law for the unmarried woman among all Arab tribes.[53] The violation of virginity brought death by the primitive method of stoning at the hand of the nearest of kin.[54] The accomplice was treated with like severity in desert practice. In the more complex agricultural civilization of Canaan there was a relaxing of discipline.[55] This does not mean that in the desert there are no violations of the sex code. Indolence prevails in the tent, and adultery is not unknown. Further, as the nomad comes in contact with city civilization, or even when he joins in the pilgrimage to Mecca, he and his are likely to become profligate. So degenerate have certain tribes become that in the vicinity of Mecca a group of Shiite Moslems hire out their houses, their wives, and their daughters to the pilgrims. But such are not the ideals or the general customs of the nomads.[56]

Daughters, however, were much less highly prized than sons. In times of hardship they were a drug on the market. During famine too many mouths to feed led to disaster. When war decimated the males, numerous females disturbed the social balance, and the marriage dowry rose to new highs. Girl babies were and are neglected. Parents are often glad if they die, sorry they were born.[57] Girls in Palestine today sometimes have names such as "The last," "Too much," "We are tired,"[58] all expressive of the perplexities involved in the unequal distribution of the sexes. In the pre-Mohammedan days, in the desert among the very poor it was not uncommon to bury the girl baby alive. The Prophet faced the situation realistically. He forbade the practice, and changed the old rule that the father should give a dowry with his daughter, to the new one, that the groom should pay a bride price to the father for his daughter.[59] This proved at least a partial relief in a serious situation. It is apparent that among the nomads the woman, by virtue of her nature, occupied a place of inferiority, which was unduly emphasized by tradition. Yet there is no question that, without the benefit of equality of status, she often ruled within the tent circle. Here, according to her worth, she was

---

[51] C. Raswan, *The Black Tents of Arabia*, 99, 100.

[52] Many illustrations are cited from various world religions in *ERE*, VI, 845–867. Cf. II Kings 3:27.

[53] Doughty, *Arabia Deserta*, I, 322. C. Raswan, *The Black Tents of Arabia*, 36. A. Musil, *Manners and Customs of the Rwala Bedouins*, 239–241.

[54] A. Musil, *Arabia Petraea*, III, 208–210.

[55] Dr. Canaan, *Journal of the Palestinian Oriental Society*, XI, 18, 184.

[56] W. B. Seabrook, *Adventures in Arabia*, 75, 85, gives examples of the rigid enforcement of the law.

[57] Père J. Jaussen, *Naplouse et son district*, 30–34.

[58] Dr. Canaan, *JPOS*, VII, 4, 169.

[59] Eldon Rutter, *Holy Cities of Arabia*, II, 59, 60.

counselor, inspirer, the creator of wholesome custom, and the director of affairs within the tribe. Legislation did not enhance her values, nor did inequalities render insignificant her real influence. In primitive life there were many Abigails (I Sam. 25:2, 3, 14-38).

The accepted sociopolitical customs of each group were impressionistic rather than rational, the result of community reactions rather than of private judgment.[60] Thus what was considered right in one tribe, or under certain conditions, might be definitely banned in other tribes, or under other conditions.[61] Each clan under the pressure of its history had developed its own taboos, and these restricted the foods to be eaten, the clothes to be worn, the marriage relations, and the acts to be performed. However, lacking agreement in some specific rules of conduct, these Arab nomads were one in fundamental principles. Virtue to them closely paralleled that of the modern soldier. Loyalty to the group stood at the top of the list. This was the law of life in the desert, and none but the most contemptible violated it. Hospitality to the stranger was equally esteemed. Alongside these qualities, which had grown out of tribal needs, self-mastery, an expression of individualism, enjoyed a like acclaim. Illustrations of this are numerous, but none is more significant than the preparatory tests, among the Druse, of the young man who wishes to become a *hakam* ("wise man"). While famished, he must fast all night, alone amid a feast. Suffering thirst, all night surrounded by the choicest wines, he must not taste a drop. Again all night, subject to the most seductive sex appeals, he must remain continent. Only those who in no way fail in these tests are worthy to sit with the wise men of the tribe.[62] Personal honor was most highly prized. Possessions were impossible, or a hindrance, and prestige and wisdom, which could be attained only by the few, were heavy with responsibilities; but honor was the right of all free men, and was esteemed on a par with life itself. It was hedged about by various and sundry rules that when violated brought deep chagrin to these proud dwellers in tents. The omission of a courtesy, the failure to recognize one's station, the violation of a convention, all were grave insults, while such indignities as cutting off the beard were unpardonable (II Sam. 10:1-5). Tribal customs, of all types, in the long run assumed ethical status.

The lament of the cynic that psychology has destroyed all our knowledge of human nature [63] expresses much less than the usual half-truth of a proverb; and half-truths, though smart, are fatal to clear discernment. The history of any people, as discovered in their traditions and language, and crystallized

[60] R. R. Marett, *Anthropology*, 146, 238, 239.

[61] That custom is the determining factor in *right* and *wrong* is vividly illustrated by E. W. Hopkins, *Origin and Evolution of Religion*, 245-247.

[62] W. B. Seabrook, *Adventures in Arabia*, 199-204.

[63] G. K. Chesterton, *Illustrated London News*, Dec., 1934, 592.

in their philosophy,[64] presents a fair picture of their mentality to the student. Naturally there are barriers to the complete understanding of the modes of thought of other people, especially when their language, history, customs, and type of life differ greatly from our own. However, during the last three centuries many of the uncertainties concerning primitive man have been eliminated by the combined research of many scholars, so that the difficulties of understanding the intellectual life of the Arab nomad have, at least in part, been removed.

Naturally, the thought processes of the seminomad in the border lands of Arabia differed in many ways from those of the modern Anglo-Saxon. This is not to suggest that his mental endowment was in any way inferior to that of the Western man of today. In potentialities they are equal, while in expression they differ greatly. It is a commonplace that the world in which the nomad lived, and the inherited culture that molded his thought and expression, had but little resemblance to ours. His world, complex as it was, was simple, restful, indolent. Ours is tumultuous, turbulent, and explosive, geared into an endless, mass-production assembly line that grinds on and on in ceaseless clatter. We think of them as being prelogical, while we have a precise vocabulary, a system of formal logic, the contribution of the Schoolmen of the Middle Ages, and an adequate background for philosophic thought. They were prescientific, though the claims that primitive man had the beginning of science that called for experiment and rationalization cannot be ignored; [65] we are the heirs of intense laboratory experimentation, with accurate standards of measurement, and have at least an acquaintance with inductive studies. Superficially it may seem that there is one kind of mind under a hat and another under a *kaffiyeh,* but the anthropologist is convinced that the more one knows about savages, the more the mental difference initially felt tends to disappear.[66] They lack our accumulation of data, but have their own, which in turn is foreign to us, while, in general, their intellectual potentialities compare favorably with those of civilized man. Within the limits of their own needs, the knowledge of desert topography, the location of distant wells and nooks of verdure, the value and nature of a sheep, the marks, the habits, and the customs of alien tribes, and the fine points of honor within and beyond the tribe, their critical faculties are alert. Beyond these needs they are largely uninterested. Within the "childlike mind" attributed to primitive man, a mentality shared by many of our own population, there is a basic uniformity in psychical responses with our own that makes the different cultural thought

64 The theory of history, that every phase of civilization is a "collective psychical condition" that penetrates all psychical phenomena, and thereby all historical events, is well illustrated in nomadic life (H. E. Barnes, *Psychology and History,* 126).

65 B. Malinowski, "Magic, Science, and Religion," in J. Needham, ed., *Science, Religion and Reality,* 19–83.

66 H. G. Seligmann, *Race against Man,* 38–62; Franz Boas, *The Mind of Primitive Man,* 113; Paul Radin, *Primitive Man as Philosopher,* 5, 53.

processes seem trivial.[67] From the folklore, the customs, and the history of the Arab, we see that he had early learned his way around in his complex world, and with great wisdom had accommodated himself thereto. Indeed he had achieved to a marvelous degree. As we seek to understand his way of thinking, we are compelled to measure him by our entirely different standards. His intellectual reactions will probably stand up under our tests as admirably as would ours under his criticism. Our analysis is for the purpose, not of condemning, but of better understanding his world outlook.

That the nomad was vague and inexact in his thinking is not surprising. Little in his life called for accuracy in numbers, and native lethargy never attacks the unnecessary. Statistics were a bore, and they gained the nomad little. To count three was easy; the trinity, father, mother, and son, was the earliest group. Five was familiar; the digits of one hand could be marked off with the forefinger of the other.[68] But beyond ten was rarely required in the simple desert life, and visible support such as the fingers was absent. The higher numbers had to them little significance; 360, one for every day of the year,[69] was their phrase for a great number, while the stars of the heavens, the sands of the seashore, multitude, myriad, or ten thousand had to do duty for the uncountable. This being true, numbers from such sources had little statistical value. They were used as symbols for great achievement, amazing courage, spectacular victory, honored age, etc. They were descriptive, not mathematical, terms.[70] The same features often found in the Hebrew Scriptures,[71] have caused undue perplexity to Western readers. When we try to

---

[67] M. Graubard, *Man the Slave and the Master*, 252–255.

[68] To count five is easy for the nomad, but to count ten he has to start all over again (Bertram Thomas, *Arabia Felix*, 189). Counting to twenty and beyond is exceedingly difficult (W. G. Palgrave, *Eastern and Central Arabia*, 21).

[69] Doughty, *Arabia Deserta*, I, 22, 43, 130.

[70] Every student of tribal life in Arabia confirms this conclusion. Doughty found a number reported as 40,000 to be actually less than 350, and from long experience concluded that the tribesman usually multiplies by ten (*Arabia Deserta*, I, 153, 343, 495). W. G. Palgrave was told that thousands had been killed in battle, but actual scrutiny proved that only two or three had been slightly wounded (*Eastern and Central Arabia*, 23). Nathaniel Schmidt in his preface to *Ibn Kaldun* notes that in *Ibn Kaldun* a certain army is put at 1,005,000, whereas the original report had only 5,000 (*Ibn Kaldun*, 2). T. E. Lawrence characterizes the Arab as follows: "They had a sheer distaste for system, and inhabited superlatives by choice" (*Seven Pillars of Wisdom*, 41, 44).

[71] Early Old Testament documents, in statistical matters, show the same mentality, and are usually vague and general, rather than definite. The people were or would be a great multitude (Exod. 1:3–10, 20; Gen. 16:10, J.). They were or were to be like the sand that is on the seashore for multitude (Josh. 11:4; II Sam. 17:11), or they would be thousands of myriads (Gen. 24:10, J). At times early tradition seemed more specific. In the wilderness the people were about 600,000 men on foot, besides children (Exod. 12:37, J.), or they were 600,000 men on foot (Num. 11:21, J.), and in our text the Philistines are reported to have come up against Saul with 30,000 chariots, and 6,000 horsemen, and people as the sand of the seashore in multitude (I Sam. 13:5). All of these and many similarly questionable figures were due to lack of interest in exactness coupled with the halo that tradition always casts on the past. The exaggerated numbers given by the authors of Priest Code and Chronicles are the result not so much of indifference to statistics as of inherited material and a definite apologetic for national and priestly ideals. They were all purposeful and are considered in later chapters.

force ancient Orientals into our theological pint measure, we do them an injustice, and are quite likely, at the same time, to obscure our own vision.

The memory of the nomad has often been stated to be unusually accurate. It is claimed that having no written records the need has developed mental retentiveness. No doubt among the Arabs there are those who have phenomenal memories, especially for those objective features that make a strong appeal to their senses. The ability to cross the trackless sand direct to a far-distant water hole, unvisited for twenty years, the sense of direction, the knowledge of terrain, and like feats, amaze the city-bred man of the West. But these are the needs of the tent dweller. That the memory of the primitive is better than that of the erudite has no basis in fact. The illiterate leisure of the roving shepherd has neither strengthened the memory nor stimulated reflection. The discipline of the schools has contributed to both. The Moslem scholar can often not only repeat the entire Koran verbatim but add thereto the interpretations of the scholars. Equally amazing achievements are by no means lacking in the West.

But the trustworthiness of the nomad's traditions and the accuracy of his genealogies are both under suspicion.[72] He is beyond question a facile raconteur. He is the master of a thousand tales, often celebrating the achievements of his fathers in a way that puts to shame our funeral orations. Legends spring up every day in Arabia as do the anemones on the hillsides. Glibly the story-teller can name his ancestry back through forty or, if you wish it, back to eighty generations; and no listener from either the East or the West has any way to check it beyond four generations. Moreover, to call for factual accuracy in the thrilling story, or in the honorable family tree, is to miss the meaning of the tale, which was laudatory and inspirational, rather than historical. To insist on an inerrant *Verbum Dei* would be to be a destroyer of the faith, just a dull-witted Westerner.

A highly imaginative people, with whom the border line between reality and illusion is as elastic as it is in childhood, they often display a childlike simplicity. Someone has said, facts will never prove anything to an Arab. The make-believe world, the world of dreams, to him is real. Most incredible tales are accepted at face value. The seals in the Red Sea are the army of Pharaoh that was drowned during the Exodus. The flippers and the tail, which are degenerate arms and legs, prove it.[73] The two bubbling springs, seven miles apart, near the eastern shore of the Red Sea are caused by the

---

[72] A detailed study of Arabic poetry has shown that here, where rhyme and rhythm are aids, the memory of the Arab is quite inaccurate (A. Musil, *Manners and Customs of the Rwala Bedouins*, 140–228, 283–285). Lawrence states that their memories for strangers and for events outside the family tree soon failed (Doughty, *Arabia Deserta*, xix). W. R. Smith, in *Kinship and Marriage*, 7–23, shows that sources for ancestry rarely run back more than two generations before the Prophet. S. A. Cook suggests the genealogies of the Bedouin may be largely fabrications (*The Old Testament; a Reinterpretation*, 74).

[73] Père Abel, *Revue biblique*, Oct., 1938, 512.

escaping breath of the drowned Pharaoh. A woman was turned into a pillar of salt, and the evidence long stood on the western shore of the Dead Sea. A kinsman became the chief ruler of Egypt. An animal gave counsel in the hour of need, or of danger. A dead warrior, left in the wilderness after the battle, with his throat cut, was revived and healed by locusts, shaded from the burning sun by a partridge, and later in an hour of crisis fought with his tribe.[74] Arabs of today expect Aurence (Lawrence) to return and lead them to victory. Even while still alive, the tradition is that Ibn Saud is already seated beside St. George, their ancient hero.[75] To raise a question concerning these or a thousand similar fantasies is to be told that with Allah all things are possible. To say that the Arab believes all such to be historical facts is to fail to understand his psychology. As he does not draw a sharp line between fact and fancy, our critical judgments are scarcely applicable to him. To conclude, on the other hand, that he does not expect to be taken literally [76] is to rob the childlike mind of its chief charm.

It is recognized that early man had the ability to generalize, but in the logical processes he was at the beginning of his career. He was uncritical, and without adequate techniques or chart. Nowhere is this more in evidence than in his judgments as to cause and effect. Even at a late date he failed to differentiate between the two, often merging the one into the other. The result of an act was often considered equivalent to its purpose,[77] and the contemporaneous was thought of as causal. Illustrations of this type of reasoning—or of unreason—are so universal that we are not surprised to find many in our Bible. A weary traveler had a strange dream; he concluded there must have been a spirit in the stone on which his head rested (Gen. 28:12–17). A child died; his father knew he had violated a taboo (II Sam. 12:15–18). A woman long barren gave birth to a boy; she had entertained an angel (Gen. 21:1–7; Judg. 13:3–7). A field was unusually fruitful; the owner had within his house a spirit-possessed box (II Sam. 6:12). While close relation between two incidents, either in time or in place, is no final proof that one is the cause of the other, yet, all too often, modern reasoning follows the same pattern of thought.

The Arab temperamentally was always highly emotional. Indolent and lethargic over long periods, when aroused he was passionate. Mass movements were easily developed, and with sufficient incentive, as booty, revenge, or religion, and a leader with a good slogan, a whole tribe was ready for action and would respond with fanatical fury. On such occasions extreme savagery sometimes prevailed. Eyes were gouged out, thumbs and great toes

---

[74] W. G. Palgrave, *Central and Eastern Arabia*, I, 121.

[75] Bertram Thomas, *Arabia Felix*, 85.

[76] A. M. Ribhany, *The Syrian Christ*, 108–110, 115–139.

[77] A. Lods, *Revue d'histoire et de philosophie religieuses*, 1927, 1–16, gives many illustrations of this prelogical mentality in the Hebrew Scriptures. Also R. H. Kennett, *The Church of Israel*, 142–147.

were cut off, and even the women joined in the orgies.[78] Restraints, such as the scant fare of the desert and the dread of blood revenge, naturally kept such outbursts at a minimum. Then the passion, so easily roused and so intense, usually subsided as quickly. These emotional qualities were natural soil for religious ecstasy. The dervish fraternities among Moslem Arabs [79] and the prophetic guilds in early Israel are perpetual testimony to this type of mentality. Doughty has remarked that among some of the desert tribes probably one-third of the people are hypochondriacs, the victims of self-delusion.[80]

Dogmatism, the child of strong emotions and narrow contacts, is the rule of the desert. The tribesman knows what he knows. His conclusions may rest on limited information and devious reasoning, but to him they are irrefutable certainties. Doubt is despised and truth has no *ifs* and *buts*. In Oriental speech phrases such as *in my opinion* and *it seems to me* are noteworthy for their absence.[81] To them there are no intermediary colors; all is either white or black, and their general attitude is expressed in the boast of a modern Wahhabi, "We are exactly in the right, and every one else is in the wrong." [82] Change is to them as unthinkable as that the stars should alter their courses; and all nature warns them that uncertainty is death. The desert has fashioned the creed of the Arab. He is the child of Allah, and all that happens is the will of Allah.

Beyond the above-mentioned characteristics there are certain mental qualities that are illumined by a study of the language of the people. The speech of the pre-Mosaic tribes, however varied their dialects may have been, was basic to Biblical Hebrew, which in turn includes a number of different dialects.[83] Certain specific linguistic features found in Biblical Hebrew are an inheritance from early days, and provide an insight into the distinctive mental make-up of the Arab. As language is "inseparable from reason" through it we may most adequately enter the thought world of any people.[84]

Arabic, the most inclusive term for the language of the forebears of the Hebrews, a product of the desert, while not devoid of musical qualities, is rugged and masculine. It is marked by a wealth of gutturals and sibilants, and

[78] Doughty, *Arabia Deserta*, I, 68. H. C. Armstrong, *The Lord of Arabia*, 13–19, 119–121. T. E. Lawrence, *Seven Pillars of Wisdom*, 416.

[79] While the organization of dervish fraternities, of which there are a number of quite different orders, did not begin for some two hundred years after the opening of the Mohammedan era, they were all rooted in religious movements that had long been in existence (D. S. Margoliouth, "Dervish," *ERE;* D. B. Macdonald, *The Hebrew Literary Genius*, 74–83).

[80] Doughty, *Arabia Deserta*, II, 5.

[81] A. M. Ribhany, *The Syrian Christ*, 185–188.

[82] W. G. Palgrave, *Central and Eastern Arabia*, 265. Doughty, *Arabia Deserta*, xx–xxii.

[83] Our Hebrew text includes literature from every period from 850 to 150 B.C., comes from various communities such as Samaria, Judea, Babylonia, possibly Egypt, and Arabia, and represents diverse schools of thought, such as folklorists, prophets, wise men, priests, apocalyptists, and skeptics. Though all save a few chapters is in Hebrew, the divergencies are equivalent to dialects (Carpenter and Harford-Battersby, *The Composition of the Hexateuch*, 101–112; Zelig S. Harris, *A Grammar of the Phoenician Language*, 67–70).

[84] W. M. Urban, *Language and Reality*, 23–49.

passion and fanaticism can easily be roused by its rhythms. As the rigors of the inhospitable steppes ever echo through its speech, it is a poor medium for social amenities, the delights of the aesthetic, or the mild enthusiasms of the nature lover. These finer qualities were not absent even in the early days, but single words and phrases, never complete descriptions, had to suffice to kindle the imagination of the listener.

The vocabulary was limited, and as in all speech it had originated in sense data; and, still belonging to the lower levels of culture, it had scarcely developed beyond the concrete. Nouns and verbs dominated, while particles, prepositions, and conjunctions, as well as adjectives and adverbs, were limited. Grammatical relations were simple and poorly defined. Predicate and subject, co-ordinated or loosely connected, held the field. Moods, conditions, and even time relations were scarcely indicated. Intonation and gesture must often have supplied this lack. It is not too much to say that the primitive Semitic language, as well as the Hebrew, could have been adequately understood only within the "speech community." [85] In these facts lay the genius of the Hebrew language. It was bare and rude, but vital. It was able to express only a limited number of ideas, but these were fundamental to existence, and to the simplest social needs. It was unfitted to celebrate the trivial, but it was adequate for rough justice, and tales of the heroic ancestors. It lacked the *ifs* and *buts* of casuistry, and was not suited to express the subtle shades of meaning in philosophy and theology, but it was a keen-edged sword in the blunt, forthright speech of reformers. If its verbal forms lacked those definite time relations, past, present, and future, that are interwoven in the very fabric of our thinking, they more than compensated by expressing the condition in the verbal idea as complete or incomplete.[86] Thus personal and social relations, in the present, constituted the norm of thought for these children of the desert. For them life was more than a mad rush between yesterday and tomorrow, ticked off in minutes, hours, and days; it was an experience that lay beneath the lights and shades cast by life's fleeting incidents. Their language could not express our ideas of infinite, eternal, almighty; but they had such meaningful words as *faithfulness, personality*—unfortunately rendered "soul" in our translations—and *life*.[87] The marked poverty of the material situation was compensated for in those things that are essential.

---

[85] This is always true, and constitutes one of the grave difficulties in any translation. It is doubly so in translating Hebrew into English. In the first instance each word and phrase can be adequately understood only in the background of the community life in which the word was used. See W. M. Urban, *Language and Reality*, 235–243. But during the seven centuries from which our Hebrew literature came, every century had its definite "speech community," and some centuries were gifted with five or more. It is no light task to know each of these. Further, the differences between Hebrew grammar and that of the classics, which is our mold, are so great that adequate adjustment has never been made in our translations. See W. H. Robinson, "Symbolism of Language," *Redemption and Revelation*, 39–56.

[86] G. A. Barton, "Semites," *ERE*, XI, 380.

[87] S. A. Cook, "Semites," *CAH*, I, 194–205, is an excellent, well-ordered article on this theme.

Still more important is the fact that they believed the *word* was not merely a symbol for a thing, but was in itself a *reality*. The name and the thing named, in some mysterious way, were believed to have an inner unity, an identity of spirit. The serpent and the word *serpent*,[88] were inseparable in spirit as well as in thought. To the primitive mind both seemed to be *anima*. Names of persons were much more significant to the ancients than to us. Even our nicknames, as Lord Haw-Haw or Soapy Sam, refer only to individual characteristics or experiences. But to the ancients the name, like the hair, the nails, or even the garment, was often considered a part of the person, and to know it was to have power over the individual. Jacob insisted on knowing the name of the wrestler (Gen. 32:29) and Moses was eager to know the name of the deity who appeared to him in the burning bush (Exod. 3:13) in order that each might succeed in his mission. The name, or the word, was immaterial and invisible, but, as with winds and plagues, that enhanced rather than diminished its power. The word, spoken or written, was believed to be endowed with magic, and had a potency beyond that of arrow or slingshot. In this lay the terror and the hope in cursing and blessing that run throughout our Scriptures. This, also, is the very atmosphere in which the idea of the inspiration of the Word of God came to birth.[89]

This brings us to what may rightly be called their primitive philosophy, that is, their earliest interpretation of the world order. Faced by problems relating to life and death, the human mind, by its very nature, insisted on answers to its perplexities that in some way ministered to continued existence. With the power of generalization, a function of the forebrain, man proceeded, almost unconsciously, to gather and organize the facts into a system. The beginnings were very simple, the conclusions were tentative, and the development was very slow. Disasters that threatened his very existence stimulated him. Experiments that turned out badly taught him wisdom, and, through reflection over long millennia, little by little the world chaos, to his understanding, began to take form. He became aware that forces outside himself had power

[88] The word *serpent* is the Hebrew *srph*, or *srf*, "to burn," which has been anglicized. In all languages many words have had their origin in imitation or in description of some characteristic of the thing or the act under consideration. The appropriateness of the word to the thing or the act easily suggested an inner relationship between the two, which in turn became the basis of a vague philosophy. One of our modern philosophers, in a very thorough discussion of this question, draws attention to the fact that in the Cratylus of Plato there is an insistence on the "existence of some intimate and primordial relation between the word and the thing" (W. M. Urban, *Language and Reality*, 52, 53). It is the personal conviction of Dr. Urban that the miracle of language, which is the foundation of intelligible communication, can be understood only on the basis of a transcendental presupposition. Cf. *Language and Reality*, 84, 251–261.

[89] The belief exists among many people that the name of a thing is a soul, a living being existing by itself; and this name-soul is thought to be of the very substance of the thing or person named. Thus the intonation of a formula, through the power of magic, will bring on the person cursed or blessed inescapable results (Geo. Foucart, *ERE*, IX, 130–136, 151b–155). This use of the divine name, and certain restrictions, are frequent in Scripture. See Judg. 9:20, 27, 57; II Kings 2:24; Exod. 20:6; and J. Skinner, *Divine Names in Genesis*, 12–14. The significance of archaic phrases and names is discussed in J. T. Shotwell, *The History of History*, 45, 46.

to do things. While any single word may be too definite and too abstract to accurately symbolize man's first glimmerings on the way to philosophy, the Polynesian word *mana* [90] has come into general use as the most adequate term for this power. Mana, then, may be described as the power attributed by primitive peoples to certain persons or things. It is an extra physical force, "hovering between the personal and the impersonal," and persons or things possessing it become sacred. In our terminology it has been spoken of as "supernatural," and its activity has been called "miraculous." But primitive man had not made the false cleavage of natural and supernatural, nor had he learned that all phenomena were orderly and law-abiding. Mana was mighty, and he was largely ignorant of the principles on which it worked. However, it was infectious, and might be transmitted from one person or thing to another person or thing. This might be accomplished not only by contact but also by gesture, song, formulas, and telepathic power. Hence those persons and things that were believed to have mana must be hedged about by taboos in order to show proper respect to the latent energy in them, and to protect the wayfarer. Thus ritual, a system of taboos, was developed out of experience, in order to control mana. As ritual was largely objective, it was subject to organization, and thus became of first importance in the ordering and development of the thought processes of peoples in the lower areas of culture. When this interpretation of world forces, confused and puerile as it was, was reached, man had planted his feet firmly on the lower rungs of the ladder that reached up to the status of modern science and religion. It was the day of small beginnings that cannot be despised. Men were seeking a more comprehensive, and a more coherent, explanation of the world order, and the relation of the parts to the whole. Many and various explanations were hazarded. Many were local and short-lived. Others made wide appeal, and some have survived to the present day. Each contributed its quota, directly or indirectly, to the ultimate solution of the problems in science, theology, and religion.

The primitive Semites passed through similar stages of thought, naturally with variations, as other groups, and remnants of these are found scattered throughout their later literature.[91] Among the experiments in reflection that made serious contributions to human thinking, and definitely influenced Israel's ancestors, only three are here considered. From the earliest days the heavenly bodies were believed to be the abodes of powers that ordered the affairs of men. The sun ruled the day, and the moon the night, while the new moon introduced the month, and the stars in their cycle determined the march

[90] An important discussion of the meaning of mana, and the important part it played in thought and religion among primitive peoples, is found in R. R. Marett, *ERE*, VIII, 375–379, also *The Threshold of Religion*, 1–32, 115–141. A briefer statement is found in E. G. Bewekes, *A Survey of Philosophy and Religion*, 7, 8. The idea expressed in mana is found among many primitive tribes, and among the Huron Indians of America is called *orenda*. Cf. J. N. B. Hewitt, *American Anthropologist*, New Series, IV, 33–46, or H. B. Alexander in *ERE*, IX, 555, 556.

[91] W. R. Smith, *Rel. Sem.* (3), 550–558, 658, 663, 671.

of the seasons. Beyond that the heavens were the home of the winds, the storms, and the rain. Before man began to think, these determined many of his activities and they still claim his profoundest speculation. On the whole, however, their movements were orderly, and predictable; hence, they were most significant in human experience, and they were reliable and undisturbing influences. They steadied, rather than stimulated, early thought.

The presence and influence of the spirits of the dead always occupied a prominent place in the thought of early man.[92] These spirits were seen, heard, and felt so often by so many positive witnesses that denial of their existence and activity would have been futile. They walked by night, and appeared especially in hours of crises. Some were the heralds of disaster, others were the protectors or champions of the tribe.

Totemism is the third type of thought to be considered. In this the clan and the clan's totem, an animal or a vegetable, were believed to be related genetically,[93] or mystically, or to have the same soul-substance.[94] Totemism has been very widespread and probably originated in the early period, when the barriers between animals and man, and between animal and vegetable, did not exist. It is assumed to have been universal and the earliest form of religion.[95]

In these and other theories, mana, the indefinite energy that did things, was giving place to or was being transformed into that which was more definite, more orderly, and more personal. Animism, that system of thought in which it was believed that a spirit—*spiro,* "to breathe"; or *anima,* "breath," "wind," or "vital principle"—was in every object and behind every activity, marked this forward step in human thinking. It was a comprehensive explanation of the universe. The theory was easily understood, was realistic, seemed supported by indubitable facts, and was adaptable to all shades of thinking. These spirits were conceived to be in all objects, animate and inanimate, in all earth forms, stones, springs, trees, beasts and birds, in the heavenly bodies, and in the less tangible phenomena, clouds, storms, plagues, famine, and disease. Man thought of them as like himself, yet different.[96] They gained names, specific characteristics, and definite location. They were invisible, but capable of assuming various forms, and were able to act for weal or for woe with greater or less efficiency. They were active in palsies, epilepsy, delusions, ecstasies, and insanity. They hovered around the functions of birth, marriage, and death, and often

92 S. Reinach, *CMR,* I, 316–331. E. W. Hopkins, *Origin and Evolution of Religion,* 67–87.

93 Savages believe themselves to be kin to their totem; each animal of the species is a brother (W. R. Smith, *Rel. Sem.* (3), 124–133). When the *jinni* cohabits with a woman, he assumes a human form (F. Maclear, *Journal of the Royal Asiatic Society,* 1929, 401).

94 E. O. James, *Origins of Sacrifice,* 21–24.

95 E. Durkheim, *Elementary Forms of Religious Life,* 87–239. S. A. Cook, *Jewish Quarterly Review,* 1902, 413–448, a judicious summary of evidences of totemism in Israel.

96 This distinction between the self and the nonself has been regarded as an intellectual achievement of first importance. It was the first step in the critical discovery of the objective world, and thus prepared the way for the interpretation of that world which of necessity must be in terms of the self (J. E. Harrison, in *Darwinism and Modern Science,* 508).

were believed to have intercourse with mortals.[97] Gradually, on the basis of location, function, or power, ancient men organized their spirit world. The great spirits in the sky, and those in stones, springs, trees, and mountains, had their definite boundaries. The spirits of the winds, storms, and diseases were less predictable, and like outlaw tribes were less socialized. The spirit of fertility, the mother goddess, called Ishtar [98] or its equivalent, and her consort, Baal, the possessor, were duly assigned specific fertility functions. Spirits of different origin, of the totem, of local phenomenon, or of a renowned ancestor or other, easily became the patron deities of the individual tribes.[99] In some such way it is possible that Chemosh, Moloch, and Qos became the tribal deities of Moab, Ammon, and Edom respectively. Such a deity was believed to be the moving spirit in the tribe. As the divine father, whether by physical or by mystical origin, he was conceived of as the provider, the overseer, the judge, and the ruler of his people. While the tribe was strong, he was strong; when they weakened and died, like his worshipers he ceased to be. When Syria perished, Adad passed out of existence; and with the fall of Babylonia, Marduk went the way of all flesh. Thus, as the deities were the reflection of the tribal or national history, so the philosophy of the people was the measure of the intelligence of its wise men.

This theory recognized the kinship of all life from the lowest to the highest, the communicability between the lower and the higher, and implied the unity of the universe.[100] Spirits great and small were believed to fill all the world, and were pressing around humanity as completely as does the ether. Man's incoming and outgoing, his downsitting and his uprising in the black tents of Kedar were ever compassed about by a great cloud of witnesses. This theory in its most refined form seemed, to the pre-Mosaic tribes, a satisfactory explanation for all phenomena, personal, tribal, and cosmic. It was sufficiently comprehensive for the wisest and fluid enough to admit the crudest of interpretations. In fact, it was accepted, almost without question, by biological and medical science from the days of Galen until the time of Galvani, who in 1780 A.D., by his theory that nerve force was animal electricity, gave it and the theological edifice resting on it their death blow.[101] Still, it seems so natural an explanation for delirium, epilepsy, insanity, and many types of hallucination that in wide-

97 In Arabia it is commonly held that certain clans and tribes are the descendants of a man and a jinniyeh (female spirit), or of a woman and a jinni. The Beni Kalb are reputed to be the offspring of a fair woman and a white hound (Doughty, Arabia Deserta, I, 130). The Ajman tribe boasted a jinniyeh as their ancestress (Bertram Thomas, Arabia Felix, 209, 269). Cf. Gen. 6:2–4.

98 Ishtar is the one divine name common to all branches of the Semites (G. A. Barton, "Semites," ERE, XI.

99 Ed. Dhorme, La religion des Hébreux nomades; Le dieu parent, 313–319. Paul Radin, Primitive Religion, 192–194.

100 Goblet d'Alviella, "Animism," ERE, I, 535–537. A. Stratton, JRAS, Oct., 1934, 715–727, a study of the supposed activities of spirits in Arabia today.

101 Sir Chas. Sherrington, Man on His Nature, 234–251. Lynn Thorndyke, History of Magic and Experimental Science, IV, 612.

spread areas it is still orthodoxy.[102] On the other hand, all branches of science are of one accord in declaring that the whole concept rests not on fact but on fancy, and even the sanctions of hoary tradition cannot prevent its collapse.

The statement that the nomad is not deeply religious, quite apart from any definition of terms, may be seriously questioned. The desert has not mothered three great religions without a subsoil that readily nourished zeal toward higher things. Its broad wastes certainly encouraged an emphasis on social values, while its brooding mysteries were congenial to the spirit of reverence, and to a profound dependence on the great Unknown. It may, however, be correct to say that, by and large, the desert dweller is indolent and complacent, and that in the routine of life he is not given overmuch to ritual practices. But if religion deals with life values, and calls for submission to the Higher Powers, in this he is by no means lacking.

The religion of any people is not only colored by their environment but is rooted in the geographic and economic conditions of their habitat. As has been said, Semitic religion is the natural growth of the soil in the Semitic soul.[103] Indeed, all the strands of life, the economic, social, political, and intellectual, were so interwoven that the preceding pages of this chapter are but the framework for the understanding of nomadic religion. The constant problem for the Arab tribes had been to integrate or harmoniously adjust themselves to the environment, both visible and invisible, so as to secure, so far as possible, a happy, continued, tribal existence. They were realists, and emphasized life as it was, not as it might be in some other realm. Their objective, as expressed in the root meaning of ye sh û 'a h, was enlargement, freedom, welfare, not, as usually translated, "salvation," with our theological implications. Life to them, it is true, was meager and hampered, but it was theirs, and to them it was good. That the food supply should be increased and storms and diseases prevented was desirable, but lethargy and faith had so conspired that whatever was their lot therewith they were content. For the solution of their problems they had a laboratory, but they were without blueprint or tutor. Their welfare (salvation) in an animistic world order had to be worked out by the trial-and-error method. Through millennia they built up their approaches and defenses to their spirit world, patiently, almost blindly, plodding toward the light.[104] Many of their efforts were futile, and much now seems to us childish, but like the gurgling lisps of early speech they were the human adventure toward abundant life, the worthy heralds of things to come. Each tribe reacted to climate, topog-

---

102 S. König, Folk Lore, 1938, 270–276.

103 Doughty, Arabia Deserta, I, 265.

104 It is growingly clear that the earliest stages in ritual were the product of social customs, which were the instinctive responses to the chase, to love, and to war. As primitive man acted before he thought, so the earliest cult practices preceded reflection on the why, and the how (R. R. Marett, Anthropology, 238, 239; "Magic," ERE, VIII, 245–251, esp. 247b. W. R. Smith, Rel. Sem. (3), 16–26).

raphy, and experience in its own peculiar way, and migrants ever and anon introduced new blood and at times strange customs. Yet in spite of local differences, there were large agreements in the religions of the tribes from south and north, east and west in Arabia in ancient as well as in modern days. The endless sands, the broad horizons, and the merciless sun have written their message deep in the hearts of the children of the steppes. The pre-Mosaic clans, from whatever region they may have migrated, beneath varied cult practices must have had much in common.

As indicated in the previous section, the earth, the air, and the sky, the spirits of the ancestors, the principle of fertility, and totemism had each, at one time or another, occupied a place in the reflection of the early Arabs. Remnants of ritual, sometimes preserved down to late days, reveal that all of these had played a part in the primitive religion of some or all of the tribes. The observance of the new moon continued down beyond the period of the exile. Ancestor worship has left definite traces in names, phrases, and customs in all periods. That fertility worship could not have been lacking is seen by its prevalence among all primitive tribes, as well as relics of phallic worship found in the Old Testament (Gen. 24:2, 9; Exod. 20:26). Totemism, which had long ceased to play any vital part in religion, may be the correct explanation of the numerous animal names of tribes. The prevalent bull[105] and snake worship[106] (I Kings 12:28; Exod. 32:3–16; Num. 21:8, 9; II Kings 18:4), as well as archaic features preserved in prehistoric rites, such as the *red heifer* (Num. 19:2–19) may very well be vestigial remnants of primitive thinking. Even the taboo on eating swine's flesh may be camouflaged evidence of totemism.[107]

Definite cult practices grew up from earliest days around each and every object of worship in order to maintain those intimate and happy relations with the various spirits that insured the well-being of the tribe. Fear of the spirits or the gods has long been considered the dominating motive in the religion of early man. Owing to our classical and eschatological inheritance, and the theory of Feuerbach that religion originated in fear, Christian writers still usually follow this pattern of thought.[108] But on the other hand, some anthropologists with abundant evidence definitely reject this assumption. Durkheim, the exponent of totemism, was convinced that early man believed the spirits were his friends, even his kinsmen.[109] Many scholars, often from divergent points of view, have come to a similar estimate of the rather insignificant place

105 In a suggestive study in which he collates the significant Biblical material, Professor Meek presents a strong case for the bull being the primitive symbol for the Joseph tribe (T. J. Meek, *Hebrew Origins*, 133–139). This being true, the probability is that it originated in totemism.

106 The serpent symbol quite possibly belonged to the tribe of Levi *ibid.*, (116–132) and may also have had a totemistic origin.

107 W. R. Smith, *Rel. Sem.* (3), 137, 138, gives a cautious, well-balanced statement on totemism. Reference is made to the red heifer on pp. 351, 354, 376.

108 J. L. McIntyre, "Fear," *ERE*, V, 797–800.

109 Durkheim, *Elementary Forms of Religious Life*, 224, 225.

fear played in early religion.[110] One of the most important contributions to Biblical studies is that of E. O. James, who concludes that ritual originated in the food quest, and that faith and hope were fundamental thereto.[111] Further, in an article on sacrifice he asserts that a yearning to enter into a sacramental union with the tribal god was the motive that lay behind Semitic sacrifice, while fear had no conspicuous influence.[112]

Cult practices that originated in the desire to enter into communion with deity, and thus perpetuate a happy existence, have been said to be the sum total of ancient religions.[113] Ritual, once accepted, soon becomes stereotyped and constitutes the framework that preserves the emotional phase of religion.[114] The forms are likely to remain static, though changes are often made in their interpretation. Hence, even in late strata of Semitic religion telltale fragments of most primitive practices may sometimes be discovered.[115]

Primitive cult rites have very frequently been spoken of as magical. But though we have no substitute for the word it is subject to serious misunderstanding. Originally it meant the learning, the ritual practice, and the religion of the Persian Magi. But in Western usage, it soon came to be associated with witchcraft, sorcery, and the like. Thus, in science and religion, magic was used for that which was inferior, and antisocial. In theology it has often been thrown into sharp contrast with religion, religion being described as submission to the will of deity, while efforts to force deity to do as man wished have been called magic.[116] But this line of cleavage, though still persisting in many quarters, is quite untenable from the standpoint of both psychology and the history of religions. Most, if not all, of the primitive rites were efforts to co-operate with deity, were accompanied by faith in the Unseen, and would be called religious, while some of the widely observed rites of the Christian religion are but degenerate forms of crassest superstitions. Magic may then be thought of as the system of primitive rites, whether of word, gesture, act, or instrument, that were believed to have some subtle connection with the source of power, even as the button has with the electric bulb. These rites originated in the natural responses of man to the stimulus of need, and were based on universal psychophysical reactions.[117] Magic, then, may rightly be considered the protoplasm

---

[110] Malinowski concludes that the idea that fear first made gods in the universe is certainly not true in the light of anthropology (Jos. Needham, *Science, Religion and Reality*, 82). Marett would admit wonder, admiration, interest, respect, and even love to be essential constituents of the elemental mood of primitive man, and considers awe the one that expresses the fundamental religious feeling most nearly (*The Threshold of Religion*, 13). G. F. Moore holds that the impulse to self-preservation was the universal, supreme, perpetual motive that lay behind the origin of religion (*Birth and Growth of Religion*, 3, 4). Cf. also W. R. Smith, *Rel. Sem.* (3), 518–520.

[111] *Primitive Ritual and Belief*, 21–48.

[112] E. O. James, "Sacrifice," *ERE*, XI, 6b.

[113] W. R. Smith, *Rel. Sem.* (3), 16–26, esp. 20.

[114] E. W. Hopkins, *Origin and Evolution of Religion*, 180–183.

[115] *Ibid.*, 180–203.

[116] For a brief study of the use of the word see R. R. Marett, *ERE*, VIII, 244b, 245a.

[117] B. Malinowski, in Needham, *Science, Religion and Reality*, 73–78.

from which art,[118] science, and religion were derived. In the beginning some rites were more adequate than others; throughout history some forms were regenerated while others degenerated. The former we have called religious, the latter magical.

The cultus of the tribes under consideration naturally was simple in form and limited in type. Places, objects, and acts that lay within their usual routine were guarded by well-known and rigid restrictions. These taboos—the Polynesian word *tapu* literally means to mark off, and in usage implies, "unlucky to meddle with" [119]—are the equivalents of the "Thou shalt not" of Scripture. Thou shalt not go up by steps unto mine altar. Thou shalt not lift up a tool upon the altar. Thou shalt not cut off the hair upon thy head. Thou shalt not touch this or that. Thou shalt not eat this or that. Thou shalt not wear this or that. Thou shalt not marry this one or that one.[120] Etc., etc. These were all negative customs that had been evolved by experience, and as such were the social disciplines at the lower level of culture. Places, objects, and acts that lay outside of the usual tribal experience as a whole, like enemies, wild animals, and spirits whose ways were unknown, were strange, and because of possible danger were to be avoided. Taboos thus were the established safeguards in primitive society, and in due time came to be considered the dictates of deity, endowed with religious sanctions.[121] It seems probable that at one time or another all or most of the taboos may have contributed a quota to tribal welfare, and some that emerged in the far past may be of permanent value to humanity. But as we scan the history of religions, it seems beyond question that most of them, like the Chinese Wall, lost their values long ago. The observance of many still sanctioned by our religion aids chiefly in intolerance and isolationism, and is a barrier to both civilization and religion.

Magic is positive and aggressive, while taboo is negative and defensive. Ordinarily it has been divided into four types: sympathetic magic, divination, thaumaturgy, and incantation. Most of these lay outside the range of interest of the Arabs of the borderland. The broad barren spaces, the sparse population, and the stagnant life were poor soil for a luxuriant growth of such exotic arts. Incantation, that is, the use of spells, or the chanting of a curse or blessing, may have occasionally been practiced, as indicated in the Balaam story (Num. 23:7–24:24), though prayer or any equivalent is very rare among the nomads.[122]

Divination by oracle, augury, or lot, in order to learn the future, could have had but slight appeal to these men. They knew the water holes, the rock shel-

---

[118] Count Begouen, *Antiquity*, March, 1929, 5–20.

[119] R. R. Marett, "Tabu," *ERE*, XII, 181–185, and *Threshold of Religion*, 85–114.

[120] Ed. Dhorme, *La religion des Hébreux nomades*, 297–311. Cf. I Sam. 21:5–23; Exod. 19:15; Lev. 15:18.

[121] Taboo has not only been accepted as the chief factor in social discipline among the most primitive tribes, but has been called the seed bed of personal religion (R. R. Marett, *ERE*, XII, 183).

[122] Ed. Dhorme, *La religion des Hébreux nomades*, 247–262. Here it is recorded that Père Jaussen in all his sojourn with the Bedouin learned of only one simple prayer, and that was addressed to the moon.

ters, the plots of grass, their friends and their enemies. The past had offered few surprises, and the future had little or nothing on which to speculate. What had been was, and what was, was to be. Existence, like the gods, was unchangeable.

Thaumaturgy, or miracle working, likewise lay beyond their ken. They were romantic, and attributed superhuman achievements to their heroes, past and present, but this was the unfettered hero worship of children. The traveling magician with bag and staff could bring no profit to them, nor could he gain aught for himself. Only in the more complex society can such thrive.

Sympathetic magic, the most primitive of all, based on the idea that like produces, or cures, like, must also have played a very insignificant role. Originating in dramatic action, in which man acted out that which he wished accomplished, thinking thereby to aid the spirits [123]—this form of magic covered a wide range of human interest. Based in inherent reflex responses of the nervous system,[124] it must have been practiced from before the dawn of human consciousness. Processions, dances related to rain, wind, war, marriage, and mimetic actions were easily developed and, owing to the feeling of actual participation in the desired result, gained an emotional authority that accepted their validity.

Times and places, owing to functional activities, and rare experiences became the landmarks of religion. The springtime for the flock, and birth, tribal initiation, marriage, and death for the family, were the axes around which life, therefore religion, revolved. Places that were essential to the physical and psychical welfare of the tribe naturally became sacred. Shrines and sacred seasons were usually co-ordinated. The springtime festival of the shepherds ordinarily would be observed year after year in the same place. Ain-Kadeish, Bab edh-Dra', Horeb, Baal-peor, and others seem to have long functioned as such sanctuaries, while others like their devotees were short-lived. Natural phenomena which were peculiar and persistent, such as a bubbling fountain or a smoking mountain (Exod. 3:2), tended to make permanent such sanctuaries, as mysterious, cosmic features have always aroused the awe of untutored tribes. But when, for any reason whatsoever, worshipers ceased, the sanctuaries and gods alike passed into oblivion.[125]

123 In Palestine today when rain is sorely needed the *rain procession,* in which water sprinkling is an important part, is religiously staged (T. Canaan, *Zeitschrift des Deutschen Palestine-Vereins,* 1913, 290; G. Dalman, *Arbeit und Sitte,* I, 1, 150–154; W. O. E. Oesterley, *The Sacred Dance,* 19–30).

124 In any public competition many of the onlookers, by their definite bodily movements, play the whole game from the side lines. The rhythmic slogans of the leader of a gang of Oriental workmen, as well as the ritual of the cheerleader in college football, are based in the same physiological fact. Primitive man turned this principle into religious channels. (B. Malinowski, in J. Needham, *Science, Religion and Reality,* 66–71).

125 Many examples of long-deserted sanctuaries might be cited, but none is better than that of Bab edh-Dra', which was partly excavated by Kyle, Mallon, and Albright in 1924. Here at the southeast end of the Dead Sea were found the ruins of a large, ancient pilgrimage center that had been a resort for hundreds of years and then, about 1800 B.C., had been suddenly deserted (Albright, *Bulletin of the American School of Oriental Research,* XIV, 5–7).

The ceremonies observed, even those of the springtime festival, which was most significant to the nomad, were usually simple, though they often lasted a week or more.[126] The rites pertaining to birth, marriage, and death were largely family affairs, and under unfavorable economic conditions were often neglected. In fact the formal side of religion never flourished among the lean, hunger-bitten men who roamed the margin of the desert land in search of food.

But two features of primary importance persist throughout their most sacred rites. One was the belief that in their sacrificial feast they entered into a mystical union with their deity;[127] the other was their conviction that blood possessed most mysterious potencies. According to their philosophy it was *anima*, and, of all the world spirits, it was among the strangest. When it flowed from an animal body, the body lost all its vitality, therefore the blood *was* the life, that is, the animating spirit, the blood-soul.[128] When it was out of the body, it was believed to be no less potent; its potentialities had but been released from its earlier habitat.

When blood was shed, and the blood-spirit was thus released from its material abode, primitive man believed that under certain circumstances this strange power might be helpful to him. In many parts of the world the blood of an enemy slain in battle, as well as the blood of a sacrificial victim, is drunk in the belief that the anima or spirit of the victim enters into and strengthens the partaker.[129] Primitive people frequently have thought that spirits and deities, like humans, had a thirst for blood,[130] and it is possible that an early form of sacrifice was an expression of this idea. A widely observed practice in Arabia is the sprinkling of the blood of the sacrifice on the newly plowed field in order to promote the fertility of the soil.[131] It is also poured out on the foundations of a new house and over the threshold, sprinkled on the doorposts, and smeared over the bodies of the worshipers for protective purposes.[132] While ideas concerning the significance of shed blood may have changed from time

---

[126] In early Arabia during the first eight days of the spring month a festival was held, during which a sheep was sacrificed, either at home or, preferably, at a sacred place; the blood was poured on a stone, and the flesh was eaten by the worshipers (J. Wellhausen, *Reste Arabischen Heidentums*, 74, 94, 105; *Prolegomena to the History of Israel*, 92, 93).

[127] W. R. Smith, *Rel. Sem.* (3), 224. E. O. James, *Origins of Sacrifice*, 120–127. J. G. Fraser, *The Golden Bough*, II, 68, 69.

[128] Within small compass, the most constructive article on the subject is that of H. Wheeler Robinson, "Blood," *ERE*, II, 714a–719. See also T. H. Weir, *ERE*, XI, 30; L. R. Farnell, *The Evolution of Religion*, 105, 110, 111.

[129] Clay Trumbull, *The Blood Covenant*, 126–134, 139–142. W. R. Smith, *Kinship and Marriage*, 284. Doughty, *Arabia Deserta*, II, 41.

[130] It was believed that life was transmitted by the letting of blood (Clay Trumbull, *The Threshold Covenant*, 194, 195). Anat, the war goddess, had a love for massacre (Virolleaud, *Zeitschrift für die Alttestamentliche Wissenschaft*, 1939, 206–208), Chemosh of Moab also (*The Mesha Stone*).

[131] Doughty, *Arabia Deserta*, I, 136.

[132] Père Jaussen, *Naplouse et son district*, 22, 37–39, and *Coutumes des Arabes*, 309, 316–320, gives many illustrations of this in modern practice. W. R. Smith, *Rel. Sem.* (3), 233–236, 337, 339, 344–346, 351, 381, 431, interprets the use of blood in ancient and modern customs.

to time, it is evident that it played an important part in primitive Semitic religion.

Man long ago learned that what could be most helpful, such as water and fire, could under certain circumstances be extremely dangerous. This was particularly true of all things in which dwelt important spirits, such as the ark, and the blood. Hence, as a protection against possible dangers, many restrictions or taboos were imposed to prevent contacts with the blood-spirit. Blood must be covered lest the spirit take vengeance on those in the vicinity (Gen. 4:10; Job 16:18). Blood must not be eaten (I Sam. 14:32–34; Lev. 17:12, 13), and capital punishment must be by stoning, so that there should be no bloodletting (Deut. 17:5, 6).[133]

The ritual prescribed for all their religious functions, however primitive and simple, was profoundly effective with the worshipers. It always was at their own level and had evolved out of their tribal experiences. The festivals—fasting was of minor importance to the nomad[134]—with processionals, dances, and music in which all joined, were never-to-be-forgotten experiences. Like the village home-coming, or better still a ten-days sojourn by the faithful at the shrine of Bernadette, tradition and expectancy co-operated to enhance their appeal. Bodily vigor was renewed, the mind was refreshed, the emotions were kindled, and in the name of religion the whole man entered into fellowship with the tribe and his god.

A due appreciation of the values in such rites is, to us, as difficult as is a just appraisal of their way of life. But we cannot forget that these people were close to the source whence three great world religions had their origins. Possessing nothing and haunted by starvation, life and religion held compensations. As the Arab who had crossed 150 miles of uninhabited, waterless desert, when asked, Who accompanied you? in his splendid simplicity answered, Allah,[135] so these destitute wanderers were sensible to some of the imponderables of life. They knew that invisible powers lay beyond man's ken, and they believed that these might become their allies in the struggle against the hardness of their lot. Faced by immeasurable forces and unknown horizons, they had learned humility and reverence, and in the field of thought had taken the first steps toward a coherent theology. They were religious; without prayer book or priest, chalice or cathedral, in loyal devotion to their kin and in the outgoing of their desire toward the Unknown, augmented by their few and simple rites, they worshiped the creator and the protector of their destiny. From sons of these tribes, and their kin, came the dogma of a jealous, not-to-be-questioned deity, the stern ethics of the prophets of Israel, the rigors of the ritual of the

---

[133] G. F. Moore, "Sacrifice," *Ency. Bibl.,* IV, 43. Doughty, *Arabia Deserta,* I, 492.

[134] Fasting as a religious exercise is widespread, and originated in a variety of causes. Its ritual, chiefly taboos, is related to women, war, the dead, initiatory rites, and disasters. It had no great significance in pre-Mosaic days (J. A. MacCullough, *ERE,* V, 759–765; J. A. Montgomery, *Journal of Biblical Literature,* 1932, 105, 183–213).

[135] Gertrude Bell, *Syria, the Desert and the Sown,* 39.

priests, the wisdom of the sages, and the flaming visions of the eschatologists. Later religion owes much to the nomad of the broad spaces of Arabia.

But we disregard history if we forget those who rebelled against the monotony and dullness of their lot and, in the restlessness of their hearts, were ever ready for experiment and for adventure. These free men, who from time to time went out, not knowing whither, were the creative spirits whom we meet in the chapters that follow.

Chapter III

⫷⫷⫷⫷⫷⫷⫷⫷⫷⫷⫷⫷⫷⫷⫷⫷❈⫸⫸⫸⫸⫸⫸⫸⫸⫸⫸⫸⫸⫸⫸⫸⫸

THE RELIGION OF THE SINAI CONFEDERATES

1250 B.C.

THE thirteenth century preceding our era was one of world confusion. Peoples everywhere were restless; tribes were persistently on the move; great empires were tottering to their fall, and the future, obscure to all, was big with promise to some. Egypt had reached the zenith of her culture centuries earlier, and long before the death of Ramses II in 1225 B.C. the speedy decline of old age had set in. Following his death, Ethiopia in the south, Libya in the west, and Syria in the north each made inroads on the ancient empire, but none had the needed vitality for wide dominion. Civilization in southern Mesopotamia, after flourishing for two thousand years under Sumerian, Akkadian, and Amorite dynasties, by 1600 B.C. was overrun by the Kassite invader, and long before the thirteenth century B.C. the glory of Babylon had passed, never again, save for one brief period, to be rekindled. About the same time the Hittite empire in Asia Minor, that for three centuries had been a challenge to the armies of Egypt, failed to halt the ravages of the northern barbarian. The Achaean Greeks in 1183 B.C.[1] after a siege of ten years destroyed the Troy of Homeric legend, and thus European influence began its definite penetration of Asiatic life. The beginning of the twelfth century B.C. marked the end of an old and the beginning of a new era. Great empires had crumbled in the dust, and petty princes alone remained to rule the shattered fragments of ancient dynasties.

This disintegration of the great powers was due to a combination of causes. Incessant wars had sapped their strength without comparable compensations. New conditions, emerging between 1500 and 1200 B.C., had added to the world tensions. The Age of Bronze was giving way to the Iron Age.[2] The superiority

[1] Dr. Carl Blegen of Cincinnati, after excavations on the site of Troy on the Scamander, over a period of seven years concluded that the seventh city, not the sixth, as previously held, was the city destroyed by the Achaean invaders, and that the date probably was 1183 B.C. (C. Blegen, *American Journal of Archaeology*, 1939, 204–228; also 1937, 17–51; 553–597).

[2] Iron was in use in a small way in Egypt in the predynastic period, though the ore is not native to the country (*Journal of Egyptian Archaeology*, May, 1932, 3–15). It has been found at a little later date in Asia Minor (*American Journal of Semitic Languages*, Oct., 1938, 437), and in Babylon (*Ill. L. News*, July 22, 1933). But the smelting process, that seems to have had its origin in Asia Minor, was not developed much before 1400 B.C. This mastery of iron, marking the beginning of the Iron Age, was momentous for the progress of civilization. Its diffusion in the different world centers naturally began at different dates (J. B. Willson, *Princeton Theological Review*, 1917, 250–276; H. C. Richardson, *A J Arch.*, 1934, 555–583). The importance of the Iron Age in Palestine, and its subdivisions, are treated by W. F. Albright, *Haverford Symposium*, 23, 24.

and availability of the new metal, which furnished a stronger and keener weapon, aroused its northern possessor to a new activity and gave him a margin of security in combat. Foreigners were now employed in Egyptian armies, either as mercenaries, or as slave soldiers,[3] and the common man was becoming conscious of his individual powers and worth. The resentment of the slave against highhanded officialdom was growing apace, and hungry hordes of barbarians were breaking down barriers and crossing frontiers to plunder the products of passing civilizations. Empires in their pride of history and faith in ancient customs, blind to the gathering storm, failed to adapt themselves to the needs of the new day, and went down before the surging tides of new life. Egypt, Babylonia, and Heth, like individuals, succumbed to the infirmities of old age.

With the decay of empire, for the time at least, went the cultural heritage of these nations. The Hittites, as well as the Horites, their eastern neighbors, had much of value in social customs, art, architecture, military technique, and religion. The Babylonians, who had inherited and in part developed, the Sumerian achievements, had attained a status in civilization, and had reached conclusions in religion that in many ways amaze the thoughtful reader today. Nor had Egypt lagged in her contribution to the beautiful, the good, and the true. In political and military science she had had no equal. In art the pyramids of Abusir and Gizeh and the statuary of Abu-Simbel are a standing testimony of her skill. In letters, she pioneered in romance, in allegory, in criticism, and in poetry.[4] Her religion, in its organization, with the sun-god incarnated in the ruling Pharaoh, and the earth forces represented by Isis—Osiris—was the most complete in ancient history. In morals, measured by the rights of the common man, the Eloquent Peasant, the Wisdom of Ptahhotep, and the Installation of the Vizier are worthy to be placed by the side of the great prophets of Israel.[5] The appeal of the Eloquent Peasant is summarized in "that good word that comes out of the mouth of Re himself: Speak truth, do truth (or righteousness), for it is great, it is mighty, it is enduring."

As the foundations of empires, that had grown top-heavy, gave way before pressures within and without, so these splendid cultures, the rich fruitage of over three thousand years of history, no longer ministered to the needs of the nations. Ancient customs lost their appeal; Re went under a cloud; and Marduk suffered a severe decline. New tribes struggled to the fore, and new norms were in the making. Mankind instinctively was registering its claims, and was laying the foundations for a new philosophy of life, and new concepts of deity were on the horizon.

[3] H. H. Nelson indicates that foreigners were in the armies of Ramses II and III, though foreign troops are not shown in the festive scenes of victory (*Medinet Habu*, 4; J. H. Breasted, *Ancient Times, a History of the Early World*, 124).

[4] A. Erman, *The Literature of the Ancient Egyptians*, xxiii–xxxv, 2–13, 131–149, 254–289.

[5] These have been translated in *The Development of Religion and Thought in Ancient Egypt*, by J. H. Breasted, 220–225, 226–238, 239–243, 250.

It was at this juncture [6] that a man leading a band of fleeing shepherds appeared on the border of Egypt. The man, Moses, a bearded priest, long habituated to the desert though unknown from contemporary, historical records,[7] in religious tradition has been all but deified. The priestly writer makes Yahweh say, "See, I have made thee a god to Pharaoh" (Exod. 7:1). The rebel band was quite insignificant. A few score shepherd clans, with their flocks, with few possessions other than clothes and tents, but weary of the dirty drudgery of brick making, were making their escape from the land of Goshen out into the hungry spaces of Sinai.

Our sources preserve the tradition that in the pre-Canaanite period the Hebrews passed through certain crucial experiences. The following four, which are self-authenticating, were landmarks in Hebrew history: The immigration of certain nomadic clans into Goshen in time of famine; their subsequent oppression and their escape into the near-by wilderness; the affiliation of these with a number of Sinaitic-Kenite clans in a covenant with Yahweh, the deity of Horeb-Sinai, under the leadership of Moses; and later the entrance of this confederacy into the land of Canaan. These are so in conformity with desert life, and so interwoven in the later history of Israel, that to refuse them validity would be hypercritical.

First, that ancestors of the Hebrews in time of drought, attracted by the better pasturage, had crossed from the desert into Goshen raises no serious question. From ancient days shepherds with their flocks had crossed and recrossed the frontiers as pasturage and group pressures had determined. Midianite caravans made regular business trips to the Egyptian markets (Gen. 37:25–36), and the sons of Jacob found their way there in time of need (Gen. 42:5; 43:15; 46:1–7). The Egyptian monuments at Beni-Hassan portray a caravan of thirty-seven Asiatics, probably traders, entering Egypt as early as 1900 B.C.[8] The Hyksos, among whom were Semites, entered Egypt from the east about 1750 B.C., overran the country, and ruled the Delta and surrounding territory until driven out in 1580 B.C. In the thirteenth century B.C., an Egyptian frontier official reported to the effect: We have finished permitting the Bedawi tribes of Edom to pass the frontiers of Merneptah belonging to Thaku, toward the

[6] The date of the Exodus is uncertain. Biblical material is indefinite, and archaeological data are not conclusive. Dates from 1450 to 1200 B.C. have been defended. Twelve hundred and fifty B.C. is a working hypothesis.

[7] Egyptian sources know nothing definite either of Moses or of the Exodus. The Pentateuch, which is of composite origin, strata dating from 850 to 400 B.C. (see any standard Bible dictionary), has preserved different traditions, none contemporary with the events but each giving its own interpretation. However, all consider Moses a member of the priestly class. His experience at the burning bush, and his commission (Exod. 3:2, 3, 5, 7, 8, J.; Exod. 3:4, 6, 9–14, E.), his long apprenticeship with Jethro, the priest of Midian (Exod. 3:1, E.; Exod. 4:24–26, J.), his official status before Pharaoh (Exod. 6:11, 12, 27; 8:7, 18, 19; 9:11, P.), his office as oracle giver for the people (Exod. 18:15, E.), all accept him as priest. The late P. document makes him a descendant of Levi in the fourth generation (Exod. 6:16, 18, 20. Cf. Gen. 15:16; Num. 25:59).

[8] I. M. Price, *The Monuments and the Old Testament*, 170. T. E. Peet, *Egypt and the Old Testament*, 65, 66.

pools of Pithom of Merneptah, . . . in order to feed themselves, and to feed their flocks.[9] Add to this the fact that people called Aperu, the equivalent of Hebrew, are referred to in Egyptian monuments five times between 1500 and 1165 b.c.,[10] and it is evident that the Biblical story falls into line with the somewhat usual movements of shepherd tribes between the Sinai peninsula and the land of Goshen. However, it is equally true that these and other isolated references throw no light on the details of Hebrew history.

The experiences of these shepherd clans in Egypt, and the Exodus loomed large in the religious traditions of the Hebrews. Certain underlying facts seem assured. Egypt is a general term such as England or France, while Goshen [11] is as definite as Devon or Normandy. It is the border district of eastern Egypt, astride the Wady Tumilat, which runs east into the depression between Suez and the Red Sea. Triangular in shape, it has an area of about seventy square miles. Pithom and Raamses (Exod. 1:11; 12:37) were its important centers. Pithom, a frontier store-city, 650 feet square with brick walls from eighteen to twenty-two feet thick, built by Ramses II, 1292–1225 b.c., was definitely identified by Professor Naville in 1893.[12] Raamses has not been identified with equal certainty. Like Alexandria, it was the name of a number of cities, each named in honor of the great Pharaoh. Petrie, in 1906, advocated Tell er-Retábeh, ten miles west of Pithom,[13] as the original site, while later, Pierre Montet discovered at Zoan (Tanis), some seventy miles north of Wady Tumilat, to the west of Lake Menzaleh, evidence that seemed to support the claim that this was the site of the Raamses of Scripture.[14] That these cities were built with slave labor was in accord with the economic pattern of the period.[15]

From this it is evident that archaeology and the Old Testament converge in determining the location, the date, and the extent of the Hebrew experiences in Egypt. The center of their occupation, from which some of the families may have wandered considerable distances in various directions, apparently was the Wady Tumilat. In prehistoric days a channel of the Nile had flowed through it to Lake Timsah, and though now long closed by the accumulated detritus, it was easily irrigated and was still more fertile than the desert. Though not so productive as the Nile Valley, to the Bedouin, who so often suffered from

---

[9] *Anastasi papyri*, VI. J. H. Breasted, *Ancient Records of Egypt*, III, 273. T. E. Peet, *Egypt and the O. T.* 65, 79, 80.

[10] S. R. Driver, *Cam. B. Ex.*, xli, xlii. J. A. Wilson, *AJSL*, 1933, 275–280.

[11] Driver, *Cam. B. Ex.*, 67; W. M. Müller, "Goshen," *Ency. Bibl.*

[12] I. M. Price, *Monuments and the O.T.*, 184, 185. Driver, *Cam. B. Ex.*, 4. That some of the bricks had particles of straw in them, while others had none, has often been stated and related, for apologetic reasons, to Exod. 5:7. More careful examination has proved that straw was in all the bricks. It is strange, however, that Pharaoh's stamp has not been found on any of them (J. G. Duncan, *The Exploration of Egypt*, 79, 80).

[13] W. F. Petrie, *The Hyksos and the Israelite Cities*, 28, 31.

[14] *Expository Times*, Feb., 1931, 232. *AJSL*, 1934, 54, 183. T. E. Peet, *Egypt and the O.T.*, 85–91.

[15] J. H. Breasted, *A History of the Ancient Egyptians*, 254, 317.

famine,[16] it was the best of the land (Gen. 47:6, 11). The soil was so rich and so well watered that it encouraged a sedentary life, while as a frontier post it was a base for army supplies, and at times called for fortification.

The date of the Exodus is tied in with the oppression, and the known facts indicate that this probably occurred during the reign of Ramses II (1292–1225).[17] The excavator has furnished the most definite evidence. Pithom was built by Ramses II, and Raamses, which may well be Avaris (Tanis or Zoan), played its most important role during the same reign.[18] Also the demand for slave labor was at its height, both for building operations and for defense work, under this noted monarch. Adding to this the fact that after his death the military might of Egypt was in decay, it would seem that the reign of Merneptah, 1225–1215 B.C., was favorable for the Exodus. In 1220 B.C. Merneptah recorded, "wasted is Tehenu, Kheta is pacified, plundered is Canaan, . . . carried off is Askelon, seized upon is Gezer, Yenoam is made a thing of nought, *Israel* is uprooted, her seed is nought. . . ." [19] Nomadic clans were constantly on the move. Those on the border of the Delta had easy access to the Sinaitic peninsula, and some spent long years away from the parent stock (Exod. 2:15–17, J.; 3:1, E.; 4:14, J.). But that an important group of Hebrews fled from the Egyptian taskmaster during the reign of Merneptah seems highly probable.

Following the Biblical story, we have good grounds for believing that the Joseph tribes, Ephraim and Manasseh, which were rated as part Egyptian (Gen. 41:45, J.; 41:50, 51, E.), and were formally adopted into the family of Jacob (Gen. 48:14–22, J., E.), constituted the essential element in the Exodus.[20] These, with a mixed multitude (Exod. 12:38, J.) composed of small neutral

[16] Starving Asiatics frequently begged permission to live in the land of the Pharaoh (Breasted, *Anc. Rec.*, III, 7, 273).

[17] That the oppression took place under Thutmose III (1501–1447) is not without supporters. Josephus quotes Manetho to the effect that the Shepherd Kings (Hyksos), after possessing the country for 511 years, were driven into a ten-thousand-acre area at Avaris (Tanis), and later in the reign of Thutmose, after a period of siege, they agreed to leave the country. Then, returning to Syria, they built the city of Jerusalem (*Contra Apionem*, I, 14, 15). Continuing the Manetho narrative the Jewish apologist definitely identifies the Hyksos with the Jews (*C.Ap.*, I, 26–30). But the Egyptian chronicle was not only vague but so inaccurate as to be of not the slightest historical value. In recent years not a few have accepted this date (T. E. Peet, *Egypt and the O.T.*, 105–125). J. Garstang, *Foundations of Bible History*, 51–66, collates Biblical, Egyptian, and archaeological material so as to date the Exodus at 1447 B.C., and the fall of Jericho at 1407 B.C. T. H. Robinson in *History of Israel*, I, 68–86, presents the same conclusion.

[18] A. H. Gardiner after an examination of Egyptian papyri concludes either that Avaris was the "House of Ramses II," the Delta capital of the Nineteenth Dynasty, or it is a town unknown to Egypt's monuments (Peet, *Egypt and the O.T.*, 85).

[19] So reads in part the Merneptah stele, found in Thebes in 1896 by Petrie. See W. F. Petrie, *Seventy Years in Archaeology*, 170–172. This is the first time the name Israel appears in any ancient record. Unlike the five other peoples named it lacks the determinative sign used for a sedentary people (G. A. Barton, *Archaeology and the Bible*, 375). They were probably a nomadic group lying somewhere north of the Esdraelon Valley, if the order of the names is indicative of location.

[20] This was cautiously expressed by K. Budde in *The Religion of Israel to the Exile*, 10. Since then many have accepted it as a working hypothesis.

clans that were only loosely attached to the main body, weary of brick making, found their way out into the wilderness.

The total number joining in the Exodus could not have been large. To defend the tradition that there were over 600,000 fighting men from twenty years old and upward,[21] which would imply a population of between two and three million, would be a piece of folly. Such highly colored traditions, a commonplace of most ancient historians, arose out of that self-glorification that delights to bask under the shadow of a renowned ancestry. But the general tone of Scripture gives quite another picture. Two midwives, who are named, sufficed to take care of the women in childbirth (Exod. 1:15-22, E.). The people were afraid to go by way of the Philistines lest they see war (Exod. 13:17, E.).[22] They were sore afraid when they saw the Egyptians marching after them (Exod. 14:10, E.), and in the desert they could prevail against the Amalekites only by supernatural or magical means (Exod. 17: 10-12, E.; Num. 14:43-45, J.). Likewise the spies reported that they could not take the land of Canaan because the people were fierce and strong (Num. 13:28, 31, J.). When we learn that the annual pilgrimage which crosses the desert from Egypt to Mecca is rarely over 5,000, but stretches out over two miles,[23] we recognize how preposterous are the above figures. Under the same arrangements 600,000 men, without their families, would form a procession 240 miles long. Rather than juggle with the statistics, to give them a semblance of plausibility and thereby seem to confirm the letter of the Scripture,[24] it would seem wiser to recognize exaggeration in numbers as a general practice of ancient storytellers and early historians.[25] The numbers of those who left Egypt at any one time probably should be reckoned in hundreds, or at most in the lowest thousands, if the known local conditions and history can be any guide to us.[26] This, as already

[21] Num. 11:21, J., states that there were 600,000 men on foot. Num. 1:45, 46, P., is more explicit, giving the number of the men able to go to war, before they left Egypt, apart from the Levites, as 603,556. Exod. 12:37, J., reports about 600,000 men on foot, besides children and a mixed multitude, as they departed from Raamses, and Num. 26:51, P., places the number of those from twenty years old and upwards able to go to war, when they were about to enter Palestine, at 601,730.

[22] A fair estimate can be made of the size of ancient armies by the fact that one of the strongest forces Ramses II ever met was that of the Hittites at Kadesh on the Orontes, in 1288 B.C., which has been estimated at not less than 20,000 (Breasted CAH, II, 142). Inasmuch as it was a drawn battle, the Egyptian army could not have been much larger.

[23] Doughty, Arabia Deserta, I, 7, 8, 61.

[24] The most noteworthy effort in this direction was that of W. F. Petrie, who by a specious use of the Hebrew numerical characters reduced the number of men to 5,730 (Researches in Sinai, 207; also the Expositor, Aug., 1905, 148-152). Not only would such a system, if used in general, produce absurdities, but even here it calls for a total of some thirty thousand in the Exodus party. Those who know the desert, and have seen thirty thousand men in camp or on the march, are likely to be skeptical.

[25] Let one illustration suffice. Manetho, the Egyptian historian, is quoted as saying that 480,000 men besieged the Hyksos who were within the walled city of Avaris (Jos., C. Ap., I, 14).

[26] The present population of the Sinaitic peninsula has been put at about 5,000 (J. G. Duncan, The Exploration of Egypt, 88-92), while the total population of all of Arabia Deserta has been put at 60,000 (Doughty, Arabia Deserta, I, 5-8).

indicated, implies that but few clans of those later recognized as integral units of the twelve tribes were actual participants in the Exodus. However, remembering that nomadic tribes were always in a state of flux, dividing, affiliating, and realigning, it is quite possible that many, if not all, of the later Israelites may have had some claim by right of ancestry, or of adoption, to belong to the nucleus of the adventure.

The Exodus caused no ripple on the stately life of Egypt. From ancient days shepherds with their flocks had come and gone as pasturage and group pressure had determined. Escape was easy.[27] Like the plagues, that are annual occur-- rences in Egypt, the physical difficulties have been greatly magnified by tradition. A night's journey brought the fugitives to the wilderness, ever ready to conceal the wanderer. Pursuit was never profitable, and the Egyptian, born and bred in the walled villages, dreaded the unknown dangers of the open wilds. But to the motley mob it opened a new page in history. It was rebellion against serfdom, a demand for freedom, an adventure in religion (Exod. 3:13–15, 18).

The significant thing that took place was in the realm of mind and heart. Some of these people were at home in Goshen, probably having sojourned there at times for generations (Exod. 1:6, 8, J.; 6:19, 20, P.). At least a few of them had close personal contacts with the natives. The mother of Manasseh and Ephraim is reported to have been an Egyptian (Gen. 41:45, 51, 52, J., E.). Moses, whose name is Egyptian, is credited with having married a Cushite woman (Num. 12:1, E.), while the priests Hophni and Phineas (I Sam. 1:3) reflected Egyptian influence by their names. Though the Hebrews were shepherds, and differed greatly in their manner of life from the Egyptian villagers, they could hardly be oblivious to the glamour of city life, and the pomp and pageantry of imperial Egypt. Even the religious life was not without its appeal. The daily consecration of the Pharaoh, who was the personal embodiment on earth of the sun-god, the dramatic fertility pageant of Isis-Osiris, and the animal worship that penetrated every nook and cranny of the land—these at least must have stimulated and satisfied the senses. Many of the people were acclimated to this seminomadic life, and all enjoyed the protection of the might of Egypt. Rebellion had its dangers. Some feared the frontier guard (Exod. 13:17, E.); others remembered the bleakness of the arid desert so, though in

27 An interesting parallel to the story of the Hebrews has been recorded by Sayce. He tells us that Mohammed Ali colonized the Wady Tumilat with Arabs from various quarters in order to develop the culture of the silkworm. They were promised freedom from military service, taxes, and *corvée*. When his successor taxed them and attempted to force them into military service, the whole colony silently departed in a single night, with all their possessions (A. H. Sayce, *Higher Criticism and the Monuments*, 249, 250). Communication between Sinai and the Delta was always unobstructed. Ishmaelite caravans made regular business trips from Palestine to Egypt (Gen. 37:25, 28). The sons of Jacob crossed and recrossed the border without any supernatural aid (Gen. 42:6; 43:15, 18, 25), and Moses and Aaron made the passage without any special difficulties (Exod. 2:15; 4:27).

distress, they responded not to the appeal of Moses (Exod. 6:9, 12, P.). To arouse those who sat complacently among the sheepfolds listening to the pipings for the flock was a task of no mean order. Yet the native restlessness of the nomad, his natural dislike for all manual labor, his resentment of any task-master, and his innate desire for freedom, all were in rebellion against the new order. But to unite even a small number of different, discontented clans into a coherent unit required a definite objective and a masterful leader. To wor-ship the god of the fathers was the objective (Exod. 3:6, 15, E.; Exod. 3:16–18, J.), and Moses, who proved to be an "innovating personality," was the man of the hour.

Moses is honored in Scripture as the genius of the revolt. The migration from Egypt, the covenant with Yahweh, the confederation of the desert tribes, and the invasion of Canaan without a director of policy would be like a stream flowing into the desert sand. The fountainhead of Jewish national conscious-ness and the name of Moses belong together. The activities of Moses, however, have been so obscured by appreciative tradition that few details remain beyond question. Contemporary documents never mention his name or even hint at any of the achievements that later were attributed to him. Our oldest records (J., E.), written some four hundred years after the Exodus, exhibit in unmis-takable ways the general features of legend. The priestly writer, in line with his theological theory, makes Moses a super-miracle man, who along with Aaron, by means of a magic rod (Exod. 7:10; 8:1–4), a handful of ashes (Exod. 9:8), or an outstretched arm (Exod. 10:12; 14:16, 21, 22, 26), is fully accredited as the vicegerent of Yahweh (Exod. 7:1). Josephus, accepting current tradi-tion, heightened still further the marvelous. The sacred scribe of Egypt pre-dicted his destiny. In an hour of disaster he was made general of Egypt's army, defeated the Ethiopian conqueror, drove him back within his own fortifica-tions, destroyed the flying serpents, by subtlety took the impregnable capital city of the enemy, and married the Ethiopian princess (Josephus, *The Antiqui-ties of the Jews,* II, ix, 2–7; x, 1, 2). Nor did the rabbis sin by silence. Ginsberg's *Legends of the Jews,* Vols. II and III, reveals the length to which devotion to a man may go. Before he was a day old he walked and talked like an adult (*Legends of the Jews,* II, 264). At four months he prophesied that he would receive the law (II, 270). When Pharaoh tried to execute him for murder, the sword slipped ten times, harmlessly, on his neck (II, 282). In Midian he was taken up into heaven, and guided through the spheres, and was also given a peep into hell (II, 307–313). Back in Egypt, the ten plagues narrated in Scrip-ture were but faint glimpses of his real power. Unseen, at will, he passed the palace guards, and before him the fierce lions became as fawning puppies (II, 331–332). At Sinai, the two tables he received contained all the Pentateuch, all the Hebrew Scriptures, all the Mishna, Gemara, and the Talmud (II, 307, 309). Indeed, all truth and all philosophy of all ages were in his law (II, 325,

326). Such glorification, in early as well as in late tradition, has sadly blurred the landmarks of history. After a detailed study of all the material, one of our most careful historians concluded that "even if Moses is an historic personality, we have at present no sure criterion by which to determine what he said or did." [28]

While we recognize fully that all conclusions must be tentative, at the same time the history of the Hebrews calls for a leader who by his personality gave abiding values to the Exodus and to the tribal affiliations at Sinai.

The Biblical story of Moses, after the incredible features have been ignored,[29] has preserved a variety of reliable information. From this we arrive at three conclusions, of a general nature, that seem to be well attested if not absolutely proved. The first is that Moses had been greatly influenced by the Kenites, who were a branch of the Midianites. This, which is the heart of the Old Testament story, fits in with local conditions and with later history. The name Kenite is akin to that of the wanderer Cain (Qain) (Gen. 4:14, 16, 22),[30] and to the clan names Kain (Num. 24:22; Josh. 15:57) and Kinah (Josh. 15: 22), and identical to that of a tribe reported to have been in the land in pre-Hebraic days (Gen. 15:19, D.). All of these, like Hobab, the Kenite brother-in-law of Moses, seem to have settled in the southland at an early period (Num. 10:29-32, J.; Judg. 4:11; I Sam. 15:16), and in the time of David were considered to belong to Judah (I Sam. 27:10; 30:29). In the days of the Judges, Heber the Kenite, whose wife distinguished herself by violating the conventions of religion, was of the family of Hobab, an affiliate of Israel (Judg. 4:11-17; 5:6, 24), and later still we find Jonadab, a descendant of Rechab the Kenite (I Chron. 2:55), aiding in the Yahweh revolution (II Kings 10:15, 23). Thus the indications are that the Kenites were loyal, even fanatical, worshipers of Yahweh, and had been an integral part of Judah before the writing of the earliest Old Testament documents (Judg. 1:16).

Moses was not only affiliated by marriage with the Kenites (Exod. 2:21, 22, J.) but spent the middle years of his life with the family of Reul (Exod. 2:15-22, J.), or Jethro, the Midianite (Exod. 3:1, E.), a priest, who evidently was a worshiper of Yahweh (Exod. 18:11, E.). He received the rite of circumcision by proxy (Exod. 4:24-26, J.), and thereby was formally adopted into the tribe and the religion of the Kenites. While here he had an experience at the burning bush (Exod. 3:2-5, J., E.), and here he dedicated himself to the task of liberating a slave people (Exod. 4:18-20, J., E.). Even his mother's

28 Nathaniel Schmidt, *Journal of the American Oriental Society*, LIII, 194–199.

29 That Moses was the adopted son in the Egyptian court in the days of either Thutmose III or Ramses II, with an option on the throne, is but a foolish fantasy. Ramses II was the father of a hundred sons, and dying after a long reign was succeeded by Merneptah, the thirteenth, with a long line of aspirants in waiting. Other features are of the same value as similar tales found in the legendary material of other people. Cf. A. Lods, *Israël des origines au milieu du viii. Siècle*, I, 193–195.

30 B. Stade, *Biblische Theologie des Alten Testaments*, I, 42, 43. W. F. Albright, *Arch. and Rel.*, 206, n. 7.

name, Jochebed—"Yahweh is glory"—preserved only by the priestly writers (Num. 26:59, P.; Exod. 6:20, P. Ed.), if correct assumes a definite pre-Mosaic contact with Yahweh religion. From these fragmentary references it seems probable that as Moses learned much from his father-in-law about tribal government (Exod. 18:17–26, E.), he also was initiated into the religious lore of Yahweh worship as he lived with the priest in the vicinity of the mount of God (Exod. 18:5, 11, 12, E.).

The second fact to be noted is that Moses came under the influence of Egyptian culture. But this side of his experience has been so highly colored by legend that the dependable features remain rather uncertain. That as a babe he was rescued from the Nile by the daughter of Pharaoh and became heir apparent to the throne has no more relation to history than that he became the general of the army of Egypt. Neither were the shepherds in the vicinity of the Nile, nor did Egyptian princesses bathe in public. That he came in contact with local superintendents or governors, and that he gained influence and authority, is within the range of probability. But unfortunately, in his relation to both the Hebrews and the Egyptians definite information is scant. One word alone, the name Moses, witnesses to Egyptian influence. *Mesu* is the Egyptian for son, as in Ra-mesu, "son of Ra," and Thutmose, "son of Thoth." This puts the impress of Egypt on him, otherwise his name is inexplicable. It so clearly follows the Egyptian name pattern, and the interpretation in Exodus 2:10, E., is so definitely a Hebrew wordplay on the incident, that there can be no serious doubt that the name is Egyptian. But where the boy was born, how long he was in the land of the Pharaohs, what contacts he may have had with the culture and the religion of the court, and in what important incidents he functioned—all the details of his activities have been clouded in the mists of legend. However, that he was in Egypt and there attained a position of influence among the oppressed clans seems a certainty.

The third fact is that Moses is fully accredited as a priest of Yahweh. Tradition, early and late, declares that he possessed and used the ways and means of the contemporary priesthood for the welfare of his people. He had a magical staff (Exod. 4:2, J.; 7:15, E.) [31] with which he performed marvels, causing plagues (Exod. 7:17, 20, E.), rolling back the Red Sea (Exod. 14:16, E.), and bringing water from the rock (Exod. 17:5, 6, E.). With his stretched-out arm he was able to bring devastating hail (Exod. 9:22, E.), devouring locusts (Exod. 10:12, 13, E.), and a pall of darkness that could be felt (Exod. 10:21, E.). When his hands were upraised as he held the staff of God, an otherwise victorious enemy could make no advance (Exod. 17:8–12, E.). Also the word of Moses had power over plagues (Exod. 8:10–13, E.), and prevailed even with Yahweh (Exod. 9:29, 33; 32:30–33, J.; 32:11–14, J., E., Ed.). Outside the

---

[31] While in the earliest records it is Moses who is the priest, and as such possesses and uses the staff, or rod, in P. it has become the rod of Aaron, who in the course of some eight hundred years' history had become the official head of the priesthood (Exod. 7:9, 12; 8:5, 16).

camp a tent was pitched in which he met with and talked with Yahweh in order to obtain an oracle for those who so desired (Exod. 33:7–11, E.), and an ark, that became a symbol of Yahweh, was ascribed to him in the later traditions (Deut. 10:1–6, Num. 10:33, 35, 36). Above all, he alone could go up into the sacred mountain, commune with Yahweh, and live (Exod. 19:3, 12, 20, 21; 34:2–4, all J.). In all this, like the priest in Arabia, he was the wonder-worker, the soothsayer, the medium between God and man. The conclusion, that he acted as a primitive priest, seems to be well grounded. Then, as a priest, he was also a member of the Levitical order, whether Levi originally was a tribal [32] or an official [33] term.

Moses, who qualified as a Levite, trained in priestly lore, was more than a magician. In his struggle to arouse a complacent people to an adventure and to mold the heterogeneous clans into a new confederacy we see a man of flesh and blood, competent in the strain and stress of enlarging vision. He inspired a few families to unite and to seek an ancient sanctuary where they might enjoy their freedom, and worship Yahweh, a new-found deity yet the God of the fathers of some of the tribes (Exod. 5:3; 3:13–17). It was a day of small beginnings, but so was that of St. Francis, of Luther, of Roger Williams, and of William Penn. That night, when a few shepherds and their families hurriedly ate their evening meal and silently turned their faces toward the land of freedom, was big with promise (Exod. 12:38, 39, 42a, J.).[34] Under the clear stars, led by the priest of Yahweh, they went out from under the yoke of their masters to shape their own destiny. They toiled across the marshy sea of rushes (Exod. 13:18; 15:4, E.) and rejoiced in the escape from the oppressor (Exod. 15:21, E.). That night will long be observed by all the children of Israel throughout their generations (Exod. 12:42, P. Ed.). It was the first step toward their emancipation.

[32] The P. Code registered Moses as a descendant of Levi, the traditional third son of Jacob (Gen. 29:34), in the fourth generation (Exod. 6:16, 18, 20; Num. 26:58, 59) while E. states both father and mother were of the house of Levi (Exod. 2:1). That the tribe of Levi, after serious defeat (Gen. 34:25–31) compensated by turning their energies into priestly channels has been suggested by J. Wellhausen, *Prolegomena to the History of Israel*, 121–151, and defended by T. J. Meek, with a wealth of cogent material, in *Hebrew Origins*, 116–144. See also G. B. Gray, *Sacrifice in the Old Testament*, 245–255.

[33] Much evidence points to the term Levi having originated as an ecclesiastical title. Micah was a Levite of the family of Judah (Judg. 17:7, 10–13). Eli and his sons, priests at Shiloh, are of the tribe chosen to be priests (I Sam. 2:27, 28), and David's sons (II Sam. 8:18) and Solomon exercised those priestly functions that later were reserved for the Levitical house of Aaron (I Kings 8:14, 55). Moreover, the process of history is never so artificial as that reported by the priestly writer, in which a tribe becomes the privileged officers of religion in place of the first-born of each family in all the tribes (Num. 3:11–13, 5–10, 41, 45). The chief dignity in the family, and the clan, and the tribe was not relinquished so easily. Further, *lawi'u*, identical with the Hebrew *lēwi*, was the official term for priest among the Minaeans at Al-'Ula in south Arabia before the eighth century B.C. (Ed. Meyer, *Die Israeliten und ihre Nachbarstämme*, 88, 89, 428).

[34] Our oldest story, Exod. 12:38, 39, 42a, J., is largely in keeping with what is known to have been the custom of parties leaving a place under similar conditions. The later document (Exod. 11:9–12:20, P.) has garbed the actual history in the full religious ceremonies of its own period. Invaluable as it is for cult practices of 400 B.C., it robs the actual Exodus of much of its reality.

The second step in the religious history of the nation was the covenant at Horeb-Sinai—Horeb, the mountain of God, according to the northern tradition; Sinai, following the tradition of Judah (Exod. 3:1; 4:27; 17:6; 33:16, E., and Exod. 19:11, 18, 20, 23, J.). Here was an ancient sanctuary, of uncertain location,[35] which had long been frequented by various neighboring, nomadic clans.[36] In the days immediately preceding our story, Jethro, the Kenite priest, who may have lived in the vicinity, like Eli at Shiloh, probably was the chief priest at the sanctuary; while like Samuel, Moses, his son-in-law and disciple (Exod. 18:5-12, 15, 24, E.), was the leader in a new and better order in a period of transition. Such a conclusion seems warranted from the fragments preserved to us in history, and it furnishes us with the background needed to understand the full significance of the work of the new leader.

Though unidentified, the mountain probably was of volcanic origin, with intermittent activity (Exod. 19:9, 18, J., E.). Throughout our narratives the "burning bush" is assumed to be in the same area, and the similarity of sound between *seneh,* "burning bush," and sinai to the Oriental would carry with it identity of essential spirit, as well as of place [37] (Exod. 3:2, 3, J., E.). Such an awe-inspiring mystery, to the ordinary observer, was the indisputable evidence of the presence of deity, and a suitable preparation for religious experiences that lay deeper than the world of sense.

The tribes chiefly concerned in the new organization consisted of two or more somewhat diverse groups. One, the Joseph tribes, Ephraim and Manasseh, and a mixed multitude (Exod. 12:38; Num. 11:4, J) that had recently escaped from Egypt, now united by a common experience, and facing common dangers, was hopeful for the success of the new venture. The other group

35 The Biblical material is confusing, owing to the dual traditions, though neither one has any definite landmark. Sinai is the name of a mountain range, while Horeb is the name of a number of peaks in widely separated areas. The priestly historian supplied an itinerary of the journeyings in the wilderness (Num. 33:5-37, 41-49), but the majority of the place names cannot be identified. An early monkish tradition which preceded A.D. 300 located the mount of the law at Jebel Musa, on the side of which the monastery of St. Catherine has been built. For long centuries this was accepted as the site of the giving of the law. But almost a century ago (1853) Lepsius questioned it on the ground of inadequate space for the multitudes of Israel, and proposed Jebel Serbal twenty miles to the northwest, which is much more imposing, and has adequate accommodation for a large caravan beneath its massive peaks. T. C. Currelley has admirably defended this location (Petrie, *Researches in Sinai,* 247-254). Another trend was inaugurated by Sayce, when in 1894 he insisted that the military guards around the Egyptian mines in Sinai would make any location in the peninsula impossible, and he sought Horeb in Midian, east of the eastern arm of the Red Sea. Arafa, north by northeast of Mecca, Araif, southwest of Ain Kadeish, and Petra (Sela) have each had their advocates. But like the birthplace of Homer, and the grave of Moses, no man knows beyond dispute the site of the mount of the law. Cf. Driver, *Cam. B. Ex.,* 177-191; *Palestinian Exploration Quarterly,* 1933-1934, 137-146; *JPOS,* VII, 186-208; J. Wellhausen, *Prolegomena to the History of Israel,* 344.

36 Peculiar phenomena, such as a smoking mountain, a burning bush, a bubbling spring, a wriggling, disappearing serpent, and the like, have ever been sacred to primitive man the world over. Before Jethro was born his fathers worshiped at this shrine, and before Moses was adopted by the Kenites men had heard voices from the heavens, and had seen visions of the Unknown.

37 G. Westphal, *Jahwes Wohnstätten nach den Anschauungen der alten Hebräer,* 2-30.

belonged to the desert, and in this the Kenites, to whom Jethro and Hobab (Num. 10:29–32, J.) and their families belonged, occupied a commanding place. Other elements in it are uncertain. Calebites must have joined the movement at an early date (Num. 13:30; 14:8, 9b, J.; I Sam. 30:14; Josh. 14:6–15, Ed.). Simeon, whose cities in the reckoning of P. are all in the south of Judah (Josh. 19:1–9), Reuben, Gad, and Machir, who long had pasture grounds east of the Jordan (Mesha Stone, line 10; Deut. 3:12–20; Num. 32:1–5, 34–38, P.) and were somewhat closely affiliated with the Kenites (Judg. 1:16; I Sam. 15:6), may have been original members of the new alliance.

These two main groups, with subsidiary clans, did not unite in any significant covenant without long and painful preparation. Then as now, tribal or national affiliations, faced by local prejudices, personal interests, and group demands, were the achievements, not of weeks or months, but of decades and centuries. Each group was composite. Its families were scattered over considerable areas, and were held together by rather loose bonds. The Kenites and their followers were wanderers, possibly ass-nomads,[38] or itinerant smiths, as the name suggests. The Joseph tribes were outlaws from Egypt. Smaller outcast clans may have attached themselves to both main groups. Few had secure pasture lands. All were on the verge of disaster. Strong neighboring tribes occupied the land, and at times were antagonistic. Amalek to the north (Num. 14:43–45, J.), Edom to the east (Num. 20:14–18, E.), the Canaanite of Arad (Num. 21:1, 2, J.), and Moab and Ammon are all reported to have been hostile (Num. 22:2–24:15; J., E.). The common danger from these enemies, who were sedentary and held the most fertile parts of the country, must have hastened the unification of the homeless wanderers. But this in turn provoked internal strife, due to differences in social and religious customs of the different clans, and the clash of personalities.

In the midst of all this struggle, our records, though late, make it clear that Moses dominated the scene. Miriam disliked her Cushite sister-in-law, and was thrust outside the camp for seven days (Num. 12:1, 10, 14, 15, E.). Aaron boasted that he had the prophetic spirit as well as his brother, but soon confessed his folly (Num. 12:2, 6, 7, 8, 11, E.). Dathan and Abiram, Reubenites, like petty politicians asserted that he had not kept his campaign pledges. They were at least silenced, if not wiped out (Num. 16:1b, 12–14, 27b–31, J., E.). On occasion, the people became dissatisfied and complained; usually they soon received their reward (Num. 11:1–3, E.; 14:2, P.; 14:3, 4, J., E.). Korah, a Levite, insisted on his priestly rights, and preferred the incense his ancestors had used to that prescribed by Moses. He and his rebel priests were duly punished (Num. 16:1a, 16–24a, 35, P.). It is true that these tales were selected in order to heighten the achievements of Moses, and the last one is priestly propaganda for the Mosaic origin of the late ritual; yet beneath all we feel

---

[38] W. F. Albright has drawn a comparison between these and the Asiatics who have been portrayed on the tombs at Beni Hassan. *Arch. and Rel.*, 99. Also the name Qain means smith.

the strain and stress that is unavoidable in every forward movement, and in all, in spite of the halo of tradition, we meet a man of like passions with ourselves, who in the daily struggle led a band of nomads toward freedom and an enlarging life.

In due time, driven by hunger and desire, these clans, the nucleus of later Israel, came together in solemn covenant at the mount of God. This occurred at one of the annual shepherd festivals, probably in the springtime, in the month of *Abib* (April) which to the nomad was the beginning of the year, and in later days became the ecclesiastical New Year [39] (Exod. 13:4; called *Nisan,* Neh. 2:1). At such a time, tribes from far and near journeyed to their ancient shrine to have fellowship with one another and with their god. Every such festival had in it something of a covenant. Family pacts were renewed; marriages were arranged; tribal experiences were exchanged, and the activities and fortunes of unfriendly neighbors were discussed. Processions, dances, and simple rites were enjoyed by all. Vows were fulfilled; the sacrifice and the feast in which all united with the deity were the climactic features of the week or more, and thus all were emotionally fused in one body, by bonds peculiarly religious.

But the festivals that followed the Exodus were different. The escape had been meaningful. The federation was growing. The leader was gaining experience and control. Hopes were stirring, and confidence in the future was becoming stronger. The processes of change and growth continued over a generation, during which the needs, the dangers, and the future of these forlorn clans were discussed in the tents of the sheikhs, as well as at the annual gatherings. Tribal integration in the wilderness was settled no more speedily, or supernaturally, than are international relations today. But through the give and take of intertribal reactions came the crystallization of a wider, better-knit, and more purposeful union, that naturally received formal sanction during one of the yearly festivals at the mountain shrine. In the inhospitable wilds of Sinai a new order was emerging.

Yahweh, the god of Abraham, Isaac, and Jacob, an old deity to some, a new one to others (Exod. 3:13-15, E.; 6:2-9, P.; cf. Gen. 4:26, J.), the god who had led the serfs out of Egypt, to whom Moses was the priest and the spokesman, was the god of a new order. The name, to those who believed that the name was a reality existing in the very essence of the person or thing named,

---

[39] It has been suggested that at a time preceding Moses the central feature of the New Year's festival was the enthronement of the god, the divine king (S. Mowinckel, *Rev. hist. et phil.,* 1926 (LX), 409; S. H. Hooke, *Myth and Ritual,* 132-139, 188, 189). Not a little Biblical material may be interpreted as reflecting the concept of a primitive theocracy. Early prose tradition, as well as the later processional Psalms, e.g., Ps. 24:7-10; 47:1-8; 68:24-26; 74:12-17, lends itself admirably to this theory. Kinship, in the tribe, and between the tribe and its god, furnished a firm basis for the covenant. If this relationship were made concrete in the pattern of kingship it would contribute to the impressiveness of the ceremonies.

was of chief significance. Such words as Elohim (God), Baal (Master), Adhonai (Lord) had long been universal terms for deity, and had approximated abstract ideas; while Marduk, Ashur, Chemosh, and Yahweh were the national or tribal gods, and were the exclusive patrons of their worshipers.

The pronunciation, the origin, and the meaning of the sacred name, however, important as all are for the understanding of early religion, are now matters of some uncertainty. That Jehovah was not the original pronunciation of the divine name is a certainty. For centuries before the destruction of the temple in Jerusalem, the four letters JHWH of the "incommunicable name" had been pronounced but once a year, and that by the high priest on the day of the atonement. Thus the correct pronunciation was easily forgotten. Not only does Hebrew phonetics permit of no such word formation as Jehovah, but this spelling is first found in a brochure by Raymond Martin titled *Pugio Fidei*, published in A.D. 1270. The archaeologist has found at least four different spellings, Yô, Yāh, Yahû, and Yahweh,[40] which contributes little to aid us in determining the earliest form. Was the shortest form an abbreviation, or was the longest form an extension of the original?

That the earliest form preceded the age of Moses is a certainty; but where it originated and how widespread it was remains a mystery. Since 1902, when Friedrich Delitzsch announced that he had found Yahweh as the name of a god in a Babylonian inscription from 2000 B.C., scholars from time to time have thought they discovered it in the ancient records of Babylonia, North Syria, Amarna, or Ras Shamra. In some cases the identification was groundless; in others it was doubtful, while in only a few, save those that were post-Mosaic, has it been probable. It may be that the name exists in the Ras Shamra tablets, or that it may ultimately be identified with Ea, of Mitanni origin, but at the present those most competent hesitate in identifying the name with the deity of any people, or with any provenience.[41] Thus at present our earliest identification of Yahweh must be with the forebears of Moses, whose mother's name, Jochebed, "Yahweh is glory" (Exod. 6:20; Num. 26:59), is a compound of Yahweh, and with his father-in-law's family, who were worshipers at Horeb-Sinai. Naturally, other Midianite clans, east of the peninsula, and affiliated clans in the south of Judah,[42] may have claimed and enjoyed the same privileges.

As for the original meaning of the word Yahweh, there is much uncertainty.

---

[40] Presentation and analysis of material at hand has been made by S. R. Driver, *ZAW*, 1928, 7–19, and H. G. May, *AJSL*, 1933, 10–14.

[41] A summary of such claims and a careful evaluation of each is found in T. J. Meek, *Hebrew Origins*, 96–99; also in A. Lods, *Israël*, I, 370–377; Max Löhr, *History of Religion in the Old Testament*, 23–39, and Albright, *Arch. and Rel.*, 63, 64.

[42] While our traditions are confusing, though no more so than are the actual tribal relations in the Near East throughout all their history, fragments bear out the suggestion that Levi, Caleb, and Judah considered Yahweh to be the god of their fathers. This tradition is early and seems creditable (A. Bertholet, *History of Hebrew Civilization*, 136, n. 3).

The interpretation given in Exodus 3:14, "I am that I am," in a source written long after the days of Solomon, is one of those byplays on a word, so loved by Hebrew writers, which expresses the theological concept of the writer but has no relation to derivation or to primitive religion. "I am that I am," or any one of the marginal readings in the American Revised Version, even the more metaphysical "I am because I am" is equivalent to "I am the unquestioned Ruler." It is authoritarianism in religion, which was widespread among the Semites, and no doubt long preceded the days of the Hebrew kingdom, but it was scarcely primitive or original.[43] It is generally accepted that the names of the gods arose out of experiences which were related to objects of sense, such as stones, trees, springs, sun, moon, and stars, and the earth powers, at work in famines, plagues, and storms, and active in vegetable and animal life. It is probable that the name Yahweh came into being in long-forgotten days through some such vital process. Was its lowly origin the "one coming down" in the rain, or in the lightning, or in the mountain storm, or in the meteor?[44] or was it derived from the more abstract idea, the "one who is," or "He is He?[45] The hypothesis that Yahweh was originally thought of as a mountain- or storm-god fits into what is known of early religious ideas, in which strange, concrete phenomena were explained as manifestations of deity.

It seems, however, most consistent with all the evidence that to early worshipers, or at least to the Mosaic tribes, Yahweh was thought of as a storm-god, dwelling on Mount Sinai, in or above the storm clouds.[46] At times he made himself known in smoke, and fire, and earthquake (Exod. 19:18, J.; 19:16, E.). His voice was in the thunder (Exod. 19:16, E.), and the mountain was so charged with his power (mana), that to gaze on it was dangerous, to touch it was certain death (Exod. 19:11b–14, 21–24, J.). Moses, his priest, so versed in his ways as to be immune from the dread danger, could alone venture into the mountain abode of the deity (Exod. 19:24; 24:2, J.).

The auspicious year for the consummation of the desired union at last arrived. The question of authority in civil affairs had, after serious conflicts,

43 *The Lord*, which in the AV, following late Jewish practice, has displaced the original Yahweh, and *the Eternal* of Moffatt, who was influenced by the French Synodal translation, are both theological substitutes that obscure early religious ideas.

44 W. R. Smith, *OTJC*, 1st ed., 423. D. S. Margoliouth, *Relations between Arabs and Israel*, 5–7, 14, 19, 20. R. Eisslen suggests a meteoric stone that later was placed in the ark and called the *kabhodh Yahweh*, "the glory of Yahweh" (*Le Monde oriental*, XXIII, 56–58).

45 The origin has often been derived from the Qal form of the verb "to be," meaning "the one who is." Recently Dr. J. A. Montgomery has raised the question, may the original form be a combination of Ya, the exclamation, and Hu, the third personal pronoun? Then Yahu would be "O He," equal to "O Allah," or "O God." Yahu would then mean "He is He," which would be basic to all theology (*JBL*, 1944, 161–163). B. Balscheit in *Alter und Aufkommen der Monotheismus in der Israelitischen Religion*, 1938, 45, following a suggestion from S. Mowinckel, propounded a similar idea.

46 Parallels to this are found among many people. Olympus in Thessaly, traditionally the early abode of Zeus and the great gods, is one of the best-known examples.

been settled (Num. 16:1b, 12–15, 25, 26, 30; Deut. 11:6). Political organization of the desert type had been achieved (Exod. 18:17–27, E.).[47] The required rites in religion had been long the common property of all the tribes.

The contracting parties assembled for the covenant were a motley and unimposing group, not the "Twelve Tribes of Israel," the descendants of one patriarch. In the desert weak clans continually merge with stronger ones for mutual aid. A qualified affiliation may be granted (Josh. 9:3–8, 11–15, J.; II Sam. 21:1–6), a fictive brotherhood may be established (Amos 1:9), or a new clan may even be grafted into an old family tree.[48] Israel was probably enriched in its growth by all three processes. Such an affiliation formed under religious sanctions created a psychological bond that might easily prove more lasting and vital than that based entirely on physical kinship.[49]

The ritual at Sinai, judging from our knowledge of nomadic custom and the narratives found in the oldest documents, was naturally of the simplest type. Cleansed garments, continence (Exod. 19:14, 15, E.), and the prohibition of all contact with the sacred mountain (Exod. 19:12, J.) were probable preliminary requirements.[50]

The shepherd's rite of the slain lamb obviously was fundamental in this compact. There was the sacrifice of the offering; the pouring out of part of the blood to Yahweh and the sprinkling of part of it on the people (Exod. 24:6, 8, E.); the solemn passing between the two parts of the sacrifice, by the representative of Yahweh and the representatives of the tribes (cf. Gen. 15:10, 17; Jer. 34:18, 19),[51] thereby pledging the loyalty of each to all, clan to clan and all to Yahweh (Gen. 26:31; Deut. 26:17–19). Mutual intertribal obligations were accepted by all contracting parties. Ancient nomadic customs must now

[47] The struggle between the democratic and the autocratic ideals, which was constant, has been preserved in one of the most ancient sources, in which Nadab, Abihu, and Aaron were coequal with Moses, the ranking officer (Exod. 24:1, 2, 9, 10, J.). See O. Eissfeldt, *Hexateuch-Synope*, 49, 50.

[48] D. Jacobson, *SBOT*, 120.

[49] W. R. Smith, *Rel. Sem.* (3), 505, 506.

[50] While the accounts of the covenant in J. (Exod. 19:3b–9, 11b–13, 20–25, 18) and in E. (Exod. 19:2b, 3a, 10, 11a, 14–17, 19) are both primitive, it is probable that both have idealized the experience. The actual ceremonies may have been even simpler than the author of J. suspected. It is probable that an observer of the inauguration of the Mosaic covenant would have been unable to distinguish it from other similar movements among Semitic tribes. So concludes A. Lods, *Israël*, I, 365. The difficulties in reconstructing the details of the scene are recognized by all. See A. B. Davidson, *Dictionary of the Bible*, ed. Jas. Hastings (five vols.) I, 512. For attempted reconstruction see A. H. McNeile, *Exodus*, Westminster Series, civ–cxxi. K. Galling, *Die Erwählungstraditionen*, 26–37, is more critical.

[51] Covenant pledges were ancient and universal, and varied in form, and record, with place and time. They became essential with the beginning of intertribal relations, and the records developed in keeping with the civilization. A boundary stone was the permanent record of the covenant between Laban and Jacob (Gen. 31:44–49). In the story of the covenant of Yahweh with Abraham, a torch and a flame passing between the divided sacrifice is the symbol of Yahweh (Gen. 15:12, 17, J.). Sometimes the sacrificial animal was dismembered, and the parts were distributed to those interested as in I Sam. 11:7. A similar ceremony has been found in the Assyrian records (Ed. Dhorme, *La religion des Hébreux nomades*, 217, 218).

be given broader applications. *Thou shalt not kill, steal, commit adultery, bear false witness* had been the unwritten law for ages, but it had been observed only within the tribe; to practice these with the alien might be treachery to one's own tribe. But now these and other like customs became the law for the new confederacy. Old feuds must give way to new friendships, and thus, though not without heartburnings, the horizon of idealism was lifted. Likewise new taboos in foods, formulas, greetings, and new duties, arising out of the new complexities and the new ambitions, must be accepted by all parties. Intertribalism cannot exist on the basis of the old tribalism.

The sacred meal (Exod. 18:12; Gen. 26:30) in which all assembled, deity, priest, and people, entered into communion, was the closing feature and the climax of the ritual. Beneath the mountain of God they had taken their vows, and Yahweh was with them, and in the mountain. Some glorious, awe-inspiring, even terrifying spectacle (Exod. 19:16, E.), some physical phenomenon on the mountaintop, a fire-belching volcano (Exod. 19:18, J.), or a crashing, blinding thunderstorm (Exod. 19:16; 24:15, E.), with some probability lay behind this poetic narrative. Such an experience, unfamiliar to most of the seminomads, could not fail to produce definite psychological results. "They saw God, and did eat and drink" (Exod. 24:11 J.). This is an epitome of an inner experience that united memories and expectancies. They were thereby, in spirit, united with the brotherhood, and with Yahweh himself. The covenant, though simple in the beginning, even similar to many others, was crucial. With the passing centuries it was repeatedly re-expressed, and even changed in essential features, under the influence of growing experience, and theological theory. Yet, so vital was this incident, and so profound was its influence on national history, that the essential fact is correctly expressed by the phrase, "they saw God." [52]

The continued presence of Yahweh with his people was one of the problems immediately related to the covenant. All religions, in one way or another, have sought to provide guidance for their adherents amid the uncertainties and the mysteries of life. Oracle giving was so common a practice that it causes us no surprise when our records assure us that at the request of Moses, Yahweh gave his promise, "My presence shall go with you, and I will lead you" (Exod. 33:14; 34:9, J.), or as a later writer phrases it, "I will send my angel before them" (Exod. 23:20–22, E.). But, further, it was necessary that in some way this guidance should be made definite and objective to the clans. Among the various means devised and used for this purpose were the teraphim, the Urim and Thummim, while the tent of meeting and the ark of the covenant both had special significance.

---

52 J. Hempel has emphasized the importance of this moment in history, but has so labored the covenant as an act of divine choice that mutual obligation and the process of development have been disregarded (*Gott und Mensch im A.T.*, 162–189). See K. Galling, *Die Erwählungstraditionen*, 36, 37; W. Eichrodt, *Theologie des A.T.*

The tent of meeting, which Moses was accustomed to pitch afar off from the camp, was explicitly for oracle giving [53] (Exod. 33:7–11, E.). When the people sought Yahweh (Exod. 33:7, E.), that is, sought an oracle, Moses entered into the tent and Yahweh descended in a pillar of cloud before the door of the tent and spoke to Moses face to face "as a man speaketh to his friend" (Exod. 33:9–11, E.). This gives it a very significant place in religion in early days. While the origin of the tent of meeting is nowhere stated, it has been suggested that it may have been a Kenite contribution, through Moses the priest, to early Hebrew cult practice.[54] If this be correct we can understand the readiness of some tribes to enter the federation, while others hesitated. An illustration of this conflict is found in the abortive effort to organize the whole community around the tent of meeting. Seventy men, elders of the people, were given official status "around the tent" and the spirit came on them (Num. 11:16, 17a, 24b–30, which may originally have followed Exod. 33:9–11, E.). But though at first this seems to have been an effort at co-operation, it was not unanimous. There were isolationists who refused to join, and remained within the camp (Num. 11:26, 27). Further, on these two men, Eldad and Medad, the Spirit came just as on the others. It was an experiment in religious organization, and the advocates of personal freedom won the day. "They did so no more" (Num. 11:25). Tribal tensions, due to divergent, inherited customs, as reflected in such episodes, were at work in early as well as in late days. To some of the clans the tent of meeting, as the exclusive symbol of the presence of deity, was a violation of their ancient religious privileges. The Spirit could no more be confined to place, or to a professional priesthood, than in the early history of Christianity (Acts 15:8).

It has been maintained by many that the sole purpose of the tent of meeting was to house the ark of the covenant.[55] This, however, seems to telescope its really important function, and ignores its possible relation to the Arabic tent of the oracle. But whatever its origin it proved to be ephemeral. Before the time of David, so far as we know, its usefulness was gone. It had served its day and ceased to be. Whether it was united with the ark of the covenant during the wilderness experience so that the functions of the two as well as their respective tribes were co-ordinated, or, as some assert, they were not united until

[53] Arab tribes frequently have a sacred tent to which the priest retires when an oracle is required (J. Morgenstern, *Hebrew Union College Annual*, V, 121–126). The same thing was true of the Carthaginians (W. R. Smith, *Rel. Sem.* (3), 37). At Delphi, Pythia sat in, or at the mouth of, a cave when she gave an oracle. In Gezer in Palestine, R. A. S. Macalister found an underground cave which he supposed had been the cell of a priest who gave the oracle through the small opening that connected it with the larger assembly room (H. Vincent, *Canaan d'après l'exploration récente*, 117, 118).

[54] J. Morgenstern, *HUCA*, V, 121–126, and *The Ark, the Ephod and the Tent of Meeting*, 131–161.

[55] This is the assumption most frequently found in religious writings. Cf. articles on tabernacle in *Ency. Bibl.*, by I. Benzinger, and in *HBD* (five vols.), IV, by A. R. S. Kennedy. M. J. Lagrange, *Rev. bib.*, 1903, 215.

the political destinies of south and north were brought together under David,[56] cannot be answered with certainty.

The ark, an oblong box four feet long by two and a half deep and two and a half wide (Exod. 25:10; 37:1, P.), according to the only measurements preserved, was of even greater importance than the tent of meeting. It played its most important role in the conquest of Canaan, and evidently belonged to Ephraim,[57] as its location in Shiloh (I Sam. 3:3; 4:3, 4) and its Ephraimitic priesthood would suggest (I Sam. 1:3; 2:11, 17). Our records, though fragmentary and interpretative, reveal the fact that from time to time the name, the physical appearance, and the function all changed in response to the development of the national and religious life.

The name by which it was known in the earliest literature (J., E.) was the ark (Num. 10:35, 36; Josh. 4:10; I Kings 8:5), or the ark of Yahweh (Josh. 3:13; 4:5, 11; I Kings 8:4), or the ark of Yahweh your God (Josh. 4:5). It is particularly noteworthy that in the earliest literature it is in no way related to the Sinaitic covenant. When we come to the Deuteronomic writings it is now the ark of the covenant, or the ark of the covenant of Yahweh (Deut. 10:8; 31:9, 25, 26; I Kings 6:19; 8:6; Num. 10:33, D.). Two centuries later, when the priests have come into power, in keeping with their theology it is now the ark of the testimony, that is, of the ten words, which are the will of God (Exod. 25:22; 26:34; 39:35; Num. 4:5; 7:89; Josh. 4:16, P.).

The workmanship and the furnishings of the sacred chest underwent similar changes, if not in fact, then in theory. J. and E. give us no light on its construction. Deuteronomy has only a passing reference in which the author makes Moses say, "I made it out of acacia wood" (Deut. 10:3). It is to the priest that we must turn for any suggestion of detail. Here we are informed that Bezalel made it out of acacia wood, and it is described as elaborately embellished, being completely overlaid with gold within and without, according to the pattern shown in the mount (Exod. 25:10–15, 40; 37:1–5, P.).

The function of the ark likewise changed with the changing times. In the earliest days it was a simple box suitable for the purpose of sheltering some sacred objects or symbols of Yahweh. Contact with these symbols soon transferred *holiness* to the box itself so that ere long the ark itself was addressed as Yahweh (Num. 10:35, 36, J.). During the wilderness period it functioned as

---

[56] In a well-ordered small volume this suggestion has been presented by Max Löhr, *A History of Religion in the Old Testament*, 46.

[57] Doughty informs us that the nomad clans usually have such a box, in which are kept the religious symbols and other prized possessions of the clan (*Arabia Deserta*, I, 227). There is general agreement that the ark originally belonged to Ephraim (J. Meinhold, *Die Lade Yahwe;* A. Lods, *Israël*, I, 369). W. R. Arnold suggested that there may have been a number of arks, each the property of a tribe (*Ephod and Ark*, 67–80). Egyptian influence in idea and construction has been maintained by E. Montet, *Histoire du peuple d'Israel*, 47. The most complete study is by J. Morgenstern, *HUCA*, V, 122–128, and *The Ark, the Ephod, and the Tent of Meeting*, 77–113.

guide to at least a part of Israel,[58] and led them in the invasion across the Jordan (Josh. 3:13–17; 4:5, 9, 18, J., E.). In Canaan, like the people, it became sedentary, and was settled in a substantial building at Shiloh (I Sam. 1:7, 9; 2:13–15; 4:3, 4). On one occasion, at least, it was taken out to battle, so that its strange power might avail in the conflict. But alas, tragedy befell both the army and the ark (I Sam. 4:5–11). In the time of David it was carried into Jerusalem (II Sam. 6:12–19), and later, when Solomon built the temple, he had it placed in the oracle of the house, the most holy place, the windowless chamber in the rear of the temple (I Kings 8:6–10; vss. 8 and 9 are from D.). So far as we know, it was the original box of acacia wood that was placed in the oracle. This occurred about 960 B.C., and no light on its later history has come down to us. Some time, we know not when, but previous to the time of Jeremiah (cf. Jer. 3:16), it disappeared. The priestly writers, some five hundred years later than Solomon, sought to bridge the gap, and a change in function as radical as that in workmanship was announced. It is now called the ark of the *testimony,* and the stones with the ten words are stated to be within it. Above it is the mercy seat, that is, the means of propitiation (Exod. 37:1–9, P.), and on either side of it are the cherubim (Num. 7:89, P.). No longer does it wander from tent to tent as in the wilderness (II Sam. 7:6), nor guide the people into new adventures, nor go out to battle as the symbol of the war-god; but within the curtains it ministers to the unfolding of the mysteries of the Unseen. Political and national life have given place to the rites and the ceremonies of religion.

Yet amid these changes, the ark retained throughout what seems to have been the earliest idea, aptly expressed in the phrase "the focus of divine power." [59] It was ever the symbol of Yahweh's presence with his people. In

---

[58] The following facts raise the important question, did all Israel enter Canaan at one time? First, the invasion of the land was both easy and frequent. The five important fords of the Jordan made it easy for any clan to cross from the east any night during the year. Amorites, Hyksos, Habiri had overrun the country in succeeding waves before the fourteenth century. Cushan-Rishathaim, Moabites, and Midianites are reported to have conquered it during the period of the judges. Second, such invasions were by small guerilla bands that captured isolated villages and slowly infiltrated deeper into the country. They were never comparable to ancient or modern organized armies that engaged the enemy in decisive battle array. Third, our literary sources, J. and E., though carefully co-ordinated by Judean editors, clearly indicate the constant conflict between north and south save for the years of the united kingdom. Different ancestry, different history, and divergent religious ideals caused this cleavage. Fourth, the story of the relation of Joshua to Moses during the wilderness wanderings as preserved in E. (Exod. 17:8–16; 32:17, 18; 33:11, E.) is vague and insignificant, while that in P. (Num. 13:8; 14:6, 7, 30, 38) is an apologetic. Behind the account in Joshua 2:1–12:24, a J., E. narrative carefully edited by D., there is every reason to recognize a definite Ephraimitic invasion of the Shechem country. The question thus is raised, was there an invasion or infiltration from the south as indicated by Judges 1:10–21, and another one, possibly earlier, from the east as in Judges 1:22–28? If so it would clarify some of our literary problems, and at the same time it would conform to the known course of history. The question has been ably presented by T. J. Meek, *Hebrew Origins,* 25–45.

[59] T. K. Cheyne, "Ark," *Ency. Bibl.,* I, 300–310.

the tribal wanderings, it was Yahweh going on before them (Num. 10:33). In battle, it was Yahweh smiting their enemies (Judg. 5:31; I Sam. 4:3, 6; Num. 14:14). In the days of Solomon, along with the tent of meeting in the most holy place in the temple, it was Yahweh conferring religious sanctions on the national union of Judah and Ephraim (I Kings 8:4–6); and under the priestly regime it became the embodiment of the will of Yahweh as revealed for the redemption of his people. Indeed, so intimate was the relation of the ark to the deity that it was his presence, or, more concretely, to many it was Yahweh himself (Num. 10:35, 36).

A question of some importance is, what was inside the ark? The earliest documents give us no hint as to what sacred object, if any, was there originally (Num. 10:35, 36; I Sam. 3:3; 4:3, 4). Deuteronomy, before 621 B.C., informs us that two tables of stone, on which the ten words had been written by the finger of God (Deut. 9:10; 10:4), and nothing more (I Kings 8:9, D.) were within it. The priest, by 400 B.C., added his contribution, and the ten words became the "*testimony* of all things which I will give thee in commandment to the children of Israel" (Exod. 25:16, 22). The ten words had thus become inclusive, and stood for the sum and substance of the will of God, as continually to be revealed through the priesthood. A further step in theological progress was made when the rod of Aaron and the pot of golden manna, which in priestly tradition were both expressly placed *in front of* the ark (the rod in Num. 17:10, Hebrew text is 17:25; and the pot of manna in Exod. 16:33, 34), in later rabbinic tradition were both moved *inside* the ark. Still later, we are carried one step farther, when in vision we are shown the ark of the covenant inside the temple of God that is in heaven (Rev. 11:19).

This diversity of statement, which records the progress of theology, is the product of history, but it fails to recognize origins and is unconscious of development. As piety continued to add to the sacredness of the ark and the objects within it, from the time of Deuteronomy on, it may be suspected that the same process had long been in operation. That ten words were written on two tables of stone by the finger of God is recognized to be the language of symbolism. Further, these words, as already indicated, were written in the hearts of man everywhere, and to an illiterate people the written form would be valueless. We also note that when Deuteronomy was written the ark probably was not in existence (Jer. 3:16), and that this reform was a definite propaganda against idolatrous practices (Deut. 12:1–13; 18:9–14). The question then arises, was there a tradition that there had been stones or some other primitive symbol of Yahweh in the ark? And if so, did the same spirit that after Deuteronomy added to the facts in the interest of the higher religion enlarge the original material, in order to avoid the semblance of idolatry, and report that on these stones the finger of God had written the ten words? It is a question to which many and diverse answers have been given.

Because of its ultimate importance, during the last half-century many widely different suggestions as to the contents and the function of the ark have been made and supported by a wealth of material. A few of the most significant of these are here noted. Some have been insistent that originally the ark was the symbol of the invisible Yahweh, and that as such it naturally was empty.[60] This is an appealing theory. Desert worship must have been simple in all its appointments, and primitive philosophy was well aware that the invisible forces in the world were mightier than the visible. Also it falls in with our own predilections. But it in no way accounts for the box, nor does it correspond to primitive practice.

Somewhat akin to this is the theory that the ark was the *throne seat* of Yahweh, held by some to be visible in the form of a bull, while others thought of an invisible Yahweh on the empty throne. Hugo Gressmann, following earlier suggestions, held that the ark was a firmly closed box, and was the throne of Yahweh Zebaoth, the God of the hosts of Israel and of the hosts of heaven, and that while he was *in* the ark, he was also *beyond* it. He proceeded to show that this explained Biblical references such as the war song (Num. 10: 35, 36), the song of the temple entrance (Ps. 24:7, 8), the cherubim looking down on the mercy seat (I Kings 8:6, 7), and Yahweh over the throne chariot (Ezek. 1:26, 27) in a way that no fetish or stone tables of the law could. Also, the fact that at times the ark was guided on its way by an unseen power added confirmation to the thesis (I Sam. 6:12). An excellent parallel is furnished by Xerxes, who had with his army on the march the sacred chariot of Zeus, which was guided by a footman, for no man dared mount the chariot (Herodotus VII, 40).[61] The author concludes that Yahweh the God of heaven was too great to be a fetish or a demon, or to be made in the image of man, and thus the religion of Israel, in the very beginning, was raised to an unusually high level.

The majority of scholars, much as they might wish to find approved modern concepts expressed in the dawn of Israel's religion, agree that "the chest was certainly made to hold some sacred object." [62] But here agreement ceases. The bones of Joseph, which had been placed in an ark and brought up out of the land (Gen. 50:24–26, E.; Exod. 13:19, E.; Josh. 24:32, E.), it has been argued, were the earliest sacred objects in the ark.[63] This is not beyond the range of

[60] R. H. Pfeiffer, in a critical attack on the idea that the national god of Israel had ever been pictured in the image of serpent, bull, or man, states his conviction in a quotation from Professor Arnold to the effect that the sacred box was a sort of shrine within which the *numen* could work its mysterious spell upon the lots while shielded from the scrutiny of the human eye (*JBL,* 1926, 211–222, esp. 220). H. T. Obbink suggests that the bulls of Jeroboam were visible pedestals of the invisible Yahweh (*ZAW,* 1929, 264–274). W. F. Albright follows suit, with archaeological support, and recognizes that there is no essential difference between an invisible deity as enthroned on the cherubim or standing on a bull (*From the Stone Age to Christianity,* 229, 230). He also believes the aniconic character of Yahweh to be vital to Mosaic religion (*ibid.,* 202, 203), and that material representations were foreign to the spirit of Yahwism from the beginning (203).

[61] H. Gressmann in Gressmann, Gunkel, *et al., Die Schriften des A.T.,* II, 1, 15–19.

[62] G. F. Moore, "Idolatry," *Ency. Bibl.,* II, 2155.

[63] D. Jacobson, *SBOT,* 177.

possibility. These people revered their ancestors, believed that the spirit of the departed remained in close proximity to the body, and that on occasion it could be effective in life. The *wely,* or tomb of the saint, among their descendants is today a sacred place which often becomes a local sanctuary. This ark (the same word is used as for the ark of the covenant) would then be a primitive reliquary that might easily have been a revered center during their pilgrimage and later.

The brazen serpent has also been claimed for this place of honor.[64] Such an object would not have been entirely inappropriate to the situation. Serpent worship has been prevalent among many peoples, and there is abundant evidence of its popularity in Petra and Palestine.[65] Excavations in almost every village ruin in the country have furnished incontestable proof of its long-continued existence in Palestine. The Old Testament likewise adds a quota of information. The sign of the power of Moses lay in the magical rod, which was even called a serpent (Exod. 4:2-4, E.), and in a later document is a monster dragon (Exod. 7:9, P.). In the wilderness Moses is said to have erected a brazen serpent on a pole for healing purposes (Num. 21:8, 9, J., E.), and it remained in the temple as an object of adoration until the time of Hezekiah (II Kings 18:4). Such objects have often been associated with vital experiences, and in some cases may have been the steppingstones to more intelligent religious views.

A more widely held theory than either of the above is that an image of Yahweh, probably in the form of a bull, may have been the original occupant of the ark, but like the serpent of Moses it outgrew its usefulness and by the time of Deuteronomy had been replaced by a more worthy object. The cogent facts and a critical review of the empty-box theory have been published by Professor W. A. Irwin of the University of Chicago.[66] Worshiping deity in the form of a bull was common among ancient people. Jeroboam I, no doubt with the approval of many of his people, made two golden calves by which they worshiped their gods (I Kings 12:28, 29). Images of deity were carried in a sacred boat in religious processions in Egypt,[67] while Arabs going into battle often carry some sacred object, such as an image of deity or a copy of the Koran, on camel back, in the Mahmal,[68] or Merkab.

[64] R. H. Kennett, *ERE,* I, 791a–793b.

[65] A general statement is found in *ERE,* XI, 399–411, by J. A. MacCullough. Much of the archaeological material coming from Palestine has been presented by S. A. Cook in *The Religion of Ancient Palestine in the Light of Archaeology,* 62, 82, 89–100, 103, 106, 116, 117, 147, 193. A compendium of serpent lore, as found in all countries, has been published by Oldfield Howey, *The Encircled Serpent.* Meyer follows Luther, who derived Levi from Leviathan, equal to Nehushtan, II Kings 18:4 (*Die Israeliten und ihre Nachbarstämme,* 120, 426).

[66] The *Crozer Quarterly,* Oct., 1942, 292–301. Hugo Gressmann in *Die Lade Yahves,* 68, rejected his earlier theory, and concluded that the ark contained a bull image of Yahweh.

[67] J. G. Wilkinson, *Ancient Egypt,* III, 573. A. Erman, *Life in Ancient Egypt,* 276.

[68] W. F. Albright, *BASOR,* No. 91, Oct., 1943. J. Morgenstern, *The Ark, the Ephod, and the Tent of Meeting,* 5–55.

Others have ventured the thesis that a stone, either a meteor, or a block from the sacred mountain, was the long-discarded original.[69] The black stone of Mecca, which for thirteen hundred years has been the chief object of Moslem pilgrimages, is a noted illustration of this practice. The belief that spirits were present in such objects was accepted without question in the Near East, and was part of the faith of the Hebrew patriarchs (Gen. 28:17-19, E.).

These various theories are not without support both in comparative religion and in Scripture. As Israel was a union of various tribes, it may well be that the ancestors of some of them reverenced the spirit believed to reside in one or other of these cult objects. To root the worship of any one of them out of religious practice would seem to require centuries of growth in idealism. The main body of Israel, in the early days, would seem to have given the place of honor in the ark to a bull image or to a sacred stone; but in the course of the revolt from Canaanite pagan worship, and the development of the higher forms of Yahwism, not completed until after the exile, such symbols, as well as the ark and the tent of meeting, were ultimately outgrown and discarded. Such seems to have been the course of history. The school of Deuteronomy believed that the ten words on two tables of stone were in the ark (I Kings 8:6-9), and P. by way of interpretation makes them the "testimony of all things which I will give thee in commandment" (Exod. 37:1-9). The tradition behind Deuteronomy must have been aware that some material object was in the ark; and if Moses did proclaim any peculiarly spiritual conception it must long have been null and void. Mosaic religion, no doubt, was simple, but some symbol of the presence of Yahweh would be in keeping with what we know of early practice. A box in which emptiness was the symbol of the god would seem to be the dream of later days, rather than the findings of the historian.

Some of the characteristics ascribed to Yahweh at this time may be suggested with a degree of certainty. In this we must neither demand too much nor accept too little. Hairsplitting distinctions, the delight and life of many theologians, were never dreamed of by nomads. But they were keenly aware of great practical issues, simplicity of life, personal freedom, the bonds of brotherhood, wariness of the alien, and submission to the inevitable that lay within the will of the unknown Powers. Like all people they endowed their deity with the qualities, even the frailties, of their own ideals.

Thus Yahweh is conceived of as speaking and acting like a sheikh, or a supersheikh. He easily became angry with his people (Exod. 32:11-14, E.; Num. 14:12), with Aaron and Miriam (Num. 12:9, 10, E.), and in an outburst of temper even sought to kill Moses (Exod. 4:24-26, J.). Yet like the Arab he

[69] G. F. Moore, *Ency. Bibl.*, I, 2155. The most recent and most complete treatment is that of J. Morgenstern, *The Ark, the Ephod, and the Tent of Meeting*, 1-5, 146-158, in which the theory of an empty shrine is supported, considering this a definite contribution of Moses, as against the earlier contention that a stone, the symbol of Yahweh, was in the ark (*HUCA*, V, 134-151). A brief summary of the various theories is found in A. Lods, *Israël*, I, 498-501.

soon repented, and to save face among the nations, at the advice of Moses, he reversed his decision (Num. 14:20–23, E.). Naturally the ethical standards attributed to Yahweh were on the level of the common practice, in which personal interest overlooked the boundary lines between right and wrong. To the endless perplexity of Jewish and Christian apologetes, Abraham, the guilty, was rewarded (Gen. 12:16, 20, J.; 20:16, E.), Jacob the tricky was smiled on (Gen. 30:30–43, J., E.), and Yahweh ordered the fleeing Israelites to despoil the Egyptians of jewels of silver and of gold, and of raiment (Exod. 3:21, 22; 12:35, 36, E.). Tribal tradition delighted, in the name of Yahweh, thus to honor the ancestors, but not a few cases reflect little credit on the moral sensibilities of the age, and are without defense in later days.

In the desert, Yahweh had begun to assume the function of a war-god, with whom might was right. The song of Miriam,[70] which is early, is a paean of triumph over the oppressor. Yahweh, however, soon became an aggressor. He was displeased with the overtimid spies (Num. 13:11, 12, J., E.). He miraculously aided Moses against the Amalekites (Exod. 17:8–16, E.), and called for the utter destruction of the ancient inhabitants of Hormah (Num. 21:1–3, J.). While early experiences have probably been glorified, the underlying fact is that Yahweh became the patron of conflict; and the fight for the possession of territory became no less important than the fight for freedom. On the ground of might alone was there even the semblance of a claim to the land of Canaan. Power politics, aggressive, often unjust, frequently brutal, demanding *lebensraum*, found its source in Israel in the growing ambitions fostered in the desert.

But there is another side to the story, a finer one, which should be neither omitted nor exaggerated. The comparative absence of the crude and the coarse, so frequently found in early religions, is worthy of note. Whether this was due to the major role played by the patriarch in tribal life,[71] to the reaction of the tribal demands for chastity, or to the editorial vigilance of late scribes, the fact is that Yahweh in the Scriptures has no paramour. It is conceivable that, as in Mohammedanism, at a later period, the good seed came from the arid soil of the wilderness life. However, under whatever influences the mother goddess was excluded from all functions in Yahwism, it was a distinctive feature, with marked ethical implications, in the religion of the Old Testament people.

Alongside this austere and masculine interpretation of the powers that ruled the affairs of men was also the kindly and the compassionate. Yahweh in the

[70] Exodus 15:21 (E.) seems to be the original nucleus of the song of Moses (Exod. 15:1–18), and may be rendered:

Sing to Yahweh, for he rose up in his might;
Horse and chariot he flung into the sea.

See Moffatt's translation.

[71] The male occupied the position of supreme importance in nomadic life; the female sometimes was of less value than a donkey. A tendency has been noted among the early Semites to change the female deity into the masculine (Père M. J. Lagrange, *Etudes sur les religions Sémitiques*, 264; G. A. Barton, *Studies in the History of Religions*, presented to C. H. Toy, 192).

beginning was the God of an outcast and distressed people, their liberator from bondage. They were of mixed ancestry, with them went a mixed multitude, and a wife of the leader was a Cushite. Families of Kenites, and other wanderers joined them in the wilderness. Human interests, not tribal, humane considerations, not aggression, were the vital bonds in their union, and the deity must reflect the noblest qualities of his people. The religion of Yahweh thus started on the ground floor of human need and human potentiality. Late tradition but expressed in the language of its day the earlier ideal when it sang, "Yahweh is a God, full of compassion and gracious, slow to anger, and plenteous in mercy, and truth" (Exod. 34:6). Yet other ideals are always at work, and Yahweh is made to say, "I will be gracious with whom I will be gracious" (Exod. 33:19, J.).

Significant, also, is the fact that Yahweh became a mobile God. While his ancient home was in Horeb-Sinai, he had brought the people up out of Egypt, had led them in the wilderness, and then had marched with them into Canaan. No longer was he confined within his mountain citadel, nor like the Baals of Canaan was he related to specific locations. He dwelt in the midst of the tribes, sharing in their conflicts and their victories, a participant in their adventures (Exod. 17:7, J.; 34:9, J.; Num. 11:20, J.; 14:11, J., E.). In this intimate, personal relationship he was emancipated from local physical phenomena such as storm clouds or volcanic activity, and took over the wider role of a people's God. By the covenant he had entered into vital relation with them in all the normal activities of their growing experiences. His presence (Exod. 33:14-23, J.), specially embodied in the ark (Num. 10:35), or as manifested in his angel (Exod. 23:20-23, E. ed.) went with united Israel. He was in the give-and-take always found in social and religious progress, and spoke through that struggle from within, the hard, the ethical way, not through the swift word from above. Later writers turned the smoldering charcoal in the elevated brazier of the chief, the common guide in the desert, into a mysteriously moving pillar and a heavenly flame; but neither Moses nor the sheikhs had the certainties that theologians read into their activities. They lit the charcoal at night, and carried it forward in the morning light. They toiled and struggled. They marched and changed their strategy. They set up tribunals, found them inadequate, and tried again. It was a wearying trial-and-error experiment, discouraging from Goshen to Baal-peor, and in it all Yahweh was involved. *My presence shall go with you, and I will lead you safely* (Exod. 33:14, J.)[72] was the rewarding hope of the new confederacy.

Yahweh, as the deity of the tribes which had formed the new intertribal union, and as such had chosen him as their God, has thereby had his range of

---

[72] No translation can do justice to this text. Literally it reads, "My faces shall go, and I will cause you to rest." Moffatt translated it, "My presence shall go with you, and I will settle you safe." Meek in the Chicago University translation reads, "I will go along myself, he said, and lead you." The original implies, "lead you safely."

interest widened and his sense of human rights deepened. His outlook, thus, is on a higher ethical level than heretofore. For each clan some of the old shibboleths, privileges, rites, and deities sacred to the ancestors must be abandoned, and new names and symbols of a more inclusive nature must be adopted. The poignancy of such decisions can easily be understood, while the ethical values that may arise from such choices can scarcely be overestimated. Beyond the required social readjustments, the pledge of loyalty to the new God, with the renunciation of the old deities, naturally lifted the worshipers to a new level of intelligent devotion, of action, and of character.[73] The comfortable, inherited routine was no longer adequate, and deliberate choice promoted the creative and awakened personalities to greater achievements. When all the people answered with one voice and said, "All the words which Yahweh hath spoken will we do" (Exod. 24:3, 7, E.), it was a portent of things to come. Followed out it will purify much of the primitive Semitic religion that in Canaan had degenerated into witchcraft, sorcery, and other antisocial practices, and it will pave the way for perpetual adjustment to the growing demands for justice and righteousness. The Hebrew philosophy of history that God was always at work within the human process is a product of this covenant (Num. 23:22; 24:8; Amos 2:10; 9:7; Hos. 12:10; 13:4; Jer. 16:14).

Jealousy is a pronounced characteristic of Yahweh from the earliest period to the latest. Such intolerance, though not unknown,[74] is rather unusual.[75] In this case it may be an expression of the well-known Semitic genius for religion. To this religious temperament must be added the fact that a union of such diverse elements called for coherence at the center. While much must remain fluid, the various tribes must accept the new leader and the new God, without qualification, if the desired end is to be achieved. Further, in early thought the wells, the sanctuaries, the flocks and herds, and the tribe itself were believed to belong to the deity, and his personal dignity, even his existence, was bound up in them.[76] As Chemosh gave the land to the Amorites, so would Yahweh give the land to the Israelites (Judg. 11:24).

These characteristics attributed to Yahweh, the God of Moses and of Israel, austere, gracious, mobile, ethical, and jealous, seem to date from the days of the desert.[77] All of these features may be found in other religions; no one in

---

[73] Ed. Meyer long ago called attention to the fact that free choice was the root of all ethics (*Gesch. Alt.*, I, 1, 105). Recently a suggestive study has shown that where national organizations have been founded on compulsion war has been inevitable; where the foundations have been laid in voluntary consent the tendency has been toward internal harmony and strength (J. R. Devanton, *Evolution of Nations*, Smithsonian Studies No. 2, 1943).

[74] Jealous deities, who refused to allow their worshipers to acknowledge other gods, are found in Egypt and Assyria, especially on the occasion of the introduction of a new religion or a new dynasty. Cf. A. Lods, *Israël*, I, 363, 364.

[75] Paul Radin, *Primitive Religion*, 254–267. Ed. Meyer, *Gesch. Alt.*, I, 1, 104.

[76] W. R. Smith, *Rel. Sem.* (3), 157–162.

[77] Brief statements of the probable work of Moses may be found in W. E. Addis, *Hebrew Religion*, 52–77; Karl Marti, *The Religion of the Old Testament*, 36–71; A. Lods, *Israël*, I, 356–361.

itself was of unusual significance; all together taken in their setting gave no more promise of religious uniqueness than did other similar movements in ancient times.[78] These were days of small beginnings. But there were resident energies; there was the demand for freedom; there were dreams and aspirations. And a man was there who had had an awakening experience, an idea, and a confidence in his God. Thus we are witnesses to a miracle of creation; out of the womb of peasant history a people was born. Israel became the people of Yahweh, and Yahweh became the God of a nation. It was a brave adventure, the expression of an inner necessity responding to an outer appeal. It was as a grain of mustard seed cast into the ground that ultimately filled the whole heavens.

The experiences in Transjordania may have contributed their share to the growing strength of the union. Our Biblical reports have preserved a few fragments that throw some light on the situation. Archaeology has given us a complete picture of the conditions in this area during this peroid. From the beginning of the second millennium until about the twelfth century B.C. there was no sedentary population from Gilead in the north to Edom in the south. The cities, built earlier by the Amorites, had been deserted, and all were now in ruins.[79] Tribes wandering in from the desert were gaining a scant livelihood. Shortly after 1400 B.C. the Habiri, or confederate clans, migrating from the north and east were crossing the Jordan and raiding the villages of Canaan.[80] By 1200 B.C. shepherds had staked out claims in Moab-Ammon territory and were beginning to adjust to village and agricultural life. The tribe of Gad, that later joined up with Machir, and part of Reuben may have had pasturage claims in Gilead for some generations (Josh. 1:12–18, D. ed.).[81]

Thus all east and west of the Jordan was in a state of flux, when Ephraim and her allies pushed up into Transjordania. They came not as a compact, well-organized army of occupation but as a few widely scattered clans, with divergent histories, yet effectively united by covenant to each other and to Yahweh. They quarreled among themselves, clashed with tribes that had preceded them (Deut. 3:1–22, late), and, unable to hold the territory, they either were absorbed or moved into other less populated districts. Yet from the long-range point of view they had made progress. The frustrations had tested their spirit, strengthened their bond of unity, added to their confidence, and confirmed their allegiance to Yahweh.

What may have been the closing episode in the life of Moses has been preserved in duplicative narratives that echo a dramatic event of crucial im-

---

[78] A. Lods, *Israël*, I, 361–364. Joachim Wach describes many religious groups of somewhat similar origin, *Sociology of Religion*, 54–97.

[79] Professor N. Glueck, *BASOR*, Sept., 1934, 16–20. W. F. Albright, *ibid.*, 26.

[80] J. A. Knudtzon, *Die el-Amarna Tafeln*, Nos. 84, 103, 286–290.

[81] This narrative is late propaganda for the theory of a united "Twelve Tribes" of Israel. Pfeiffer places it about 550 B.C. (*Introduction to the O.T.*, 304).

portance (Num. 25:2, 3b, 4, J.; and 25:1, 3a, 5, E.). At Shittim Israel played the harlot with the Moabitish women, by pairing themselves off in the sex orgies of Baal at Peor; or in more religious terms, some of the Israelites participated in the fertility rites that were part of the worship of the Moabite deity. Two types of religion thus faced each other. In concrete form the Moabite religion was a violation of the basic principle of the worship of Yahweh: *thou shalt have no other gods before me.* It was a challenge to leadership, and a test. The result was drastic. The guilty ones, at the command of Moses, were hanged in public as a sacrifice to Yahweh; but like a censored message no hint is given as to the casualties on the other side. It would be strange if the Moabites did not demand an eye for an eye, and if some of the Hebrews did not suffer for the faith that was in them.[82]

These migrants, as they camped before the Jordan preparing for the crossing, were rather nondescript, and at a low level of both culture and religion. But they had assets of which they were proud. They had a new intertribal alliance; tribes out of Egypt, tribes out of Midian, and clans out of the south and the east were bound together by treaty—a source of strife, but also the leaven that promised development in both culture and religion. They had a new law, the expansion of old custom, a new ritual, the enrichment of ancient ceremony, a new ideal, and a new purpose. All these were gathered round a new symbol, the ark, and were consecrated to a new God, Yahweh. The central group in this movement was harsh as the desert, passionate in its loyalties, and aggressive in its aims. They faced the land of promise with its strange civilization with confidence in the name of Yahweh.

[82] It has been suggested that Moses may have suffered martyrdom at the hands of the mob. That he was buried over against Baal-peor, that no man knows the definite place of his burial (Deut. 34:6), and incidental references that lay a peculiar emphasis on Baal-peor lend some color to the theory (Hos. 9:10; 12:13–13:1) (E. Sellin, *ZAW*, 1928, 26–33).

Chapter IV

THE RELIGION OF THE CANAANITES. 1250 B.C.

WHEN the nucleus of the Joseph tribes crossed the Jordan, to them it marked the beginning of a new era. Similar movements out of Arabia, from the north and the east, like the sand of the sirocco, were ever breaking over the borders and settling on the hills and in the valleys of Canaan. The Amorites, a Semitic people, to whom the Abraham clan belonged, had drifted down from the northern mountains, wave after wave, from 2200 to about 1800 B.C.[1] So numerous were they that they took possession of the hill country, which for many centuries was known as the land of Amuru (Num. 13:29; Josh. 24:8, 18). Hurrian colonies, non-Semitic tribes, the Horites of the Old Testament (Gen. 14:6; Deut. 2:12), early in the second millennium B.C. migrated from northern Mesopotamia and in small groups made their homes in Palestine, especially in the south.[2] Somewhat later, the Hittites (Exod. 3:8, 17, J.), whose leaders were Indo-European while the majority of the population was a mixture of widely divergent cultures, during the second half of the second millennium B.C. extended their sphere of influence from their centers in Asia Minor and Syria down to the border of Egypt. Their activities on the borders of Palestine continued for centuries, and were so memorable that the name Hittite was used anachronistically for all their kin (cf. Gen. 23:3, 5, 7, 10, 16, 18, 20; 25:9, 10; 49:29, 32; Num. 13:29).[3] The Hyksos, likewise a mongrel, largely non-Semitic people from the north, invaded the land, occupied the strategic centers, and strongly fortified the chief cities, while they ruled lower Egypt from their capital in the Delta, from 1750 to 1580 B.C. In a real sense they governed Palestine during this period.[4] Within two centuries of their expulsion from Egypt, and the ensuing Egyptian rule in Palestine, the

---

[1] G. A. Barton, *Archaeology and the Bible* (6th ed.), 150, 151.·

[2] E. A. Speiser, *Mesopotamian Origins*, 120–163, and *JAOS*, XLIX, 269.

[3] The influence of these people on the laws and religion of Palestine was enormous. Knowledge of their history and their customs has been growing apace during recent decades, showing conclusively that the Old Testament owes much to them. The following studies are important: A. E. Cowley, *The Hittites*. D. G. Hogarth, *Kings of the Hittites*. A. Götze, *Das Hethiter Reich*. J. Garstang, *The Hittite Empire*. E. O. Forrer, *PEQ*, 1936, 190–203; *AJSL*, 1932, 137–169. Bedrich Hrozny, *Archiv Orientalni*, Vols. I-VIII. Ed. Cucq, *Le Droit Babylonien et les lois Hittite*. M. San Nicolo, *Beiträge zur Rechtsgeschichte in Bereiche der Keilschriftlichen Rechtsquellen*, 48, 96–105. E. H. Sturtevant, *JAOS*, 1934, 363–406. A. T. Olmstead, *History of Palestine and Syria*, 115–128, 216–244.

[4] T. E. Peet, *Egypt and the Old Testament*, 67–77. R. M. Engberg, *Chicago Studies in Oriental Civilization*, No. 18.

Habiri—equivalent to 'ibrî or Hebrew [5]—appeared on the scene. These invading bands plundered much of Syria and Canaan, causing widespread confusion among the local rulers.[6] A century later the Aramaeans, Semites from the northwestern mountains, were on the move and soon were masters of the city-states of Samal, Aleppo, Harran, and Damascus, while their influence extended even beyond the borders of Palestine (cf. Deut. 26:5).[7] To these must be added the Philistines, a sea people of European stock, migrating from Crete and shortly after 1200 B.C. settling in the southwest of the country, who ultimately gave their name to the whole land.[8] Each of these ethnic units contributed social customs, religious rites, as well as its life blood to the basic culture of Canaan.

"Canaanite" has come to be the blanket term for this complex of Aryan-Hamitic-Semitic stocks, the product of two thousand years of interracial cross-fertilization of which Old Testament writers were so conscious.[9] The land was well populated and commerce was active and varied. Many were sheep raisers, others were farmers, while weavers, carpenters, and tinkers met the local economic needs. A few were potters, while all classes indulged in trade of a sort. The rulers, their retainers, and many of the chief families lived in cities, built on hilltops, secure behind massive stone walls.[10] From 1600 to 1200 B.C. each city, with its surrounding hamlets, maintained its independence as a petty feudal state, under an Egyptian inspector, who collected tribute for the overlord. Squabbles between cities, corruption on the part of officials, evasion of tribute by unwilling subjects, and general disintegration of Canaanite vitality was the inevitable result.[11] Nevertheless the culture of the land remained

---

[5] B. Gunn, *Annual of the American School of Oriental Research*, XIII, 38; Albright, *Arch. P. and B.*, 132. Opposed by Ed. Dhorme, *La Religion des Hébreux nomades*, 80–85.

[6] J. A. Knudtzon, *Die el-Amarna Tafeln*, esp. Nos. 279–290. A. T. Olmstead, *History of Palestine and Syria*, 185–193.

[7] E. Kraeling, *Aram and Israel. Origins*, 1–37; development of the city kingdoms, 38–139.

[8] H. H. Hall, *CAH*, II, 295–352. E. Stahelin, *Die Philister*.

[9] When the Hebrews entered Palestine not only did they find tribes quite distinct from each other in history and culture, but they became acquainted with traditions that in a vague way preserved memories of prehistoric peoples like the Anakim, Avim, Emim, Zamzumim, Rephaim (Deut. 2:10–12, 20, 21), and heard tales of more recent invaders such as the Horites, Hivites, Hittites, Amorites, and Canaanites (Josh. 3:10), as well as of less significant clans, as Jebusites, Perizzites, and Girgashites (Josh. 3:10).

[10] The report of the spies that "the cities are fortified, and very great" (Num. 13:28; Deut. 2:12, 22), has been amply verified. At this period the cities usually occupied only from six to ten acres, and seemed impregnable. Tell en-Nasbeh was protected by cyclopean masonry, wall, tower, and revetment being thirty-five feet wide at the bottom and twenty-nine feet at the top, while on the outside, at least in one place, the wall rose more than forty feet. (W. F. Badé, *Excavations at Tell en-Nasbeh*, 15–23). The walls of Jericho, in the late Bronze Age, 1600–1200 B.C. were double, the outer one being six feet thick and the inner one twelve, both made of sun-dried brick and rising to a considerable height, while the area enclosed was less than six acres (J. Garstang, *The Foundations of Biblical History*, 130–133, 145–147). For Shechem, see *ZDPV*, 1926, 49, 229, 304. For Gibeah of Saul, a small city, in reality a citadel, probably destroyed by the judges, see Albright, *BASOR*, Dec., 1933, 6–12. For a general summary, see M. Burrows, *What Mean These Stones?* 136–140.

[11] This state of decadence is elaborated by A. Bertholet, *History of Hebrew Civilization*, 80–84, 113, 114; also Albright, *From the Stone Age to Christianity*, 154–157.

of a high order. Their substantial dwellings, their great storage vaults, the permanent water supply, the happy social life within the city gates went far toward satisfying the pressing human needs. But the ability to unite and to resist invasion had been forfeited by the long dominance of petty local interests. Two thousand years on the highway of the great civilizations, to which they were ever subject, had molded their customs, their religion, and their politics, and had largely determined their destiny.

The religion of the Canaanites was as complex as were the ethnic and cultural elements [12] in the country. Both the forms and the motivating spirit run far back into prehistory. Preceding the middle Bronze Age, which began about 1800 B.C., they had inherited many concepts and cult practices, that paved the way for later and more highly developed ceremonies.

The cult of the dead, a primary witness to the consciousness of human values, was one of the earliest and most fundamental expressions of popular religion. Unquestioned evidence for its existence is found in all ancient cemeteries, and in Canaan these carry us back not less than a hundred thousand years.[13] While the dead have been disposed of in a number of different ways, two types were in use in Canaan. Cremation, a method used by many people in many lands,[14] seems to have been practiced in parts of Canaan in early pre-Semitic days.[15] This was a means of freeing the spirit of the dead from its local habitat, and at the same time relieving the living from the possible disturbance of its ghostly visits.

Cave burial had been in existence from the earliest days, but with the invasion of the Amorites, a Semitic people, it rapidly became the prevailing practice.[16] Like cremation it expressed a belief in continued human values, but unlike it, it emphasized the unity of the person, in whom acting, thinking, and willing were inseparable from the body. More concrete in form than cremation, and providing opportunities for personal devotion to the departed, burial has ever made a strong appeal to the popular mind. Rites of purification and symbols of personal worth were gradually developed accrediting the dead in the courts of the beyond. Meat and drink, implements of the chase and of war, and prized personal possessions were placed in the tomb for the use and pleasure of the deceased. Thus provided, and the body often carefully preserved after the manner of Egypt, the dead was fully equipped for the ongoing

---

12 Summaries of the contributions of the various ethnic groups to the religion of Canaan are found in A. Bertholet, *History of Hebrew Civilization*, 65–76, 97–113; S. A. Cook, *The Religion of Ancient Palestine*, 90–149; Albright, *From the Stone Age to Christianity*, 169, 170, 175–179, also *Arch. and Rel.*, 71–83; W. C. Wood, *JBL*, 1916, 14–133.

13 The skeletal remains of nine persons, carefully arranged in burial in the cave of the kids, to the south of Mount Carmel, found by T. D. McCown prove to be at least 100,000 years old. See *Bulletin of the American School of Prehistoric Research*, IX (1933), 9; C. C. McCown, *The Ladder of Progress in Palestine*, 31–42.

14 E. S. Hartland, *ERE*, IV, 423, 424, 425; R. Munro, *ERE*, IV, 466; S. Langdon, *ERE*, IV, 444, 445.

15 R. A. S. Macalister, *Excavation of Gezer*, I, 286. G. A. Barton, *Arch. and Bib.*, 220, 228.

16 W. R. Bennett, *ERE*, IV, 497a–500; Père Ed. Dhorme, *La Religion des Hébreux nomades*, 102–124 (see Gen. 23:4–6, 9; 25:9; 49:29; 50:30).

of life. These ancient burial rites, so varied and often so elaborate, were the product of devotion to the departed, and the permanent monument to a belief in the hereafter.[17] Crude and commonplace as some of these may seem to us, they were so important in the growth and development of religious ideas that they have been rightly, and dramatically, called "the first steps in faith." [18]

The Hyksos, who dominated the land from 1800 to 1580 B.C., added confusion to complexity. Religious symbolism multiplied; the serpent, the dove, the incense altar, and the symbols of the mother goddess became the vogue, and fertility rites of many types flourished. Then, when in 1580 B.C. Egypt regained her ascendancy, many of her forms of worship were observed in the local city-states; and at military posts, such as Beisan, great temples [19] were erected, and imperial religious ceremonies were established.

The cultus of Canaan, and its underlying theology, at the end of this period, 1200 B.C., though complex and syncretistic can be understood, in general, when we co-ordinate the findings of archaeology with the illuminating phrases that are found in the Old Testament. The sacred tree, the upright stone, the spring, frequented by a spirit, had long been sanctuaries where seekers after well-being had found illumination, protection, and the answer to their quests (Gen. 28: 18). Hillside altars were numerous; and community open-air shrines, such as Gilgal, and Bab edh-Dra', where seasonal pilgrimages united kindred groups in social worship, were ancient sacred places. Some of these, owing to strategic location, strange local phenomena, or the peculiar competence of the priesthood, gained an importance that eventually overshadowed their neighbors. History was ever revising its judgment, and the old often had to give way before the new. Gezer and Gilgal lost their hegemony to Shechem and Hebron, and both of these in turn were eclipsed by Jerusalem. An occasional unroofed temple, because of economic development and foreign influence, had invaded the field of religion long before the entrance of the Hebrews. Such had been built in Sidon, Tyre, Ras Shamra, Beisan, Shechem, Megiddo, and probably at other places [20] before the end of the late Bronze Age.

[17] Detailed studies on burial rites as found among many aboriginal tribes and often preserved in present-day ceremonies are found in ERE, IV, 411–511.

[18] W. C. Graham and H. G. May, Culture and Conscience, 61–99. See also S. A. Cook, The Religion of Ancient Palestine, 90–149, and M. Burrows, What Mean These Stones? 239–242.

[19] The influence of temples, such as those found and described by the excavators of Beisan, on the religion of the subject people must have been enormous, and permanent. For a summary of the finds see Alan Rowe, Museum Journal (Museum of the University of Pennsylvania), March, 1927, 9–45; Dec., 1927, 414–442; PEQ, Apr., 1927, 68–84; Père Ed. Dhorme, Rev. bib., Jan., 1927; Fitzgerald, PEQ, 1931, 59–70.

[20] In the excavations at Tell en-Nasbeh Badé uncovered what he considered to be the foundations of an early Canaanite temple (PEQ, 1930, 12; W. F. Badé, PEQ, 1932, 204–208; A. Thiersch, ZAW, 1932, 73–86). Conclusions questioned by Albright, Arch. and Rel., 65, and McCown, BASOR, No. 98, 2–15. The Ras Shamra tablets tell the story of the erection of an unroofed temple in that city about 1400 B.C. (R. Dussaud, Revue de l'histoire des religions, 1931, 353–408; 1932, 245–302; 1935, 9–35). See also Albright, JPOS, 1934, 101–132. That building temples to the gods was an ancient practice throughout the country is seen in S. A. Cook, North Semitic Inscriptions, 19, 32, 48.

Baal, the master, and his consort Baalat, known under various names,[21] were the deities of vegetation, and were worshiped in order that fertility of flock, field, and family might be assured. That the gods should go in pairs, male and female, was normal in all early religions. Primitive man could not think of the creative powers in other terms, and even a late priestly writer has preserved the myth that must have been common among the Hebrews, viz., that God made man in his own image, "male and female created he them" (Gen. 1:27; 5:2). Such conclusions must have seemed axiomatic to the early philosopher.

Further, it was seen that all the world forces, visible and invisible, were marvelously interrelated. The heavens ruled the earth and its productivity, as well as man and his destiny. The sun rising and setting bounded his day, and the moon determined his night and his months. Ursus Major, pointing eastward in the spring, south in summer, west in autumn, and north in winter, ordered his seasons, and thereby in the springtime brought heat to the soil and to animal life, causing the fish to spawn, the lioness to whelp, and the domestic animals to produce after their kind. Toward this most desirable of all objectives religion sought to co-operate with the gods, and working on the principle of sympathetic magic, universally approved by the ancients, devised rites and ceremonies to secure the needed benefits to the individual, the family, and the community, and at the same time to satisfy the esthetic and economic interests of the priesthood.

Festivals which were lavish, social, and sensuous embodied the culmination of such ritual, particularly that provided for community religion. There were three such festivals: the beginning of harvest, when unleavened cakes were eaten and the sickle was officially thrust into the ripe grain; the conclusion of the wheat harvest; and the final harvest, that of the fruits, grapes, and olives.[22]

The ritual observed, while very simple in the beginning, under foreign and priestly influence gradually became extremely elaborate. The oldest ceremony may have been a "wave offering"[23] (Deut. 24:19; Lev. 19:9), in which the first sheaf of the harvest was presented to the god of the harvest; but soon the first fruits of the ground, the grain, the wine, and the oil (Gen. 4:3, 5; I Sam. 1:24; 21:6; 10:3), became the stated obligation of the farmer to the god of the

---

21 The relation of Baal to the soil and his significance for religion are discussed by Père Ed. Dhorme, *La Religion des Hébreux nomades*, 321–332. For Baalat, and the names under which she was known in the O.T., Asherah, Astarte, and Anat, see J. B. Pritchard, *Palestinian Figurines in Relation to Certain Goddesses Known in Literature*, 59–83.

22 Our sources of information for these festivals come from the literature of neighboring peoples, Babylonian, Hurrian, North Semitic, Ugaritic, that had strongly influenced Canaanitish life. But beyond all these the O.T. is the chief and most accurate witness. These three agricultural festivals were appropriated to Yahweh worship by the Hebrews, who, no doubt, rejected some of the local rites and added others. Thus, in the main, the early O.T. codes preserved much of the pre-Hebraic Canaanite cult. For an interpretation of these festivals, and Canaanitish influence on the Hebrews, see A. H. McNeile, "Exodus," in *Westminster Commentaries,* xlvi, lvi, lxv, lxxxiii, 140–142.

23 S. H. Hooke, *The Origins of Early Semitic Ritual,* 51.

soil, just as naturally as the tithe was his tribute to the feudal lord. Such offer-ings were dedicated to Astarte,[24] the goddess of fertility, with appropriate rites, which were always suggestive to the initiated. Her symbols, pillars and posts, were beside every altar (Exod. 34:13; Deut. 12:3; Judg. 6:26); and the sacred trees,[25] associated with the tree of life, the forerunners of the sacred groves notorious in Antioch for licentiousness,[26] readily ministered to the service of the goddess.

The autumn festival, which concluded with the celebration of the "begin-ning of the year," [27] was the most impressive of all. When all the farmer's ac-counts had been balanced, and the old year was closed officially, the stage was set for the future. The pageantry and responses, the sacrifices and vows ap-pealed to mass emotion and at the same time strengthened the individual for the tasks that lay ahead. Strange as such ceremonies might seem to us, they contributed no little to the joy, the hope, and the confidence of the Canaanites of ancient days.

These harvest festivals were each related to fertility functions, and as such were linked up with the changes of the seasons. The autumn, at the end of the third quarter of our year, had its religious counterpart the world over in harvest home, or thanksgiving, at the conclusion of which, as above noted, the Hebrews observed Rosh Hashana. Springtime, the close of the first quarter of our year, at an early date was observed as a shepherd festival (Exod. 12:21–27; 3:18; 7:16). Later, with a new meaning, it became the Jewish Passover (Exod. 12:15–20, P.), and still later the Christian Easter. The closing cycle of the year, the fourth quarter, beginning with the winter solstice, December 23–25, was to primitive man most important of all. Though not referred to in the Old Testament until late, the rites connected with it must have pene-trated Canaanitish life and thought.

"Tammuz worship" is the name under which this most alluring fertility cult was known throughout Palestine. While differing greatly in details, in

---

[24] Astarte is the western pronunciation of Ashtart, of which the plural is Ashtaroth. Ishtar is the Babylonian and Assyrian, and Athtar the South Arabian. Originally thought of as the mother goddess, and the protectress of her people, she ultimately became the goddess both of war and of fertility. Among the warlike Assyrians her chief function was war; but among the Canaanites, where triumph over the invaders was impossible, she compensated by devotion to fertility. She was the giver of the grain, the wine, and the oil, and the inciter of sexual passion (G. F. Moore, "Ashtoreth," *Ency. Bibl.*; S. R. Driver, "Ashtoreth," *HBD* (five vols.). In Greek religion Aphrodite had the same functions.

[25] Sacred tree in the Hebrew is *'elón,* or *'eláh,* and comes from the same root as the word for god (Père Ed. Dhorme, *La Religion des Hébreux nomades,* 149–159).

[26] Fr. Cumont, *Les Religions orientales dans le paganisme romain,* 4th ed., 109, 258, 259. N. Perrot, *Les Representations de l'arbre sacré sur les monuments de Mesopotamie et d'Elam,* 1–143.

[27] The origin and the importance of this observance has been suggested by S. H. Hooke, *The Origins of Early Semitic Ritual,* 51–56. Its significance is still preserved in Rosh Hashana, the Jew-ish new year.

essentials it was similar to Isis-Osiris worship in Egypt, and the Attis-Cybele worship of Asia Minor.[28] In mythology Dumuzi, the Sumerian god—Tammuz is the Akkadian equivalent—was the consort of the mother-earth-goddess. In the autumn the procreative powers failed, it was believed, because he had descended into the underworld. His consort Ishtar, with her devotees and all nature mourned his absence (see Ezek. 8:14; Amos 8:10; Jer. 22:18; Zech. 12:10). Seeking him, she followed him into the underworld, divesting herself of one after another of her garments as she passed through each of the seven stages to the lowest and chief circle of Sheol. Finding him there, she bargained with the mistress of the nether world that he should remain on the earth six months of the year, and finally, at the winter solstice, she started back with him, reclothing herself stage by stage, on their journey to the upper world. This mythology expressed, in dramatic form, the dying and reviving of the vital energies in vegetable and animal life; and the priesthood perfected suggestive ceremonies symbolizing death, burial, and birth in order to aid the powers of fertility. Some of the rites beyond question would be called licentious; but on the whole they were appealing. To many they were utterly convincing and thoroughly idealistic (see *The Golden Ass,* chap. xi); and in fundamental principle they were an endeavor to keep in line with reality. It has been said that all was carried out with "solemnity and decorum well-fitted to soothe the troubled mind and ease the burdened heart."

Community rites, such as human sacrifice and child sacrifice, were too much an integral part of Canaanitish custom to be omitted from any résumé of their religion. The one was believed to ward off grave disaster, and the other was the guarantee of security to a chief building or to a city wall. Such practices, probably taken over from the pre-Semitic population,[29] though gruesome and inhuman in the extreme, were accepted and long observed by various Semitic groups. Moabites, Phoenicians, Carthaginians, and not a few Hebrews were so convinced of the superior efficacy of such offerings that they made them the supreme evidence of their devotion.

The cultus related to the religion of the individual and the family was pitched to the same key as that of the community. Clay figurines, symbols of the nude goddess (four to eight inches in length, some coarse, others re-

---

28 Tammuz ritual is described by T. G. Pinches, "Tammuz", *ERE,* XII; Graham and May, *Culture and Conscience,* 80–99, 119–139; S. H. Hooke, *The Origin of Early Semitic Ritual,* 10–18, 28–44, 70; Albright, *Arch. and Rel.,* 84–92. Isis-Osiris worship, by J. H. Breasted, *The Dawn of Conscience,* 94–110; Apuleius, *The Golden Ass,* chap. xi. Attis-Cybele worship, Lucian, *De Dea Syria,* 6, 15; Grant Showerman, "Cybele," *ERE,* IV, 374, 375. A brief statement of widespread fertility worship is found in Joachim Wach, *Sociology of Religion,* 262–268.

29 That human sacrifice in its origin was non-Semitic is supported by Ed. Meyer, *Gesch. Alt.,* I, ii, 345, and E. A. Westermarck, who considers it Aryan in origin and notes that it is never found among savages but only among the semicivilized (*Origin and Development of Moral Ideas,* I, (434–447). For Canaanitish practices, see S. A. Cook, *Religion of Ancient Palestine,* 82–85.

fined, and all of them emphasizing the idea of reproduction),[30] have been found in every tell and in many levels in Palestinian excavations. Introduced into Palestine as early as 2000 B.C.,[31] they became exceedingly numerous between 1700 and 1300 B.C.,[32] and were never entirely absent during the history of Israel. They were used as talismans to insure conception, and as votive offerings to the goddess.[33]

The serpent, strangest of creatures, hence an excellent subject for mythology, in many lands has been believed to be the incarnation of an earth spirit, and subject to the mother goddess.[34] On the one hand it easily became a symbol of procreation, and thus was sacred to the female, while with equal appropriateness it became associated with the powers of the lower regions [35] (Wisd. of Sol. 2:24; cf. Gen. 3:1-5). The frequency with which it has been found on cult objects dedicated to the goddess leaves no doubt but that in Canaanitish worship it was a symbol of fertility. It is equally certain that for centuries after the conquest it was popular among the Hebrews, even within the court circles (II Kings 18:4; Num. 21:4-9; cf. Gen. 3:1-24).

The sacrifice of virginity as an act of devotion to the mother goddess, the giver of all life, probably found a response among the Canaanites. That it formed a part of the religious ritual among a few of the nations in early days is beyond dispute.[36] It had been practiced in Babylonia,[37] where, guided by the same fundamental principle, *qedeshoth,* that is, temple prostitutes, were dedicated to the service of the goddess with the sanction of church and state.[38] That the Canaanites were no whit behind their kinsmen in their veneration

---

[30] Nudity, which was based on the belief that things are best the way God made them, was a primitive and widespread expression of religion. The reverse is, what man has made is contaminated and contaminating. Hence at sacred places shoes should be removed (Exod. 3:5); in sacred dances garments should be discarded (II Sam. 6:20); hair should not be cut (Num. 6:5); and temples should not be built (II Sam. 7:6, 7) (W. R. Smith, *Rel. Sem.* (3), 687). On the same principle good people have insisted that railroads should not be constructed, anesthetics should not be administered, surgical operations should not be performed, and have opposed almost every advance in science and philosophy.

[31] Edw. Pilz, *ZDPV,* 1923-1924, 129-168, 260.

[32] Albright, *Arch. and Rel.,* 74-78. It is interesting to note that as yet none of these plaques has been found in early Israelite levels in central Palestine (*ibid.,* 95-119).

[33] G. Contenau, in *La Déesse nue babylonienne,* 82-101, has collected a wealth of material that throws light on this subject. The relation of these cult objects to passages in the O. T. is treated in *Religion of Ancient Palestine,* 123-227, by S. A. Cook. See Pritchard, *Palestinian Figurines,* 83-87, for conclusions.

[34] Graham and May, *Culture and Conscience,* 82-85.

[35] The part played by the serpent in primitive religions has been treated by many writers. The following are important: J. A. MacCulloch in *ERE,* XI, 399-411, esp. 409-411. E. Sjöquist, *Arch. für Religionswissenschaft,* 1933, 308-359. R. H. Kennett, *Deuteronomy and the Decalogue,* 13. S. Reinach, *CMR,* I, 67-76; II, 396-400.

[36] Ed. Meyer, *Gesch. Alt.,* I, I, 27; I, II, 345.

[37] Herodotus, I, 93, 199. Strabo, XI, 14, 16; XVI, 1, 4, 20; XVII, 2, 46.

[38] D. D. Luckenbill, *AJSL,* Oct., 1917, 1-12. J. C. Gadd, *History and Monuments of Ur,* 92. G. F. Moore, *Ency. Bibl.,* I, 337a. S. N. Kramer, *Proceedings of the American Philosophical Society,* LXXXV, 293-323. Albright, *Arch. and Rel.,* 74-78. Barton, *Hebraica,* IX, 131-165; X, 2-23; 27-60; *ERE,* XI, 378-384.

of the goddess of love is amply attested by archaeology, and the Scriptures [39] (Num. 25:1-5; Gen. 38:15-24; Deut. 23:18; I Kings 14:24; 15:12; 22:46; Amos 2:7; Hos. 4:14; Ezek. 16:30-34).

The number and the organization of the officials of religion naturally kept pace with the type and complexity of the civilization. As each village in Canaan was independent, each sanctuary tended to develop its own local priestcraft. Eli at Shiloh, in the next period, probably reflects the earlier practice, and though the priesthood would be hereditary, it waxed and waned in response to the incidents of history.

Beyond the priest, and the *kedheshim* and *kedheshoth* who were associated with local sanctuaries, there were those who specialized as seers, interpreters of dreams, fortunetellers, oracle givers, necromancers, healers, and miracle workers. At times individuals or groups became spirit possessed and in trance or ecstasy spoke or acted as impelled by the spirit. Features of these types have been common throughout the country in all ages, and are the background of much in early Hebrew history. Thus, all was in a state of flux. Neither the activities of the individual nor those of the local shrine were fully standardized, and change for the worse or the better was always possible.

Legend and mythology, the expression of the intellectual history of the people, went hand in hand with the cultus. The local residents had their histories and their heroes; and these, whatever their origin, Horite, Amorite, Hyksos, Habiri, Aramaean, or other, like St. George and the Dragon in later days had been thoroughly assimilated and had become *Canaanite*. Ancestral figures, such as Cain, Abraham, Ishmael, Jacob, Esau, Shechem, and priestly sheikhs like Melchizedek, were honored in different parts of the land by tombs, place names, and tribal traditions. Nor were they lacking in mythologies. The tales of the gods, their loves and quarrels, their creative acts and their frustrations, the number of their progeny, their names and their histories, their relations with the children of men, their desires and demands—all these, with much diversity, were common property throughout the ancient Semitic world. [40]

Each of these religious aids contributed its quota to the individual, family, and tribal welfare. All phases of cultus and thought gathered round the desire

[39] Add to the nude figurines the serpent images, the *qedeshim* among the temple personnel at Ras Shamra (see Virolleaud, *Syria*, XVIII, 159-164), the *qedeshoth, qedeshim,* and the *zoneh* of the O.T., and the proof seems complete. There is an excellent article on the goddess in Canaanite folk religion by J. B. Pritchard in the *Crozer Quarterly*, Apr., 1944, 106-117.

[40] A cross section of the mythology that flourished in northern Syria between 1500 and 1400 B.C. is found in the Ras Shamra tablets. El was the father of gods and of men. Asherah, his wife, bore him seventy gods and goddesses. Baal and Anat, his wife, were the most important pair, and their chief function was related to fertility. Mot, the god of death, slew Baal because of jealousy, and Anat in turn slew Mot. This myth, which is akin to that of Tammuz, has been vividly interpreted by Cyrus H. Gordon, *The Living Past*, 113-155, also *The Loves and Wars of Baal and Anat*. See also Albright, *Arch. and Rel.*, 84-92; J. Morgenstern, "The Divine Triad in Biblical Theology," *JBL*, March, 1945, 15-37.

for an increase in flock and herd, a bountiful harvest, a large and vigorous family, and the prosperity of the community as a whole, the great realities of daily existence. The symbols and the ceremonies had stood the test of long experience; and personal testimony of their worth was given by neighbors and by priests. Flocks had been multiplied; crops had become abundant; health had been restored; women long barren had borne children; and the gods, pleased with human sacrifice, had hurled back the conqueror (II Kings 3:27). Their talismans had been effective; their prayers had been answered. Such was the way of their fathers, the will of their god.

To the Canaanites, both the worship and the mythology kept alive memories of the sacred past and provided a long-established philosophy of life that gave them divine assurance for their earthly pilgrimage. To them it was good. But to the invading nomad, guided by the voice from Sinai and disciplined by the austerities of the wilderness, much of it must have seemed a strange hocus-pocus, a degenerate travesty of true religion.

Chapter V

◄◄◄◄◄◄◄◄◄◄◄◄◄◄◄◄◄◄✦►►►►►►►►►►►►►►►►►

THE RELIGION OF THE INVADERS. 1250-1030 B.C.

T HE differences between the resident Canaanites and the invading clans can scarcely be overestimated. The Canaanites had everything—population, resources, organization, fortifications, and culture. The Hebrews had nothing. They were uncouth, unarmed, hungry shepherds. But they were vigorous of body, clean in morals, fanatical in religion, and united in purpose. The imponderables, hope and determination, were theirs.

Crossing the Jordan was as decisive to them as crossing the Rubicon was to Caesar. The physical difficulties have been very greatly magnified by the storytellers. There were five chief fords in the lower Jordan, any one of which was passable at most seasons of the year.[1] Before the venture was launched there had been a period of preparation at Shittim (Num. 25:1–5). Spies had penetrated the chief frontier city and the surrounding territory (Josh. 2:1–24). Finally the ark, the symbol of Yahweh, had been placed in the forefront of the invaders (Josh. 3:3, 8), and thus the biological urge, that led the "have nots" to exploit the accumulated riches of civilization, was transmuted into a religious quest guided by the God of the fathers. This psychological factor, the will to victory on the part of a united group, sanctioned by the presence and the authority of Yahweh, was of utmost importance.

The newcomers, however, in language, shepherd life, customs, and world view had a common background with the natives. The language spoken by both was Semitic; that of the desert people was the purer, while Canaanitish, of which there were a number of local varieties [2] differing from each other in pronunciation, vocabulary, and grammar, was the more cultured. Probably a third of the inhabitants of Palestine in those days were shepherds, while the dominant strain in the blood stream was Semitic. All, of both groups, held essentially the same animistic outlook and were firm believers in the power of magic. Thus the common heritage furnished a bridgehead from which the immigrants could at least approach the older civilization.

Two hundred years, more or less, passed from the time the Ephraimitic

---

[1] G. A. Smith, *Historical Geography of the Holy Land*, 336, 337. T. K. Cheyne, "Jordan," *Ency. Bibl.* J. Garstang, *The Foundations of Biblical History*, 135, makes the unnecessary suggestion that a landslide may have temporarily dammed the river. Physically there was no need of the unusual. Moabites (Judg. 3:12–17), Midianites (Judg. 6:1–5), Ephraimites (Judg. 12:5, 8), Gileadites, Israelites (I Sam. 11:3, 9–11), and many others at all periods in history crossed whenever they wished.

[2] Zelig S. Harris, *The Development of the Canaanite Dialects*.

tribes crossed the Jordan until the beginning of the monarchy. But though the literary sources are meager (Judges, Joshua, and I Samuel) and the episodes are summarized and telescoped, the general picture is both clear and reliable. To this, Palestinian archaeology has added much that throws light on the trends and activities of the period.[3] Gradually the Hebrews adjusted themselves to the new environment. Through tedious generations they learned the way of the farmer, the businessman, and the city dweller. The conquest was a process, not a capitulation. Infiltration of the pasture lands, an occasional raid, called a battle, but only of the guerrilla type (Judg. 3:16–29; 7:15–25; 9:42–49; 21:19–23), treaties contracted with neighboring sheikhs (Josh. 9:3–5), villages burned in extreme cases (Josh. 7:2–8:29), and the natural assimilation by inter-marriage with the natives (Gen. 33:18–34:21, Judg. 8:29–32; 11:1–3; 21:19–33; Josh. 8:30) [4] all went on apace. Freed from the interference of outside powers, Hebrew and Canaanite together unconsciously were working out in Palestine a new design of life and order. In addition to these perpetual social tensions, the influences of topography, climate, soil, and diet [5] so different from those of the desert, inevitably contributed to mold the conqueror into the ways, even the religion, of Canaan.

Owing to the overthrow of the strategic fortress of Jericho,[6] the successful raids against open villages,[7] and a couple of major campaigns, one in Esdraelon (Judg. 4:1–5:31) and the other in the hills of Ephraim (Judg. 7:9–8:28), Yahweh, the God of the shepherds, like his people, had become a Deity of the warpath, Yahweh of hosts. Such a change of function was inevitable, if either people or Deity was to continue to make progress. Such was the law of life. Peace societies may have been vocal, and isolationists [8] were in the land. But

[3] Every one of more than a score of excavations has contributed its quota to the better understanding of the age. Only in the reports issued from each site can the wealth of significant material be found. But excellent summaries have been presented in: W. F. Albright, *From the Stone Age to Christianity*, 2–220; S. A. Cook, *The Religion of Ancient Palestine in the Light of Archaeology*, 84–152; A. Bertholet, *History of Hebrew Civilization*, 141–147; J. Garstang, *Foundations of Biblical History*, 105–115; M. Burrows, *What Mean These Stones?*; C. C. McCown, *The Ladder of Progress in Palestine*, 68–308.

[4] Two types of marriage seem to have been practiced: the *beena* marriage, a primitive tribal type in which the wife and her children remained with her own people (Judg. 15:1); and the *Baal* marriage, which was Canaanitish and, disregarding old tribal affiliations, undermined the very existence of the clan (J. Morgenstern, *ZAW*, 1929, 91–110; 1931, 46–58).

[5] C. C. McCown, *J. Rel.*, 1927, 520–539. C. A. Mills, *Climate Makes the Man*. E. D. Starbuck, "Climate," *ERE*, III.

[6] J. Garstang reports that walls of Jericho belonging to 1600–1200 B.C. may have been destroyed by earthquake and by fire (*Foundations of Biblical History*, 140–148.

[7] Tradition attributes the destruction of Ai to Joshua (Josh. 7:2–8:29). Excavation shows that the site was in ruins from 1800 to 1200 B.C. (W. F. Albright, *BASOR*, No. 56, 11; R. Dussaud, *Rev. hist. des rel.*, 1937, 125–141). Either the name Ai had shifted to some near-by place, or tradition was confused.

[8] The early chapters of the J. document are propaganda for the nomadic way of life as opposed to city civilization with its musicians, metal workers, and crime (Gen. 4:2, 3, 17, 21, 22). The Nazarite vow harks back to desert practices (Num. 6:2–5), and the Rechabites exalted a limitation of nomadic life into a religious principle (Jer. 35:2–19). These remnants of ancient customs indicate antagonism against the new civilization.

eventually the war lords, always aggressive, won the day. Deborah is quite cynical about those who at the watercourses of Reuben had great searchings of heart (Judg. 5:16); and the inhabitants of Meroz were bitterly cursed because they came not to the help of Yahweh in the slaughter of the natives (Judg. 5:23). Thus it came about that in Canaan the sword of Yahweh and of Gideon became the popular slogan in Israel (Judg. 7:20).[9] This idea is dramatized in the vision of Joshua as he stood before Jericho and saw the captain of the host of Yahweh with a drawn sword, who declared, "The place whereon thou standest is holy" (Josh. 5:13–15, a late passage). By the time this was written the land was Yahweh's, the sword was his symbol, and his authority must not be questioned. This belief had at an early date permeated all phases of Hebrew religion.

The ark, originally the sign of the guiding presence of Yahweh (Num. 10: 33, J.), led the people into Canaan (Josh. 4:7; 5:13, J., E.); then it led the victory procession around the city of palm trees (Josh. 6:7, 8, 11, J., E.). Still later it was carried as a talisman into battle against the Philistines (I Sam. 4:3–5), and in the slogan, "Up, Yahweh, let thine enemies be scattered" (Num. 10:35, J.), it was the symbol of conquest and destruction.

Ruthlessness, in the exercise of discipline in the exigencies of war, is a common characteristic of the military chief. So, in the occupation of Canaan, Yahweh came to full stature as a bloody war lord. The tradition, that has been gloried in, is that the cities were laid in ruins (Josh. 10:20, 26, 28), that men, women, and children were slaughtered (Josh. 6:17, 21; 8:29; 9:24), that kings and princes were hanged, mutilated, and quartered (Judg. 1:17, 25; 7:25; 8:21; I Sam. 15:33) at the behest of Yahweh (Josh. 11:6–15, J., E.). The early songbooks, the book of the wars of Yahweh and the book of Yashar (Num. 21:14, 15; Exod. 15:21), were the product of this spirit. In later history the heartless brutalities of Jehu and the disciples of Yahweh were a ghastly commentary on this phase of early religion (II Kings 9:24, 27, 33; 10:7, 11, 14, 23–27). These brief phrases uncover horrors of religious wars that all but rival the revelations of modern concentration camps.

As war was justified by its victories, the God of war was enriched by the spoils. The silver and gold, the vessels of brass and of iron became sacred to him (Josh. 6:19), and the trophies of war went to adorn his dwelling, or to reward his priests (I Sam. 5:2–5; 21:9; II Sam. 5:21, RV). So Yahweh, in song and story, is presented as an aggressive war-god and is made responsible for atrocities the very defense of which remains a permanent blot on any system of thought. Surely the ancient apologists made god in their own image when under the guise of piety they credited him with the blood lust of their own passions.

It is true that the idea of a god of power was congenial to desert life where

---

[9] Yahweh of hosts is a war phrase meaning "Yahweh commands the armies of Israel." It was popular and is found in the O.T. 278 times (J. Hempel, *Gott und Mensch im A.T.*, 33–37).

man seemed so puny and the forces of nature were so irresistible. Also it was an easy, though superficial, interpretation of the jealous God of the covenant. Authority now had come to be based on might, and the question of right was definitely ignored. The covenant at Sinai had involved mutual considerations, but military authority was unilateral. The free choice of a democratic people, the ethical basis of the Mosaic covenant, was in process of being scuttled in the interest of military efficiency, national unity, and the priesthood. Failing to recognize the rights of those beyond their own confederacy, they were undermining the rights of those within the tribe.

However, recognizing that humanity, owing to a prevailing indolence, is always profited by the shock that sets in motion a stagnant idealism, it must be admitted that war has reached some objectives not easily attained in peace. If distressing and far-reaching consequences went hand in hand with aggressive warfare, it is equally true that values scarcely to be gained otherwise were developed thereby. It is recognized that courage, loyal co-operation, and unselfish devotion to the cause of humanity, social and psychological virtues apart from which there can be no higher idealism, are developed more surely through the grueling necessities of war than in the more relaxing ways of peace. While the complacencies of a comfortable life threaten the noblest ideals of humanity, conflict calls to the heroic, stirs those immediately interested to their emotional depths, and releases energies that may accomplish the impossible. The ease-loving Arab finds no ride too long, no risk too great, if adventure, spoil, or revenge be the prize.[10] Not only is man strengthened physically by the hard, muscle-building demands, but mental activities are keyed up, and even the moral fiber is toughened to the realities of life, rather than brutalized by the casualties of battle.

Further, the co-ordination of clans and tribes in a larger whole, otherwise well-nigh impossible, was thereby achieved. The song of Deborah, which antedates the founding of the kingdom, reveals the disintegration due to local tribal rule, while the larger federation assures security and progress. The rulers had ceased in Israel, the highways were unoccupied, commerce was imperiled by robbers, and lawlessness was unchecked (Judg. 5:6, 7). But Deborah, in the name of Yahweh, united six tribes against the foe, while four were severely censured for not sharing in the conflict. This was a crucial incident. Civilization, culture, even religion itself was in the balance. When "every man did that which was right in his own eyes" (Judg. 17:6; 18:1; 19:1), authority backed by force was needed for the greatest benefit to the greatest number. The war leaders, Deborah (Judg. 4:1–5:31), Gideon (Judg. 6:11–8:21), and Jephthah (Judg. 11:1–12:7), by inciting the tribes to fight were the forerunners of the kings, and paved the way for the larger and more law-abiding kingdom of Israel. The willingness to observe law and order for the general welfare of the community had at least been accelerated by the discipline of the sword.

Conquest, that had rapidly expanded the borders of Israel, gradually brought

10 A. Musil, *Arabia Petraea*, III, 369-398.

Canaanite villages, either as allies or as servants, under the rule of the conquerors and their God. Bloodshed, struggle, and compromise marked the
course of such triumphs. Zealous Yahweh worshipers called for unconditional
surrender and the extermination of the enemy (I Sam. 15:32, 33; Judg. 2:2;
Deut. 7:2). Canaanites were no less savage, and mutilated and enslaved their
victims (Judg. 1:5–7; 8:18, 19; I Sam. 11:2). Israel at times fought Israelite and
Canaanite without discrimination (Judg. 8:1; 9:5, 36–40, 44, 45, 47–54; 20:19–
21, 25–48; 21:8–12). Compromise often became the order of the day, as the
natives were allies (Judg. 4:17, Josh. 6:22, 23; 9:3–27), or were kinsmen by
marriage (Judg. 8:29–31; 9:1, 2). Virgins of a defeated enemy often were desirable, and as such were saved alive (Deut. 21:10–14, Judg. 21:12–14, 21–23).
Thus many Canaanitish clans, in the ordinary course of history, naturally became identified with Israel.

While Yahweh was becoming a war-God, and like his protégés was taking
the captured and affiliated Canaanites into his family, constant conflict raged
between the two religions. To the city dweller Yahwism was uncouth, barren,
and intolerant, and so remote from his daily life that it satisfied none of his
religious needs. His sense of the social, the human, and the esthetic found little
in the shepherd religion that appealed to his sense of devotion. To him there
was a great gulf fixed. Nor was Baalism, the essential religion of the villager,
attractive to the newcomers. To them much of it was repugnant. The endless
and intricate ritual was as meaningless to the simple-minded man from the
desert as are the ceremonies of the Latin or Greek churches to the uninitiated.
They were spectacles, highly entertaining, sometimes seductive, occasionally
revolting, but on the whole tiresome and scarcely religious. The social revelry
at the festivals, the accredited religious votaries, male and female, and the ac-
companying sex orgies to most of the chaste tribes were disgraceful. Nor were
the activities of the Baal priests, the officials of religion, acceptable. They
usurped the old-time prerogatives of the head of the family, and had established an aristocracy in religion. The democracy of the desert never loved the
vested interests of an entrenched hierarchy.

Further, the two systems fundamentally were quite incompatible one with
the other. To the shepherd, an offering of the first fruits of the ground, the first
cluster of ripe grapes and the sheaf of grain, lacked the essential element of
true religion. It provided neither the sacrificial lamb nor the sacred meal in
which the worshiper entered into a living union with Yahweh. Even more distasteful to him was the fact that the grain, the wine, and the oil were tribute
to deity, the equivalent of a tax.[11] This was commercial; that of the shepherd,

[11] The meaning of *minhah* is "gift," "tribute," "offering," and is used for the tax paid by the
vassal to his lord (Judg. 3:15, 17; II Sam. 8:2, 6), or as an appeasement gift to a possible enemy,
or to a friend (Gen. 32:13, 18), or as a gift to deity (Judg. 6:18; Gen. 4:3). On the other hand
zebah, the word used for "sacrifice," or the slaying of the lamb, carries in it the idea of a sacrificial feast in which the community and the deity enter into a mystical union. See W. R. Smith,
Rel. Sem. (3), 240–243.

Hebrew or Canaanite, was mystical. Baalism, as nature worship, with its social and sex emphasis, was pitched on the lower levels, and, aiming at prosperity by means of magic, the human was prostituted to the material, and idealism was seriously hampered. Yahwism placed the emphasis on the personal relation to the spirit world, and left the higher nature of man free for future achievement in the world of spirit.

There were three quite distinct, though not always clearly separate, reactions on the part of Yahweh worshipers in the long conflict with Baalism. A few were irrevocably hostile to every departure from the practices of the desert life. To them custom and religion were inseparable. The experience at Sinai was final. Many others, however, soon lost interest in the old pledges and principles as they enjoyed the larger, fuller life of Canaan. The third class, probably only a few in any generation, sought to maintain and to interpret the democratic and ethical ideals of the wilderness in the midst of the new agricultural and commercial environment.

. The first group was definitely antagonistic to Baalism, and had no liking for the Canaanites, the restrictions of civilization, or the intricacies of priestcraft. They were nomadic in spirit and culture, and refused to become the slaves of the plow or the servants of Baal. Tired muscles, nomadic ideas of human dignity, and the religion of the fathers conspired against the toils of farm life and the snares of the local festivals. The quiet life in the tent in out-of-the-way places, the sheep, the long hair, the milk and the curds were the symbols of the way of Yahweh whom they would not forsake. They were sure that the sacrifice of Abel was acceptable to Yahweh, while the fruit of the ground offered by Cain was abhorred (Gen. 4:3, 4). Convinced that their religion was all-inclusive and final, they refused to compromise with evil or to bow down and worship other gods. Considering themselves the only true worshipers of Yahweh, their loyalty was intense, intolerant, and at times fanatical. No doubt they were sincere, and thanked God they were not as other men were; but they became, in the course of centuries, the fossil witnesses of a rapidly receding past.

The second and largest group consisted of those who did not take the old-time religion either so seriously or so literally. Rejoicing in victory, they easily floated along with the tide accepting life as it came. With eyes on the mess of pottage, without too great difficulty they made the transition to agriculture, and more or less complacently conformed to the worship of Baal, the god of the farmer.[12]

During the period of the judges marked progress was made by the Hebrew shepherds in their transition to the sedentary life. Gideon (Judg. 6:11) and the

---

12 As in Canaan Baal and Baalat were believed to be responsible for all fertility, whoever learned to farm, or married into a Canaanitish family, in the very nature of the case became a worshiper of the Baalim, performing the usual fertility rites (C. R. Bowen, *The Living Bible*, 62–64).

men of Beth Shemesh (I Sam. 6:13) were wheat farmers, while Saul was a plow boy (I Sam. 11:5). Three of the judges, Jair, Abdon, and Ibzan, were honored, not for delivering Israel from an oppressor, but for the number of their sons, and grandsons, and for the wealth they derived from farms, trade, and conquest (Judg. 10:3, 8, 9).

This cross-fertilization of culture that continued throughout the whole period, by the ordinary give-and-take in social life, almost completely changed Yahwism. Micah, a man of substance settled in the hill country of Ephraim, was sure Yahweh would do him good because he had installed in his house of gods a Levite of the house of Judah (Judg. 17:13); and the report was current that the ark of Yahweh brought signal blessing to Obed-edom, and to all his house (II Sam. 6:12). Measures of meal, of wine, and loaves of bread, all the products of agriculture, ultimately were considered acceptable to Yahweh by most Israelites (I Sam. 1:24; Judg. 13:19, 23; I Sam. 21:7). The cult dances, featuring various phases of fertility, were always popular with many, and gained at least semiofficial status in some quarters (Judg. 11:34; 21:19–21; II Sam. 6:13).[13] Even the harvest festival at Shiloh, celebrated so joyously by the maidens, had become, without any qualms of conscience, the feast of Yahweh (Judg. 21:19). Nor could this process of confiscation stop short of appropriating the three farm festivals sacred to the Baalim, with most of their ritual, to Yahweh, the victorious (Exod. 34:22, 23, J.; 23:14–17, E.). Sacred places, long centers of the fertility cult, where altars were *built* or *shaped*, in disregard of the earlier custom, when the earth mound or the unhewn stone alone was legitimate (Exod. 20:24; Judg. 6:20; 13:19; I Sam. 6:14; cf. Judg. 6:24, 26), and where temples, presided over by an established priesthood, were erected (I Sam. 1:1–3:31; 21:2–5, 7; Judg. 17:5; 18:30; 9:27)—these became the property of Israel, and thus centers of Yahweh worship. It is noteworthy that at the end of the period it was in one of these temples that Yahweh delighted to make himself known (I Sam. 1:17; 3:1–21).

This progress is epitomized in the story of Gideon, which though but an incident in the struggle of these centuries, and now in legendary form, preserves the spirit of what was actually happening throughout the country (Judg. 6:11–8:32). Gideon was a Hebrew farmer who, in danger of losing the hard-earned product of his labor (Judg. 6:13), ventured to make an offering of unleavened cakes, a strictly Canaanitish requirement, to Yahweh. This innovation, bloodless though it was, worked, for Yahweh signified his acceptance of the gift by fire (Judg. 6:21). Thus encouraged, he took a second step and built an altar to Yahweh, who again looked with favor on this departure from desert custom, for the altar was named *Yahweh is peace* (Judg. 6:24). Emboldened, Gideon went still farther in extending the claims of Yahweh. With his retainers he made a night raid on a neighboring Baal altar, smashed it, and

---

13 Such dances were very ancient, and owing to the belief in magic were considered essential to the success of the farmer (A. E. Crawley, *ERE*, X, 356–362).

cut down the Asherah. Then as a crowning act, on the top of the stronghold he built an altar and by use of the Canaanitish burnt offering he dedicated it to Yahweh [14] (Judg. 6:25–27). This was both aggressive and revolutionary. Gideon became the champion of Yahweh (Judg. 7:20), but Yahweh was no longer limited to the desert and the rites of the shepherd; he was the God of the stronghold, of settled village life, and of the threshing floor (Judg. 6:26, 36).

Such changes were the result of no playboy dreams, but had been attained only through years of bitter antagonisms of rival religions. This struggle, and the ensuing assimilation in which Baalism, as well as agriculture, was, at least in part, winning the day, went on subtly but irresistibly during the whole period. Physically, socially, and religiously the invaders were being pressed into the Canaanitish mold by all the powers that be. Climate and soil, tyrant-like, drove many from the tent to the mud dwelling. Farming, with its ample returns, persuaded many to hard labor that, in turn, stimulated the nerve centers and roused ambitions never fostered in the desert. City life contributed a number of quite revolutionary features. Marriage was no longer limited by tribal interests, but became an affair of caste controlled by wealth and office; and authority was not the paramount privilege of the elder; the gifted leader, the priest, and the king were on the way.

The intellectual life of the land was a ferment to the newcomers. At the festivals and in the city gates they heard the folk tales of Nimrod and Noah, of Abraham and Sarai, of Lot and Laban, of Jacob and Esau, of Daniel and Job, and many others, all of them forefathers of the Canaanites. Mythologies like-wise were heard and pondered. The creation of man, his relation to the animals, the origin of pain, toil, sorrow, and death have been the concern of all thinking men. Why plagues, and pestilence, and drought? Why so many languages, and so many tribes? Why the thunder, the lightning, and the storms? Questions and answers alike had welled up from community consciousness and were the precipitate of age-long reflection, perfected by the criticism of succeed-ing generations. Behind Canaanite folklore and mythology lay the best thought of Sumerian and Babylonian, Amorite, Horite, and Arab reflection. It was composite, not individual; corporate, not private intelligence. It was Canaanite, and now it became the legitimate inheritance of the Hebrew community. On the face of it these facts suggest that, though the Israelites conquered the Ca-naanites, the culture and the religion of the latter in the end vanquished the former. It is quite possible that for the majority of the invaders this was literally true.

[14] The burnt offering, in which all was consumed on the altar by fire, probably was agricultural not nomadic in origin. It is unlikely that the nomad ever felt constrained to provide a holocaust, so foreign to his way of life, as an offering to his deity. He reached the peak of exaltation in the sacred meal, in which he communed with the deity of his tribe. That the whole burnt offering was a gift to deity has been argued at length by Père Lagrange, who concludes that the gift idea lay behind all sacrifice (*Etudes sur les religions Sémitiques*, 243–274).

In reality, however, Israel had conquered in religion no less than in war and in national organization. There were within her, at all times, those who never forgot the independence, the justice, the chastity, and the human dignity, the chief rewards of the desert life, even when they enjoyed the greater abundance of Canaan. These men, rarely named by tradition, were not so narrow as the Nazarite, nor so indifferent to humanity as the multitude. With the former they insisted on loyalty to Yahweh and to the ideals of the fathers; with the latter they believed religion was not incompatible with prosperity. Living in the midst of conflicting claims made by the religious leaders, they learned to distinguish between ancient custom and human rights, and between the externals and the essentials of religion. Aided by daily experience, their outlook broadened until the olive groves, the wheat fields, and the vineyards came within the domain of genuine religion, and Yahweh could live and breathe in city, court, and temple as surely as in the camp of the nomad. Under the influence of such men, acting from complex, not simple, motives, two things happened: much of the Canaanitish cultus was rejected; some of its central features were adopted by Yahwism.

Much of the cultus of the settled population was alien to the shepherd life and therefore came immediately under the ban. Injunctions such as, "Thou shalt not boil a kid in its mother's milk" (Exod. 34:26), and "Thou shalt not offer the blood of my sacrifice with leavened bread" (Exod. 34:25), resulted from the same type of reasoning that at times has refused to use hymns, organs, and modern translations of the Scripture in Christian worship. Our god does not look with favor on innovations.

Many of the Baal rites were licentious, the odious violation of long-honored tribal ideals, and thus aroused deep-rooted hostility. Unchastity (Exod. 22:16, 17; Deut. 22:20–30), incest (Gen. 19:33–38; Deut. 27:20, 22, 23; Lev. 18:6–18; 20:17), homosexuality (Judg. 19:22–26; 20:8–35; Lev. 18:22), and bestiality (Exod. 22:19; Deut. 27:21; Lev. 18:23),[15] vices that prevailed at caravan and cult centers, were a stench in the nostrils of many.

Some of the customs were condemned as they violated human rights and privileges and degraded man to, or below, the level of the beast. The commercial activities of Canaan, that lay on the pathway between corrupt civilizations and had no unified government, had undermined tribal relations, so that the dignity, the freedom, and the equality of all men, so vital to desert life, had become secondary to property interests. Israel was following in her footsteps. War had contributed to the current demoralization, and in her transition from tribal to national life confusion reigned. The strong prospered at the expense of the weak, and human values sank low in the scale in the new, and larger,

---

15 While our records in their present form are late, some of them after the eighth century B.C., they express toward these questions the attitude of the tribesman, ancient or modern, Hebrew and Canaanite alike, who has been uncontaminated by city civilization or who has revolted against it.

civilization. *Every man did that which was right in his own eyes* (Judg. 21:25) well expressed the mounting tide of self-interest that disregarded the old standards. Hebrew legislation, guided by the Sinaitic tradition, insisted that proper consideration be given to the stranger, the widow, the orphan, the poor, and the distressed (Exod. 22:21, 22, 25, 26). *A man is of more value than a sheep* is axiomatic in any social group.

Some of the honored religious rites were rejected on the same basis, that of humanity. Child sacrifice, once so prevalent in the land, was, in theory, acknowledged as an obligation to deity. *The firstborn of thy sons shalt thou give unto me* [16] (Exod. 22:29; 34:19; 13:1, 2; Num. 3:11–13, 40; 8:17) was the primitive law that in later times was reinterpreted in terms of Levitical service (Num. 3:12), while the early practice was repudiated by thoughtful men who were no less pious than their ancestors. Yahweh never required the father of the faithful to sacrifice his first-born son, said an ancient tale that discredited this early, inhuman interpretation of the will of God (Gen. 22:1–13). Human sacrifice, an effort made in the hour of despair to appease an angry deity,[17] is reported to have been offered by leaders such as Jephthah (Judg. 11:31, 39, 40), Samuel (I Sam. 15:33), David (II Sam. 21:7–9), Ahaz (II Kings 16:3; 17:17), and Manasseh (II Kings 21:6); but under those influences of civilization that tone down the rigors of paganism, and the human interest of the prophets, this gruesome devotion to the gods was disregarded (I Sam. 15:20, 22), then denounced (Mic. 6:7), and finally, like child sacrifice, was rejected as unacceptable to Yahweh (Deut. 12:31; Lev. 18:21; 20:2, 3).

Many popular superstitions, such as divination, sorcery, witchcraft, and necromancy,[18] which were largely foreign to desert life, and were antisocial and anti-Yahwistic, sooner or later officially came under the ban (Exod. 22:12; Deut. 18:9–14; Lev. 19:26, 31; 20:6; I Sam. 28:7, 9). Moreover, the very name

16 The same verb is used here as in Exod. 22:30, where sacrifice is implied. For the significance and the development of this custom, see S. R. Driver, *Cam. B. Ex.,* 105, 235, 409, 410.

17 See A. Lods, *Israël,* I, 102, 112, 114. G. F. Moore, "Molech, Moloch," *Ency. Bibl.,* III.

18 The statement attributed to the woman at En-dor that Saul had cut off from the land those who had familiar spirits, and wizards (I Sam. 28:9), no doubt represents the attitude of many Israelites, and may have had the support of the king. However, many primitive methods of learning or determining the future that had long been in use in Canaan were only slowly outgrown by Israel. The shooting of arrows, under prophetic direction, was considered a means to military achievement (II Kings 13:15–19). Dreams were long believed to be supernatural revelations (Gen. 37:5, 9; 40:8; 41:1; Dan. 2:2, 25–45; 4:4–27). Incubation, that is, spending the night in the vicinity of a shrine so that the visitor might be granted some specific boon by the deity dwelling in the sacred place, seems to have been a religious practice of special importance. At Bethel Jacob had a vision (Gen. 28:12); and again at Peniel, tradition reports that he was blessed and saw God face to face (Gen. 32:24–32). At Shiloh Yahweh appeared to Samuel in the night, revealing himself (I Sam. 3:3, 4, 10, 24); and at Gibeon, where there was a great high place, Yahweh appeared at night to Solomon, giving him a wise and understanding heart and riches and honor surpassing that of all rulers (I Kings 3:4–14). Incubation was a widespread religious custom (see Louis H. Gray, "Incubation," *ERE,* VII) and its prevalence in the Near East has been significantly confirmed by the Ras Shamra tablets. The most complete interpretation of this phase of Oriental ritual is that by Julian Obermann, in Supplement to *JAOS,* April–June, 1946, 1–30, "How Daniel was blessed with a son. An Incubation Scene in Ugaritic."

Baal, meaning "master," and the gift of grain, and oil, and wine, which was a "tax" to deity, were most distasteful and irreligious to the early, freedom-loving disciples of Yahweh. All these, the name, the licentious rites, the superstitions, the inhumane tendencies in economics and religion were alien to and, at least in part, were rejected by the moral sense of Israel's leaders.

While religion was thus cleansed of much that was unwholesome, all this was negative, and by itself could never provide a victorious program. Acceptances were even more important than rejections. Out of the prolonged conflict between the two types of religion, the creative minds of Israel and of Canaan, all of them anonymous, were learning that the observance of the agricultural festivals, the dedication of the first fruits of the fields as a tribute to deity, the installation of an informed and efficient priesthood at permanent sacred places for social and national worship enriched the life of the people and promoted national well-being. Such features, all of them Canaanite in origin, refined and purified in the passionate fires of religious antagonisms, were ultimately adopted, no doubt with a sense of achievement, into the worship of Yahweh.

Though the resultant religion, like the social and economic life of the land, seemed closer to Baal of Canaan than to Yahweh of Sinai, yet the spirit was that of Yahweh, while the forms were those of Baal. If the hands belonged to Canaan, the voice surely was that of Israel. Three underlying principles, the peculiar gifts of Yahwism, deserve repetition. First, life alone counts in the desert, where man stands supreme and possessions become a burden. Human rights can never become obscured in Yahwism. Second, owing to the long experience in the tribal tent, parental authority had become an elemental social attitude that was inescapable and gave stability amid the conflict of cultures. *Honor thy father and thy mother* was a watchword in Hebrew religion from the time of Moses to Ezra, even down to the present, and nowhere else has this demand been more insistent (Exod. 20:12; Deut. 5:16).[19] As moral discernment, which is the product of social relations, has its roots in family life,[20] the ethical implications of this law of the family are very far-reaching. The home, the essential unit of moral growth, was thus safeguarded from the too hasty intrusion of foreign elements, and respect for gray hairs laid strong foundations on which the future could safely build. *Thou shalt worship no other god* (Exod. 34:14; 20:3, 5), the third factor, was the leitmotif that dominated the religious issues of the day.

These three principles, the primacy of the human, respect for parents, and unswerving loyalty to the God of the covenant, learned the hard way in the tent, in Egypt, and at Sinai, inspired and directed the insistent drive that re-

[19] The pronouncement of the death sentence on anyone guilty of smiting or cursing father or mother is an indication of the severity of the law (Exod. 21:15; Lev. 19:2; 20:9). S. Spinner in a lengthy study has declared that honoring father and mother was all but unknown outside of Israel in the ancient world (*Herkunft, Entstehung und Antike Umwelt des Hebräischen Volkes,* 509).

[20] J. H. Breasted, *The Dawn of Conscience,* 120–129.

jected the grossest elements of Baalism and at the same time appropriated the finest. Like the Canaanites themselves Baalism was split up into **local factions**, and like the worshipers some of the Baal altars were destroyed, others were taken over by Yahweh, while in the end Yahweh ruled through the length and breadth of the land. As the two people had coalesced, so had the two religions. Though there were dissenting cliques, both Israelite and **Canaanite**, yet a new unity of life and religion, different from either parent stock and not the sum total of the two but a new entity, had come into being.[21] This notable achievement, of which neither Samuel nor Saul was conscious, laid the groundwork and created the ideal for the new task, the adventure in kingship.

[21] In a study of composite civilizations it has been laid down as a general principle that in all such unions there occurs a new form of social grouping, the result of compromise on the part of each original unit. A new group emerges, differing from each of the originals, which is not merely the addition of the two, but a new unit (B. Malinowski, *The Dynamics of Cultural Change*, esp. 41–51, 64–72).

Chapter VI

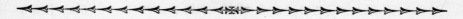

THE RELIGION OF NATIONALISM. 1030-931 B.C.

ISRAEL, under the rule of Saul, David, and Solomon, was molded into a unity, and for a hundred years flourished, from 1030 to 931 B.C., as the united kingdom. This was a new thing under the sun for those people and for that country. From Dan to Beersheba, and from the Shephelah to beyond Jordan, an area slightly over six thousand square miles with a population probably a million in round numbers, became one nation ruled by a native king. The independence of the country, which was not achieved until about 1000 B.C., resulted from two factors. The great empires, exhausted by costly foreign wars and internal conflicts, were disintegrating; and the leaders of Israel, by appealing to the Sinaitic confederacy in the name of Yahweh against the alien yoke, gained the coveted freedom and then established the kingdom. The ambitions of the few, which gave direction to the wishes of the many, after long and patient endeavor were crowned with success.

Deborah, Gideon, Abimelech, and Jephthah were but symptoms of a growing demand for freedom from foreign rule and for internal unity. Samuel was foremost in laying the foundations for the new regime (I Sam. 9:1-27). The conference of thirty sheikhs, probably at Mizpah, was neither a hastily arranged dinner engagement nor an emergency act initiated by Yahweh. The yearly tribute to the Philistines, the irritating presence of foreign customs collectors, the encroachments and arrogance of an alien neighbor had long rankled like a festering thorn in the side of Israel. The time was ripe for revolt. Saul, the daring son of a landowner of some importance living within sight of Samuel's home, through a stirring episode at Jabesh-gilead had become a heroic figure in the hill country (I Sam. 11:1-11). The desperate need and the intrepid leader had arrived on the stage together. Samuel, the old prophet, supported by a majority of the assembled leaders, promoted and in the name of Yahweh sanctioned Saul as leader in the fight for freedom (I Sam. 9:25-27).

That there were local bickerings and bitter dissensions, largely suppressed by ancient censorship, is evident. According to the record of a late writer, there was a reactionary group that insisted that such an innovation was apostasy and a direct violation of the will of Yahweh (I Sam. 8:4-9, 19, 20).[1] Neverthe-

---

[1] I Sam. 8:1-22; 10:17-27a, comes from a late writer who attributed it to Samuel, either following tradition or in order to give it authority. While it is in violent contrast to chapter 9, it no doubt represents the attitude of many from the earliest days toward a growing desire for self-rule. In the days of Deborah (Judg. 5:16, 17, 23), of Gideon (Judg. 8:22, 23), and of Jotham (Judg. 9:7-20) there was antagonism to all such activity.

less, it was a prophetic hour in religious history when it was said to Saul, "On you and on your father's clan is the desire of all Israel" (I Sam. 9:20). It was the dim gray dawn of national consciousness that gave direction to the covenant at Horeb and thrust Israel out into the current of world history. It was a democratic demand for freedom, that in a new situation called for a reinterpretation of the will of Yahweh.

But it was a hazard. Not only was there dissent among the Hebrews, but it was rebellion against the Philistine overlords, and the chances of success seemed slim. The Philistines were seasoned soldiers, well armed (I Sam. 17:4–7), skilled in forging weapons (I Sam. 13:19–23), and effectively organized in a five-city league, either subject to or allies of Egypt. The Israelites, on the other hand, had few weapons (I Sam. 13:22), lacked facilities either to make or to repair them, and were divided by conflicting interests and traditions. Each tribe was proud of its ancient freedom, and every city secure behind its own walls boasted of its independence. Many were complacent; the tribute was light, and even victory would not be worth the cost.

But the spirit of freedom was at work; the bond of Sinai was not altogether forgotten, and the presence of Yahweh in history was assuring. Songs such as those of Miriam, "Sing ye to Yahweh, He is mighty" (Exod. 15:21), and of Deborah, and slogans such as "the sword of Yahweh and of Gideon" (Judg. 7:20), under vigorous leadership kindled the spirits of many for the new endeavor, which succeeded far beyond expectation.

Saul, the spearhead of the movement, was the founder of the kingdom. He drove the Philistines out of the hill country, cleared the land of revolters, and before the northern citadel of Bethshan so fought the enemy that though he and three sons died on the battlefield the oppressor never again wandered so far from his home base. David, though like his predecessor never free from trying and even vicious opposition,[2] built shrewdly and wisely on well-laid foundations. He united most of the discordant elements (II Sam. 3:36), captured the city of Jerusalem, extended the boundary lines (II Sam. 8:1–14), and proved to be the organizing genius of the new nation. Solomon, who erected a gorgeous superstructure on this foundation, appears in the full-dress regalia of an Oriental monarch (I Kings 5:1–10:29). He drafted the captives and the poor for his many profitable projects (I Kings 5:13–18; 9:20, 21). He was a merchant prince of international renown trading in horses and chariots (I Kings 10:14–17, 28, 29), in spices and precious stones, in jewels and gold (I Kings 10:1–13). As an industrialist not only did he build palaces, temples,

---

[2] While in large measure Saul's difficulties had been caused by David and the Philistines, David had trouble with his rebel band, who thought of stoning him (I Sam. 30:6), with the house of Saul, that long opposed him (II Sam. 3:1, 6), with Michal, who upbraided him for indecency (II Sam. 6:20), with the prophet, who rebuked him (II Sam. 12:7–12), with Absalom, who rebelled against him (II Sam. 15:4, 10–12), with Shimei, who cursed him (II Sam. 16:5–8), and with Sheba, who publicly stoned him (II Sam. 20:1–2). These are only illustrative of the tensions ever present in the growth of the new organization.

and ships, but he worked extensive iron mines, and built and operated a unique smelting furnace at Ezion-geber.[3] He controlled at great profit the lines of transportation by land (I Kings 9:17–19) and by sea (I Kings 9:26–28) so that his wealth exceeded that of all the kings of the earth (I Kings 10:14, 23). This, the glory of Solomon, was the climax of the venture of kingship. The way of life had kept pace with industry. A generation ago Saul plodding behind the plow had been the hero; now Solomon in robes of state, riding in the Egyptian chariot or seated on the ivory-inlaid throne, was the acme of perfection. The alluring pageantries led by the dancing women and the richly garbed priests, marching to exotic music, the daily prodigal court dinners, with thirty oxen and a hundred sheep as the *pièce de résistance,* and the architectural splendor of palace and temple made Jerusalem a glamour city, while throughout the land Judah and Israel dwelt in safety, every man under his vine and fig tree all the days of Solomon. A nation had been born, victorious in battle, prosperous in commerce, renowned for culture, glorious in religious symbolism, and influential in world affairs. The ambitions of empire had been achieved, and tribalism was merged in nationalism.

It was a never-to-be-forgotten era to the people of Palestine. Agriculture was developed, trade flourished, and prosperity hitherto undreamed of was enjoyed by all. Opportunities for personal gain were multiplied and the standards of living were raised. Native sons, for service or good behavior, were elevated to the rank of princes. The arts, architecture, sculpture, music, and dancing, were cultivated. Social activities opened a new chapter in the life of the capital. Princesses from Sheba, Egypt, and Phoenicia graced the court and set the styles (I Kings 11:1–3). All the amenities of civilization were in vogue, mellowing the more rigid and broadening the narrower interests of earlier days. Law and order pervaded the scene (I Kings 4:2–19). The old rabble-rousing prophet bands were not encouraged, and the spirit of rebellion was not tolerated (I Kings 11:26–31, 40), while in the interests of justice an effort seems to have been made to establish a system of weights and measures [4] (II Sam. 14:26). Religion, however, occupied the central place in all these changes. The temple within the walls of the court high above the old city, with its cultured priesthood and carefully ordered worship, a royal sanctuary, was the epitome of this new life. A smoothly running government cared for the needs of all classes, firmly controlled the irresponsible and the

---

[3] One of the most illuminating of all archaeological discoveries is that of N. Glueck at Tell el-Kheleifeh, a short distance north of Ezion-geber. In 1938 he uncovered a smelting and refining plant with a complicated system of flues and air channels constructed so as to utilize the strong, prevailing wind for firing. It was built and operated in the days of Solomon, and the abundant remains indicate there was great activity in smelting copper and iron, and in the manufacture of articles of merchandise (N. Glueck, *BASOR*, No. 71, 6, 7; No. 72, 10, 11; No. 75, 8–14; No. 79, 2–18).

[4] D. Diringer, *PEQ*, July–Oct., 1942, 82–104.

intransigent, and provided for the religious needs of the nation. This was the golden age of Israel, and the achievement of the kingship.[5]

Kingship in Israel, successful though it was, was a violation of the traditions and the ideals of both the Hebrew nomad and the Canaanite city dweller. It even destroyed the sociopolitical system of both, and brought in religious ideas and practices quite foreign to early Yahwism. But out of dire necessity, as the patriarch had slowly given way before the local judge, so now the judge yielded place to the leader of the army, who became the chief of the new and larger unit. His achievements were the measure of his power, and this in turn assured his sanctity.

Neighboring nations, particularly its nearest neighbor, Egypt, that through local governors had ruled the country from 1580 to around 1100 b.c., in all likelihood furnished the basic pattern for the concept and ceremonies connected with the royal office. When Saul had been anointed by the prophet as the representative of Yahweh (I Sam. 10:1), he became another man (I Sam. 10:6). As the anointed one, he was a Messiah, and as such his person was considered sacred (I Sam. 24:6; 26:9; II Sam. 1:16). He was an incarnation of the spirit of Yahweh (I Sam. 10:6). Anointing as a religious ceremony was practiced long before the days of the Hebrew monarchy. A prince of Nuhassi, near Aleppo, in one of the Amarna letters[6] reports that Thutmose III of Egypt had appointed his grandfather king and "had poured oil upon his head." Oil—that is, the fat—is widely used in hot climates for its refreshing and sanitary values. It was self-evident that in some way the essence or the spirit that was in the oil was effective. From this it was an easy transition to the belief that in using sacred oil, the oil that belonged to the sacrifice, there was an actual transfer of divine power to the recipient (cf. I Sam. 16:13).[7] As there is no evidence that anointing had attained a religious significance in Babylonia or Assyria,[8] but it had long been an essential in most important Egyptian rites, it is obvious that Egyptian and Canaanite customs lay behind the Israelitish innovation.[9]

The full significance, to the Israelites, of the anointing and the kingship is hard for us to appreciate. Among primitive tribes and ancient nations the king was ofttimes believed to be a god. Indeed, until very recently kings have

---

[5] The development of nationalism has been interpreted by Louis Wallis in *The Bible is Human*, 80–140.

[6] Knudtzon, *Die el-Amarna Tafeln*, No. 51.

[7] In ancient practice the sacramental principle, viz., that divine life was actually transmitted to the anointed one by the sacred act of anointing, was the controlling factor. See A. E. Crawley, *ERE*, I, 549–554, esp. 550.

[8] M. Jastrow, *ERE*, I, 557a. Since Dr. Jastrow wrote his article much new material has come to light; but the writer is not aware of anything that would change the statement.

[9] This is a fact now generally recognized (A. Bertholet, *History of Hebrew Civilization*, 113; A. Lods, *Israël*, I, 135–137; C. R. North, "The Religious Aspects of Hebrew Kingship," *ZAW*, 1932, 8–38, esp. 14.

usually been considered superior beings, while in the ancient world view it was thought they were possessed by a divine spirit which endowed them with supernatural powers (I Sam. 10:6, 7, 9; 16:13), so that they became sons of God (II Sam. 7:14; Ps. 2:7; 89:26) and were accepted as gods. The voluminous literature on this topic cannot even be suggested, but it is beyond cavil that from the earliest days among Egyptians, Sumerians, Akkadians, Hittites, Cretans, Greeks, and Romans kings were often worshiped as gods. Many were deified after their death,[10] while many were acclaimed to be gods during their lifetime,[11] and not infrequently rulers were declared to be the physical progeny of the gods, or the goddesses, or of both. No doubt some of this language was official and referred to kingship rather than to the king. In other cases we may have the laudatory phrases of the courtier to one in power, and such must be listed as flattery. But all such fit into the ancient philosophy that explained all unusual activities, achievements, and qualities of body or mind as directly due to some relation with the spirit world. That the gods had begotten the kings was but a part of ancient world thought that was nearly universal.

In such an atmosphere it could hardly have completely failed to influence the thinking of that small but ambitious nation seated astride the pathway of ancient empire. That the Hebrews were susceptible to foreign influence is apparent here as elsewhere. Even as Israel demanded a king, that they might be like all the nations (I Sam. 8:5, 20), so the rite of anointing and its significance may be credited to well-known practices in Canaan and in Egypt. By virtue of his kinship, his personal valor (I Sam. 11:6-11), the choice of the assembled tribes guided by Yahweh (I Sam. 10:19-24), and the anointing oil (I Sam. 10:1), Saul the first king was fully accredited. Thus, he was not simply the military leader, but he and his successors after him became organically one with Israel, and by the spirit one with Yahweh (I Sam. 10:6, 9; 11:6). Thus in himself the king united the human and the divine in a mystical com-

[10] A relief from Medum, Egypt, is evidence that Snefru, Egyptian Pharaoh *ca.* 2900 B.C., was deified (*Bulletin of the University of Pennsylvania*, Vol. 3, No. 6, pp. 174, 175). See also Ed. Meyer, *Gesch. Alt.*, I, II, 105, 106. J. Garstang provides evidence that among the Hittites the dead king was thought of and honored as a god (*The Hittite Empire* 7, 8, 106, 107, 112, 113, 117, 224).

[11] This general fact is stated by H. H. Nelson as follows: "The ruler himself was a god, the son of the deity who dwelt in the temple" (*Biblical Archaeologist*, VII, 51). By the end of the fourth Egyptian dynasty, 2750 B.C., the Pharaohs were declared by the priesthood to be the bodily sons of Re, that is, they were begotten by Re himself. From then on every Pharaoh was asserted to be the bodily son of the sun-god (J. H. Breasted, *Anc. Rec.* II, 187–212). A. Erman, *Literature of the Ancient Egyptians*, 5, emphasizes the act of physical begetting. The same conception is occasionally found in Babylonia. Kings were the sons of the mother-goddess, fashioned by her in the womb and suckled by the holy milk (C. J. Gadd, *History and Monuments of Ur*, 63, 64; see also 17, 122, 123). It was a common idea throughout Mesopotamia (J. Hempel, *Gott und Mensch*, 134); and G. Contenau, *Manuel d'archéologie orientale*, I, 287, 288, traces the idea back to the Sumerians (294). It is common knowledge that in Greece Alexander was deified. (E. R. Bevan, *ERE*, IV, 525–528), and that emperor worship was common in the Roman Empire (*ibid.*, 529–532; J. Wach, *Sociology of Religion*, 289–294).

munity. He was the mana-possessed person[12] in the nation, having been transformed by the spirit of Yahweh (I Sam. 10:6, 9; 16:13; 19:23).

As the head of the state, and the incarnation of its will, the king by his acts was the cause of famine (II Sam. 21:1–6), drought (I Kings 18:2, 18), plague (II Sam. 24:12–15), war, and exile (II Kings 17:21–23; I Kings 13:34; 14:16; 15:26, 34; 16:13, 26).[13] David believing that his act was the cause of the plague could say, "Lo, I have sinned, and I have done perversely; but these sheep, what have they done? let thy hand, I pray thee, be against me, and against my father's house" (II Sam. 24:17). *L'Etat, c'est moi,* in a mystical as well as in an authoritative sense, would accurately describe the solidarity of king and people during the united kingdom.

The king was also the vicegerent of Yahweh, and had the power to stay the plague, relieve the drought, and ward off the famine through priestly rites. As the anointed one his person was inviolable (I Sam. 24:6, 10; 26:9, 16, 23; II Sam. 1:14, 16; 19:22). Throughout the period he was the supreme judge, arbitrarily appointing and dismissing the officers of church and state (II Sam. 8:15–18; 11:15; 20:4–6; I Kings 4:2–19), and his achievements were definitely identified with Yahweh, while in oaths the king and Yahweh were co-ordinate (II Sam. 11:11; 14:19; 15:21).

More light is thrown on this question when we consider the priestly functions of the king in early religions. David when bringing the ark up to Jerusalem wore the priestly ephod and assumed the chief role in the processional (II Sam. 6:14, 16). In the formal organization of the kingdom his sons were chief priests, a fact obscured by translators and commentators in the interest of late theology. Solomon at the dedication of the temple was chief priest, and as such made intercession for the people before Yahweh, and turning to the assembly in the name of Yahweh blessed the waiting throng (I Kings 8:5–8, 22, 28–30).[14] From certain features in our story, aided by knowledge of the ritual of Israel and that of neighboring nations, it has been inferred that this ceremony took place on the equinoctial New Year's Day, at the exact moment when the rays of the rising sun penetrated through the temple doorway to the ark, protected in the darkened chamber in the rear, and fell directly on Yahweh, or on his image. It is also suggested that

[12] W. Eichrodt, *Theologie des Alten Testaments,* I, 235–240, gives an admirable statement of this concept. Also Ed. Dhorme, *La religion des Hébreux nomades;* 313–319.

[13] The expressions in these illustrations were more meaningful to the ancients than to us. We recognize that the responsibility of the leader is greater than that of the common man because of his official standing. The early Hebrews added to the kingly influence the belief that he had a peculiar power for good or for evil that we would term magical or supernatural. For long centuries even the Western world believed there was miraculous power in the king's touch (cf. II Kings 5:6).

[14] The story as we now have it comes from some three hundred years after the event, and is a Deuteronomic interpretation. However, the priestly function of Solomon, which is clearly indicated, is historical and is not open to question. Early rulers throughout the world were priest-kings, and divided responsibility came only with the increased complexities of civilization. The "Defender of the Faith" still a title of the king of England, witnesses to the historic fact. See M. Buber, *Das kommende Königtum Gottes,* 45–86; also C. R. North, *ZAW,* 1932, 17–21.

at that moment Solomon, as priest-king, stood within the holy of holies it-self, in the very presence of Yahweh, to whom he made supplication for the kingship, the dynasty, and the nation for the new year.[15] This was the apogee of the kingship.

A priest-king, between the nation and Yahweh, was the incarnation of both. That he, with the dynasty from which he could not be separated, was considered divine by most is not to be doubted; and in a land surrounded by nations in which deification of kings was common he would easily be thought of as God by the masses. A number of passages, understood by historians as always referring to a definite individual, to the Davidic dynasty, or to the nation, lend themselves to the same general interpretation. *I will be to him a father, and he shall be my son* (II Sam. 7:14) to those acquainted with Egyptian theory would naturally convey the idea that the ruling house of Israel had been adopted to sonship by Yahweh. The statement *Yahweh said to me, Thou art my son, this day have I begotten thee* (Ps. 2:7) would like-wise be considered a claim comparable to that of the deification of the Pharaoh. A curious phrase preserved by the Chronicler may be reminiscent of this be-lief. Describing the coronation of Solomon it is said, "All the assembly . . . bowed down and worshiped Yahweh, *and the king*" (I Chron. 29:20). Here so far as language can indicate the king is on the level with Yahweh and is the object of worship (cf. I Chron. 28:5; 29:23; II Chron. 9:8). Similarly, *To us a child is born, to us a son is given; and the government shall be upon his shoulders, and his name shall be called Wonderful, Counsellor, Mighty God, Everlasting Father* (Isa. 9:6) to those acquainted with Egyptian, Babylonian, or Greek mythology might very easily be interpreted in the cur-rent pattern of deification.[16] Remembering that the united kingdom of Israel came to an end some 2,668 years ago, and that the concept of kingship since

15 J. Morgenstern, *Amos Studies,* I, 227–232, esp. 230. Owing to the translation of much ancient historical material and recent research among small tribes long stranded in the backwash of civiliza-tion, it is becoming clear that among many peoples, early Babylonians, Egyptians, and others, the new year was believed to be a time of supreme crisis that could be happily entered only by unusual religious rites. The death of the old year and the birth of the new one—a cosmic fact—was paral-leled, or symbolized, by the deification and installation of the king at the beginning of the year, and by his sacrifice at the year's end, or his sacrifice in symbol with his annual reinstatement in office. The general theory with much illustrative material has been set forth by J. G. Fraser, *The Dying God,* 9–46. In recent years many interpreters have been at work on the considerable ritual that has been placed at their disposal. The following are merely suggestive: S. Mowinckel in *Psalmenstudien,* Vol. 2, interpreted a number of Psalms in the light of this theory. H. Zimmern in *Der Alte Orient* summarized Babylonian material in "Das Babylonische Neujahrsfest." K. H. Ratschow in *ZAW,* 1935, 176–180, gathered up Egyptian material. S. H. Hooke, in *Myth and Ritual,* 1933, was responsible for an important symposium on the general field, and in 1938 pub-lished *The Origins of Early Semitic Ritual,* which is of special value. An interesting study of Psalm 47, on the enthronement of Yahweh as king, by J. Muilenburg, is in *JBL,* Sept., 1944, 235–256.

16 Deification, as a popular expression of value, is not altogether lacking in this rationalistic age. Millions of youths in Europe, but a few years ago, with the devotion of martyrs worshiped Der Führer. Farther to the east, an emperor was long, officially and popularly, honored as a god; while closer home among the two million claimed to be followers of a noted religious leader in our largest city are many who call him God. Nor is this an isolated phenomenon in Christianity.

then has been revolutionized, we need not be surprised if Hebrews sometimes subscribed to ideas quite untenable to us. Three commanding figures
had ruled Israel. They had brought unity and prosperity, and had awakened
hope, and pride, and patriotism. These men were worthy of wholehearted
devotion, and merited the highest expressions of their age. Their achievement, the united kingdom, furnished the pattern for all later ideals. That
kingdom was to be established forever in power, in justice, and in mercy
(II Sam. 7:14–17). The city of David became the model for social architects
for succeeding generations. It was to be the city of truth, with boys and girls
playing in the streets thereof (Zech. 8:3–5), and later still, lying four-square,
with walls of jasper, gates of pearl, and streets of gold, it was the shining
symbol of the kingdom of God (Rev. 21:2, 18, 21). The Messiah, the anointed
of Yahweh, in the dark days of national disaster, was the expected deliverer
of the faithful (Zech. 4:6–10; Isa. 9:6, 7; 11:1–5; Ezek. 34:23; 37:24; Jer. 23:5;
30:9). But kings and princes failed, and then hope was transferred to Yahweh
himself, who would become king over all the earth.

But these visions of righteousness and justice, of permanency and peace,
all go back to and are built on the foundations laid by the three kings of the
United Kingdom. The glory of Solomon eclipsed that of all others; it was he
who established the golden age of Israel. The question may have been asked,
and also answered: If Pharaoh was deified, then why not Solomon? [17]

If the kingship came into being amid struggle, the temple not only met with
stiff resistance but also was the product of divergent cultures. It had long
been lying in embryo in the heart of the nation. Its germ was in the aspiration that ever insists in giving appropriate form to religion, whether in the
simple institutions of the shepherd or in the elaborate structure of the Assyrian
temple. For Israel in the wilderness, religion found suitable symbolism in an
ark and a tent, the perpetual pledge of the presence of the God of the fathers.
In the new land these shrines looked shabby alongside those of the Egyptian
deities. With increasing wealth, Israelites with esthetic and priestly interests
assumed that Yahweh was worthy of a habitation in keeping with the culture
of his worshipers and comparable with those of Baal or Dagan. As a witness
to the religious vitality of Israel, houses of a simple type were erected at Shiloh,
Nob, Bethel, and Shechem for the more adequate service of Yahweh. After
Jerusalem was captured by David, the patron of religion planned a temple,
but was prevented by the objections of influential leaders (II Sam. 7:4–9).
Solomon succeeded where his father failed, and with never-to-be-forgotten
ceremonies dedicated to Yahweh the new, imposing temple. Within the

---

[17] C. R. North has summarized the O.T. material on the subject and concludes that while the
facts do not necessarily exclude divine kingship, the onus of proof rests on its advocates. However,
it would seem that if we were Israelites living shortly after the days of Solomon, thinking in the
concepts of those days, the burden of proof would rest on other shoulders (North, *ZAW*, 1933,
21–38).

temple was the oracle (*debhir*) or the holy of holies (I Kings 6:16; 7:50; 8:6), where Yahweh with his sacred symbols was kept within the dark chamber of mystery. This, the holy place, and the temple were holy (I Kings 8:10; Isa. 66:20; Ps. 138:2). Jerusalem, a sacred place probably before the time of Melchizedek (Gen. 14:18; Josephus, *The Wars of the Jews,* VI, 438), became the holy city of the Hebrews (Exod. 15:13; Joel 3:17; Dan. 9:24), and ere long the land captured by the raiding bands became to them the holy land (Josh. 5:15; Zech. 2:12; I Sam. 26:19; II Kings 15:17).[18] In the course of the centuries Israel was fast becoming like all the nations round about. For four centuries more the temple continued to be the center of Israel's religion, and its rites, its symbols, and its architecture responded to the ever changing economic and political demands of the hour.

The temple of Solomon was distinctly a royal sanctuary, neither a sacred place for all who wished to worship, as of old, nor a priestly shrine as in the later days.[19] It was within the court area; near by were the palaces of the king and the queen, the harem, the hall of justice, and the arsenal, all of which were enclosed within the walls of the citadel (I Kings 7:12). Solomon himself was the priest-king of Yahweh (I Kings 8:12–14, 62–66), and only through him had the people access to the national God.

This was a radical breach with the past, quite definitely departing from the early democratic nature of religion.[20] Nevertheless, it was the bearer of certain important values. It forged the bonds of a national, religious unity, and the people were united with Yahweh in the person of their king. Further, Baalism, the old nature worship at the high places, under the splendor of the new national sanctuary lost some of its influence. Though it long continued to function in many places, its prestige was limited and its type of worship was modified more or less consciously. Civilization was civilizing religion; humanity was being freed from the cruder phases of life and lifted to higher levels of mental and moral activity.[21]

Because of its proximity to the palaces and the presence of an expert priesthood, certain restrictions were inevitable. The old freedom of agricultural sanctuaries, the rude cult songs, the familiar social contacts, and the highly emotional features that often merged into orgies—all such naturally were either modified or suppressed by the more orderly and reverent rites appro-

[18] A general idea among primitive folk was that the earth was sacred to the deity of the locality. Sargon took soil from the sacred city of Babylon for the foundation of the temple built at his new capital at Agade (C. J. Gadd, *History and Monuments at Ur,* 44). Naaman asked for two cartloads of earth, so that on this soil in Damascus he could worship Yahweh (II Kings 5:17). The same idea is expressed in the cry of David, "They have driven me out this day that I should not cleave to the inheritance of Yahweh, saying, Go, serve other gods" (I Sam. 26:19).

[19] Even two centuries later the sanctuary at Bethel in the north was considered a royal sanctuary (Amos 7:13).

[20] This followed as a natural consequence of the new political organization (G. F. Moore, *The Birth and Growth of Religion,* 46–49).

[21] *Ibid.,* 94.

priate to the *esprit de corps* of the court life (cf. II Sam. 6:20; Amos 7:12, 13). Features that belonged to demon worship, sorcery, and witchcraft, and many of the cruder magical rites, in the very nature of the case could have no place in the worship in the city temple.[22] Old rites, those belonging to the agricultural festivals, were either ultimately abandoned, as the feast of the new moon (I Sam. 20:5, 6, 18, 24; II Kings 4:23), or reinterpreted, as the spring festival of the shepherd and the farmer, which as the Passover was made commemorative of the Exodus (Deut. 16:1–8; II Kings 23:21–23). New ceremonies were added to meet historical demands (II Kings 16:10–16; Ahaz an ally of Assyria has a new type of altar placed in the temple) or for the enrichment of the worship, as was deemed wise. The developments were roughly similar to a change from the camp meeting to the cathedral. They were neither all loss nor all gain.

The temple, by the abundance and variety of its symbolism, all of which was freighted with long religious history, cast its spell, with varying reactions, over all the land. All the ritual, because of its antiquity and its relation to the essentials of religion, was well suited to arouse in sympathetic minds the sense of awe and to impress on the worshiper the fact that he was within the shadow of the powerful, ever-revealing presence of Yahweh, the God of the fathers. We cannot here indicate in detail the wealth of rite and imagery that was unified in this enrichment of Yahwism. Phoenician architects laid their skill, the product of a thousand years, on the altar of Yahweh (I Kings 7:13–47).[23] Babylonian mythology, Egyptian religious art, Horite, Hittite, and Canaanite contributions were also placed under tribute. But from whatever source derived, this temple was Yahweh's temple, and the resultant religion was the religion of Yahweh; it was worship neither of the Baal of Canaan nor of the Baal of Tyre.[24] It is equally certain that the Yahwism of Solomon was not that of Moses. Of Yahweh it might be said, I am a part of all that I have met.

The temple, as it stood on the hill within the present temple area, in its main lines has been reconstructed by competent scholars.[25] In front of it was the great rock altar, that met the primitive requirements (Exod. 20:24–26) and in later tradition was claimed as the Mount Moriah of Abraham (Gen. 22:2, 9) and the scene of the staying of the plague in the time of David (II Sam. 24:18). Thus it was provided with sanctions appropriate to the place for the chief sacrifices at the time of dedication. Westward, beyond this rock, the temple was oriented, perhaps so accurately that at the spring and autumn equinoxes the first rays of the rising sun penetrated directly into the holy of

[22] See W. Eichrodt, *Theologische Studien und Kritiken*, 1937, 1–27.

[23] All the evidence points to very strong Phoenician influence (J. Morgenstern, *Amos Studies*, I, 228–231).

[24] It is significant that in the Davidic period we find fifteen names that are compounds of Yahweh (C. R. North, *ZAW*, 1932, 34).

[25] I Kings 7:1–8:9 is the basis for reconstruction (B. Stade, *Geschichte des Volkes Israel*, I, 311–343, which has been followed by A. R. S. Kennedy, "Temple," *HBD* (one vol.).

holies.[26] This was a regular feature in all sun worship. While it would injure none, any more than does the orientation of many of our churches, or our use of Sunday—the day of the sun—for worship, it would probably aid many in their devotions.

Flanking the doorway were the pillars, Boaz and Yakin (I Kings 7:13–22), which, standing free without any structural function, served either for decoration or more likely as religious symbols. There are strong reasons to believe that they were related to the Asherah poles dedicated to Astarte, that stood beside the high places in Canaan.[27] Fertility rites were so prevalent in all the country that, had there been no recognition of them in the temple, many worshipers would have felt the loss as seriously as if all evidence of the cross were removed from Christian churches. While the temple undoubtedly represented a trend away from the primitive and the vulgar toward the cultural, it was not motivated by puritanism, and its influence would not be lessened by the presence of old symbols. Their unquestioned importance is indicated by the fact that on official occasions, such as coronation, and covenant making, the king stood by the pillar, *as the manner was* (II Kings 11:14; 23:3; II Chron. 34:31).

Beyond the pillars was the doorway, the entrance into the precincts sacred to Yahweh. In ancient times, doors to palaces, and temples, and city gates, owing to the belief in the presence and activity of innumerable spirits, were usually protected by word and by spell.[28] The threshold was sacred to the deity to whom at the time of construction sacrifice, sometimes that of a child, had been offered to frustrate the evil spirits [29] (Josh. 6:26; I Kings 16:34). Thus the threshold was sacred and must not be trodden on (I Sam. 5:1–5; Zeph. 1:9; and I Kings 18:21, "How long will you leap over both thresholds?"). Probably sprinkling the blood of the sacrifice on the doorposts of the house (Exod. 12:7, 13), on the horns of the altar, and around the base (Lev. 1:5;

26 See footnote 15. J. Morgenstern, *HUCA*, X, 3–148. F. J. Hollis, *Myth and Ritual* (S. H. Hooke, ed.), 87–96.

27 W. R. Smith, *Rel. Sem.* (3), 487–489; G. A. Barton, *ERE*, I, 350–351. The suggestion has been made that originally they may have been symbols of the female principle, and then as decorations expressed a mental attitude (E. D. Starbuck, *ERE*, 829b). R. B. Y. Scott has proposed that they may stand for sentence-names setting forth dynastic oracles on the royal chapel, Boaz meaning, "In the strength of Yahweh shall the king rejoice," and Yakin, "Yahweh will establish his throne forever" (*JBL*, 1939, 143–149). This hypothesis, which has much in its favor for the Solomonic temple, may be but the adaptation, to a new use, of an ancient symbol. In no way does this interfere with the interpretation that basically the pillars were related to fertility worship, and stood in place of the Asherah (S. A. Cook, *Religion of Ancient Palestine*, 167).

28 The important role that the door of the home or of the temple, or the gate of the city, played and still plays in the religious life of the Near East has lost most of its significance to us. On the outside were innumerable foes, visible and invisible; within, when the entrance was adequately protected by religious rites, was peace and security, because of the protecting power of the gods. A suggestive summary of these facts has been made by J. A. MacCulloch, "Door," *ERE*, IV, 846–852.

29 Such customs were world-wide. See C. H. Trumbull, *The Threshold Covenant*, 21–23, 45–48, 66–77, 94–108, 261–263; Sir A. Evans, *Mycenaean Tree and Pillar Cult*, 55, 83–87; Père Jaussen, *Coutumes des Arabes*, 309, and *Naplouse*, 92.

3:2), were but variants of the same principle. Flanking the approaches of ancient temples, especially in Babylonia and Assyria, great animal forms of bulls, lions, eagles, or dragons, the incarnations of guardian deities, were placed to prevent the intrusion of malevolent spirits.[30] Thus, by check and double check, the ancient abodes of the gods were believed to be immunized from the ever present powers of evil. Likewise the entrance to the temple of Yahweh was carefully guarded by the initiatory sacrifices, the ensuing rites, and the court officials. However, in the course of history, as in all institutions, under the pressure for more and still more officials a "threshold guard" was established (II Kings 11:4, 11; 12:9; 22:4; 23:4).

All the other cult objects and ornaments in and around the temple were calculated to awake memories, stimulate emotions, and give direction to the national religion. Most of these, like the pillars and the threshold, were ancient symbols adapted and incorporated into the worship of Yahweh. The history and meaning of many of them, though well known, cannot here be elaborated. Moreover, two factors contribute to some uncertainty as to the exact number of such objects that were there at the time of the dedication. First, our sources are all late, and some of them have been edited by interested priests.[31] Second, the temple and its furniture were undergoing continuous change throughout its entire existence. In the reign of Rehoboam, Shishak of Egypt stripped the temple of much of its gold and ornaments (I Kings 14:25, 26). Later it would seem that Queen Athaliah had introduced the worship of Baal into the precincts of the temple, if not into the temple itself (II Kings 11:18), all of which was drastically removed when young Joash came to the throne. In the days of Amaziah the temple was again looted of its treasure (II Kings 14:13, 14), and Ahaz, shortly after ascending the throne, made a thorough reconstruction of the interior, remodeling it after the pattern he had seen in Damascus (II Kings 16:10-18). Hezekiah, the reformer, in the interest of higher worship discarded the serpent of Moses (II Kings 18:4); but Manasseh turned back the wheels of progress and reinstated old pagan altars and ritual (II Kings 21:4, 5; 23:4-12); which, in turn, were cleaned out of the sanctuary by Josiah. With changes recurring so constantly, it is little wonder that the ancient writers did not always give us complete details.

The table of showbread—bread of the faces, or presence—in all probability occupied a place of importance from the beginning (I Kings 7:48). Israel had long been familiar with it (I Sam. 21:5, 6), and it was in common use among

---

[30] G. C. Maspero, *Life in Ancient Egypt and Assyria,* 198, 199, 220. A. H. Sayce, *ERE,* II, 587–589.

[31] This is very evident in I Kings 7:48–51—a general summary—in which such a feature as the golden altar (48b) has no function. Though Solomon was immensely wealthy, the use of pure gold in this section savors of tradition rather than reality. A critical study is found in C. F. Burney, *Notes on the Hebrew Text of the Book of Kings,* 99–103. Cf. Pfeiffer, *Introduction to the O.T.,* 377–385, 387, 388.

their neighbors.[32] Likewise the brazen serpent must have enjoyed sanctuary here at an early date (II Kings 18:4; Num. 21:8, 9). The perpetual light, also, may have contributed to the symbolism enjoyed by the faithful. The ten candle-sticks (I Kings 7:49; II Chron. 4:7), though found in late sources, may by this time have superseded the lamp, which in the days of Samuel was kept burn-ing all night at Shiloh (I Sam. 3:3), and may have been the forerunner of the seven-branched candlestick described in the late priestly regulations (Lev. 24: 1–4; Num. 8:1–4; Exod. 25:31–40, all P.; Exod. 27:20, 21; 30:1–8; II Chron. 13:11) and in use in the post-Ezra period (I Macc. 1:21; 4:49; Jos. *Ant.*, III, VI, 7).[33] The light in the temple was no doubt influenced by the lamp that in the house of the well-to-do in the Near East was kept burning day and night. Surely the abode of deity was as deserving as that of the wealthiest of men.[34] But as both light and fire, as seen and felt in the sun's rays, the lightning flash, and the volcanic fire, were of divine origin, interpretation, in the course of the centuries, exalted the humble household vessel to a place of dignity in religious thought. Light, thus, became the symbol of the presence of Yahweh. The early philosopher ultimately developed the idea that the god of light—that is, of the day—triumphed over the god of darkness—that is, of the night—and thus the perpetual light and the perpetual fire (Lev. 6:9; II Macc. 1:18–36; Jos. *Wars,* II, XVII, 6) became symbols of the victory of the God of light over the powers of darkness.[35]

The altar of incense probably was not to be found in the first temple, and it may not have gained recognition until after the time of Ezra. It is true that the burning of incense was an ancient practice among Israel's neighbors,[36] but we have no reliable reference to it in pre-exilic Hebrew literature,[37] while in the exilic period both Jeremiah (6:20) and Ezekiel (8:11) scorn its use. But within

---

[32] Primitive man believed that the spirits of the departed, and the spirits of the unknown world, needed sustenance the same as human beings. So they provided food and drink for them; and in later days, when the spirit world was thought of as organized under a chief or a god, the old practice was continued. The showbread in the temple was a memory of this primitive idea. Even in the exilic period Israelites provided food for the queen of heaven (Jer. 44:19) and for Gad (Isa. 65:11). See W. H. Bennett, *ERE*, XI, 452, 453.

[33] For interpretation and history see S. R. Driver, *Cam. B. Ex.,* 328–330; E. Schürer, *History of the Jewish People in the Time of Jesus Christ,* I, 281, 282, 290; A. R. S. Kennedy, "Tabernacle," *HBD* (five vols.), IV, 663.

[34] Primitive man found it easier to preserve both light and fire than to kindle them anew, which was apparently the reason for the perpetual light A. R. S. Kennedy, "Candle," *HBD* (five vols.), I, 348.

[35] Important articles bearing on this topic are found in *ERE*: J. Batchelor, I, 242; A. E. Crawley, VI, 26–30; J. A. MacCulloch, VIII, 47; W. Cruikshank, VIII, 62.

[36] In prehistoric times the burning of certain woods and gums was found to be pleasing as a deodorant and effective as a disinfectant. These strange values easily assumed religious significance at an early date among the Arabians, Egyptians, Babylonians, and others (J. A. MacCulloch, *ERE*, VII, 201–205; S. A. Cook, *The Religion of Ancient Palestine,* 61, 62; G. F. Moore, "Incense" *Ency. Bibl.,* II, 2165–2168).

[37] G. A. Smith, *Jerusalem,* II, 307.

three centuries, under the careful guidance of the priests, it had become an essential part of the worship of Yahweh (Exod. 30:1–10, P. 2; I Macc. 1:21, 22; 4:50; Jos. *Ant.*, III, vi, 8; III, x, 7), and contributed its quota to the emotional satisfactions of the devout.

The brazen, or molten, sea, that stood outside of the main building, east of it and to the south, in all probability belonged to the time of Solomon [38] (I Kings 7:23–26, 39b; II Chron. 4:1–5, 10). It was a curious object. The brazen bowl, fifteen feet in diameter and eight feet deep, rested on the backs of twelve oxen, three facing each of the points of the compass, each on a pedestal four and a half feet high. The total height of the construction was about sixteen feet. Though it contained 16,600 gallons of water (I Kings 7:26), or 25,000 (II Chron. 4:5), or even less, it served no utilitarian purpose. To some it may have been ornamental, but unquestionably it was magnificently symbolic, an embodiment of ancient mythology. Oxen, in the Near East, always typified that superb vitality believed to be an expression of the gods of creation. Their orientation toward the four corners of the earth indicated their rule in the world of totality; while the great sea was witness of the primeval ocean out of which the world was created.[39] Thus the vital forces of the universe and the incomprehensible mysteries of all life were tellingly objectified. In part, at least, it was familiar to all. The oxen, that had been sacred symbols long before the days of Jeroboam (I Kings 12:28–30), seem to have won a place in the religion of united Israel. Later writers rejoiced to think of Yahweh as the bull of Jacob (Gen. 49:24; Isa. 1:24; 49:26; 60:16; Ps. 132:2, 5, AV, "Mighty One"). Moreover, it opens an important page in the history of religious thought. In the far-off, undated days, man was reflecting seriously on how the world and the life therein came into being. An answer that reveals acute observation has been preserved in early Babylonian literature, an adaptation of still earlier Sumerian philosophy: "The primeval abyss, their begetter, and the roaring sea, who bore them," from these came all life.[40] This explanation, taken over from Canaanites or from Phoenicians and symbolized in the molten sea, was Israel's

---

[38] This sea seems to have been too alien to the life and thought of Israel to have become important in her religion. In fact it receives scant notice throughout history. Ahaz set the sea on the pavement, and removed the brazen oxen, probably to use the metal for some more pressing service (II Kings 16:17; see II Kings 25:13, 16). Ezekiel in his reconstruction of worship has no place for it; and the Chronicler, who adds to its holding capacity 50 per cent, endeavors to give it practical significance by placing the washing lavers beside it (II Chron. 4:1–6; Exod. 30:19, P. 2).

[39] Water has been held to be sacred, and springs, rivers, and the ocean were believed to be the abodes of deities, by most peoples of the ancient East. Hence water has functioned in many ceremonies and has occupied a central place in mythology (James, and Mercer, "Water," "Water-Gods," *ERE*, XII, 704–716; G. A. Barton, *Arch. and Bib.*, 304). The closest parallel to the molten sea seems to have been in the temples in Babylonia (Jastrow, *The Religion of Babylonia and Assyria*, 653), where the great basin, called "the deep," or *Apsu*, was placed between the ears of the bull (A. H. Sayce, *The Hibbert Lectures*, 1887, 63; see also H. Zimmern, *ERE*, II, 314; G. A. Smith, *Jerusalem*, II, 65, 66). W. F. Albright, *Arch. and Rel.*, 142–149, gives the cosmic interpretation; and I. Benzinger, *Ency. Bibl.*, III, gives a complete study of the Biblical material.

[40] G. A. Barton, *Arch. and Bib.*, 287.

first lisping of *the spirit of God hovered over the face of the waters* (Gen. 1:3). Hebrew genius had the bravery to take this massive symbol and place it in the temple court, thereby assuming, or perhaps asserting, that Yahweh, the covenant God of Israel, not Marduk was the source of vitality and national prosperity.

The holy of holies, or the oracle, a square chamber from which all light was excluded, occupied the western end of the temple building, and was the objective toward which all the other features converged. This darkened oracle, a cube of thirty feet, may preserve a hint of origin, which so often, like the oracle at Delphi, was a cave; but here it indicates the separation of Yahweh from all contact with the profane, and emphasizes the mystery of the divine. In general design and significance it was similar to its counterparts in Babylonia [41] and in Egypt.[42] Within the oracle were the cherubim and the ark, in which there may have been some symbol of Yahweh.[43]

The winged cherubim (I Kings 6:23-28; 8:6, 7; II Chron. 3:10-13), each fifteen feet in height, with a wingspread of fifteen feet, like the oxen were ancient and widely known symbols of functions of the gods. Similar composite forms, strange combinations of parts of human and animal anatomy, all the products of the fertile imagination of early races, have been found among the Aegeans, Assyrians, Babylonians, Egyptians, and Hittites.[44] Amid great diversity of forms there is an underlying similarity that suggests a common origin far back in prehistory. While the meaning of the word cherub as well as its original home are both uncertain, it is probable that the temple cherubim derived their general form from Babylon, via North Syria and Phoenicia. Their function clearly was to guard the ark, in which was the presence of Yahweh (I Kings 8:7). Later they guarded the tree of life (Gen. 3:24), while in Isaiah, the seraphim, an Egyptian word for beings comparable to the cherubim,[45] were the watchers of the threshold. Still later, in Ezekiel, the cherubim could not be distinguished from the Assyrian bull colossi, the symbols of the great gods of the Assyrian empire (Ezek. 1:5-25; 10:1-22). If these monstrous creations erected in the Solomonic temple did come from pagan sources, the

[41] In the Babylonian temple there was a small sanctuary, the most holy place at the end farthest from the entrance, in which the image of the god was set up (H. Zimmern, *ERE*, II, 317, 318, on Babylonians and Assyrians). In Assyrian temples the same was true, and one inscription explicitly states that the holy image of the deity "must not be brought out to profane the light of day" (A. Leo Oppenheim, *Bib. Arch.*, Sept., 1944, 54, 56).

[42] H. H. Nelson, *Bib. Arch.*, Sept., 1944, 44-53.

[43] J. Morgenstern, *Amos Studies*, I, 229.

[44] General discussion of cherubim is found in *ERE*, III, 508-513, by R. W. Moss; *Rev. bib.*, 1926, 328-358, 481-495, by Ed. Dhorme and H. Vincent; and I. Benzinger, *Hebräische Archaeologie*, 267, 268, 368, 386, 387. For facts concerning their place in Aegean religion see D. G. Hogarth, *ERE*, I, 145, and Sir A. Evans, *The Palace of Minos at Knossos*, I, 709-721; II, 482, 785, 786. T. K. Cheyne believes that the cherubim of the temple were influenced by Hittite sculpture (*Ency. Bibl.* I, 741-745. For a brief summary see J. Skinner, "Genesis," *International Critical Commentary*, 89-90.

[45] G. B. Gray, "Isaiah," *ICC*, 105, 106.

genius of Hebrew religion in due time acclimated them and made them subject to the will of Yahweh (Ezek. 1:22–25).

The ark bearing the presence of Yahweh was now sheltered under the protecting wings of the cherubim. It had begun its long journey amid simple surroundings, accepted by a few fanatical followers with simple ideas about life and religion. Because the covenant was based on free choice there had been capacity for growth. In the land of Canaan the ark had become the symbol of war and conquest. In the home of Obed-edom it gave the assurance of agricultural prosperity (II Sam. 6:11), and soon it journeyed to the city where for years it remained housed in the tent (II Sam. 6:12–19). Now at last, no more to wander from tent to tent among the tribes, it was sheltered in darkness, an unseen testimony of the Invisible who had guided his people from the beginning (I Kings 8:12, 13). Here, secure from profane contact (Lev. 16:2), it soon became the national oracle in which forgiveness, guidance, and benediction were sought and secured for the new year. The presence of Yahweh was the glory of the temple, and the temple was the glory of Israel.

To this end the growing strength and coherence of the nation had moved, more or less consciously, ever since the days of the invasion. Religion had kept pace with economic and political development, and with the passing of the years had abandoned crude and inadequate rites for more meaningful ceremonies. Yahweh, who had united strange tribes in the desert, and later had appropriated the land, the altars, the festivals, and the mythology of the Baalim, now called on Kenite and Canaanite, Hittite and Horite, Ephraimite and Judahite as a corporate body to worship on the holy hill of Zion. The assembled throng, gathered from the four corners of the land, by hallowed word and magic sign of the priest-king [46] were fused into a mystic brotherhood (I Kings 8:12b–14). Expectancy was fulfilled in ecstasy as people, priest-king, and Deity in spirit became one in the bond of religion. The temple, a rich composite gleaned from neighboring nations, stood as the monument of national growth, and was the herald of a new chapter in religion. If it was the seal of approval on the long and bitter struggles of the past, it was equally the sign of things to come.[47] It was the glory and the bond of Hebrew nationalism.

[46] A king, though only a figurehead, actually binds together great congeries of people to whom he is the symbol of those interests and loyalties that most easily arouse their deepest emotions. But in the ancient Near East, with its belief in the supernatural power of the priest-king, the emotional response to the above event would be beyond expression. See G. H. Mead, *Mind, Self, and Society*, 311–317.

[47] J. Wach emphasizes the fact that this national cult was something entirely new to Palestine, and was therefore of great significance (*Sociology and Religion*, 92–95).

Chapter VII

THE RELIGION OF THE REACTIONARIES.

931-830 B.C.

THE death of Solomon brought to an end the golden age in the history of Israel. The experiment in kingship and the interrelated adventure in worship had succeeded beyond expectation. Three kingly characters, each peculiarly fitted for his task, had each contributed to the formation of the small yet noteworthy kingdom of Israel. But on the death of Solomon violent reaction that had long been fermenting in out-of-the-way places broke loose, and the glory of empire passed, never to be regained. The drive of culture had been stayed by the drag of pastoral folkways. The North seceded, continuing with fluctuating success for two centuries, and then suffered eclipse; while the South, a small territory some thirty miles in diameter, centered in Jerusalem, held on through four centuries of hope deferred before country, city, and temple were laid in ruins, and the people were scattered to the four winds of heaven. The nation perished, but the people and the religion survived.

The apparent cause of the disruption of the kingdom was the attitude of the arrogant, snobbish son of Solomon. But topographic, economic, and racial differences, to say nothing of recent innovations, divided the North from the South. Public opinion prevented David from building a temple to Yahweh; serious objections were raised when he proposed a national census, and during the closing years of his reign groups were in rebellion against the growing centralization of power. Beneath the prosperity of Solomon's reign the storm had been brewing. The sullen drudgery of a growing army of slaves; the smoldering rebellion of the North, resentful of princely favors conferred on the South; the passing of blood revenge, which was a personal privilege as well as a religious obligation; the rising wrath of a multitude who saw the religion of their fathers discredited by the spectacle of a priest-king, a propagandist for strange rites—all grievances came to a head when Rehoboam refused the request of the council at Shechem (I Kings 12:1–15).

The reaction was immediate and disastrous. The slogan of the North, "To your tents O Israel" (I Kings 12:16), was a call back to the shepherd life, a reversion to type. Two fragments of a little nation, hostile each to the other, independent and arrogant, fought over the disintegrating inheritance of the kingdom of Solomon. National strength was sapped. Industry was paralyzed; caravan commerce was lost, and international amity was forfeited. Shishak of

Egypt overran the country, reducing both North and South to servitude (I Kings 14:25-28),[1] and thus in the clash of ideas, the old against the new, the accumulated achievements of a century were in large measure nullified. Religion, as symbolized by the temple worship, with its appeal to eye, and ear, and heart, suffered a severe setback. The shields of gold were replaced by brass (I Kings 14:25-27), and the ritual probably deteriorated in like measure. The North under Jeroboam I officially withdrew all patronage from the Jerusalem temple and established sanctuaries to its own liking (I Kings 12:28). Worship had to keep in step with political life, and naturally reverted to type. The king in conference appointed priests from among the common people, established high places throughout the land, set up golden bull images of Yahweh at Dan and Bethel, and proclaimed an autumn festival, with appropriate sacrifices, similar to that held in Jerusalem (I Kings 12:28-33). To many in the northern kingdom, that is, Israel, this was a great day, a day of freedom and of return to the religion of the fathers. The common man had come into his own; democracy had been re-established; and Yahweh worship, stripped from alien elements, had been restored.

This, none but the disputatious would deny. Jeroboam was supported by Ahijah, "my brother is Yahweh" (I Kings 11:29-31), and his own devotion to the Deity of the covenant was indicated in the name of his son Abijah, "my father is Yahweh" (I Kings 14:1). Yet while all was antagonistic to the temple worship, and its promoters considered that it preserved Yahweh worship, it differed vastly from the old desert ritual. *Once on the move you can never go back* is a truism in all ages. Three hundred years in Canaan, influenced by topography and climate, food supplies and neighbors, commerce and culture, had been at work subtly molding the life pattern and the worship of the inhabitants of the North. So altars were built, houses for worship were erected, a priesthood was organized, and harvest festivals were sanctioned. It was Yahwism, but it was again on the highroad to civilization.

Under the competent leadership of Omri and Ahab (887-842 B.C.) in the northern kingdom, commerce was developed, Samaria was built and made the capital of the kingdom, and friendly relations were established with Tyre and Jerusalem to the advantage of all concerned. As part of the good-neighbor policy, Queen Jezebel came to Samaria, and her daughter Athaliah was married to the king of Judah.

Jezebel was a true daughter of Ittobaal, a priest of Baal, who by revolution had seized the kingship of the city of Tyre. Coming to Samaria as queen, she naturally brought with her her own deities, male and female, that she, like Solomon's wives (I Kings 11:8), might worship according to her custom, that

---

[1] The contemporary Egyptian records on the temple at Karnak, which have been verified by the Shishak monument found at Megiddo, furnish evidence that the North as well as the South suffered invasion (I. G. Matthews, *Old Testament Life and Literature*, 127).

is, according to the dictates of her own conscience. The worship was sensuous, appealing to the esthetic, and indulging in the highly emotional. It was the religion of her court, and thus in some quarters at once became the fashion. It was missionary and was making inroads in the country, apparently having established itself on Mount Carmel after having destroyed a Yahweh altar (I Kings 18:19, 30). Thus Yahwism again was in danger of taking color from the environment, and Baal and Baalat of Tyre, who were only the old fertility gods decked out in city clothes, were pressing their claims for allegiance.

Many were captivated, thrilled with the new and more cultured rites of religion. These were days of great national prosperity, due, in part at least, to the alliances with Tyre and Jerusalem. Many delighted in the fine apparel, the brimming banquet bowl, and the ivory palaces that vied with those of Solomon. Good people, thoroughly modern, easily learned the formulas of good society, which was the first cousin to religion; and even the priests of Yahweh, so recently selected from the common people, had quickly mastered court etiquette and now four hundred of them played the sycophant before royalty (I Kings 22:6). But not a few were indignant at this growing paganism, and more than one was intolerantly belligerent. As when rebellion against the Solomonic hierarchy swept the country, so now when Tyrian Baalism is a challenge to Yahwism, the spirit of reaction is again abroad.

Elijah, the Tishbite,[2] a man of the desert, fiercely hostile to the enervating amenities of civilization and a zealous peripatetic for Yahweh, saw clearly what was happening under the rule of Ahab and his wife, and with fiery energy denounced the growing apostasy. Though a free lance, he was the spokesman for a school of prophets (II Kings 2:3, 5, 7). For years, probably for decades, he had assailed the court religion and had been a troubler in Israel (I Kings 18:17). Finally, as so often happens in Palestine, rain failed throughout the land for a succession of years. The brooks dried up; famine brooded on the hillsides; and death entered every hamlet (I Kings 18:1-5). The cause of the disaster was certain to every group. The prophets were positive it was due to the Tyrian Baalism at the court; Yahweh was greatly displeased. Jezebel was equally sure the catastrophe was a punishment for the prophetic campaign, led by the elusive Elijah, against her gods; Baal was angry. So Ahab the king, who was held responsible for the welfare of his people, sought far and wide for this insurgent and his allies (I Kings 18:17).

Elijah, however, was not daunted, and, meeting Ahab, charged the king and his father's house with the national calamity because of their disloyalty to Yahweh (I Kings 18:18). But stranger far was his assertion that Yahweh, the God of the desert, and not Baal, had withheld the rain clouds, and only he could

[2] Tishbite (I Kings 17:1; 21:17), derived from Teshub, originally the name of a Horite deity, is evidence of mixed racial inheritance.

bring them up again from out the deep.[3] The feud between these two types of religion had been long and bitter. Transitions had been slow, and conclusions came only after age-long conflict. The Carmel contest was the dramatic epitome of this struggle, and its significance was not so much in the fire falling from heaven as in the fact that the desert prophet, clad in the hairy mantle, in the name of Yahweh could cause the heavens to turn black with clouds and wind so that there was a great rain (I Kings 18:45). His ancestors of two centuries earlier would have disowned him as an unscrupulous apostate to Baal.

The story of the contest on Carmel, it is generally agreed, was written within fifty years after the event. By this time the dust of battle had cleared, and the inner significance of the episode could be more accurately appraised, while at the same time tradition had been busy dramatizing it. Neither Elijah nor Jezebel was conscious of the turn of the tide in religion in the North. Nor was either aware of the power of the prophet to call down fire from heaven.[4] Jezebel, without any inhibitions, swore that she would have his life within twenty-four hours (I Kings 19:2); and the hero of yesterday, convinced that he had failed and despairing of his life, fled to the far south by night, and prayed for death (I Kings 19:4-8). When Yahweh visited him he complained, "I, even I only am left, and they seek my life to take it away" (I Kings 19:14). Like many a pioneer in literature, art, and science he had achieved a victory of which neither he nor his generation was fully conscious. This, however, was the turning point in the defeat of Tyrian Baalism, and the triumph of Yahwism.

The conflict now entered its second phase. Though often overshadowed by the supernatural haze that enshrouds the Carmel story, the results of the experience of Elijah at Horeb were of signal importance (I Kings 19:11, 12). Here we see the mind of the prophet at work. His conclusion is that Yahweh was not in the wind, the earthquake, or the fire, but was in the hushed whisper. The interpretation is given, and is clear. Achievement is attained not by stormy denunciation, nor even by fire from heaven, but by subtle propaganda, through underground channels; by carefully laid plans for revolution among the disaffected, and by the dagger for those who stand in the way of the purposes of Yahweh (I Kings 19:15-17). Hence the mission of Elijah from now on was to

---

[3] This was a revolution in thought; and Yahweh thus takes over the function of Baal, the god of agriculture. Here for the first time Yahweh is the giver of rain (I Kings 18:18; 44). It is found again in the creation story of J. (Gen. 2:5), and later it is a common assumption (Hos. 2:10; Deut. 28:12). This was a crucial forward step in the struggle toward monotheism. See J. Hempel, *Gott und Mensch*, 56.

[4] Many attempts have been made to rationalize the fire called down from heaven in the Carmel story (I Kings 18:19-24). It has been suggested that Elijah used the "sacred fire." This looked like thick water, and when in the warm sunshine water was poured on it, "a great flame was kindled" (II Macc. 1:19-36; cf. R. H. Kennett, *O.T. Essays*, 1928, 81-104). But it seems more likely that our story is the result of that legendary activity that always endeavors vividly to portray important events and extraordinary characters. The later Elijah stories, calling down fire from heaven on the two bands that were sent to capture him (II Kings 1:10, 12), and his ascent in a chariot of fire (II Kings 2:11), seem to be of the same type. They were popular efforts to convey to posterity the measure of a great man.

lay plans for the assassination of Ben-hadad of Syria, to conspire for the anointing of Jehu as king over Israel, and to train up a successor to himself whose word and work would be fiercer and more inexorable than his own (I Kings 19:15-17). It was a fierce commission, as fierce as were the worshipers of Yahweh. Its interests were as wide as were their interests. Yahweh was still a jealous God; but no longer, as held by the Nazarites, was he thought of as a desert God, or as an isolationist. National life had thrust Israel into an international world, and the unprovoked war with Syria (I Kings 15:18-20) had threatened her very existence (I Kings 20:1-3) and incurred inescapable responsibilities. The boundaries of Yahweh's interest now reached far beyond the sheepcote to the cities of Samaria and Damascus, and beyond the simple tent of Jeroboam's day to the palaces of Omri and Ahab.

Strange things were and are done in the name of religion. Elijah's program was faithfully carried out. He himself was responsible for the first act. It was gruesome; treachery, lying, and murder, without any apology, were perpetrated in the name of Yahweh (II Kings 8:7-15). The second act, the anointing of Jehu as king over Israel, culminated in the slaughter of two kings (II Kings 9:24, 27, 28), the atrocious slaying of a Tyrian queen, the treacherous butchery of the priests of Baal, and the ruthless massacre of the princes of both the North and the South (II Kings 9:30-10:28). This blood bath, which vies with the worst acts of modern mass murder, no doubt sent a thrill of exultation through the ranks of the school of the prophets. They had achieved the will of God, and tradition records that Yahweh gave his blessing to Jehu: "Because thou hast done well in executing that which is right in mine eyes, and hast done to the house of Ahab according to all that was in my heart thy sons of the fourth generation shall sit on the throne of Israel" (II Kings 10:30).

These bloodstained annals are marked by deadly sincerity on the part of the heralds of Yahweh. To Elijah and his school, religion and culture were inseparable. Hence any alliance with a foreign nation was intolerable, as it naturally led to an adoption of their deities. Yahweh was jealous, hence the Baal temple in Samaria was an abomination to the prophet (I Kings 16:32). When Ahaziah, king of Samaria, sent to Baal-zebub at Ekron to inquire as to his son's recovery from sickness, his death was construed as punishment for thus slighting Yahweh (II Kings 1:1-4).

Loyalty to Yahweh alone was the primary interest of Elijah. In this he was akin to the prophetic guilds, with whom tradition linked him so closely (II Kings 1:8; 2:2, 3, 5). He had strange habits, appeared and disappeared at will (I Kings 18:10-12), saw visions and heard voices (I Kings 19:9-14), possessed a magic mantle (II Kings 2:8, 13, 14), and like some members of the dervish fraternity was a master wonder-worker (I Kings 17:1, 5, 14-16, 21-24; 18:30-34; II Kings 1:10, 12). But though his Yahweh was not yet speaking with the accents of the ethical prophets, he had long ago forsaken the desert. The story of Naboth's vineyard (I Kings 21:1-20), so often loosely interpreted, makes this quite clear. The question of justice is not considered, and lying, treachery, and murder are passed over without comment. But the violation of an old Canaanitish custom, the family right of entailed inheritance,[5] that was the unpardonable crime. That economic and social needs, in the expanding national life, should in any way interfere with the customs of the past was unthinkable to this reactionary. Yet, by this very claim, Yahweh had become an agricultural God.

The story of Micaiah ben Imlah, so far as our records show, is of like import. He was a seer of visions (I Kings 22:17, 19–23) who under spirit influence (I Kings 22:14, 24) always spoke evil concerning Ahab. No question of social justice is involved. But he insisted that he was the true spokesman for Yahweh (I Kings 22:14), apparently uncorrupted by court influence. But this formal phrase, "Yahweh saith," used by all the prophets, in itself gives us no information. However, not only did the editors place the narrative alongside the Naboth story, but it fits into the framework of the Elijah movement, which was the destruction of the Omri-Ahab dynasty on the ground of Baal worship.

Probably unlike Elijah, he lived in Samaria (I Kings 22:9, 13, 17), and may have been hospitable to city life; but like his illustrious contemporary, he stood a lone figure against four hundred parasite court prophets, and pronounced ruin on Ahab. While the reason for this is nowhere explicitly stated, it is most probable that the ground for his curses was Ahab's partnership in Tyrian Baalism, which was so deeply resented throughout the land. There is no evidence that he was an advocate of desert life, or that he was antagonistic to militarism or to the kingship as such. Nor did problems of social ethics occupy his attention. The overthrow of Baal and the reinstatement of Yahweh in the seat of authority was his main objective. He was an ally in the program to wipe out the last vestiges of the hated, seductive, alien, court worship.

These heroic leaders, the spokesmen for a considerable number of less courageous souls, roused the common people to the dangers of the hour, the insidious encroachments of Tyrian Baalism. Their appeal to the God of the fathers, always a heart-warming slogan, was winged with memories. Tradition had forgotten the slow, painful progress and the many setbacks, and had rainbow-hued the achievements. It illumined the spell of Horeb; it glorified the crossing of the Jordan; it resounded with the fall of Jericho and the conquest of the land (I Kings 18:31, 36). The past, thus interpreted, carried in it the promise of the future. Loyalty to Yahweh, a jealous God, who had wrought such great wonders, assured the nation of abundance, prosperity, and victory over Syria. It was an appeal to tradition, to a formula, and to a name. But what a name!

The name was the old name Yahweh, but the religion was no longer that of the shepherd wandering over the desert. Yahweh was now the God of the land of Canaan, of her people, of her customs, her feasts, her villages, and her cities.

---

[5] This law, now found in Leviticus 25:23–25, like the land itself originally belonged to the Canaanites (H. Schaeffer, *Social Legislation of the Primitive Semites*, 43, 169).

However, theirs was not the religion of Amos and Isaiah, at least so far as our records show, but they were on the side of the angels. They faced the task of their generation: to stem the growing tolerance in high places for an alien and enervating worship. The odds seemed against them, but as lone individuals they recklessly defied the might of state and church. They were intolerant and belligerent, and at times their tactics were remorseless. But they strove not in vain. They hastened the overthrow of foreign intrigue and the death of alien despots, and made the name of Yahweh to be feared throughout the land. Henceforth Yahweh, not Baal, is honored and worshiped by high and low alike, at least officially, throughout the North.

During this century (931–830 B.C.), while religious reaction flourished in Israel, the South was more quietly undergoing a series of reforms. Judah, now centered in Jerusalem, while much smaller and much less fertile than the North, had whereof to boast. The temple, that lay in the heart of the city, like a diamond in a circlet of gold, was her glory; the pride and joy of all, it compensated for the smallness of territory and the poverty of soil. Indeed it played a role that might have been impossible in a united and flourishing empire. As the worship was the chief care of kings and priests, reform rather than revolution prevailed. After the secession of the North its physical glory was dimmed. The lavish expenditures of Solomon's day could not be continued, and drastic curtailment in appointments and personnel was essential. Shishak, the Egyptian invader, made his contribution toward simplicity by carrying off the treasures of the palace and temple, notably the golden shields of the temple (I Kings 14:25, 26).

From the partial details that have been preserved by the Deuteronomic editor, the kings, Asa, Jehoshaphat, and Joash, are credited with reforms of considerable moment during this century. Asa (917–876 B.C.) removed the idols his father had made and the abominable image for an Asherah which Maacah his mother had made (I Kings 15:12, 13). He is credited with bringing into the temple the things he and his father had dedicated to Yahweh (I Kings 15: 15.) Jehoshaphat (876–851 B.C.) removed the sodomites (I Kings 22:46), and the priestly panegyric of later centuries describes him as a patron of religious education and the organizer of a priestly, judicial system (II Chron. 17:6–9; 19:8–11; cf. 20:23).[6] Joash (836–796 B.C.) became king of Judah as an aftermath of the Jehu revolution. In the North the Yahweh party had succeeded, as already noted, but at a great price. The carnage had swept across the border and had engulfed the South. Jehu had treacherously murdered forty princes of Judah (II Kings 10:13, 14), and Athaliah had retaliated in kind. Yahweh

---

[6] While the first intimation of this activity comes from more than four hundred years after the king's death, it is suggestive, and may be based in fact. A detailed study of the problem has been presented by J. Morgenstern, who is convinced that a small law code was introduced at this time (*HUCA*, IV, 1–138).

had appealed to the sword; and Baal took up the challenge. The desolated and enraged daughter of Jezebel destroyed all the royal seed save little Joash, who had been concealed from her wrath (II Kings 11:1-3). Then followed six years of feverish tension. Religious riots in the city gates; stealthy plotting behind closed doors; bribery by officials, and underhand tactics; and at last the Yahwists proved the more efficient and staged the final act. The young prince, a protégé of the priests, was crowned king, and Athaliah, regal in her doom, was ostentatiously slain (II Kings 11:13-16). The house of Baal, his altars, and his images were destroyed, and Mattan, the priest of Baal, was slain (II Kings 11:18). Thus Yahweh had acquitted himself valiantly, and the temple was cleansed of the Baal abominations. Twenty-three years later the temple was repaired at considerable cost, and the record states that no vessels of gold or silver were provided for the service, and that no trespass- or sin-offerings were required (II Kings 12:4-16). But though the sanctuary no longer had the glamour of the days of Solomon, it perpetuated the worship of Yahweh. And it is quite within the range of probability that its inner values increased in measure as its outer splendor decreased. Reform from within and pressure from without had united to change and to cleanse its rites and ceremonies. The reign of Joash, the climax of a century, initiated and dominated by a zealous priesthood, was a victory for Yahwism as notable as the triumph of Jehu in the North. It is true, treachery and assassination had played their part, but these were palliated, if not gloried in, in the name of traditional religion. The struggle had ended; the goal had been reached. Now the pent-up emotions of the loyal were liberated and all could rejoice that Yahweh, the jealous God, again held undisputed sway in the ancient city of Jerusalem.

While the forms and the spirit of religion in Judah were thus being molded by the forces of history, a much less drastic but no less effective propaganda for national Yahwism was under way. Mythology and folklore, which are the products of social processes, and present ideas, attitudes, and ideals, often personalized, rather than incidents in history or the biographies of heroes, had long been in circulation in Canaan. Much of these had been absorbed and even Hebraized by the Hebrews, and had been blended with their own peculiar heritage, which likewise had been sifted and idealized.[7] During this period scribes were at work, probably in various centers, or schools, reducing to written form those parts of their tradition that were of particular interest to them. This purposeful activity was a gradual process that profited by natural selection and informal editing before it attained the form in which it now exists in the Hexateuch. Our J. document, an early product of these composite labors, in its ethical and religious outlook is on the same general level as the Elijah and Micaiah narratives. There is no great interest in social ethics, such as is

---

[7] While folklore often may have small resemblance to factual history, it is the best gage to the life and the spirit of a nation. See C. R. Bowen, *The Living Bible*, 75-91.

found in the great prophets, or in individual ethics, as lying, stealing, and murder are in good form if in a good cause or directed against a foreigner. But it is a collection of the best stories and might well be designated the faith of the common man in Judah at the end of this period.[8]

The stories in the J. document are unified by a threefold purpose: Yahwism is vindicated; the national claim to the land is assured by the promises of Yahweh to the fathers; and a legal code for the worship of Yahweh is prescribed. Some of its chapters (Gen. 2:4a–4:26, and much of 6:1–11:9)[9] make a telling appeal for the life and religion of the seminomad. The theme that unites these odd stories, whatever the date of their origin, is that farming and city building, working in iron and brass bring strife, sorrow, and chaos, while the life of the shepherd is the ideal, and the lamb is the offering acceptable to Yahweh. These tales are a challenge for the simple life and for simple worship as opposed to a highly developed civilization. To many this was the good life, and the way of Yahweh.

Further, in the long ago, Abraham, Isaac, and Jacob had occupied the land and had built altars to Yahweh at Shechem, Bethel, Ai, Hebron, Beersheba, Mahanaim, and Penuel, and thus the land was theirs by right of settlement. Moreover, again and again Yahweh had promised to them and to their posterity the land as an inheritance for ever and ever (Gen. 12:1–3; 13:14–17; 15:7, 18, 19; 17:2, 4–8; 22:15–17; 26:3, 4; 27:27; 48:15–19; 49:1–27), making it theirs by divine right. While this was religious fiction, rather than actual history, it nevertheless expressed the hopes and the idealism of the people of Judah at this period, and beyond question was effective in future history.

The third important feature was that the ritual decalogue (Exod. 34:14–26, J.), a summary of rites and taboos, that in the long struggle between Baal and Yahweh had won the general approval of leaders and people in Judah, had now been put into written form. This marked an advance in culture, and was a token that the leaders in Judah were convinced that the correct worship of Yahweh was of prime importance to the nation. It no longer left religious practices to the haphazard decisions of local communities, or to be wholly controlled by priestly interests. Rites and ceremonies were standardized for all the land, and thus contributed to the unification and strengthening of the

---

[8] The evidence that lies behind the judgment that the Pentateuch is of composite origin, as are all other lawbooks, and is the product of generations of devout leaders, may be found in any standard Bible dictionary, such as Hastings, or in greater detail in volumes such as A. T. Chapman, "An Introduction to the Pentateuch," in *Cambridge Bible for Schools and Colleges;* S. R. Driver, *An Introduction to the Literature of the O.T.;* R. H. Pfeiffer, *Introduction to the O.T.,* 129–289. An interpretation of the religious values of the early documents is presented by G. C. Mansfield, *The Book of Yahweh.* See also Chas. Weynon, *The Creation Story in the Light of Today;* C. R. Brown, *The Story Book of the Early Hebrews;* Jas. Strachan, *Hebrew Ideals;* Laura Wild, *A Literary Guide to the Bible.*

[9] These and a few other sections of similar import have been separated from the J. document. Pfeiffer considers them a late insertion in the Hexateuch (*Introduction to the O.T.,* 159–167).

national bonds. These rites and taboos became the signposts of orthodox Yahwism, and established a wall between the loyal worshipers of Yahweh and those who through an appeasement policy temporized with Baal.

The first requirement was, "Thou shalt worship no other god, for Yahweh, whose name is Jealous, is a jealous God" (Exod. 34:14). Later a practical implication of this, that marriage with foreigners, which would inevitably lead to the tolerance and worship of other deities, should be prohibited, was added by an editor (Exod. 34:15, 16). Further, the firstborn of flock and family or a substitute must be offered to Yahweh as an evidence of devotion (Exod. 34:19, 20). Then came the demand to observe the three agricultural festivals before Yahweh (Exod. 34:22, 23), and to outlaw a number of current practices, such as molten gods, blood mixed with unleavened bread, and boiling a kid in its mother's milk (Exod. 34:17, 25, 34).

Like the people themselves this law was composite. Its roots ran back into pre-Mosaic tribalism; it was dominated by the spirit of the desert covenant; and, while it denounced the cruder Baal practices, it reinterpreted others and incorporated them into Yahweh worship. By its spirit of compromise and its inclusiveness it set the pattern for later legislation in both the South and the North.[10] While it was brief, and nonethical, it revealed the discriminating judgment of the leaders, who amid the clash of religious ideals were the advocates of the higher levels in worship. It was prophetic of the further elimination of the primitive and the acceptance of the more universal in the onward march of revelation. In it were all the joys of a credo, the satisfactions of a definite pattern in worship. It was the measure of religion among the common people of Judah and might well be termed the Magna Charta of Old Testament religion.

Thus by 800 B.C., as the result of the never ceasing conflict, Yahweh became firmly established as the God of two small nations, Judah and Israel. While there were many differences between South and North both in life and in religion, the similarities were even more fundamental. As a family may have its internal bickerings and yet unite against all the world, so were both nations united in Yahwism. Yahweh, not Baal, was the God of the land and of the two peoples. He was still Yahweh of the desert; the jealous God of the sheep and of the tribe; the God of human dignity, and equality. Yet he had become the God of the farmer, the giver of the grain, the wine, and the oil; the God of the festivals, and of the kindly social life; the God of plenty, and of the higher standards of living.

The Elijah-Jehu revolution had stayed the excesses of Canaanite paganism and had discredited the very name of Baal. The worship of Yahweh had been established officially in both nations, and in both the ritual demands of Yah-

---

10 This ritual decalogue was incorporated in the North in Covenant Code (Exod. 21:1–23; 19; cf. esp. 22:28–31; 23:14–19). Comparison between the various codes that indicates relationship is found in R. H. Pfeiffer, *Introduction to the O.T.*, 210–270.

weh had been, or were in process of being, formulated. The glory of Solomon had passed, but the essential spirit of a growing civilization, the social and commercial processes, the orderly and unified rites of worship, the priestly organization and the kingship had, formally at least, been brought under the jurisdiction of Yahweh. In Judah they gloried in the temple, and in an approved and written ritual. In Israel they prided themselves in their freedom, and displayed a fierce loyalty to Yahweh, who had brought them up out of the land of Egypt. In both, the name Yahweh had a history that was both vital and plastic, and aroused deep-felt emotion that was easily enlisted in any venture. Both gloried in the promise, "Ye shall be holy men to me" (Exod. 22:31, E.; Exod. 19:6; Lev. 11:44).

Chapter VIII

THE RELIGION OF THE LAYMEN. 763-700 B.C.

THE early years of the eighth century B.C., in both Israel and Judah, were marked by unusual prosperity. A strong ruler sat on each throne, Jeroboam II in Israel, 781–740 B.C., and Azariah (Uzziah) in Judah, 783–751 B.C., and wisely they were affiliated, politically and religiously. Though lacking the splendor of the days of Solomon, the immediate prospects were most favorable. The cities were populous, palaces were resplendent with ivory and gold, revelry and banqueting rejoiced prince and peasant alike, and for the well-to-do a summer holiday in the Lebanons and a winter respite in Memphis added to the fullness of life. Religion, secure with its written charter—the ritual decalogue in the South in 850 B.C. and a similar document introduced into the North about 750 B.C.—kept pace with the social life. Ritual was punctiliously observed, sacrifices were lavish, and the festivals were thronged with devout and happy worshipers. These were good days in Samaria and Jerusalem, and a grateful people rejoiced that Yahweh so greatly favored them as a nation. The promises of the Jehu revolution in the North and the reforms of Joash in the South were being realized to the satisfaction of all. It paid to offer sacrifices morning and evening, to beautify the temple, and to bring the tithes into the treasury.

The more thoughtful, however, had to admit that somehow these expectations had been long delayed. After the days of Elijah Syria had continued her ravages on the country, scourging it in 856, 855, and again in 853 B.C. (I Kings 20:1–34; 22:3). Even after the crowning of Jehu, the champion of Yahweh, state affairs had gone from bad to worse. In 842 Jehu paid tribute to Assyria, and in 837 Hazael, king of Syria, had reduced Gilead and Bashan to Syrian provinces (II Kings 10:32, 33). Moreover, Assyria, with capital at Nineveh, had turned greedy eyes toward the west, and by 797 B.C. had sent six military expeditions against Damascus and her neighboring allies, so that preceding the reign of Jeroboam II the affliction of Israel was bitter (II Kings 14:26). For almost a century the political intrigue fathered by Elijah had reaped the whirlwind.

But at last the war clouds lifted, and the leaders of the established religion of both lands were highly gratified. They had an ancient and worthy inheritance. On the honor roll were the great and the good from Noah to Elijah. In office were priests trained in the traditions of Yahwism, devoted and eager to serve. They beautified the worship, improved the daily service, multiplied sacred days, added to the priesthood as required, and could report increased attendance at the festivals and no lack of funds in the treasury. With great satisfaction they assured the nation that all was well, and all rejoiced in the abiding presence of Yahweh in their midst.

But there were rebels in the land; guileless, God-fearing laymen like Amos (763 B.C.) and Hosea (740 B.C.), who without mercy scored the business activities and the religious practices of those in power; a villager named Micah (720–700 B.C.), who visited Jerusalem and in flaming speech denounced prophet and prince, judge and priest, and pronounced judgment on Jerusalem; and an Isaiah (740–700 B.C.), who associated with the official classes but was no less critical than others of the outer and inner life of his fellows. These four men, appearing at the height of the country's prosperity, were the drastic critics of the existing order, the prophets of national disaster. Yet, they and those whom they opposed were in agreement in important basic principles. All were worshipers of Yahweh, whose existence and power were never questioned. They all believed that both Israel and Judah were his people, and that loyalty to him brought national prosperity, while disobedience would bring disaster. The prophets and their opponents alike were sure that the presence of Yahweh had been with his people throughout their history, and that he revealed his will to them from time to time.

The mutual acceptance of such vitally important ideas made for a happy relationship with their fellows. But, owing to the convictions of the great prophets as to what was right and wrong, and their appreciation of human values, their interpretation of the above-mentioned principles was in violent antagonism to that of the officials of their generation. We call them reformers, and pay them homage. In their own day they were rabid iconoclasts, violently attacking the accepted standards in business, society, government, and religion; and they paid the price.

As destructive critics of the time-honored institutions of their own day the land was not able to bear all their words (Amos 7:10, 16; 2:12; 5:10; Hos. 6:5; Mic. 3:12; cf. Jer. 26:22, 23). Even today their speech sounds harsh, and their principles would spoil business, land representatives of the law behind the bars, and disrupt the smooth routine of Christian worship and propaganda Vagueness and concealing rhetoric never dulled the edge of their criticism. To root out and to pull down was the primary part of their mission. They dealt in personalities as well as with principles, and a *Thou art the man* often sped the accusation to the heart of high officials in church and state (Amos 2:13; 7:11, 17; Hos. 5:1; Mic. 3:9–12; Isa. 3:16; 7:10–17). Passionate preachers of uncomfortable truths, they rebuked the great, defied the strong, and roundly cursed the obdurate. They were free lances, a most disturbing element in ancient Palestine, radicals who today would scarcely be tolerated in Christian society. Their individual messages have been so often and so fully interpreted that only a cross section [1] of their most significant contributions is here presented.

Business practices that were prevalent throughout the land have never been more savagely, or more justly, assailed. Their approach to the problem was based on no economic theory, at least not on one that would be valid today; nor did they think in terms of abstract justice, as such. They were simple-minded men, whose judgments were conditioned by apparent human values. In all cases of injustice, someone, a human being, was suffering. These men were sensitive to much that lay beneath the surface and passed unnoticed, or at least went unheeded, by the well-to-do official classes. The hunger fare of the poor, the hopeless despair of the debtor, the unequal struggle of the widow and orphan were but the witnesses to the loss of freedom, the frustration of hope, and the violation of human dignity. They were inhuman; they were wrong. But this was only the dark background of the easy profits of the money-lender, the revelry of the banquet chamber, the scarlet and fine linen of prince and king, and the pomp and pride of the priest. This glaring inequality between the classes was unjust; such had not been the custom in Israel's early history; nor was it related to the needs, and the essential nature, of man. Hence justice for the poor was the ever repeated cry; a just balance, a fair wage paid promptly, no usury, humane consideration for the unfortunate, and kindness toward the needy crowd the pages of these spokesmen for humanity. Scorn was poured out on the greed of the rich, the arrogance of those in power, and blistering words were hurled at the women for their ostentatious luxury (Amos 4:1–3; Isa. 3:16, 17). Businessmen, especially those in the upper brackets, were held responsible for the twofold human tragedy, suffering and debauchery, and the swiftly coming destruction which each prophet saw like a thundercloud on the horizon.

These laymen, for such were Amos, Hosea, and Micah, have been called the conscience of the nation; they might also be called the champions of the under-privileged classes. Their messages were a reinterpretation, in the new and complex environment, of the old principle found in the mores of all early societies, *thou shalt not steal*. The rights that belong to humanity are older than the opportunities for private gain, and are deep-rooted in the very nature of society. But they need to be reinterpreted in the ever changing environment, or the lust for gain on the part of the strong may for a time defy an underlying

---

[1] It is no accident that the English-speaking world has more competent interpretations of the prophets than of any other part of the Hebrew Scriptures. The prophets majored in human interest, and democracy ever turns back to one of its sources. Among worth-while books are A. F. Kirkpatrick, *The Doctrine of the Prophets*, an old book but still rich in meaning; G. A. Smith, commentaries in *Expositor's Bible*, volumes on *The Minor Prophets* and *Isaiah*; J. M. P. Smith, *The Prophets and Their Times* (2nd ed. by W. A. Irwin, 1941); Fleming James, *Personalities of the Old Testament*.

law of social integrity. "Business was made for man, not man for business" might have been a slogan of the prophet.

Kings and princes fared no better than did the businessmen at the hands of these troublers of Israel. The kingship, originally promoted by the most farseeing prophet of the day, and accepted by local leaders, had been sanctioned officially by Yahweh (I Sam. 9:1–10:16). Naturally, however, though not recorded in the early documents, there were those who gravely shook their heads at such a radical innovation, and it was not long before some four hundred lawless fellows formed a raiding band that threatened the very existence of the venture (I Sam. 22:2, 8; 20:31). Within a hundred years, sanctioned if not led by a prophet of Yahweh, the kingdom was split in two (I Kings 11:29–31), and thenceforth neither North nor South for any considerable time was free from the shackles of a foreign power. Even more discouraging was the fact that many of the kings were incompetent, some were a disgrace to the office, and only a few, according to religious ideals, were considered worthy. Hence what were real values seemed to be overshadowed by failure. Further, it was inevitable that sharp criticism should come from the prophets, who were free men and had been nurtured in an atmosphere that encouraged freedom of speech. Micaiah ben Imlah voiced the dissatisfaction of many (I Kings 22:19–25), and a later writer expressed prophetic disapproval when he penned the objections that tradition attributed to Samuel (I Sam. 8:1–22; 10:17–27). Amos was accused of conspiracy against the king (Amos 6:1–8; 7:10, 11), and Hosea, bolder than the others, asserted that kings had been a snare to the people and had never been set up by Yahweh (Hos. 7:3–7; 8:4; 13:10, 11). This, written about 740 B.C., is the earliest certain date for a clear-cut utterance against the kingship. History, the final arbiter of all institutions, had failed to approve the early hopes of the prophets. Isaiah, from his opening vision on, considered Yahweh the supreme ruler in the domain of men, and in conference with the intractable Ahaz announced the end of the kingdom (Isa. 7:13–15). Such judgments were but the prelude to the later hope that the Prince of Peace, whose kingdom would be established in justice and righteousness for ever and ever, would at last sit on the throne of David (Isa. 9:6, 7; 11:1–6). When the nation was in the throes of disintegration, prophetic idealism, again reinterpreting history, leaped forward to a vaster kingdom under a King of Kings with whom was neither variation nor shadow that is cast by turning. Their denial that the kingship had been inaugurated by Yahweh was the result of a growing awareness of the ways of the Eternal in the affairs of men. History has always brought about the collapse of institutions, and prophets have ever been striving to build anew and better out of the ruins of the past. In a wider context one of our scholars in cryptic Oriental language has said, "The king is the last of the gods, and the first of men." [2]

2 W. F. Petrie, *Personal Religion in Egypt*, 45.

The sons of the prophets, who were believed to be possessed by a divine spirit whereby they could see things hidden to others, could foretell the future, and could perform amazing feats, physically and mentally (I Sam. 10:9-11; I Kings 18:8-12; II Kings 2:8; 12-15), and were usually considered sacrosanct, did not escape the wrath of these radicals. Amos scornfully repudiated the very name prophet, declaring himself to be a layman unrelated to any school (Amos 7:12-16); and from then on seers, visionaries, and *nabhi* (prophets) lost caste in Israel. Isaiah called the prophet a teacher of lies (Isa. 9:15, 16), who reeled with strong drink, erred in vision, and stumbled in judgment (Isa. 28:7). While Micah, a rustic from Moresh-gath, charged the prophets with selling out for a meal ticket (Mic. 3:5-8). His message, on the other hand, was one of justice, even to tell Jacob his transgression, and Israel his sin (Mic. 3:8). This onslaught against the prophet, now branded as false, and against the ancient guild of prophets was later without mercy carried to its climax by Jeremiah (Jer. 23:14-40).

The priest, however, had to bear the brunt of the most serious charges against the religious leaders of the day. Three of these prophets were countrymen, who had little knowledge of, and less appreciation for, ritual that to them was meaningless. On the other hand the priesthood, a sacred institution, had been strengthened in the South in 850 B.C. and in the North by 750 B.C. by the publishing of the ritual decalogue (Exod. 34:14-26, J.; and Exod. 20:23-26; 23:10-19, E.),[3] which placed the three agricultural festivals under the care of Yahweh. This, the putting of customs into written form, which was ultimately an aid in purifying the ritual, could easily be used by the priesthood to vulgarize the worship in the interest of popularity and profit. Now the ritual had sanctions; Bethel and Gilgal, Dan and Beersheba, Hebron and Jerusalem could now appeal to a recognized code in support of their own interpretation of cult practices. Altars flourished on every hilltop; incense became popular; new moons and solemn assemblies were set apart; sacrifice every morning; meal offerings and freewill offerings became the order of the day. Molten and graven images, stocks, stones, and poles were set up as objects to aid worship, while witchcraft and soothsaying flourished on the side. Assyrian influence came in under Ahaz in 734 B.C. (II Kings 16:10, 11), and priests found it convenient to understand and to cater to the preferences of Ashur, the god of the victor, while even the temple in Jerusalem was remodeled to accommodate the sun-god (II Kings 16:10-19; 23:4, 5, 11, 12). Under foreign domination local tribal types of worship gained a lease on life, and Moloch, Chemosh, Milcom, and all the Baalim again gained in popularity (II Kings 23:13). Rites that were barbarous and brutal, such as prostitution, sacred to

---

[3] J. Morgenstern thinks the ten words representing the chief principles of Yahweh worship in the North were formulated by Elijah and his followers (*HUCA*, IV, 54-91).

the fertility cult [4] but hateful to those imbued with desert ideals, and child sacrifice, seem to have been revived under pagan influence (II Kings 23:10). The Jehu-Jeroboam dynasty, which had enthroned Yahweh in the seat of Baal, so far as we know had made no attempt to purify the ritual, and in the South under the pro-Assyrian Ahaz priests in high office had heartily cooperated with the political needs. Within the established order all seemed to prosper. The sacrifices were ample; the priestly appointments were well cared for; and the sacred tithe was acceptable to the servants of Yahweh. All were contented, all was well.

But to these prophets, untutored men from the countryside, the whole show was nothing less than damnable. They were scathing in their criticism and absolute in their insistence that such abominable rites had never been instituted, and could not be countenanced, by Yahweh. Amos cries out in the name of Yahweh, "I hate, I despise your feasts and your solemn assemblies," and then stated that they never offered burnt offerings and meal offerings . . . in the wilderness (Amos 5:21–25). Hosea is unequivocal, "I desire goodness and not sacrifice; and knowledge of God rather than burnt offering" (Hos. 6:6). Isaiah, a little later, in the South, asks, "To what purpose is the multitude of your sacrifices? . . . I delight not in the blood of bulls, or of lambs, or of he-goats. . . . Who has required this of you, to trample my courts? Bring no more vain oblations . . ." (Isa. 1:11–17). Micah joins the chorus stigmatizing all the worship as the hire of a harlot (Mic. 1:7; 3:11). These were stormy words, an icy blast against the most sacred rites of the day, but proclaimed by four such men over a period of some sixty years they redeemed Yahwism from the corruptions native to Baalism and fundamental to magic.[5]

[4] See chapter iv, footnotes 36–40. Some ancient peoples believed prostitution to be a sacred duty. The Hebrew words qedeshoth and qedeshim mean "those set apart," or "the holy ones," translated in English versions by "prostitute," "sodomite," and "harlot" (I Kings 14:24; 15:12; 22:46; II Kings 23:7; Deut. 23:17, 18; Hos. 4:14; Gen. 38:21, 22), but "male and female votaries" would be more accurate. Also zoneh, usually rendered "harlot" may have been the Canaanite word for priestess. See D. Nielsen, Altarabische Mond Religion, 192; H. G. May, AJSL, 1932, 73–98; W. C. Graham, AJSL, 1931, 208. For a general statement see W. R. Smith, Rel. Sem. (3), 612–618; and for its importance, E. A. Leslie, Old Testament Religion in the Light of its Canaanite Background, 168–193. That such persons were in good standing in Baalism, and were even officials, cannot be doubted. Then when Yahweh displaced Baal as the god of agriculture it would not be easy to exclude all the undesirable elements from popular practice. Statements such as those found in Genesis 34:31, 39:15, Joshua 2:1, 6:22, I Samuel 2:22, Amos 2:7 suggest, if they do not prove, that down to the days of the prophets there were Yahweh worshipers who paid their respects to these courtesans.

[5] These clear-cut statements have long been a thorn in the side of the commentator, who has often dulled their edge by tortuous exegesis in the interest of a theory of inspiration. Had the prophets so intended they themselves would have inserted the needed ifs and buts to secure this end. Face to face with the powerful priesthood they declared that their interpretations of the Yahweh religion were mutually exclusive. It is evident that this was also the priestly understanding of the attack. L. Waterman, "The Ethical Clarity of the Prophets," JBL, Sept., 1945, 297–307, is a clear-cut exposition.

While the rulers, civil and religious, were blamed for the corruption and the coming calamity, the common people not only suffered but were held to be equally culpable. It is true they were followers, not leaders, but because of this they escaped neither disaster nor censure. The people were like the priest (Hos. 4:9), all were adulterers (Hos. 7:4). The city would be destroyed for the transgression of Jacob, for the sins of the house of Israel (Mic. 1:5). "From the sole of the foot even unto the head there is no soundness in it" (Isa. 1:6); they were "a people of unclean lips" (Isa. 6:5), who refused the waters of Shiloh (Isa. 8:6), and would not seek Yahweh (Isa. 9:13). This was the law of tribal solidarity in which all were on a basis of equality—an equality in sharing the necessities of life, an equality in suffering in common disasters, and an equality in the responsibility for the weal and woe of the tribe. It was the primitive law; but it is also fundamental to all social existence; it is just. All are bound up in one bundle of life.

These prophets were builders as well as uprooters, and in this they were as radical as they had been in their assaults on the fully established institutions of their day. That Yahweh primarily was a moral being was one of their far-reaching contributions to religious thought. This was correlative to their interpretation that the leaders were doomed and that the existing institutions had not been founded by Yahweh because both leaders and institutions violated human rights and dignity. Building on what to them was axiomatic, they concluded that Yahweh was as fair-minded and as just as was man himself. In the world of men, where right was paramount, God himself must be the embodiment of right. This was a step forward in the realm of religious ideas. In the wilderness, Yahweh had been the God of people, and his interests had been largely limited to human welfare. In the days of conquest, he became a war-God, and thereby took possession of the land. By the time of Elijah and Jehu, he had dogmatically become the God of agriculture and commerce. In this process, the grain, the wine, and the oil came to the fore and began to push man out of the picture. Might was on the throne in war, in business, in politics, and in religion; and the weak were bought and sold for private gain (Amos 8:4–6).

These, the ethical prophets, began to build on the foundations of the past, but they did not accept the *status quo* as final. That Yahweh was the God of history, the God of the desert, the God of the conquest, the God of the farmer, the businessman, and the nation, was an unquestioned part of their inheritance. But that he was interested primarily in social ethics was their distinctive message. The existence and the power of deity no good Semite ever questioned. Amos, like Elijah, was confident that it was Yahweh who gave and withheld the rain, and created and destroyed the produce of the land (Amos 4:6–9; 7:1–7), and that the land from the top of Carmel to the bottom of the sea was his (Amos 9:3, 4). Hosea climaxed these claims when he dogmatically asserted "I [Yahweh] gave her the grain, and the new wine, and the oil, and her silver and gold" (Hos. 2:8), thus broadening the domain of orthodox Yahwism.

Such a conclusion, that the land and its produce belonged to Yahweh, could not fail to introduce many changes in living and thinking. A great gulf lay between the days of Moses and those of Isaiah. The barren life of the desert had given way to the kindlier atmosphere of the court. Food supplies were more abundant; men were more virile; the population was greatly increased; luxuries of earlier days were now necessities; all life had become more complex, and all was now within the domain of Yahweh.

Yahweh, as the God of civilization, was now declared to be a kindly God. The Elisha stories (II Kings 2:1-25; 4:1-6:22; 8:1-15; 13:14-21), save that strange one of the boys and the bears (II Kings 2:23, 24), and the judgment on Gehazi (II Kings 5:27), while they read like legends are all expressions of a kindly, helpful spirit. Hosea makes *hesed,* leal love, the chief characteristic of Yahweh, whose loving-kindness he never ceases to celebrate.[6] Out of his matrimonial tragedy grew the conviction that Yahweh was as loving and forgiving as was man at his best. As the conjugal relation was the most inclusive and most ideal in social life, so in religion the relation between Yahweh and Israel was as husband and wife (Hos. 11:1-4, 8). Wayward as Israel was, God would never give her up. He had taught her to walk, dandled her in his arms, and bound her to himself with the bonds of love. Rarely, if ever, has the all-embracing mercy of God been more poignantly or more ethically expressed. The finer features of civilization was the soil in which such sentiments were nourished.

This belief was no idle sentiment with Hosea. It reached backward as well as forward. If Yahweh were kindly, then some things had been done in his name that were unworthy of his nature. The swift utterance, *I will avenge the blood of Jezreel on the house of Jehu* (Hos. 1:4) gives us a clearer insight into the progress of religious ideals than is found in many a modern volume. Elijah and the prophets of Yahweh had inspired, directed, and blessed the revolution of Jehu; but the history of a hundred years cast suspicion on the claims of the earlier prophets. Hosea challenged the judgment of his predecessors and pronounced destruction on the house of Jehu, and an end to the house of Israel. It was a bloody cycle; and even a kindly deity knew no other way than bloodshed by which to mete out justice to the guilty.

That Yahweh was just and righteous, as well as kindly, was insisted on as axiomatic by these prophets of the Assyrian period. In this, as in nothing else, they were united, and spoke in such resounding tones that all the Western world has been compelled to listen. It is true that laws—mores—governing

---

[6] A fine study of Hosea's use of the word for loving-kindness, showing its reciprocal and ethical connotation, its human-divine quality, was made by N. Glueck, "Das Wort hesed," *Beihefte ZAW,* 47.

social and economic relations are found the world over, among the most primitive and the most cultured people. Stealing, lying, breaking faith, and killing (Hos. 4:2) are primary taboos functioning within all tribes for their self-preservation. They are the products of social life, depending on no special revelation. Even gangsters observe them or in time are self-destroyed. In Israel, from the earliest days, loyalty to such rules, probably unwritten, had been implied,[7] if not pledged, within the tribal bounds in the name of Yahweh. But the desert application of "thou shalt not steal," where sheep and camels were the chief consideration and the operation of the law was within the federation, never extratribal, had in it little or nothing that was definite for the more complex commercial and international life in Palestine. Our prophets not only preached justice and righteousness, good words but vague, but they widened and deepened the scope of primitive custom and translated stealing, lying, cheating, and murder into the inescapable details of petty action in their own daily environment. The light weight, the scant measure, bribetaking, holding back wages, taking advantage of the unfortunate, coveting fields, planning and plotting for higher prices, all such are acts that come under the jurisdiction of Yahweh, and are hateful to him. Justice was no flaccid theory, glorified by rhetoric. It had become a two-edged sword, cutting into unearned profits and laying bare the greed for gain by judge, and priest, and prince. *This act is unjust,* and *thou art the man,* were the uncomfortable words of the prophet.

As already indicated, these men had denounced ritual as of no avail, but now, if possible, they went farther, and made social ethics the essential, even the sole, requirement of Yahweh. "What doth Yahweh require of thee, but to do justly, and to love kindness, and to walk humbly with thy god?" (Mic. 6:8.) Such comprehensive phrases summarize the central emphasis of the great prophets. To priest and early prophet alike such pronouncements were scandalous, to the businessman they were impudent, offside interferences of impracticable theorists, and to religion they were revolutionary. That God, the creator of the universe, the upholder of all things by the word of his might, should have no interest in the fragrant incense, the smoking sacrifice, and the blood of bulls was unforgivable heresy; but that he should busy himself about the quality of the wheat on the market, the peck measure, and the daily wage seemed utterly childish.

Nevertheless, such a conception was far from puerile. Right appeals to

---

[7] Evidence seems to show that the decalogue, Exodus 34:14–26, which has to do exclusively with rites and ceremonies, was the earliest written code of law in both Judah and Israel. The date at which the ethical decalogue, Exodus 20:2–17, was put into code form is far from certain. Was Hosea 4:2 the summary of a code already extant, or was it the basis of a later formulation? However, on any count, the essential features of this code were a part of the social inheritance of each tribe of the federation long before the time of Moses. The period at which it was written, while important from a cultural point of view, is of much less significance than its early origin, which is assured.

depths in human nature that never respond to the dictum of might, whether in church or state. It has in it a creative drive for human welfare quite foreign to that of brute force. The terrible meek has a penetrating quality that pierces where no bayonet can reach. Might, which triumphs by brawn and brain, brings victory to the strong and the shrewd, but carnage ceases only when the strongest have eliminated all competitors. It is the law of the jungle, of the animal nature, and is suicidal. Right is the law of the higher, the moral nature of man, in which resides his chief superiority over the lower creation. Recognition of the inherent rights of others, and co-operation with them, not carnage, is the law of human progress. Right, social justice, that knows no boundary lines of color or creed, race or ritual, age or sex, while expressed most clearly by Amos, underlay the judgment of all. Yahweh was still a jealous God, but he was no respecter of persons. *The eyes of the Lord Yahweh are upon the sinful kingdom* (Israel), *and I will destroy it from the face of the earth* (Amos 9:7, 8a), the words of Amos, though toned down by ancient censorship (cf. Amos 9:8b), were a trumpet blast shattering the sleepy optimism of petty tribalism that so often has pervaded religious institutions. Character, not tribal origins, national history, or perfected ritual, was the only salvation for the nation (Amos 9:7). This emphasis, by implication, paved the way for the brotherhood of man, provided a sound basis for internationalism, and was the foundation of ethical monotheism. Yahweh Zebaoth, the early war-God (I Sam. 17:45), was thus converted, and, influenced by Isaiah's vision of Yahweh, "high and lifted up" (Isa. 6:1–3), later writers interpreted him as the God of the stars and the angelic hosts of heaven (Amos 4:13; 5:27; Isa. 47:4; 48:2; 54:5; 61:15).

The method of divine revelation was likewise reinterpreted by this group. Again they were revolutionary. As they believed God to be a moral being, so his revelation to man, or man's approach to him, whichever way the problem may be stated, must be ethically conditioned. Even as their conclusions concerning social ethics and the nature of Deity were the result of personal convictions, rising out of daily experiences, so in the field of psychology, their belief was that man's understanding of God came through reflection on the facts observed in history and society; that is, God spoke to men through their intelligence.

Their contemporaries had inherited and used many and varied devices for ascertaining the will of deity (Isa. 2:6). Physical nature was believed to unfold the future to those initiated in her secrets. The wind rustling in the leaves (II Sam. 5:24), the flight of birds, the actions of animals (Num. 22:27), the eclipse of moon or sun (Amos 8:9; Joel 2:10, 30, 31), the stars in general, and in particular falling stars, and the conjunction of stars (Judge. 5:20; Num. 24:17; Isa. 47:13; Dan. 2:47), and many other features were held to be portents of things to come. The early priests, who often were oracle givers,[8] had definite ways and means of settling many practical problems, that is, of finding out the will of God. Methods such as waters of bitterness as a test for adultery (Num. 5:11–31), the marks on the liver of the sacrificial animal (Ezek. 21:21), inquiring by the teraphim (I Sam. 19:13, Gen. 31:19; Zech. 10:2, Ezek. 21:21), casting the sacred lot (I Sam. 14:36, 37, 40–42; Josh. 14:2; 15:1; 16:1), the use of the ephod (I Sam. 30:7, II Sam. 5:19), and the Urim and Thummim (I Sam. 14:18; 22:18; 23:6, 9; 28:6) were well-established, priestly means of learning the will of God. The early prophets emphasized the place of strange and abnormal experiences as a means of, and evidence for, revelation. Dreams were believed to have special import (Gen. 28:12–19; 37:5–11; 41:15–25; Judg. 7:13; I Kings 3:5; Dan. 2:38; 7:1); voices heard at sacred shrines were accepted as divine (Gen. 28:13–15; I Sam. 3:4, 6, 10; I Kings 3:5); spirits of the dead, in times of crises appeared in order to utter warnings (I Sam. 28:15; Isa. 8:19), and abnormal psychical experiences, such as ecstasy, trance, and coma, induced by exercises indulged in by the prophetic guilds, were the popular channels through which people learned the divine will (Num. 12:6–8, E.).[9]

In marked contrast to this, two facts stand out in bold relief. Prediction, as such, never occupied the attention of these moral reformers. They pronounced judgment on the nation, but this was in no way akin to clairvoyance. The signs of the heavens were not their sources of inspiration, but the market place furnished them with information. Destruction for the corrupt nation was certain; but the how and when were indefinite. They believed, with others, that famine, plague, and war were due to the displeasure of God; but they argued that Yahweh's anger was caused, not by lack of blood of bulls and goats, but by injustice and inhumanity (Amos 7:1–9; 8:4–10). Hope for the future was also proclaimed, at least by Hosea and Isaiah. But this was not a program for future ages,[10] it was a statement of faith in a moral Deity.

The second fact to be noted is that the popular methods of learning the

---

[8] *Kohen,* the Hebrew word translated "priest," in Arabic means "soothsayer" or "oracle giver," which may be the original meaning of the Semitic word.

[9] It should be noted that during and following this period all such methods suffered decline in Israel, for a considerable time, and most of these methods were prohibited (Deut. 4:19; 18:10, 11; Exod. 22:18; I Sam. 28:9; Lev. 19:26, 31; 20:6) (G. Hölscher, *Die Propheten,* 89–132, 143–173; J. Wach, *Sociology of Religion,* 331–374).

[10] Statements that most closely approach definite predictions are Amos 7:14–17, and Isaiah 7: 13–17. In the case of Amos, the prophet about 760 B.C. declared to Amaziah, the priest, that his wife would become a harlot in the city, and his sons and daughters would be slain by the sword. This was a curse, couched in the general terms of conquest and captivity. But the North did not go into captivity for almost forty years, and even then Samaria did not greatly suffer. Isaiah's message was to Ahaz in 734 B.C., stating that Damascus and Samaria would be overthrown within some three or four years (Isa. 7:18). Damascus fell in 732, and Samaria capitulated in 722 B.C. Taken as divinely inspired predictions both were inaccurate. Taken as the expressions of the certainty of doom on iniquitous peoples, both are unimpeachable. Not only is it unhistorical, but it is unethical as well to treat these reformers as the seers of a future far beyond their own horizon. They were greater than all who read "the signs of the times." They proclaimed the way of right, which is the way of God (S. A. Cook, *The O.T.; a Reinterpretation,* 108, 172; A. B. Davidson, *Theology of the O.T.,* 379).

will of Yahweh are either disregarded or indignantly rejected. The priestly practices are never mentioned with approval, and the prophetic guilds were scorned as timeserving sycophants (Amos 7:14; Mic. 3:5, 7). Amos unhesitatingly denied that he had anything in common with these guilds. He was a layman, a sheepherder, who was aware of the moral degeneracy of the nation and could not escape the conviction that vengeance was sure (Amos 7:14, 15). Micah definitely repudiated all ecstasy, but was full of the spirit of justice, to denounce transgression and sin, which was the spirit of Yahweh (Mic. 3:7, 8). Hosea's revelation came with the suffering years, in which through the tortures of disillusionment he learned that Yahweh was a kindly, forgiving God. Throughout his book there runs the peculiarly appropriate refrain, "My people perish because of lack of *knowledge*" (Hos. 4:6). This knowledge embraced experience and reason. It was wisdom of the highest type; and that wisdom was accessible to all. Isaiah speaks in the same strain. *Come let us reason together* (Isa. 1:17) is a call for good judgment, which is the court of appeal in which all ethical problems are finally settled. An equally enlightening judgment is recorded by a later writer; *Your teacher shall not be hidden* (Isa. 30:21), which is an assurance that the days of necromancy, mystic vision, and audition, in which the subject of hallucinations is granted an unutterable revelation, no longer set the test of inspiration. The teacher, with full knowledge of that which has gone before, will lead the way.[11]

The revolutionary conclusions of these four men were arrived at through normal intellectual processes. They claimed no superior gifts, had no esoteric, preparatory training, were the recipients of no special information through trance or ecstasy. They had observed the daily activities in the market, in the city gate, in the courts of justice, and at religious assemblies. They were stirred to the depths by the savage greed of business, the shady practices of judge and priest, the callousness of rulers, and the consequent suffering of the poor and needy. They knew beyond peradventure that man's inhumanity to man could not go unpunished. Sensitive to human needs, and passionately religious, each was certain that his message was axiomatic, inescapable, God's truth.

The visions they saw (Amos 7:1-9; Isa. 6:1-12a) and the voices they heard

---

11 The inspiration of the prophet is a theme of perennial interest. In early days all who acted strangely, possessed abnormal powers, uttered peculiar phrases, or spoke under great emotional strain were believed to be spirit-possessed. This theory not only became the ready explanation of all sorts of emotional upheavals, but in turn it led to the cultivation and the increase of such phenomena. Because of impressive features and supernatural claims, popularly it became the blanket theory for the origin of all Scripture. No doubt in Palestine war slogans, funeral dirges, paeans of good will, and religious oracles have from ancient days been chanted by spirit-possessed men. But that this in any way explains the inspiration of these eighth-century B.C. messages is far from convincing. Even a superficial acquaintance with them, even with Micah 3:8, suggests no "access of ecstasy," as some would imply (T. H. Robinson, *Expositor,* 1921, 217–230), but unequivocally witnesses to a matter-of-fact appreciation of justice, mercy, and humility, and a moral courage to denounce all who violated these human ideals.

came through personal reflections on everyday experiences, rather than from the heavens; and their phrases, "Oracle of Yahweh," and "Thus saith Yahweh," [12] were their inner convictions that such was right, couched in the stock phrases of the day, rather than the claim to the supernatural. Nowhere has this superb consciousness been more boldly expressed than in, *But as for me, I am full of power, by the spirit of Yahweh, . . . to declare to Jacob his transgression* (Mic. 3:8). It is this profound conviction that lay behind the change from the first to the third person, from the I to Yahweh, so often found in the prophetic books. The I and Yahweh are co-ordinate and are interchangeable because in the mind of the speaker his statements are beyond question, hence divine. In every human need and human right was heard the voice of Yahweh.

The commitment of their judgments to writing was a further innovation made by these men of affairs, or by their disciples. Earlier, folk tales and ritual codes had been put into written form; and now the convictions of these laymen on business ethics and international policies were deemed of permanent value. This was the beginning of a new order, the writing prophets, and marked an advance in religious development. It was a movement away from the incidental and the transient, the oracular and the ecstatic, toward the ethical and the reflective. To the disciples (Isa. 8:16) the written word of their masters must have been a bond of unity and a source of strength. To the Amaziahs and the Jeroboams, in all ages, these booklets have been disconcerting. Clash of opinion between those in authority and the common people, in understanding and applying their principles, has always been present. But through travail ideas are born, grow up, and conquer; and only thus do human potentials finally receive recognition. It is probable that, as the result of such conflict, local customs, ancient modes of thought, even the sterling convictions of individual prophets may have proved to be untenable; but justice, kindness, and humility—against these there is no law. They are universal, eternal principles, the Word of God and the essential features in the religion of the laymen.

---

[12] A detailed study of such words and phrases as used by these prophets has been made by S. Mowinckel, who concludes that all their experiences were states of heightened mental concentration due to the tension of ideas; that their messages were the expression of moral law; and that the stock phrases carried no specific content (*JBL*, 1934, 199–227; also J. Hempel, *Gott und Mensch im A.T.*, 95–104).

Chapter IX

THE RELIGION OF CO-OPERATION.
DEUTERONOMY. 621 B.C.

HE year 701 B.C. marked the end, so far as we know, of the active ministry of Micah and Isaiah, the last of the prophets of the Assyrian period. The result of the conflict, which for sixty years had raged between the prophets and the priests, is left largely to the imagination, as no literature now extant appeared for more than seventy years. A few scraps of history, schematic but revealing, light up the years preceding 621 B.C. In 701 B.C. Jerusalem suffered grievously at the hands of Sennacherib. If the little city was not reduced to ruins, it certainly was desolated, and Hezekiah paid an impoverishing tribute to Assyria (II Kings 18:14–16; 19:29–31). Overflowing disaster had indeed come, and to many the prophets had been vindicated (Isa. 7:20–25; 1:7–9; Mic. 3:12). But others, no doubt, attributed the calamity directly to the disrupting activities of these hard-hitting radicals.

For sixty years the Assyrian claimed the allegiance of king and country. Manasseh ruled Jerusalem from 686 to 641 B.C. and, like Ahaz of earlier days, promoted Assyrian sun worship, as a matter of good judgment if not of political necessity (II Kings 21:1–9). That he was said to have shed innocent blood very much (II Kings 21:16) is testimony to the religious strife within the city itself. Amon succeeded Manasseh, and two years later was murdered by members of the court, who in turn were slain by the people of the land, who set Josiah, a boy of eight, on the throne (II Kings 21:19, 23, 24). It was a bloody period, continuously in the throes of revolution and counterrevolution, until the crowning of Josiah in 639 B.C. The eighth-century prophets, in part at least, were responsible for the unrest. In the name of Yahweh they had split the nation in two. They had emphasized the ethical, humane, and democratic in religion, while the hierarchy had insisted that cultus had priority in Yahwism.

Under Assyrian dominance, when tribute to the foreigner and homage to his gods were required, new problems and a new line of cleavage appeared. Necessary and desirable as this subservience seemed to be to those in authority, it must have aroused the criticism of many. The rise of an anti-Assyrian party in both politics and religion was inevitable, and ultimately mutual interest could not have failed to bring the disciples of the prophets and the political insurgents into an alliance against the common foe.

Neither had the prophets lived and labored in vain, nor were the harsh results of the Assyrian regime without compensation. An objective observer during this period probably would have reported that both Judah and Yahwism had passed their zenith and were on their way out. But in religion, as in warfare, there are always the imponderables that ultimately determine the issues of the battle. While the kings and their court were proving their loyalty to Assyria, Yahwism, both old and new, was on trial. The zeal of many of the followers of the prophets must have been tempered by the lessons of history, while among the anti-Assyrian party many may have accepted the importance of ethics in religion. Thus, at least a partial *rapprochement* was achieved between two otherwise hostile groups.

All those, whether classed as anti-Assyrian or as Yahwists, who before the rising tide of terror had fled to the underground, were definitely united by a common danger and by an undying purpose. Where they lived, in caves, in palaces, or in the wilderness, how they worked, or what were their names, we do not know. But a little imagination assures us that they lived, and worked, and served the cause of Yahweh. Persecution, by its very violence, toughened the fiber that otherwise might have remained flabby. The storm, that tested the inner qualities of a man, had broken over Judah and had winnowed the chaff from the wheat. Those who daily risked their lives for their religion came from all walks of life, from the various controversial groups, and in the face of death learned to know each other better. Faced by a common enemy, and stirred by a common loyalty, superficial differences were held in abeyance, and essential principles were emphasized. Persecution was a purifying agent, and Judaism by losing its life was saving it.

A second factor contributing to the consolidation of the anti-Assyrian movement was the writings now in possession of the unknown leaders. A number of important rolls were in existence and were carefully preserved by the disciples of Yahweh, though no details have been preserved by history. The J. and the E. documents preserved in popular form much of the history and the idealism of South and North, respectively. Both were written before 722 B.C. and shortly thereafter, following the usual Semitic custom, were united in one continuous narrative. An edition of early ritual requirements of Yahweh is found in each of these (Exod. 34:14-26, J.; Exod. 20:23-26; 23:10-19, E.). The demands were simple, and stringent. Yahweh was a jealous God to whom many pagan rites were intolerable. In fundamental principle it was hostile to all foreign worship, hence Assyrian worship came under the ban. In this, all Yahweh worshipers could heartily unite. Moreover, though it was priestly, it was so simple in its requirements that if these had been the limit of the rites in the days of Amos and Isaiah, it is doubtful if their attacks on the sacrificial system would have been so violent. The writings of the prophets from Amos to Isaiah had also been inherited by these outlawed worshipers of the God of their fathers. Thus they were well furnished to bring up to date and to rewrite the religious constitution of Israel.

Prevented from public expression of their religious devotion, naturally their private reactions were intensified. Thus diverse groups, with a common goal, for more than a generation quietly operated in secret. It was a small melting pot; the heat and pressure were intense; the time, fifty years, seemed very, very long; yet from it emerged that which probably could never have been achieved so speedily and so effectively in any other way, an agreement between divergent programs, a synthesis between layman, prophet, and priest. This was embodied in an early draft of Deuteronomy, written possibly about 650 B.C. and found in the temple when it was undergoing repairs in 621 B.C., the nucleus of our book of Deuteronomy.

This "Book of the Law," when found, created a furor in Jerusalem (II Kings 22:3-19). Hilkiah found it, and read it; Shaphan read it, and then read it to the king, who in dismay appointed a representative commission to pass judgment on its worth. They took it to Huldah, the aged prophetess, who after conference with the committee pronounced it to be authoritative, and the herald of coming destruction (II Kings 22:15-20). It was brief, stirring, denounced injustice and false worship, and harked back to the days of the covenant with Yahweh. To those who had been hoping and working for the advancement of true religion, and for the uprooting of the pagan rites that still flourished in the country, it was a godsend, a weapon with which to win the final stages of the religious war.

Deuteronomy, since the days of Chrysostom, Athanasius, and Jerome, has been recognized as being, or as having within it, the book of the law discovered in 621 B.C. Some of it is pre-Mosaic; [1] a section of it is ascribed to Moses (Deut. 31:9-24); while scattered through it are many Canaanitish laws that had been adapted to the growing needs of Israel (agricultural festivals, Deut. 16:8, 9-11, 13-17; tithing, 14:22, 28). Throughout its pages the influence of the eighth-century prophets is clearly discerned, and centralization of worship (Deut. 12:5, 11, 14; 16:2, 5, 6, 11) was an interpretation, based on the deliverance of the city from the ravages of Sennacherib in 701 B.C. (II Kings 19:32-34), that such was the express will of Yahweh.

In its present form the book is composite.[2] The body of the volume, chapters 11-26, 28, because of content naturally falls into two parts, chapters 11-17,

---

[1] Many of the food taboos (Deut. 12:23; 14:7, 8, 10, 12-17) and five or more of the regulations of the ethical decalogue (Deut. 5:16-20) are social and come from earliest days; the demand for chastity (Deut. 22:13-29) originated in early tribal life; the treatment of the household slave (Deut. 15:12-18), the Levirate marriage (Deut. 25:5, 8), and the principle of blood revenge that underlay all punishment (Deut. 19:1-13; 24:16) are all prehistoric practices.

[2] The facts leading to this conclusion have been clearly presented by G. A. Smith in "Deuteronomy," Camb. B., i-xciv.

and 18-26, 28. There are two introductions, each quite different from the other, 1:1-4:44a, and 4:44b-10:22; while chapters 27 and 29-34, are appendices. Though chapters 11-17 are quite adequate to account for the reforms described so vividly in II Kings 22:1-24, it is possible that the roll found in the temple by Hilkiah consisted of 4:44b-26:19; 28:1-68, and that apart from minor editorial notes Deuteronomy, in essentially its present form, was complete by 600 B.C.

Yet, though beyond doubt the book is composite, parts of it originating in different periods and even in different sections of the country, none the less it has a marked unity. The editors had a definite theme to which available material was made subject; they had a philosophy of religion supported, they believed, by all history. Hence, to them the book was a convincing, commonsense interpretation of history and a final expression of the will of Yahweh.

The prophet, the apostle of righteousness, succeeded in having his attitude incorporated in every part of the book. His message, that sometimes had been general, is now reduced to cases and rules. To love your neighbor is a prophetic injunction; to put a coin in the hand of the needy neighbor is the rule of the priest (Deut. 15:8). Civil regulations repeating those in C.C. (Exod. 21:1-23:9), that originated in the activities of judge and priest, occupy a large place in the body of the book, but they have been so revised as to make life more tolerable for the unfortunate.[3] Here we find the prophet and the priest have worked together for the common good of the community.

The progress that had been made toward human welfare is easily recognized by a few case studies. The law for the slave (Exod. 21:1-7, E.) has been changed in Deuteronomy (Deut. 15:12-18; 23:15, 16; 24:15, 16) for the betterment of both male and female. The rights of woman are now safeguarded as never before (Deut. 22:13-21; 24:1-5), and even the maidens who are captured in war must receive what was considered decent treatment (Deut. 20:14; 21:10-14). Prostitution, which was organized as an expression of devotion to the deities of fertility, and all forms of unchastity (Deut. 23:17, 18; 22:22-30) were put under the ban. Yahweh, not Baal, was the giver of the grain, the wine, and the oil (Deut. 28:4, 18, 51), and Yahweh, who had come from the desert, was opposed to every form of sexual vice (Deut. 23:2; 27:20-23).

Many other laws that were expanded to meet the growing needs likewise reflect a more just or kindlier attitude toward those in distress. The poor must be adequately aided (Deut. 15:7-11); gleanings should not be meager (Deut. 24:19-22); servants should be paid promptly (Deut. 24:14, 15); usury must not be exacted from the brother, but the foreigner may be made to pay (Exod. 22:25; cf. Deut. 23:19, 20, where the addition is found); an escaped

---

[3] A comparison of the laws in the two codes is tabulated by C. H. Briggs, *The Higher Criticism of the Hexateuch*, 189-235; and the relation between these two, and to the code of Hammurabi, is suggested by R. H. Pfeiffer, *Introduction to the O.T.*, 210-221.

slave must be shielded (Deut. 23:15, 16); while newly married men, and those who were fainthearted, were to be relieved of military service (Deut. 20:7–9). The guilty were not to be punished beyond endurance (Deut. 25:1–3), and fathers shall not be put to death for their children, nor children for their fathers (Deut. 24:16). Those guilty of manslaughter were to be protected against rash judgment (Deut. 19:1–18, cf. Exod. 21:12–14), and care must be provided for their families. The sojourner must be treated justly, even with good will (Deut. 24:17, 18; 16:19; 10:18, 19; 1:17), and beyond all, ample provision must be made for the Levites (Deut. 18:1–5; 26:12; 16:11; 12:12, 17–19), even for those who have hitherto been officiating in cities outside of Jerusalem (Deut. 18:6–8). Amid the many petty details a warm human interest pervades the whole, but in no case does this degenerate into sentimentality. As Yahweh is no respecter of persons (Deut. 16:18, 19; 10:17, 18), justice for all is the first demand. In all this, the priest has been sitting at the feet of the prophet, learning from him. Religion is an intensely human concern, in which good will, and love, and justice are the highest expressions of loyalty to a living Yahweh.

But there is another side, we might say another voice, in the book. From beginning to end, there is a ringing call to worship; and that must be worship of the one and only God, at the one and only sanctuary (Deut. 6:4; 12:5–14; 16:5–17). Throughout previous periods worship had usually been legitimate at many shrines all the way from Dan to Beersheba. But the experiences of recent centuries had shown two things: the one, that with many shrines, each independent of all others, pagan practices easily crept in causing confusion in ritual and disturbing the national loyalties; the other, the Assyrian armies had destroyed most, if not all, of the sacred places of the South, save the temple in Jerusalem. Thus both necessity and history pointed toward the centralization of worship in Jerusalem. Best of all, in spirit this had the sanction of Moses, when all the wandering tribes had been united around a common sanctuary (Deut. 12:12–14, 18, 21; 14:24–27; 16:6, 11, 12; 26:11; 27:5). That Jerusalem was the place that Yahweh, their God, had chosen (Deut. 12:5, *et al.*) was now apparent to all.

Here the three chief festivals were to be observed (Deut. 16:1–17) by "all your households" your sons, your daughters, your menservants, your maidservants, the Levite within your gates, the sojourner, the fatherless, and the widow (Deut. 12:7, 12; 16:11) in joyous social banqueting before Yahweh, your God. The slaughter of animals for food, which occurred only on special occasions, such as the arrival of a guest, a marriage, or a death, and hitherto had always been considered a religious act that must be performed at a sanctuary, now becomes a domestic affair that may be carried out at home (Deut. 12:15, 16, 20–23). Thus a concession to human convenience removed from priestly control an ancient religious rite.

The ritual was pruned of many of the grossest foreign elements; the high places on the mountains and under every green tree were to be destroyed, the altars to be broken down, the pillars dashed in pieces, the Asherim burned with fire, the graven images hewn down, and the names of their gods destroyed out of the place (Deut. 12:2, 3, cf. II Kings 23:4–20). All divination, sorcery, enchantment, augury, child sacrifice, all abominations must be banished [4] (Deut. 18:9–14), and all idol worshipers must be put to death (Deut. 17:2–7).

At the same time, provision had been made for the observance of the whole range of offerings, burnt offerings, sacrifices, tithes, heave offerings, vows, freewill offerings, and the firstlings of the herd and flock, with fitting ceremonies, in which it is probable that all excess in ritual had been banned (Deut. 12:6). It is noteworthy that the Passover is given a place of special honor. Originating in an early festival of the shepherd (Exod. 3:18; 5:3), it is now bound in with the *Mazzoth,* or unleavened bread, of the farmer,[5] and is to be observed, "that thou mayest remember the day when thou camest forth out of the land of Egypt all the days of thy life" (Deut. 16:3). While certain very primitive regulations, such as the removal of all leaven from within their borders during seven days, and the consuming of all the sacrificial flesh before the morning (Deut. 16:4), were retained, two changes of fundamental importance were made. The slaying of the Passover lamb, which earlier had been strictly a family affair (Exod. 12:21–23, J.), now becomes centralized as a national observance (Deut. 16:5). Also the two nature festivals, now united, are made to commemorate an event in national history, "the day when thou camest forth out of . . . Egypt" (Exod. 16:3). Religion thus was lifted from the worship of deity in nature to a higher plane, in which God was recognized at work in human experience. It was a new departure, and "Surely there was not kept such a passover from the days of the judges that judged Israel, nor in all the days of the kings of Israel, nor the kings of Judah" (II Kings 23:22).

The law, the result of arduous toil and composite judgment, was well ordered, and no disregard of obligations was to be tolerated. The priest, the Levite, co-ordinate terms in Deuteronomy (Deut. 17:9, 18; 22:5; 24:8), even those who had officiated at the local, now outlaw, shrines (Deut. 18:6–8, cf. II Kings 23:9), were to be freed from financial worry (Deut. 12:12, 19; 18:1–

---

[4] A number of definite taboos have been recorded. Some of these were reactions against pagan customs such as cutting the flesh and making a baldness between the eyes for the dead (Deut. 14:1), and wearing garments of the opposite sex, a rite sanctioned at certain religious festivals, that promoted license (Deut. 22:5) (G. A. Smith, "Deuteronomy," *Camb. B.,* 260). Other taboos, such as mixing seeds, yoking together the ox and the ass, mingling wool and linen in a garment, (Deut. 22:9–11) are ordered because of the belief that God had created each species to produce seed after its kind (Gen. 1:21, 24, 25), and had instructed man aright as to how to plow, to seed, to harvest, and to thresh (Isa. 28:24–29). Crossbreeding, and all types of mixing of stuffs, was prohibited.

[5] A detailed discussion of the origin of both of these religious festivals, their union and development is found in *Ency. Bibl.,* III, 3591–3598, by I. Benzinger.

8; 14:28, 29), so that the proposed reforms could be successfully carried through. As in the past disloyalty to Yahweh had seemed the cause of all disasters, it was now decreed that such things must not happen again. Idolatry, which included all types of disloyalty, not only was proscribed, but was to be rooted out; and to achieve this end a savage system of espionage was devised. Each member of the community was called on, in the name of Yahweh, to search everywhere for apostasy, to mark any secret disloyalties in his own family, without mercy to kill brother, son, daughter, wife, or friend (Deut. 13:6–11), and to reduce to ashes any village that had forsaken Yahweh (Deut. 13:12–18). It was ferocious, a primitive scheme to stamp immorality, idolatry, and alien worship out of the community forever (Deut. 13:5; 19:16–21; 21:18–21; 22:13–30). It was the reaction of an anti-Assyrian party that for political and religious reasons had been suppressed under the strong hand of Manasseh. They had organized, may have been active in intrigue, or even in regicide (II Kings 21:23, 24), and had worked out a constitution and a program. Their confidence was rooted in the covenant idea, which tradition had pushed back to the days of Abraham (Gen. 15:1–18; 22:16–18, E.; Gen. 12:1–8; 13:14–17, J.) and had reaffirmed in the pledges at Horeb (Deut. 17:2–7; 11: 21–25). The history of five hundred years had broadened the vision, and recent persecutions had intensified the hope for a religious commonwealth that embraced all Israel, both North and South.[6]

The program called for isolation from all other peoples, as such contacts had always led to corruption in life and worship. The remembrance of the Amalakites was to be blotted out (Deut. 25:17–19) and the Canaanites, a blanket term for all the early inhabitants of the land, were to be utterly destroyed (Deut. 7:1, 2). No mercy was to be shown toward them, nor were marriages of son or daughter to be contracted with them (Deut. 7:3, 4, 16). Ammonite and Moabite were to be excluded from the assembly of Israel until the tenth generation, some three hundred years (Deut. 23:3); while Edomite and Egyptian might be granted citizenship in the third generation (Deut. 23:7, 8). Amid these marital and religious restrictions it was legitimate to take to wife any desirable woman captured from an enemy, after certain mourning rites had been observed (Deut. 21:10–14). Within the brotherhood no interest must be taken (Deut. 23:19, 20), nor was unclean meat to be sold to a member of the community (Deut. 14:21); but such rules did not apply to strangers. Business interests felt the need of a double standard.

The essential idea was rooted in early family life, which emphasized solidarity within the clan and tribe and stood aloof from, indeed often was in antagonism to, all who lay beyond the family circle. The mind of the priest,

[6] Like the prophets, the authors of Deuteronomy never recognize the division of the kingdom. In arranging the cities of refuge, the land is divided into three parts, Transjordania, Samaria, and Judah, with a city, or if necessary two, for each part, a sure sign that the writers thought of the land as united, at least in the religion of Yahweh (Deut. 19:1–10). The same is true in the Blessing of Moses (Deut. 33:2–29), written by 750 B.C. Here all the tribes are reckoned in Israel.

absorbed in the affairs of deity, rites and taboos, genealogies and festivals, and the spirit of the prophet, concerned with the affairs of men, justice, chastity, and human dignity, had co-operated to produce this comprehensive program. Thus nationalism had become a religion, and Israel a holy people, unto Yahweh their God. "Yahweh thy God has chosen thee to be a people for his own possession, above all peoples that are upon the face of the earth" (Deut. 7:6; 14:2, 21; 26:17–19; 28:1–6, 9–13).

Instruction in national history, in correct rites of worship, and in correct social conduct was to be carried out so that the program might be effective. "Thou shalt teach the commandments, the statutes, and the ordinances diligently to thy children, and shalt talk of them when thou sittest in thy house, and when thou walkest by the way, and when thou liest down, and when thou risest up" (Deut. 6:7; 11:19; 4:9; 6:20–23; 32:7). "Thou shalt bind them for a sign upon thy hand, and they shall be as frontlets between thine eyes. And thou shalt write them upon the door-posts of thy house, and upon thy gates" (Deut. 6:8, 9), and shall "lay up these my words in your heart and in your soul" (Deut. 11:18). You must remember, and not forget, to the end that "ye shall observe to do all the statutes and the ordinances which I set before you this day" (Deut. 11:1, 32). Thus, there was provided an informal system of religious education, which called on all responsible members of the community, in the name of Yahweh, for the future of the nation to exercise their gifts. That the program might meet all future emergencies, the priests at Jerusalem were to have final jurisdiction over all difficult cases that might arise, but they were required to teach according to the tenor of the law (Deut. 17:8–13); while assurance was given that there would always be a prophet, or a succession of prophets, who would make known the will of Yahweh (Deut. 18:15–19). This whole educational program, though built up on the work of earlier prophets and priests, was a decided advance in both scope and spirit over the achievements of the ancestors. Well was it said of this law code, "It is not too hard for thee, neither is it far off. It is not in heaven. . . . Neither is it beyond the sea. . . . But the word is very nigh unto thee, in thy mouth, and in thy heart, that thou mayest do it" (Deut. 30:11–14).

Deuteronomy, with its safeguards against false worship, its genuinely human interests, and its appeal to the inner nature, stands near the top of those books that have been of greatest influence in the world. To its authors it was final; for their purpose infallible, the Word of God. *Cursed be he that confirmeth not the words of this law to do them* (Deut. 27:26), and *Lay up these words in your heart, . . . and teach them to your children. . . . There shall no man be able to stand before you* (Deut. 11:18–25), express the conviction that these commands came from Yahweh, the God of Israel's history, from Horeb on down through the ages. *Ye shall not add to the word which I command you, neither shall ye diminish from it,* found in Deuteronomy 4:2, and again at the beginning of the demand to wipe out all idolatry and idolaters, without mercy (Deut. 12:32), may not have been in the earliest draft of the law, but it fittingly expresses the belief of the unnamed collaborators who set up this program to insure national security.

This book, found in the eighteenth year of the reign of King Josiah, and accredited by the royal commission, became the chart for Judah's faith and conduct in 621 B.C. Before the assembled multitude the roll was read; the king solemnly pledged himself to walk after Yahweh, to keep his commandments, and his statutes, and his testimonies with all his heart, and to confirm the words of the covenant that were written in the book; and all the people stood to the covenant (II Kings 23:1–3). Cold words are these, but the response was electric; the long-awaited day of vengeance had come. Destroy the abominations of Baal and Assyrian worship; tear the Asherah out of the temple; throw down the houses of the temple prostitutes; smash the high places throughout the country, and around the city; desecrate the altar of Moloch in Tophet; burn the chariots of the sun-god, and slaughter the horses of the sun; wreck and grind to dust the sanctuaries of Chemosh and Milcom; rip off the roof altars of the Assyrian deities (II Kings 23:4–14). It was a wild orgy of destruction, the wrath lust of a mob let loose against the symbols of a long-hated tyranny. But Bethel and the cities of the North, if a late editor can be trusted, did not escape the whirlwind (II Kings 23:15–20). High places were destroyed; altars were broken down; the Asherah was burned; and sepulchers were rifled and the bones were burned on the altars. Nor could the religious leaders of the old regime evade the fury. The false priests at the high places in Judah and around Jerusalem and the priests who had burned incense to Baal and the host of heaven were exterminated (II Kings 23:5), and in all the cities of Samaria "he slew all the priests of the high places that were there, upon the altars" (II Kings 23:20). It was a gruesome, bloody reform, vying with that of Jehu; and again it might be written, the streets of Jerusalem ran blood. Revolutions have ever been most thoroughgoing among those who have a genius for religion.

Nevertheless, it was a new day, a birth day in Israel; and birth, that is always accompanied by pangs, is also marked by joy and jubilation. The Passover was celebrated, such a Passover as had never before been known in Israel (II Kings 23:21–23). It was a sacrament, a holy communion, gladly participated in by those who had harkened so diligently to the voice of Yahweh, their God, to observe and to do all his commandments (Deut. 28:1). By fulfilling the radical conditions they had removed the curse that had overshadowed them (Deut. 28:15–68) and had become a holy people who now could claim prosperity in flock, in field, and in family, and freedom, leadership, and prestige among the nations of the world (Deut. 28:2–14).

Slaughter and destruction for the gratification of passion is devilish; but the excision of a tumor, the removal of a chronic criminal from society, or the wreckage of a death-trap building may be the first step to health and happiness. The Deuteronomic purge was drastic, but its program did not stop there. It prescribed a constructive outline for religion that was comprehensive, vital, and even unique. The king, the chief figure in the new order, must possess a copy of the law, and must read therein all the days of his life (Deut. 17:14-20). Priest and prophet were reconciled, and ethics and religion had been blended in one. The teacher, whose interests combined history, ethics, and ritual, was set to work, and intelligence displaced the old ecstasy and vision. The people, few and impoverished, but purified and strengthened by suffering, united in pledging loyalty to Yahweh—"our God is Yahweh alone"(Deut. 6:4; II Kings 23:3).

This totalitarian co-operation was due in part to the long repression under Manasseh, during which warring schools of Yahweh worshipers had learned to live together; but the book itself had healing power. It called for justice for all, and made provision for the unfortunate. One motif, love, not legalism, dominated all its requirements. One holy place, where ritual could be safeguarded, was solemnly set apart for the worship of all; and the one book, the book of the covenant, now became an authentic guide for all the needs of life. Thus as one people they responded to the call to love Yahweh, their God, with all their heart, and with all their soul, and with all their might (Deut. 6:5). This was one of the thrilling moments in religious history. Sobering as its gory prelude had been, the pledged covenant was even more serious. The war had been won; will the victory be lost?

One fact, at least, becomes immediately clear. So great was the enthusiasm for this reform that in the course of a generation (621–600 B.C.) a group of disciples had carefully worked over the history of Israel, both North and South, and had transformed it into sacred history. Availing themselves of the abundant source material at hand, and guided by the thesis of Deuteronomy—that evil brought punishment and obedience brought material prosperity, freedom from plague, and victory—they gathered together and edited much of our present Genesis, Exodus, Numbers, Joshua 1:1-12:24, and all of Deuteronomy, Judges, I and II Samuel, and I Kings. In these books we have a philosophy of history, rather than history. Implicit in this is the belief that religion is part of the stream of life and is never quite apart from it, that Yahweh is found in human experience and is the God of history.[7]

The book was a peculiar treasure, and the Jews became the "people of the book." From this were derived two results: First, learning, loving, and obeying the commandments beyond question shaped the destiny of Israel. It was their chief bond of unity and strength when, in 597, and again in 586 B.C., the country was ravaged, the city destroyed, the temple razed, and those who escaped

---

[7] S. A. Cook, *The O.T.; a Reinterpretation*, 185, 186, considers that in Deuteronomy there is "a high social morality, a noble humanism . . . ; and common humanity is the motive for . . . various requirements."

the edge of the sword were scattered, impoverished, and exiled. They had the book. Its emphasis on conduct and character, its attacks on pagan worship, its appeal to racial pride and hope, and its insistence on the presence of a just God immunized the leaders against much of the immorality, idolatry, and superstitions in the religions of the nations. It is not too much to say that Deuteronomy aided greatly in the organization and the preservation of Judaism.

The other result was different, and looks beyond provincial values to basic principles in religion. The Deuteronomic school held a twofold view of history. One, that in the long run the good always prospered in the material sense, and that the evil were always punished in this life; the other, that all history converged to prove that Israel was the chosen people of God. Both conclusions were based on a limited observation of the facts of history; and both were false. The one ignored the essential nature of man; the other was the product of wishful thinking. Both are current theories among most primitives; but nowhere have they taken deeper root, especially the second one, than in certain sections of Judaism, and in sects of her daughter religion Christianity. By placing the emphasis on things which are material, and by reducing deity to a local partisan they were prejudicial to the deeper moods of man and the higher ranges of religion. Both were vigorously combated by later writers in the Old Testament, but they appeal to prejudice and to the things of sense, so they persist. The program that was serviceable to tide over a crisis carried with it incentives and aims that were of a low order and thereby became a barrier to progress. It laid strong foundations for the hierarchy but, in like measure, it hampered the free spirit of the prophet. It was the response to a good book, but the book was neither final nor infallible.

The religion of co-operation, based on mutual compromise, aroused an overwhelming response. For more than a decade an infectious confidence in the national future swept the country. The people had performed the will of Yahweh and thus were assured of their deliverance. Then clouds began to gather, and darken. Within a decade the storm broke; the end had come. Jubilation had been short-lived; the promise had failed. But the book, a conspicuous monument to religious co-operation, remains.

Chapter X

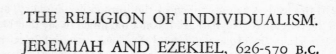

THE RELIGION OF INDIVIDUALISM.
JEREMIAH AND EZEKIEL, 626-570 B.C.

Jeremiah is known to us chiefly through the book that bears his name, and that, following the translation of Kimchi, appropriately opens with the phrase "the *history* of Jeremiah" (Jer. 1:1). As with many notable personalities, tradition, eager to add to his achievement, greatly distorted his figure. Unfounded legends credited him with concealing the sacred fire, the tabernacle, the ark, and the altar of incense in a rock chamber in the mountain from which Moses had beheld the heritage of God (II Macc. 2:1-8), and ascribe to him, as well as to Baruch, a number of booklets that neither furnish information nor add to the stature of the prophet.[1] Thus outside the book bearing his name we have no reliable information.

The book of Jeremiah, in which there is much confusion, was the result of a long process. It was not until twenty-two years after the beginning of his public ministry that he dictated to Baruch, a friend and scribe, a résumé of his early oracles (Jer. 36:1-31). The personal experience of the years between 626 B.C. and 604 B.C., it may be assumed, not only determined the selection of the material but even changed the expressions and the emphasis. When the first copy was burned by an irate monarch (Jer. 36:22-25), a second roll was written, "and there were added besides unto them many like words" (Jer. 36:32). This, the nucleus of our present book, is probably all contained within the following chapters: 1-9; 11:1-12:16; 14:1-17:18; 22:1-19; 25:1-14. Jeremiah lived and taught at least eighteen years longer, during which time Baruch continued as scribe and editor for his master. He is usually accepted as the author of biographical material that is marked by Deuteronomic phraseology and speaks of Jeremiah in the third person. By 586 B.C., the close of the activity of the prophet, he had compiled various of his oracles, giving them an historical setting, combining them into booklets such as Jeremiah, chapters 13; 18-20; 23: 9-22; 27-29; 30-31; and, uniting these with the earlier booklet, had edited the collection as a whole. But the process of interpretation and accretion continued for four hundred years. Chapters 40-49, the oracles against the nations, found in the Septuagint following Jeremiah 23:13, and chapters 50-52 are with good reason considered to come from the scribes.[2] The clearest evidence of continued editorial activity comes from the Septuagint, which was not translated earlier

---

[1] See R. H. Charles, *Ency. Bibl.*, I, 252, 256.
[2] F. Schwally, *ZAW*, VIII, 177-217, who has been followed by many.

than 200 B.C., and lacks some 12½ per cent, or 2,700 words, of what is found in the Hebrew text. Scribes never intentionally omitted; they often added for the sake of clarity. This seems conclusive evidence that even four centuries after the death of Jeremiah and Baruch, editors were still treating Jeremiah generously.[3]

The oracles that unequivocably were from Jeremiah can be segregated and appreciated only by the disciplined student. In 1901 B. Duhm, guided by a rigorous method, insisting that the poet wrote nothing save what was in the *kinah* measure, assigned some sixty short poems to the prophet. These, as polished and interpreted by Duhm, shone with rare splendor, and this critical work was the beginning of new Jeremianic studies. Much has been done, but the end is not yet.[4] The result is that we are able to see and here Jeremiah at work, and follow him in his personal reactions in four crises in his life, during crucial national experiences. His oracles are gems of rarest beauty. The vigor, the terseness, and the realism of the illuminating phrase, the simplicity of the metaphor, the lyric beauty of the poems, so attuned to the melodies of nature, and the wistful poignancy ever throbbing through the verse, these place him in the front rank of poets (cf. Jer. 2:13, 24, 32; 4:11, 23–29; 5:8; 8:14–9:1; 15:5–9). His awareness of world movements, his withering judgment of religious officialdom, his faith in the competence of the individual, and his unwavering confidence in the triumph of right, these place him among the great prophets of all ages. His personal response to the highest and holiest in the human heart, integrated in the shrinking sensitiveness and the granitelike courage of his character, make him an outstanding leader in religion among a people without superior in religious leadership.

Jeremiah, of whom we know more than of any other Old Testament character, was born about 650 B.C. His early childhood was spent under the cloud of Manasseh's pro-Assyrian rule. His home village, Anathoth of Benjamin, that lay some three miles north by northeast of Jerusalem, had a priestly tradition through the disinherited Abiathar (I Kings 2:26, 27). Manasseh died in 639 B.C., and within two years his successor, Amon, was murdered; the murderers, in turn, were slain, and the boy prince Josiah was placed on the throne (II Kings 21:18–26). These were disturbing days for responsive youth. Political tensions and religious ferment were everywhere. Problems of party prestige and national destiny, of loyalty to Canaanitish Baal, to Assyrian Ashur, to Egyptian Amon, or to pro-prophetic or pro-priestly Yahwism were vehemently

[3] Conventional phrases such as "saith Yahweh," and "the word that came from Jeremiah from Yahweh saying," the former found sixty-four times, and the latter ten times in the Hebrew but are absent from the Septuagint (A. S. Peake, "Jeremiah," in *Century Bible Commentary*, I, 65–67). Also long sections such as 10:6–8; 29:14; 30:10–12; 33:14–26; 39:4–13; 52:28–33, found in the Hebrew, are lacking in the Septuagint. F. Giesebrecht, *Das Buch Jeremia*, xix–xxxiv, presents a detailed study of the differences between the two texts.

[4] A critical analysis of the book and an estimate of the important contributions made to the study since the beginning of the century are found in R. H. Pfeiffer, *Introduction to the O.T.*, 500–511.

discussed in the village byways by heated partisans. After the crowning of King Josiah, the party in power wisely developed internal resources and quietly laid the foundations for co-operation between conflicting parties. Such schemes prospered, owing to the decline of Assyria, which was hastened by schism within and hostilities beyond her borders. Gradually preparations for the restoration of an acceptable worship of Yahweh in Jerusalem were completed.

Jeremiah, restless and vigorous, listening to the claims and counterclaims of rival parties, familiar with the teaching of earlier prophets, sensitive to the voice within that scorned the base and acclaimed the noble, was learning to discriminate in the realm of human values. In the thirteenth year of the reign of King Josiah, 626 B.C., though a youth, he could no longer restrain himself. Certain facts were beyond dispute. The current practices of the nation and the international movements proclaimed the doom of his people. Cheating and lying in the market place, inhumanity and immorality on every hand, altars to the gods of the nations everywhere, temple women and parasite priests in the temple were the heralds of ruin. Yahweh, who had led his people in the wilderness, and brought them into a garden, had been loyal; but they by their iniquities had forsaken the living waters for broken cisterns, and had behaved like slaves rather than freemen (Jer. 2:5, 6, 13).

On the national frontiers he saw the gathering storm. The Scythians, an invading horde from the far north, were desolating the lands, laying waste the cities, and spreading panic among the peoples.[5] To Jeremiah it seemed that these, like earlier invaders, would swarm over the land, pillaging and slaying (Jer. 1:11–15; 4:5–9, 20), and like the eighth-century prophets he believed such disasters were punishment for the prevailing social injustice, which was evidence of disloyalty to a righteous God (Jer. 4:18, 22; 5:1, 4, 25–29).[6] To him as to his predecessors a drastic change in human relations was the required evidence of true religion, and the only surety of deliverance.

Thus for five years, in oracles probably recited first at Anathoth and later in the streets of Jerusalem, he called on the people to repent, and thus escape the Scythian terror that was on the horizon. Chapters 1 to 6, written twenty-three years after he began to preach, contain the residuum of his messages during these years.[7] Chapter 1 indicates the inner conflict of the prophet before and

---

[5] Herodotus informs us that between 630 and 624 B.C. they threatened Egypt and were bought off. There is no evidence that they molested the peoples living on the hills of Palestine (Herodotus, I, 103–107).

[6] While the worship of Baal, and various religious rites such as burning incense are attacked (Jer. 1:16; 3:2, 3; 2:8, 20, 23, 27, 28), this may indicate the attitude of Baruch, the editor, who was influenced by both the phrases and the ideas of Deuteronomy. It is clear that the burden of the prophetic message from 626 to 621 B.C. was on justice and truth (Jer. 5:2).

[7] It is evident that we now possess only the gist of these early oracles. Poems originally recognizing the Scythian, a loosely organized rabble (Jer. 4:5–8), as the agent of destruction by 603 B.C. were rephrased to suit the Babylonian army that was then to be feared (Jer. 4:13, 19–21, 29; 5:15–17; 6:1–6, 22–26). As stated by G. A. Smith, material cogent in 621 B.C. had lost much of its significance before 603 B.C., and vice versa (*Jeremiah*, 111–134).

during his long ministry. It is condensed; a phrase reveals a scene; a sentence crystallizes within it an act; and a paragraph covers the life drama of the prophet (Jer. 1:4–9). Reluctant to speak, timid, distrustful of his own ability, and conscious of antagonisms, nevertheless the inner conviction that he was ordained to be the spokesman of Yahweh was inescapable.

The prophets of the preceding century, Hosea in particular, were his masters. Self-evident facts showed that Judah was corrupt; a good man could scarcely be found (Jer. 5:1); and profligacy had become the norm (5:1–5, 30, 31; 6:7, 13, 14), so that the people considered themselves innocent (5:11, 12; 2:23, 35). That destruction was inevitable was the deduction drawn from history, prophecy, and inner conviction, in all of which Yahweh was ever at work. But Jeremiah shrank from being the mouthpiece of the curses of an angry God. The emotional conflict between doubt and certitude, between desire and duty, has been summarized as a conversation with Yahweh.

It is an interesting dialogue permitting us, beneath the Oriental phraseology,[8] to catch a glimpse of the mental processes of one peculiarly sensitive to the moral and spiritual problems of his people. While the leaders, occupied with daily routine, were indifferent to moral issues, Jeremiah saw the swiftly approaching doom as the result of national wickedness. His higher self cried out, Your duty is to warn the leaders of the menace and call them to repentance. His lower self replied, I am too young for so great a mission. The higher self argued, Duty is not a matter of years, it is a question of understanding. The lower self answered, I am afraid of the leaders; they are intrenched in office, and have power; I am alone. The higher self responded, Duty has always been matched by power to perform; such was the law before you were born. The lower self, It is quite gratuitous; they will not listen. The higher self, Open your eyes and look (Jer. 1:11, 13) on the power of Yehweh. He, the God of nature, of armies, and of morals, has touched your lips, and it is his words that are in your mouth; go, for he is with you to deliver you.

His sincerities were deep enough to triumph over his disinclinations, and his faith strong enough to conquer his diffidence. To warn was gratuitous, to refuse would have been ignominious.

This inner struggle—or the call of the prophet—bears a general similarity, with marked differences, to that of Isaiah (6:1–12). Isaiah saw Yahweh, "high and lifted up," a transcendent Deity; while to Jeremiah, here as elsewhere (Jer. 1:6; 6:11; 11:19; 12:1; 18:20; 20:7, 17), Yahweh is immediate, intimate, and immanent; "his hand . . . touched my mouth" (Jer. 1:9). These two expressions by two of the great religious leaders in Israel but emphasize different aspects of similar experiences. Neither should be forgotten—the inner voice

---

[8] Frequently repeated phrases such as "The word of Yahweh came unto me" (Jer. 1:4, 11, 13) and "Yahweh said to me" (Jer. 1:7, 9, 12, 14, 15) are purely formal, and express strong personal conviction. See P. Volz, in *Kommentar z. A.T.*, 2.

that is sovereign, and the vision of the "enduring power, not ourselves, that makes for righteousness." These two are phases of the same thing.

The voice within never ceased asking Jeremiah, What do you see? And the answer, I see an almond tree (Jer. 1:11), a boiling pot (Jer. 1:13), a potter at work (Jer. 18:2), good and bad figs in the market place (Jer. 24:1-3), in each case furnished a telling expression of the "word of Yahweh." He brought to mind incidents in national and international history, the wilderness experience (Jer. 2:1-3), the Egyptian bondage (Jer. 2:6, 20; 7:22-25), the entrance into Canaan (Jer. 2:7), the Assyrian campaign (Jer. 2:18, 36), the destruction of Shiloh (Jer. 7:12-14), the Scythian and Babylonian invasions (Jer. 1:14, 15; 4:5-8; 5:15-17), the Egyptian army on the frontiers (Jer. 22:15-17; 37:5-10), and therein he read the judgments of the Eternal. These pages are crowded, not only with historical material that may have come from the pen of Baruch, but with clear-cut convictions derived by the prophet from factual evidence concerning high officials such as Pashhur (Jer. 20:1-6), Coniah (Jer. 22:24-30), Jehoiakim (Jer. 36:29-31), the prophets Hananiah (Jer. 28:1-17), Ahab, Zedekiah, and Shemiah (Jer. 29:21-32), and Nebuchadnezzar (Jer. 25:9). But it was the sight of the abominable iniquities and the heartless inhumanities rampant in every quarter that dominated all his utterances. "As a cage is full of birds, so are their houses full of deceit. . . ." An astonishing and horrible thing has happened; the rich have waxed fat at the expense of the poor, the prophets have been false, the priests have ruled for profit, and "my people love to have it so" (Jer. 5:25-30). All such, by their very nature, were self-destroying (Jer. 3:9; 5:25; 6:7), and as it was axiomatic that justice was inescapable, even in his imprecations he identified himself with Yahweh (Jer. 11:12, 22; 15:15; 17:18; 18:19; 20:11). No vision or hallucination, only observation and moral sense were needed for such conclusions.[9] He could not escape nature, nor history, nor himself, nor Yahweh, who was

---

[9] Within recent years it has been suggested that Jeremiah was the subject of ecstasy and hallucination similar to members of the prophetic guilds, and that his oracles were the product of such experiences (G. Hölscher, *Die Propheten*, 294, 295). It is true that such abnormalities were commonplaces in Palestine, and were held to be the work of spirits. Such phenomena, then, would not only be accepted as evidence of the activity of a spirit, but the prevalent belief itself would contribute to the phenomena. In such an atmosphere, ecstasy would be an easy and effective method of approach for the prophet, and a few of Jeremiah's phrases and acts lend themselves to this interpretation. But other facts in the situation loom large. One is that the language of the day had been inherited from primitive times, when the séance was common, but as in all language the meaning must be determined in its own setting. Jeremiah, like the ethical prophets, used the phrases, "I saw," "I heard," "Yahweh showed me," "Yahweh said to me," but these were used in reference to common sights, everyday experiences, or personal convictions that were axiomatic; that in these he was the victim of ecstasy or of hallucination is discredited by the very nature and the content of his oracles. Much soberer is the interpretation of S. A. Cook, "The prophets were not mystics— there is for them no *unio mystica*—they were intensely realist and rationalist. Yahweh was *within* all that was real and rational; and it was his 'word' rather than any spirit of ecstasy that moved them" (*The O.T.; a Reinterpretation*, 188, 189).

revealing himself in all. The clearest-eyed of his day, likewise he was the bravest of the brave.

The spirit of his early messages, 626–621 B.C., is summarized in the call, "Stand ye in the ways and see, and ask for the old paths, where is the good way; and walk therein, and ye shall find rest for yourselves" (Jer. 6:16). These paths, as the whole context shows, were to be found in the teachings of the writing prophets, whose ethical and religious ideals the youth had absorbed, becoming aflame with their self-evident and vital teachings. With burning words he demanded that the nation put away its futile worship (Jer. 6:20) and return to Yahweh in truth, and in justice, and in right doing (Jer. 4:4). It was the old message, but the voice was new. His interrogatives: Has Yahweh been unrighteous (Jer. 2:5)? Have the isles of Kittim, or Kedar, changed their gods (Jer. 2:11)? Is Israel a slave (Jer. 2:14)? imposed self-judgment on the guilty. His illustrations: Israel is a wild ass in her heat (Jer. 2:24), or a stallion roaming at large (Jer. 5:8), were unforgettable and unforgivable comparisons. His accusations, from which none was exempt (Jer. 5:21, 23, 26–30), cut deep like a whiplash into the quivering flesh; while his personality carried with it terror to the guilty. They fought against him, but did not prevail (Jer. 1:19).

The year 621 B.C. as intimated in the preceding study was the beginning of a new era for Israel, the dream of a new nation. The book of Deuteronomy, a co-operative venture of priest and prophet, was accepted as a constitution, embodying a statement of faith, for the community.

Jeremiah was thus faced by a serious dilemma. For five years he had been condemning public morals and denouncing public worship (4:3; 6:18, 20). But the emphasis in this program was different. Here cultus stood on almost an equal footing with righteousness, though not ahead of it. It was radically divergent from the demands he had so vehemently reiterated during the past five years. A sensitive soul, he must have been sorely perplexed as he faced the immediate issue. To forsake the old paths, which were so full of values? To join hands with those whom he knew and whom he had attacked so unsparingly? To adopt a compromise in religion, and unite with the fickle throng that today stood with the king? Or in this upsurge of popular patriotism to stand alone? It was a trying, testing time. The roll, however, emphasized justice; it was kindly toward the widow and the orphan, the poor and the slave; and it demanded that many of the abominations in the ritual should be removed. To stand alone, a voice crying in the wilderness, or to join actively in the official reform that had caught the imagination of the multitude? To stand alone, like Elijah and Micaiah, or to co-operate with the accepted institutions of the day? And the prophet, not yet thirty years of age, with what misgivings we know not, joined the national movement for the improvement of morals.[10] It was an adventure in the trial-and-error method, the only method by which the will of God has ever been made known to mankind, and history alone can declare its value.

Thus the die was cast, and Jeremiah made an itinerary through the villages of Judah, preaching the words of the covenant (11:1, 6). Unanimous as the acceptance of the book of the covenant was reported to have been (II Kings 23:3), it would be too much to believe there had been unhesitating approval. Further, whosoever ventured to tell the villagers that the shrines of their ancestors were no longer legitimate, owing to the new, national worship of Yahweh, was likely to stir up opposition. That many of these high places had been laid in ruins in 701 B.C., and that later they had been defiled by pagan rites, would weigh but little against the preferences and prejudices of the local inhabitants.

Jeremiah, never ingratiating, added nothing to his popularity by advising the villagers that rites and ceremonies outside of Jerusalem were no longer permissible. At Anathoth, his home village, the storm broke. The home people had long listened to his tirades against their time-honored practices. His old neighbors had suffered from his stinging epithets and were annoyed at his arrogant assumptions and indignant at his unbridled egotism. His present demands, that they should do away with the local altar and disestablish the native priesthood, passed the limit of endurance. So they plotted, "Let us cut him off from the land of the living," and through perfectly natural channels, his own eyes and ears, Yahweh revealed this plot to him (11:18, 19).

What a shock to a godly man, doing his duty in the light of conscience, to meet with such a reception from his own people! And these people he knew: easygoing, complacent, traditionalists; punctilious in local worship, commonplace in morals, grown wealthy through wickedness (12:1-3). They, an indolent, corrupt community, sought to slay him, the single-minded, conscientious servant of Yahweh. His mind was in a turmoil, and in an emotional outburst, in the name of Yahweh he cursed them: Let war and famine slay their young men and maidens, so that there shall be no remnant left to them (11:20-23). Nothing less than total annihilation of the stubborn, provincially minded natives of Anathoth could be the will of God.

Natural as it was to doom the antagonists by the power of the magic curse, a new problem not so easily settled was thereby introduced. The people of Anathoth prospered in spite of his curse, and in face of the explicit teaching of Deuteronomy 28:15-19, 20-68, which was a summary of the religion of the

---

10 Old Testament students are divided as to whether Jeremiah took any part in this reform or not. A. B. Davidson, "Jeremiah," *HBD* (five vols.), II, p. 570, and others dissent, as a formal championship of Deuteronomy would have been very unlike him; and those sections of the present Jeremiah that have been taken as supporting his activity on behalf of the reform are the work of Deuteronomic editors. More recently J. P. Hyatt finds evidence suggesting that the beginning of the prophet's ministry was not until after the reform (*JBL*, 1940, 499-513). The majority, however, still hold to the older position (G. A. Smith, *Jeremiah*, 134-161).

fathers and the prophets; while the good, notwithstanding the age-long promise of prosperity, suffered. Wherefore doth the way of the wicked prosper, was his heart-felt wail.

Jeremiah had inside information on this problem, that was not in accord with the inherited view of the ethical responsibilities of Deity. Nor was he alone in this skepticism. Zephaniah, a contemporary, intimates that there were those who were convinced that Yahweh will do no good, neither will he do evil, or, as Moffatt reads, "The Eternal never does anything" (Zeph. 1:12), that is, God is not responsible for either prosperity or calamity. Later, Habakkuk, Job, and Jesus each objects to the traditional theology.

Jeremiah, after his exasperating experience, approaches the problem with a fine reverence: "Righteous art thou, O Yahweh, . . . yet I would reason the cause with you" (12:1). Thus, by definitely raising and clearly stating the problem, a long step was taken toward its solution. The insistent seeker always finds light, even though it only dissolves his illusions, and plunges him into deeper perplexities.[11] Jeremiah's question was not answered, but Jeremiah himself was. He learned a lesson. How long he waited before light came is uncertain, but the wisdom of the years is expressed in, *If you have run with the footmen, and they have wearied you, how can you contend with horses? And if in a peaceful land you have sought shelter, what will you do in the flood tide of the Jordan* (12:5)? A theological question had been asked; another question, much more profound, a test of character, was the only answer.

Jeremiah was to learn through long years that conflicts of ever increasing intensity, with high and low, were his destiny. Life with Yahweh was not lived on a sequestered inland lake, or in a shady shepherd vale. It was out on a wind-swept ocean, where ever and anon storms, that tested the courage, endurance, and wisdom of the sailor, lashed the face of the deep. Life led up from the peaceful pasture lands, by a succession of ever higher hilltops, up to the still higher peaks and broader visions that lay beyond. The struggle never ended, but strength and vision came as its reward.

Jeremiah, by this experience, was brought to an abrupt stop, and for thirteen years, from 621 to 608 B.C., we can find no sure word of or from him. Yet, while he was silent, the destiny of nations was rapidly unfolding before his eyes, and his judgments were being re-formed. The Scythians had disappeared. The Medes from the eastern mountains marched west, and in 612 B.C. they leveled Nineveh to the ground. A few years later the ancient nation of Assyria passed off the stage of history. Nahum, a Hebrew patriot, described

11 Madame Curie seeking to free radium from pitchblende failed 5,676 times before success crowned her efforts, but her first question was no less important than her final experiment. So first questions concerning origins of the world, man, sin, the moral order, and redemption, and primitive conclusions, though never final, were worthy steps toward the light.

the fighting in the streets of Nineveh with the detail of an eyewitness who took peculiar delight in watching the prancing horses and bounding chariots as they drove over the great heap of corpses piled in the broad ways (Nahum 2:3–3:19). Yahweh had wreaked his vengeance on the bloody city. The Chaldeans—Neo-Babylonians—from southern Mesopotamia, by 626 B.C. were moving toward world empire. Forming an alliance with the Medes, they followed up the Median destruction of Nineveh by overthrowing Harran, the new Assyrian capital, in 611 B.C., and later still attacked Carchemish, the capital of an Aramaean state.

Egypt, likewise, bestirred herself, and under Pharaoh Necho began dreaming of world conquest. In 608 B.C., spurred on by the events in the north, in order to intercept the conquering Chaldean army Necho sent his forces up along the border of Palestine. Good King Josiah seems to have become the victim of his religious theories. He had proved his devotion to Yahweh by observing to do all the commandments of Yahweh (II Kings 23:3–25). The prosperity of the following thirteen years seemed to confirm the assurances of the book (Deut. 28:1, 7, 13). Hoping for the establishment of the promised, glorious kingdom, in which Samaria and Judah would again be one (II Sam. 7:12–16), he led his handful of soldiers against the Egyptian army at Megiddo (II Kings 23:29). It was a heroic adventure in faith; but it proved to be an act of folly, founded on sand. Yahweh did not unleash his thunderbolts, nor did he palsy the arm of the enemy, as folklore loved to picture ancient ventures. Josiah was slain; the army was scattered; a new king was anointed, and in three months was removed by Necho, who replaced him by the pliable puppet Jehoiakim, who collected a heavy tribute for his Egyptian master (II Kings 23:31–37). Thus the high hopes fostered by the reformation were crushed, and Israel's dream of nationhood passed into the twilight zone. The thesis that obedience to the commands of Yahweh would insure prosperity at home and victory abroad had not been sustained by the realities of history. Defeat, grinding taxation, humiliation, subjugation had been the rewards of this devotion. A deathblow had been dealt to the old theology that suffering and tragedy were always commensurate with sin.

Jeremiah, during these years of silence, was observing, reflecting, and learning. Certain tendencies implicit in human nature came to light during this decade. The enthusiasm of the mass reform movement cooled off rapidly in some quarters. When the villagers returned home from Jerusalem the perspective had changed. The city was now fifteen or twenty miles distant, and centralization of all worship suggested hardships; the appeal of the local sanctuary also had gained with proximity. Here the old-time religion, of the family, and the village, had always been observed. To annul it would dishonor the ancestors, a most irreligious deed.

Even in Jerusalem some priests were not enthusiastic over some phases of the law. Provision had been made that Levites from the village shrines should participate in the rites and the benefits of the central sanctuary (Deut. 18:6-8), but objections from some source prevented this from becoming the practice (II Kings 23:9). Nor could a competent priesthood have been quite happy with the restriction, "Thou shalt not add thereto, nor diminish therefrom" (Deut. 12:32). Indeed, within a generation a priestly group promulgated Holiness Code (Lev. 17–26), which is largely interested in rites and ceremonies not even mentioned in Deuteronomy. This was a protest against the inadequacies of the earlier law. Also interpreters went to work, and at an early date introduced the phylacteries and the *mezzuzoth,* symbols by which the law, "Thou shalt bind them as a sign upon your hand, . . . and write them on the doorposts of your house" (Deut. 6:8, 9), easily degenerated into a formalism feared by all prophets. In the same spirit, the book soon came to be considered the infallible Word of God, and they became the "people of the book." Thus with an inviolable temple and an infallible book many believed themselves to be immune from all danger.

Jeremiah, who during these crises was close by, if not actually living in Jerusalem, was sensitively alert to the bland indifference of the strong toward the welfare of the underprivileged, the swing toward ritual by the priesthood, and the shallow national hope that rested on a false hypothesis. The death of Josiah must have clarified his vision, and may have crystallized his convictions as to essential values in life. The experiment of 621 B.C. had failed. Its leaders had erred, and confusion reigned. The guideposts so carefully set up, so wholeheartedly adopted, had led to a false hope, and to disaster. The leaders had been sincere, but sincerity alone is never enough. Jeremiah had co-operated, but he had been wrong. To repent, and to acknowledge his error was a test of character. He reversed his judgment of earlier years and proved his integrity.

Now, if ever, was the opportune time for the right word, the essential emphasis. He could not withhold, and his message in this crisis is preserved in chapters 7:1–8:9; while 26:1–24 provides the biographical background. His pronouncements, at this time, are in line with his characteristic approach. To pluck up and to break down was the commission, and never did prophet face so ominous a task more heroically. He was now convinced that he knew both the cause and the cure for the national disease. The elemental place of human conduct in religion had been obscured for many by the well-ordered symbolism, while the voice of the living God had been stilled by the words of a book. Both temple and book were in the care of the hierarchy, who with ever increasing efficiency exalted Deity to the seventh heaven while they took over the supervision of his interests on the earth. To many that was an easy solution to a serious problem; the temple tithes, the vows, the festivals, the phylacteries, and the *mezzuzoth* were not too onerous for so great a benefit. Indeed it was attractive. There was an odor of sanctity throughout it all, and it relieved the perplexed individual of all personal responsibility.

But Jeremiah was of a different mind. To him it was substituting cere-monial for character. It made the individual an automaton, nodding a sleepy assent to prescribed formulas and routine, rather than a growing personality, growing by reflection, discrimination, and decision on questions of right and wrong. It made religion an affair of an unreal, other world, rather than a life in relation to the world of men. His message was forthright. It consisted of one theme: Amend your ways and your doings, and I will cause you to dwell in this place (Jer. 7:3), with two negative illustrations: Trust not in the temple or in the book, for such a trust is false and fatal.

Standing at the entrance of the temple on a feast day (7:2; 26:2), addressing the assembled throng of worshipers, he accused them of stealing, murder, adultery, false swearing, and idolatry (7:9, 10). With biting sarcasm he de-nounced their whole sacrificial system, declaring that Yahweh neither com-manded nor desired it (7:21–24), and then pronounced the most harrowing doom on the people (7:32, 33) because they had put their trust in the temple, which they had reduced to a shambles and a den of robbers (7:4, 11). The temple in which they trusted would be destroyed like Shiloh (7:12–15). To thus speak of the temple, which had been planned by David, built by Solomon, purified by Asa and Hezekiah, proclaimed inviolable after 701 B.C. (Isa. 37:33–35; Jer. 7:4), and rededicated by Josiah—the temple that was the chief glory of Judah—was nothing less than blackest heresy. Brave words, but in this hour of national crisis not comforting.

Whatever the wounded feelings or the rising resentment against him may have been, the prophet knew no restraint. Indeed, he added fuel to the fury. With equal plainness of speech he lashed out against the book of the law, the adoption of which he had promoted thirteen years earlier.[12] He considered it the work of the false pen of the scribes. Priest and prophet by providing a superficial remedy had proclaimed peace, peace when there was no peace (8:8–10). By its very nature, which was legal, it rejected the living word of Yahweh, and history had already proved it to be a delusion. The desire of Yahweh was that people should "listen to my voice," turn from the council of their evil heart, and go forward and not backward (7:23, 24).

Such unmeasured condemnation of the chief joys of religion was too much to be quietly endured by religious leaders in any age. Freedom of speech was the child of democracy, but sometimes the child must be silenced, if neces-sary by force. Jeremiah's outspoken criticism roused to white heat the anger of those whose life interests and religious functions had come under fire. The priests and the prophets, backed up by the rabble, seized him in the new gateway of the temple. Hastily, a semiformal court was instituted and the prophet was put on trial for heresy (26:8, 9).

12 While commentators long understood Jeremiah 8:8 as referring to scribal laws or scribal inter-pretation of the law, it is now recognized by many that it is the book of Deuteronomy that is here attacked (G. A. Smith, *Deuteronomy*, 159; W. E. Addis, *Hebrew Religion*, 201; W. R. Smith, *Old Testament in the Jewish Church*, 203, 295).

The trial, as reported by Baruch, reveals the strong personal antagonisms of the times. The priests and the prophets, those who had participated in the reform and had continued active in its administration, were united against the rebel and demanded that he should suffer the death penalty (26:7, 8). Jeremiah sternly called them to repentance, otherwise all the calamities spoken should befall them; then he added, However, I am in your hands, but if you put me to death my blood will be on you, on the city and on all the people (26:12–15). The boldness of the man and the terror of the curse tended to temper the violence of many. The princes then intervened and, backed by the fickle mob, supported the cause of the accused, arguing that he was not worthy of death for he had spoken in the name of Yahweh (26:10, 16). Some of the elders, by making an appeal to precedent, supported his cause (26:17–19). They called to mind that a century earlier Micah had declared that Zion would be plowed as a field, and Jerusalem would become heaps, and the house would be as the high place of a forest, but Hezekiah did not put him to death (26:18, cf. Micah 3:12). Finally, Ahikam, one of the princes, took the affair into his own hands, and declared they would not give him up to the people to be put to death (26:24).

The crisis was past. The priests and the prophets had lost their case. Jeremiah was free. The reform of Josiah, that made the temple and the book central in religion, had, first by Josiah's death on the battlefield and now by Jeremiah's triumph, suffered a severe setback. A victory for freedom of speech and for moral obligation in religion had been achieved. This was a landmark in the history of religion, a testimony to the operation of the spirit of truth and light in the hearts and minds of men. Happy the man who, in the very citadel of the enemy, withheld not his witness to the unpleasant truth.

Landmarks in personal religion or in theological thinking often make but slight impress on contemporary history; and triumphs in democracy only slowly change the currents of life. The priests and the prophets, for the moment, were checked in their purpose, but they were not reconciled to the outcome of the trial. Nor does the history of Judah indicate that religion now moved to a perceptibly higher level.

Jehoiakim, the Egyptian appointee to the throne of Judah in 608 B.C., was a luxury-loving, greedy, heartless tyrant, who after ten years on the throne deserved nothing better than the burial of an ass (22:13–19; 36:30; II Kings 23:37). Owing to Nebuchadnezzar's victory over Pharaoh Necho in 605 B.C. he became a vassal to Babylonia. Three years later he rebelled against his overlord, thus plunging the country into war that ended in the fall of the city and the captivity of ten thousand of the chief people of the land in 597 B.C.

These were dismal days for the restless patriot. For more than twenty years he had warned of approaching ruin and had called to repentance; but the response had been negligible. He had joined the great reform; but that had proved futile. Now restrained from going to the temple (36:5), a new venture appealed to him. He dictated a résumé of his early teaching to Baruch, the scribe, which might be called the first edition of his sermons. When completed, this roll was read by Baruch in the court of the temple on a special feast day in 603 B.C. (36:9, 10). When this was reported to the princes, they wished to hear it. The threatened ruin so staggered them that they insisted it should be read before the king. When Jehoiakim heard it, in spite of protest he contemptuously cut it up and cast it on the fire in the brazier, while of Baruch and Jeremiah it is said, "Yahweh hid them" (36:9–26).

This burning of the books, the sabotage of private judgment in the interest of class privilege, was of no avail. Jeremiah knew no compromise. He re-edited his oracles, and added beside them many like words, among which was a curse on the meddling king (36:29–31). This second edition of Jeremiah, with its magical curse appended, was the permanent record of his messages, all of which grew out of personal experiences with the problems of his day. It was his counterpropaganda against what he believed to be self-destroying national iniquities. While it was written for contemporary life, it is of the greatest value to us as a revelation of the character and the inner experience of a great prophet. It is witness to the belief that truth shall not perish from the earth while man remains.

From 602 B.C. to 597 B.C. all was confusion in the history of Judah. Jehoiakim rebelled against Babylon; Syria, Moab, and Ammon attacked Jerusalem; and then Nebuchadnezzar with the Babylonian army laid siege to the city. The city was in uproar. The war party blindly struggled for independence, while an anti-Babylonian party no doubt aided them (27:1–11). And there were also the traditional Yahwists, who, like Hananiah, abetted the noisy, patriotic group by their popular pronouncements (chap. 28). While some cast their eyes longingly toward Egypt (42:1–17; 43:1–7), there were others who, like Jeremiah, were openly pro-Babylonian (37:13; 38:2, 17; 40:4). *Their gods were as numerous as their villages* (2:28) expressed the completeness of the national disintegration.

Jeremiah, though at times a fugitive from the king, may have continued his public ministry during these years. If so, it was the old message in a new form. Three parables, the linen girdle (13:1–11), the potter shaping the clay (18:1–12), and smashing the clay vessel in Tophet (19:1–13), may, provisionally, be dated in this period. The teaching of each is clear, though neither the time nor the details of the acts are certain. Judah without Yahweh, like a discarded loincloth, decays through lack of use; Yahweh, as the national potter, is limited by the texture of the clay; and Judah, like an earthen vessel, will be smashed in an unclean place. The symbolism of each of these appealed to the eye and to the imagination, and was no less impressive than an inspired oracle; but to those who were not skeptical concerning the all but universal belief in the power of magic they were effective instruments in accomplishing their teaching.

When Jeremiah broke the clay vessel in Tophet in the name of Yahweh, in symbol he was bringing about the ruin of the city. To make this known to all, he then repaired to the court of the temple, and there restated in detail the horrors that were coming on the city (19:10–15). Pashhur, the chief officer of the temple, could not tolerate such a shattering attack on city morale and national religion. Indignant at such pessimism, he slapped the prophet's face and consigned him for the night to the stocks in the upper gate of Benjamin in the temple court (20:1–6). Sitting on a hard, backless bench, legs stretched straight out, ankles clamped in a wooden vice, his neck pinioned in a collar (29:26), Jeremiah, stiff, paralyzed in body, suffered throughout the long, cold night. On the morrow, when the officer released him from his agony, pent-up emotion broke out in such a fury that Pashhur, now nicknamed "Terror-everywhere," became a walking symbol of the coming destruction.

But once away from public gaze intense reaction was inevitable. He, the mouthpiece of Yahweh, had ever been the victim of man. If he announced the coming doom his life was in jeopardy. If he was silent, a tempest raged within. Whatever he did brought on suffering. Duty and desire were ever at war and he always paid the penalty. For vigor of expression, depth of feeling, and intelligent understanding of the operation of the revealing spirit, we have here a classic (20:7–12, also 15:10, 15–21; 17:14–17; 1:9). Yahweh was with him a mighty warrior, and prevailed. Such was the summary of Jeremiah's religious experiences; his deepest response to the highest he knew gave him the sense of the conquering presence of the Invisible. With him the "I" and Yahweh were integrated in his personality.

Jerusalem capitulated to Nebuchadnezzar in 597 B.C., ten thousand of the principal men were carried captive to Babylonia (II Kings 24:10–14), and Zedekiah, a vassal to Babylonia, was placed on the throne. The city had suffered for her sins and by the scourge of Yahweh had been purged of those who had led her astray. Thus purified and chastened the faithful hoped for better days ahead.

But these bewildered leaders, together with the weak-kneed king, probably eager to achieve but devoid of good judgment, in 593 B.C. joined with Edom, Moab, and Ammon, Tyre and Sidon in a plot against their new masters. This was a violation of their oath of fealty to Nebuchadnezzar, considering an international treaty nothing more than a scrap of paper (II Kings 24:20–25:1; cf. Jer. 27:3). Thirty years of frustration had neither muzzled the prophet nor dulled his sense of the right. He denounced this move with symbol and speech. He sent bands and bars to the intriguing kinglets and declared that unless the nations served Nebuchadnezzar, his son, and his son's son, they would be destroyed (27:2–10). He then made a similar announcement to Zedekiah and Judah urging them to bring their necks under the yoke of the king of Babylon, and serve him, and his people, and live (27:12). But the prophets, encouraging the revolters in their desire for freedom, were assuring them of success (27:13, 18).

Again Jeremiah found himself in conflict with the popular prophets. Hananiah was the spokesman for the majority. In the temple in the presence of the priests and all the people, he declared: "Thus saith Yahweh of hosts the God of Israel, I have broken the yoke of the king of Babylon. Within two full years I will bring again into this place all the vessels of Yahweh's house, . . . Jehoiachin the king, . . . with all the captives of Judah . . ." (28:2–4). He then took the bar off Jeremiah's neck, and broke it (28:10, 11). It was a dramatic scene, heartening to the audience. But to Jeremiah it was perplexing. Hananiah, the son of a prophet, a leader in his own right enjoying the confidence of the people and sincere, was speaking in the name of Yahweh. Jeremiah seemed bewildered, hopeful, but not fully convinced. May it be so, was his reply (28:6). Then appealing to history he noted that prophets in the past had prophesied *against* many countries, and *against* great kingdoms, announcing war, and calamities, and pestilence (28:8). But should a prophet speak peace, only the future could give assurance that he had spoken the truth (28:9). Having so said, he went his way (28:11). He must again reflect on all the facts, sense the situation, and wait to see what Yahweh would answer (cf. Hab. 2:1). In due time the conviction was deepened that Hananiah's words were false, and that the exile would not be over in the near future, for Yahweh had put a yoke of iron on the necks of all the nations that they should serve Nebuchadnezzar (28:14).

The controversy between these two prophets was as to the duration of the exile. One was positive it would be over in the near future, that is, within two years. The other saw every reason to believe the Babylonian empire would outlast the lifetime of the living. This clash of ideals and of judgment occurred in 593 B.C., and the captivity continued until 538 B.C. Hananiah was wrong, while Jeremiah was right. He had made himself clear by a number of converging statements. At the time of the controversy, 593 B.C., he had asserted that the yoke of Babylonia was one of iron, and was too strong to be shattered within a couple of years (28:14). The same year, whether before or after is uncertain, he stated that the Babylonian rule would continue under the son and grandson of Nebuchadnezzar (27:7), an indefinite period, probably over forty years. The same year he wrote a letter to those in exile counseling them to settle down, marry, build houses, plant vineyards, etc., for only after "seventy years" had been accomplished on Babylon would Yahweh restore the captivity (29:4–10; 51:59). This figure is again used in what is generally considered editorial work (25:11–14).

As these evidently are general, not specific, statements, they are correct. The captivity technically ended when Persia conquered Babylonia in 538 B.C., that is, fifty-five years after the prophetic altercation. But if we insist that the seventy years (29:10), and that the nations would serve "him and his son and his son's son" (27:7) are precise, then our case is hopeless. The captivity ended in fifty-five years, not in seventy; and five rulers, the last one, so far as evidence goes, being no relation to Nebuchadnezzar, and not three, ruled Babylonia before her fall. Hananiah's declaration of a speedy return was the result of a hasty conclusion based on wishful thinking and cheap religion that banked overmuch on the good graces of Yahweh. Jeremiah's statements were founded on the well-known factors in the case, the international military situation and the state of morals in Judah. Using the same good judgment that may be used today, he could not see the defeat of Babylon within that generation. He was a statesman, with moral insights and a long view of affairs, neither a petty politician, eager for popular applause, nor an ecstatic, who in trance or vision received specific information of things to come. To so judge him is to misread the book and to discredit the man. On the other hand, to treat these numbers as symbols and thereby to uncover a secret chart of world history down through the ages has been attempted many times. But such has long been shown to be a folly pursued only by those who have been ignorant of history. Later, in Apocalypticism, we get a glimpse into this activity.

Many and contradictory voices, caustic debates, bitter hatreds, savage curses, each offering a panacea for the distress, each claiming to be the word of Yahweh, all contributing to a hopeless confusion, clamored for attention in Jerusalem. Jeremiah, caught in the conflict of diverse opinions, ultimately laid down certain criteria of true prophecy. He was critical-minded, had learned much through harsh experience, and fortunately for us his judgments have been preserved. The *false* prophets, whom he condemns, were in good standing in the best society, they were ardent patriots and zealous in religion. They belonged to the nationalist, orthodox, conservative party of the day. They, themselves, did not violate the ethical standards; nor did their messages fall below the level of that recognized throughout the land. *False,* as we use the word, may be too harsh; national or official would be a more correct description. But neither official rank nor profession of orthodoxy was in itself a guarantee of truth.

Jeremiah considered these patriots blameworthy on three counts. First, the false, or national, prophets followed the methods of primitive religion, such as dreams, visions, ecstasy, spirit manifestation, in order to obtain knowledge of the will of God (27:9; 29:8). Such methods had been in almost universal practice, and made a strong appeal to the general public. In early Hebrew religion, under the influence of Canaan, such means had been considered quite legitimate in Yahweh worship (Gen. 28:11-17; 32:24-30; 37:5-7; 40:5-20; Exod. 3:2-12; Num. 22:34; I Sam. 3:3-14), and at times may have provided minor values. Jeremiah scored those who had visions and practiced divination (14:14; 23:16), and he had nothing but contempt for those dreamers who peddled their dreams about in public. All such were straw, and what has straw to do with wheat (23:26–28)? These do not profit the people at all (23:32). The appeal to the weird, the inexplicable, the mystical, to Jeremiah provided no evidence of the value of an oracle, while the use of the slogans, "oracle of Yahweh," and "thus saith Yahweh," carried no weight to the serious-minded (23:21, 22). In this, Jeremiah brought out into sharp relief what was implicit in earlier teaching. The prophets had denounced those who, by resorting to witchcraft, soothsayers, and wizards, had rejected the Word of the living God (Isa. 2:6; 8:19; Mic. 5:12, cf. 3:6, 7). Deuteronomy 18:9–14, where all such foreign cults are prohibited, is of uncertain date; it may or may not have been earlier than Jeremiah. The tradition that Saul banned necromancy and the like (I Sam. 28:9), and the law in Exodus 22:18 against sorcery, probably express an early reaction of the Hebrews against such pagan cults. Jeremiah, however, carried the ban farther than his predecessors, and made it more inclusive. Yahweh, as the ever present, living God, required no intermediaries in his ministry to the needs of his people, and the devotees of foreign deities were not to be tolerated.

No less serious was the second charge, that these false prophets stole their messages from others, either their predecessors or their contemporaries, and paraded them as the word of Yahweh (23:30). To Jeremiah, prophesying was much more than the repetition of the words of others, or an assent to popular demands; it was the response to an inner conviction, arising out of the needs of the hour, that such was right, and thus the will of the God of righteousness. All through his life there had been, as it were, a hand putting words into his mouth (1:9), a fire burning in his bones (20:19; 23:9), a voice within, challenging and counseling him. Unless one had thus stood in the council of Yahweh, he was not equipped to prophesy (23:18, 22). In this he was in general agreement with his predecessors, the great pre-exilic prophets. Their oracles had not been the hackneyed platitudes of court officials. Micaiah refused to repeat the accepted formulas and faced the storm alone (I Kings 22:26–28). Elijah and Amos left the beaten pathway and the religious leaders of the land to their own hurt. The messages of Hosea and Isaiah were fashioned by their own experiences, and Micah was full of power by the spirit of Yahweh. Language, content, and outlook of each differed from those of the others, but each preached righteousness and insisted he knew this to be the will of the living God.

Furthermore, these peculiarly personal sermons were always directed to the local community as warning, reproof, or comfort, to meet the specific needs of the hour (23:21–23, 33). With changing conditions and with growing knowledge the conceptions and outlook of the true prophet must grow in adequacy. He must learn, not only from the failures as well as the triumphs of his predecessors, but from his own mistakes as well. Even Yahweh changes his mind when he finds the clay intractable (18:5–10). Thus to meet the changing conditions from day to day the living God was ever near at hand

(23:18–23, 36; 31:31–34). But the repetition of the formulas of the past or the slogans of the present did not measure up to Jeremiah's standard of prophecy.

However, the all-inclusive charge against these false prophets was that they spoke out of their evil heart (23:16, 26). Their vaunted *dreams* were born in deceit (23:25, 32). They preached smooth things, peace, peace, an echo of wishful thinking (23:17; 28:1–4, 9; 8:11), and were a strength to evildoers, an encouragement to the lawless (23:14, 17). By ignoring human rights they brought disaster on the people, and under the cover of pious claims they were false to Yahweh (23:17, 31, 32). The word of Yahweh was like a fire that burned up the chaff, like a hammer that broke the rock in pieces (23:29); and such, also, must be the words of the true prophet of Yahweh. Thus underneath the changes in the prophetic message, from decade to decade and from age to age, lay justice, mercy, and truth, the unchangeable rights of humanity, and the responsibility of the man of God always to call evildoers to repentance (23:10, 22, 29, 39, 40).

Following the first captivity, 597 B.C., when ten thousand of the flower of the land were deported, the common people, the underlings, the oppressed, and the poor came into positions of power and privilege. Jeremiah, always observant, soon learned a lesson in human nature. These people, previously always defended by the prophets as being the victims of the guilty ruling class, now, in large measure, were entrusted with the economic, political, and religious life of the city. Enjoying the prestige, and charged with the new responsibilities, these, the *nouveaux riches* proved to be even worse than the old aristocrats. They were like rotten figs, so putrid they were a stench in the nostrils, as well as unfit to eat. They were a horror, a reproach, a taunt, a curse among all people; hence, by the Word of Yahweh they would be wiped off the land (24:1–3).

Not only were these new leaders inexperienced, but, lacking firm leadership, each group clamored and fought for privilege and profit regardless of the rights of others. In the hour when co-operation and wisdom were most essential, each faction like a wolf pack was at the throat of every other group. At the edge of the abyss, Jeremiah alone had the vision. He faced the patent facts of Babylonia's military strength and imperial ambitions, read the hand of Yahweh in history, and pleaded for submission to the conqueror, asserting that Nebuchadnezzar was the servant of Yahweh (25:9; 27:6; 43:10). But his voice was drowned by the mad chorus demanding national independence. When good judgment was most needed, pressure groups, ignorant of world powers and forgetful of history, disregarded all the signals, and rebelled a second time against their overlord.

It was fatal. In 588 B.C. the Babylonian army invested the city. War, pestilence, and famine slowly closed their deadly grip on the people. Skin shriveled on the bone; starving mothers boiled their own children for food (Lam.

4:8–10); and after a year and a half the rebellious city was breached, and laid in ruins, and temple and palace alike became lairs for jackals (9:11; 10:22). Many of the leaders were deported (52:28–30), and Gedaliah, a Jewish prince, appointed administrator of the desolated district, as Jerusalem was uninhabitable made Mizpah his headquarters. Two months later, Ishmael, a harebrained rival prince, treacherously slew Gedaliah, a number of the chief Jews, and the Babylonian guard (41:1–11; II Kings 25:23–26). Thus ended the kingdom of Judah, and the Holy Land became a waste of briars and thorns (Isa. 7:25).

Throughout these years of growing chaos, Jeremiah was ever in the tragedy. On one occasion the leaders, hoping to avert disaster by an appeal to the supernatural, turned religious and sought to placate the wrath of Yahweh by liberating the slaves as required in the law (Deut. 15:12–14; Jer. 34:8–10). Great was the joy in Jerusalem when shortly thereafter the Babylonian army lifted the siege and went south to meet an approaching Egyptian force (37:5, 11). Then, the desired objective having been accomplished, the masters pressed their slaves back into servitude (34:11–16). The anger of Jeremiah rose to fever heat and in the name of Yahweh he doomed the princes, the priests, and all the people to the sword, the pestilence, and famine, to be tossed to and fro among all the kingdoms of the earth (34:17–22). Such words angered the leaders and comforted only the slaves. The princes, who earlier had defended him, now lost patience, and because of his well-known pro-Babylonianism charged him with treason. He was caught leaving the city, accused of being a deserter, imprisoned, and finally thrown into a pesthole (37:11–16; 38:3–13), from which he was finally rescued by an Ethiopian slave (38:7–11).[13]

Another memorable incident occurred about this time. A relative in Anathoth, of whom nothing is said when the prophet's life was in danger in his native village, lost confidence in real-estate values, and put up for sale some property (32:6–15, 16, 24, 25). Jeremiah, who had the prior right of purchase, though certain the city would fall and the land would be devastated, bought the field, and then buried the deed of purchase, a clay document, in an earthen jar in a corner of the field (32:11–15). In this spectacular way he registered his unwavering confidence in Yahweh and his conviction that, though the captivity would be of considerable duration, it would bring the exiles to repentance, and that ultimately Yahweh would bring his people back from exile to dwell in the land forever (32:36–44).[14]

Everyday experiences were rich in revelation to this wide-awake prophet. He had closely observed the new rulers in Jerusalem, and also had contacts

---

[13] Chapter 38 may be a duplicate of 37:7–21, in which the stories of the arrest and the interview with the king are two traditions of the one event. See J. Skinner, *Prophecy and Religion*, 256–259.

[14] This section is generally recognized as coming from the pen of Baruch, and is a fair presentation of the views of the prophet.

with the princes, the craftsmen, and the smiths who had been carried captive in 597 B.C. (29:1–14). The comparison between these two groups was striking. The former were like putrid figs, but the latter, who were in captivity, had learned the hard way. The heart-rending suffering of the exile had wrought, at least for some, a work of purification, and had given them a juster sense of the permanent, human values. They were like the luscious first-ripe figs, and with a heart to know Yahweh, they were the people of God (24:1–10). From the ordinary facts of everyday life Jeremiah was slowly, but surely, learning the ways of God with men.

When in 586 B.C. the city fell, the Babylonian conquerors gave Jeremiah the choice of honorable residence in Babylonia, or of going whither it seemed good and right to him to go (40:1–4). Good and right? That had been his guiding star for forty years. When he chose to go to Gedaliah, and to dwell among his own people, crushed and desolated as they were, the new Babylonian rulers provided him with victuals, and gave him a present (40:5, 6). A prophet was not without honor save in his own country.

When, after Ishmael's unbelievable folly in the murder of Gedaliah, the pitiable remnant of distracted Jews begged an oracle from him, he advised them to remain in the land and face the consequences of their stupidity (42:7–22). Stubborn to the last, they charged him with falsehood and treachery, and fleeing to Egypt, in order to escape Babylonian justice, they carried the old prophet with them, as a sort of mascot (43:1–7). Here, at Taphanes, virtually a prisoner, a broken man to whom his people had never given heed, he found that the old idolatrous practices flourished anew, and unable to restrain himself he attacked with all his old-time vigor the sins of the people.

But these refugees were stiff-necked and rebellious. Not only did they continue in their evil ways, but by appropriating the basic thesis of the prophets and of Deuteronomy they argued that when they had served the queen of heaven (in the days of Manasseh) they had prospered, but when they had left off burning incense to her, they had been consumed by the sword and by famine (in the days of Amon and Josiah, 44:15–19). So far as our records go [15] Jeremiah, quite ignoring the actual history, and with little cogency, merely repeated the inherited theological argument (44:20–23). But he had another arrow for his bow, and he directed the shaft against the women, who were the devotees of fertility worship (44:24, 25). This was too much. Earlier he had alienated, one after the other, priests, prophets, princes, rulers, and people, and now the women were the butt of his attack. Jeremiah, an old man in a strange land among a hostile people, was alone; alone, but with a good conscience; an iron pillar against the whole land. "They shall

[15] It is evident that this whole section comes from the Deuteronomic editor, Baruch probably, hence it may be the attitude of the editor, and not that of the prophet, whose emphasis was moving toward inner values rather than the material, and toward individualism rather than nationalism.

fight against thee; but shall not prevail, for I am with thee" (1:18, 19; 15:19, 20). Tradition says he was slain by the irate Jewish colony, a martyr to his convictions. Be that as it may, the book of Jeremiah, the workmanship of not a few interpreters, is a lasting memorial to one of the great religious heroes of the centuries.

The new covenant seems to have been the final step, the culmination in Jeremiah's thinking (31:31–34). While in its present form this passage has come from the hand of an editor, possibly Baruch, many critics consider it to be essentially Jeremianic.[16] Though he had changed his emphasis more than once, a peculiarly personal note runs through all his teaching, and this gains in clarity and depth with the passing of the years. At the close of his life, all the material assets and national institutions had been swept away, and man and God alone remained. The need of the hour and the hope of the future was that which was imperishable, the law written in the heart. That lay beyond the reach of the invader, the control of priest and prince, and the power of evildoers.

This law written in the heart required no Torah, canonized by an emotionally conditioned populace and then easily subverted by legalism (8:8), "for they shall teach no more every man his neighbor" (31:34). Nor were manuals of worship, altars, and a temple, that so often became ends in themselves (7:4, 12–15), required to aid the spirit of man in communing with his Maker, "for they shall all know me" (31:34). Nor was residence in the Holy Land essential to the highest religious life. Such an idea was primitive (I Sam. 26:19), and might become a fetish. Those remaining in Judah after the first captivity were like putrid figs, and would be completely wiped out, while those exiled in pagan Babylonia could serve and enjoy the presence of the living God (24:1–10; 29:11–14). True religion was not rooted in the soil of Palestine, but in the hearts of men and women.

Even the elect nation, strictly speaking, was no longer a tribal entity. Religion had become personal. Many Jews, priests, prophets, princes, incompetent rulers, the Egyptian refugees, had become worthless outcasts. Jeremiah now saw clearly that each one "shall die for his own iniquity" (31:30; 17:10; cf. Ezek. 3:16–21; 33:10–20), and thus, as individualism became the basis of election, tribalism lost its earlier importance. It was fitting that the man who throughout his life so often stood alone should be called the father of individualism.[17] Likewise, by way of later interpretation, the doors were thrown

16 Among noted O.T. scholars such men as Cornill, Giesebrecht, Peake, Skinner, and G. A. Smith hold this position. See G. A. Smith, *Jeremiah*, 374–380.

17 Early religion, which was controlled by the pattern of primitive society, had been tribal and had emphasized solidarity. But under military achievement, the development of industry, and the growth of society and government, each of which provided opportunities for the strong and the gifted, the individual gradually emerged from the group. Parallel with this the ethical teaching of the prophets likewise distinguished between individuals. The fall of Jerusalem, when each individual was left to shift for himself, was the final incident that furnished the demand for individualism in religious thinking.

open for universalism. It is true that in the book of Jeremiah the promise of the future is limited to the Jews in exile (23:7, 8; 29:14), and the new covenant is with the house of Israel (31:31, 33), but the logic of the teaching broadens out the old boundary lines. Nebuchadnezzar was the servant of Yahweh, and a kindly Negro slave was assured of the protection of Yahweh (39:15–18). To do justice and righteousness, and to judge the cause of the poor and the needy, on which no race has any monopoly, was to know Yahweh (22:15, 16). Thus, by expansion, *all* may ultimately embrace all races, tongues, and creeds.

Religion, thus, by explicit statement and by implication, was freed from the old-time limitations of tribe, soil, altar, temple, institutions, and book. A glorious liberation for those who were sensitive to the inner voice and responsive to the sense of justice, to which man everywhere, in the depth of his moral nature gives assent (Rom. 1:18–20). Liberating religion from all externals, at the same time the new covenant strengthened and democratized it by placing responsibilities squarely on the shoulder of the individual, and purified and deepened it by making it a matter of conscience. The new covenant, the law written in the heart, was one of the great visions of religion.

Underneath and interwoven in the religion of the prophet lay his theology, of which two features need to be mentioned. Within the limits of his inherited assumptions Jeremiah's God was democratic. As with all ethical teachers, he was no respecter of persons. He condemned high and low alike irrespective of office or of power. He repented as occasion warranted, and changed his mind with changing circumstances (18:9, 10; 45:4). Indeed he was peculiarly human, at times becoming angry, and even leading the prophet astray (15:17, 18; 20:7, 8). Yet such expressions are less anthropomorphic than realistic, for above all, to Jeremiah Yahweh was felt to be a vital, living presence dwelling in the human heart. He was the *living* God, not only as with fertility worship in the lower ranges of life, but especially in the higher areas of social and religious relations (10:10). "By the living God" was his favorite form of oath (4:2; 5:2; 12:16, *et al.*), and revealing phrases such as "living word" (8:9), "living water" (2:13; 17:10, 13), "near at hand" (23:23), "in the midst of Israel" (14:8, 9), "searching the heart and the reins" (11:20; 17:9, 10; 20:12) ever recur in his messages. *Closer is he than breathing, and nearer than hands and feet* would express the seer's conviction of Yahweh's relation to himself. The "I" of the prophet, and Yahweh, at times were interchangeable, and in his highest moments Jeremiah identifies himself with Yahweh. He is an excellent illustration of what our leading American interpreter of mysticism has said: "To find God, we only need to be prepared to see, and feel, and find what fringes the inner margins of ourselves." [18]

Jeremiah, the man, however, was greater than his theology, significant as that is for all ages. His words were written in flesh and blood. He thundered

[18] Rufus Jones in *Contemporary Religious Thought*, T. S. Kepler, ed., 194.

his judgments against the sins of his people, but the lightning struck deep within his own bosom. He was in perpetual pain because of their stubbornness (8:18, 21, 22; 15:18), and their tragedy caused his tears to flow day and night (9:1; 10:19). Suffering at their hands, he interceded for them until their blind obstinacy made prayer of no avail (7:16; 11:14; 14:11–13; 15:1). He loved his people with his whole heart and at times even identified himself with them in *our* wickedness (8:18–22; 14:20, 21). His wound was incurable, because of *my* children (10:19, 20), and his heart was broken, and his bones shook like a drunken man because of the prophets (23:9). This deep sympathy for his own people expressed itself at times in impatience with them, and a desire to escape from them (4:31; 8:21, 22; 9:1, 2); and again his imprecatory explosions, that later became a model for the imprecatory Psalms, arose out of the agony of ill-requited love (12:3; 18:21–23; 15:15; 17:18; 20:12). Privileged, at last, to choose where he should spend his declining years, neither a lodge in the wilderness nor a seat at the table of Nebuchadnezzar appealed to him. He and his people, a suffering, shattered remnant, were one. Not only did he suffer with them, but he suffered for them. He became in Israel a supreme example of the suffering servant. He was despised and rejected, a man of sorrows and acquainted with grief; yet by his knowledge he made many righteous. Uncompromising in ethics, all-encompassing in human sympathy, and foundational in his understanding of God, throughout the years he lived and served. His message was vital; and he was its incarnation. By this token he was the greatest of all the prophets.

That Jeremiah stood alone in a very real sense is correct. Like a lofty windswept pinnacle on a mountain crest, he faced the storms alone, without a peer. But though harassed at every turn, he had secret admirers, friends, and disciples. Baruch never left him. Uriah the prophet was like-minded (26:21–23), and Ezekiel, a younger contemporary who lived in Jerusalem, by every evidence of phrase and idea was his disciple.

Only a small part of the present book of Ezekiel seems to have come directly from the poet-prophet himself.[19] Much to the detriment of the original material, commentators and editors for more than four centuries continued to interpret and enlarge the genuine Ezekiel, so that much of worth has been obscured by these secondary contributions. However, as the result of critical studies, chiefly in our own day, a degree of certainty has been reached as to the core of the teaching of the prophet. Those sections that, owing to phrase, form, and content, are evidently the work of interpreters and compilers, are valuable for the thought of later days, but at this stage in Ezekiel studies it seems wise to use only those passages that have stood the keenest critical tests. As a result the prophet emerges as a clear-cut figure, with a vigorous and coherent

---

[19] In 1939 the writer, in "Ezekiel," *American Commentary* series, summarized the results of critical studies up to that time. Since then an important contribution has been made by W. A. Irwin, *The Problem of Ezekiel,* in which the critical studies have been carried to a new conclusion.

message. Indeed one of the recent interpreters has called him *ein Mann von ganz monumentaler Grösse*.[20]

From the reasonably certain minimum of the oracles of Ezekiel the following conclusions seem assured: His emphasis on social justice, though specific acts occupy but small space, is as forthright as that of the earlier prophets (Ezek. 2:3–5; 3:16–19; 11:2, 3; 21:24, 25; 22:1–4; 32:10). He carried on an active campaign against the rulers in high places, the princes, priests, and prophets (12:8–11; 13:1–5, 17–19; 34:1, 2). Idolatry was to him disloyalty to Yahweh, and he attacked it more fiercely than had his predecessors. The prevalent pagan rites were an abomination, and *filthy images* gathers up his contempt for the work of men's hands (6:1–5; 11:2–6; 13:17–19; 14:1–3, 6; 15:1–5; 23: 1–3, 5; 36:18). The Holy Land had become unclean (22:23, 24), and had even sinned against Yahweh (14:12, 13), while worship abroad, at least for a time, was acceptable to Yahweh (21:1–3). For a worthy life the new heart was indispensable (11:14–16), and individualism is expressed as clearly as in Jeremiah (18:1–4; 33:7–9). In his picture of the all-engulfing ruin that was overwhelming the nation, no prophet was ever more devastating. His symbolism is like a canvas of twisted bodies of the slain, the hollow cheeks and glazing eyes of the starved, and the frantic refugees in flight to the wilderness (4:1, 2, 9, 11; 5:1–3; 12:1–11). His oracles are replete with horror. Dead bodies are stacked before the idols, and dry bones are scattered around the altars (6:5). The sword of Yahweh, drawn from its sheath and sharpened for slaughter, is buried in the flesh and drips with Jewish blood (21:5–7, 9–11). More gruesome still is the oracle of the caldron. The choice of the flock are dismembered, and flesh and bones are packed into the boiling caldron. Heap on the wood, make the fire hot, boil well the flesh, and make thick the broth, and let the bones be burned (24:10; cf. 24:1–5, 9, 10). Terrifying and inhuman as these judgments were, Ezekiel insisted that they were the word of Yahweh, and would be performed (12:21–23, 26–28). In all this he felt the responsibilities of a watchman who had been specially commissioned by Yahweh to sound the warning whether the people listened or whether they rebelled (2:7; 3:11, 19; 33:7–9). At the same time, he walked so consistently in the footsteps of his greater master that the eating of the roll (3:1–3) might well indicate his intimate knowledge of an edition of the book of Jeremiah.

Thus Jeremiah was not left without a witness. Nor did Ezekiel live and write in vain. His message was treasured by disciples, who collated, brooded over, and under changed conditions, apparently in Babylonia, reinterpreted his teachings and reconstructed the hope of Israel. Differing as the student usually does from his teacher, these men, like Christian leaders who in response to the question, "What would Jesus do?" provide their own program, laid their best gifts at the feet of one whom they honored as master. Thus the book of Ezekiel, in its present form, is enriched by the views of disciples and editors as well as those of the master.

[20] V. Herntrich, *Ezekielprobleme*, 130.

Chapter XI

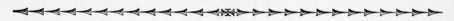

THE RELIGION OF THE INTELLECTUALS.

550-100 B.C.

THE year 586 B.C., for Israel, marked the end of one age and the beginning of another. The Jewish nation was uprooted, the Holy City and the temple were destroyed, and with the passing of Jeremiah prophecy had completed its fullest and finest expression. However, while the same emphasis on social ethics and human rights is rarely heard again, it is equally true that these men had sown seed that continued to germinate wherever it fell in all succeeding generations. All strands of later Hebrew thought have interwoven in them much of the sturdy morality of those whom their fathers rejected.

The old with its urgent dream of empire had passed, and the new had not yet taken form. But so profoundly serious were the leaders, and so definitely democratic, that within two centuries three widely divergent schools of thought, each claiming to be authoritative, arose within Judaism. As faith in armies and fortresses had perished, energy had been turned into intellectual and religious channels. Battles had been lost, but ideals had been purified, and the direction of ambitions had been changed. These three movements, each rooted in earlier history and each interrelated to and reacting on the others, were reinterpretations of phases of Judaism. For our purpose, they may be designated the philosophic—to use the term loosely, and comprehensively— the legalistic or priestly, and the apocalyptic, which was an extension of the messianic. These, the striking evidence of the vitalities of Judaism, grew up side by side, one or the other in different areas or in different periods, gaining prestige, and all together contributing to the sum total of Jewish religion.

The philosophic movement, which without prejudice we have ventured to call the religion of the intellectuals, had, as always in the world of thought, varied aspects, and many crosscurrents. This was the age of reflection for the Jew, and many problems of a practical and semispeculative nature called for attention. Of these, four of religious significance are of importance: the number and the character of the gods, the explanation of suffering, the oneness of humanity, and what is wisdom, or the problem of knowledge.

Monotheism, the dogma of one God, one of the fine expressions of Hebrew thought, underlies the philosophy of all these schools, and for more than a century had been implicit in Hebrew thinking.[1] As justice, the central idea of the great prophets, by its very nature was of universal application, so Yahweh, as an ethical Deity could function as the God of social relations among any people in any clime. Similarly, the law written in the human heart opened the door as wide as humanity, and Yahwism, freed from race and soil, was ready for monotheism. With the fall of the city and the scattering of the people, theories of the inviolability of the temple and the permanency of the kingdom lost their significance. The virgin daughter of Zion had fallen, fallen to rise no more; but in that very act the boundaries had been lifted to far horizons, and new ideals were born.

Despoiled of possessions, the captives in Babylonia had an inheritance that took on splendor in the new background. The worth of their religion, with its human interests and its intense loyalties, loomed large under the shadows of the great Babylonian temples, with their armies of officials ever busy carrying out elaborate and often meaningless rites. Thus religion to not a few of these Jews became their life. Judaism was superior to anything in Babylonia; and Yahweh possessed qualities that were absent in Marduk. Right looked Might in the face, and knew it was the superior; Idealism was victor over Materialism.

Within fifty years of the fall of the city, a thinker, or better a theologian, who was also a poet broke the silence with a song that marks a climax in the religious thought of the Old Testament (Isa. 40-55). Monotheism is here expressed as a dogma. While still the shepherd of his people, just, kindly, and compassionate, Yahweh is the everlasting God, the Creator of the ends of the earth, and like unto him there is none else (Isa. 40:12, 28).[2] Idols are considered as nothing. They are made by a carpenter from a piece of wood, and are plated by a goldsmith. They give no information, and do nothing (Isa. 40:18-20; 44:12-20). But Yahweh has measured the waters in the hollow of his hand, and meted out the heavens with the span, and weighed the mountains in scales, and the hills in a balance (40:12-17), and has raised up one from the east (41:2) to be his shepherd to perform all his pleasure (44:28). Not only in

---

[1] Monotheism, which has been aptly described as *imperialism in religion* (J. H. Breasted, *Development of Religion and Thought in Ancient Egypt*, 315), has appeared at various times in widely separated areas. It has taken various forms, each being the product of local history. In Egypt in the fourteenth century B.C., under Akhenaton, a monotheism was introduced in the priestly court circles, a protest to the conventionalized ritual and a return to the realities of life (*ibid.*, 315-343). When Assyria was at the height of her power, Ashur gained the supreme position in her pantheon. He was military chief (Zimmern, *ERE*, II, 313). Greece attained a philosophic monotheism under Plato, in the fourth century B.C., as a response to the intellectual demand for the co-ordination of the facts of the universe (L. R. Farnell, *ERE*, VI, 419, 420). For a general statement of the problem see Josiah Royce, *ERE*, VIII, 817-821. For development of the idea in the O.T. see T. J. Meek, *Hebrew Origins*, 176-203. Bruno Balscheit in an excellent study suggests that O.T. monotheism grew out of three influences, the prophetic, the priestly, and the theological, at work in the history of Israel (*Alter und Aufkommen des Monotheismus in der israelitische Religion*, 72, 73, 135-139).

[2] Professor S. Blank has shown that in this section, while Yahweh still retains a special relation to Israel, he is no longer considered her national God, but is equivalent to the universal God (*HUCA*, XV, 1-46; see also J. Morgenstern, *JBL*, LXII, 269-281).

nature and in history is he the ruler, but in the realms of strife, calamity, and morals there is none else. The proud boast is, "I form the light, and create darkness; I make peace, and create evil; I am Yahweh that doeth all these things" (45:7, cf. 41:2, 3; 49:23). "I am the first and the last; and beside me there is no God" (44:6).

This was an astounding conclusion. That thoughtful men, aware of the conquering might of Babylon and the opulence of her culture, and acquainted with her gorgeous, seven-storied, rainbow-hued temples, their majestic symbols of deity, their impressive ritual, and their stately priesthood, should dream that the God of the captive Jews was the director of the nations, the upholder of the universe, and the only true God, was more marvelous than crossing the Red Sea or the capture of Jericho. Nevertheless, on the basis of human values, it was an irrefutable conclusion. As man was greater than the things he made, as mind and heart were superior to flesh and blood, as human ideals outlive material splendors, so Yahweh, who lived in the hearts of just men everywhere, to his people towered above the gods of their masters. This was heartening beyond words to those who first heard or read this message. That their God was above all gods, and that he had not forgotten them but was directing the march of armies for their liberation (Isa. 44:26–28; 46: 1, 2; 46:12–47:7, 40:1–4) comforted many, and gave the zealous courage to face new tasks.

Further, not only was the ethical teaching of the prophets reaffirmed, but Jeremiah's conclusion, that the fountain source of true living lay within rather than without, was accepted and expanded. The people of Yahweh had no city, no temple, no army, but they had that wherein they could glory. Rewards and punishments no longer belonged to the bread-and-butter level of Deuteronomy, but were transferred to that inner life which transcends the outer. Under the force of circumstances, personality took priority over property, and confidence in God outweighed the momentary evils. Later, this judgment took its classic form: "For though the fig-tree shall not flourish, neither shall fruit be found in the vines, . . . and there shall be no herd in the stalls; . . . yet I will joy in the God of my salvation" (Hab. 3:17, 18). This triumph over externals through the strength of inner experience is again celebrated in a little poem: Though the Lord give you scant bread and a dribble of water, never again shall your teacher hide himself from your eyes (Isa. 30:20). Here was the recognition that man does not live by bread alone, and that all the splendor of Babylon could not satisfy the human heart. Might had ruled the world of the Dinosauria in the Jurassic period; but to humans of the later era social and moral values stood supreme. Thus around 500 B.C., from the most unexpected source came the unequivocal conclusion that there is but one God in the world of nature and of man, and that God is Yahweh of the Hebrew captives. This conclusion was derived, not from the incidents of history, nor from the things of sense, but from the ideals at work within the social order, that right outlives might, and that the forces of the inner man are master of externals. This conviction, that the universe at its core was essentially sound, an assumption of faith rooted in the moral nature of man, was a high-water mark in ancient religious thought.

This dogma, so confidently affirmed, and at the moment so comforting to the Jew, ultimately carried in its train questions of a profoundly serious nature. Skepticism as to Yahweh's interest in the daily activities of men had long existed. Yahweh does neither good nor evil, said some in the days of Zephaniah (Zeph. 1:12); and by the time of Malachi, cynicism had gone so far that some acted as though Yahweh could not distinguish between a sickly and a sound sheep (Mal. 1:8). Beyond this, the character of such a Deity was called in question. Could an all-powerful God, who ordered or permitted the disasters that so often overwhelmed good men and good nations, be wise and just? Jeremiah and Habakkuk had both reverently raised the question, but this age-long problem came to its acute expression in the poetic dialogue in the book of Job.

The theme of this poem,[3] as well as the literary form, is in no way, save the use of proper names, integrally related to the prose. Is there disinterested goodness, is the question in the latter; the character of God comes under scrutiny in the former. The question, Is God just? at heart was theological, but to the poet-philosopher life itself was bound up in the idea of God, and was of life and death import. With telling phrase, a compelling rhythm, and cogent reasoning he challenged the sacrosanct conclusions of the centuries, and even impugned the justice of the Most High.

The progress of thought in the poem is so easily followed that, for those who read, an outline is scarcely needed. Job accuses God of tyrannically compelling man to live when he would rather die (3:23), of unceasingly torturing him (7:19, 20), of breaking him without cause, and destroying him even when he is perfect (9:17, 20, 21), mocking at the pains of the innocent (9:23), and he climaxes his outburst by asserting that Deity is arbitrary, irresponsible, and immoral (19:6-12).

The three friends—Eliphaz, a gentleman, courteous and gracious, a scholar of wide wisdom and mature judgment, who has had a profound mystical experience (4:1-5:27; 15:1-15; 22:1-30); Bildad, a traditionalist, who repeats what he has learned from the fathers (8:1-22; 18:1-21; 25:2, 3; 26:5-14 ?); and Zophar, a layman, rough and brutal, who asserts that the ways of God are beyond comprehension, and then assumes that he knows that if Job would set his heart aright, he would again be at peace and prosperous (11:1-20; 20:1-29) —each rebukes and rebuffs the sorely distraught sufferer. Without any intimate knowledge of the cause of the distress, and with no sympathy for the mentally

[3] The poem, written possibly in the early part of the fourth century B.C., consists of Job 3:1-27: 23; 29:1-31:41; 38:1-42:6. Additions such as the speeches of Elihu, 32:1-37:24, and the poem on Wisdom, 28:1-27, with minor editorial interpretations were made later. Full discussion is found in Pfeiffer, *Introduction to the O.T.*, 667-683, who considers it preceded Second Isaiah.

perplexed, thus never coming to grips with the real issue, each one with grow-ing exasperation reiterates the time-honored assumptions of the ancients. No doubt these men rendered a service to many of their generation. They were bulwarks for the faith of the fathers, and in a period of turmoil and uncer-tainty they quieted many timid souls by affirming in familiar phrases the old patterns of thought.

Job, on the other hand, amid the intellectual crosscurrents of his day was eagerly searching for the foundations of the faith of generations yet to be. Wide observation of individual and national history disclosed the stark contradic-tions between the facts of experience and the accepted theological theory. The grave injustices suffered by the best cried to high heaven against the powers that be. No good man, had he the power, would permit what was of daily occurrence under the role of the Almighty. His speeches [4] came out of the depths of a divine despair that reached the climax of audacity. The passionate and unrestrained assaults against the character of Deity, or rather against ortho-dox theology, came from one who never questioned the existence or the power of God. It was the cry of faith in ultimate realities, that dared to face the most serious of questions.

It is noticeable that following the paroxysm of his agony, apparently ex-hausted by his emotional outbursts, he calmed down and modified his attitude. He declared his confidence in his ultimate vindication (16:18–22; also 19:25–27, though these verses are so mutilated there is no dependable translation; the AV has no support), and closed his defense by a detailed statement of his manner of life (31:1–40). This is the final apologetic for his faith. It is the *I know* of religion.

The poet then dramatically introduces Yahweh, who answers Job out of the whirlwind (38:1–39:30), and points to the marvels of the physical world, and the Creator's knowledge of and care for the animal world (38:39–39:30). Job admits his incompetence, his ignorance, and even his lack of interest and care for the animal creation. He is silenced (40:3–5), and in answer to Yahweh's question, Wilt thou condemn me that thou mayest be justified (40:8)? he confesses that he has been speaking about mysteries that were too wonderful, and repents in dust and ashes (42:1–6). The eloquent rhapsody on the maj-esty and mystery of nature, in description comparable to the finest in Words-worth, wrought its magic spell over the weary mind of the frustrated seeker. Allah is great, greater than we, and Allah is wise is the testimony of the uni-verse, and this was given as a final answer to the restless inquiry into the inequalities and the suffering of humanity.

This conclusion is only the old familiar one couched in new terms. It rests on a wishful selection of the facts of nature, and is silent about those crushing, deadly forces in the universe that ever grind on oblivious of men and morals.

---

[4] Job's speeches are found in Job 3:1–26; 6:1–7:21; 9:1–10:22; 12:1–14:22; 16:1–16; 19:1–29; 21:1–34; 23:1–24:25; 27:1–23; 29:1–31:40.

Nevertheless, it marks a forward, though not final, step in thinking. It has brought a set of new facts into consideration, and has widened the outlook of religion. It is on the way to an understanding of the great mystery. Beyond that we are enriched by the clarity of vision and the bravery of expression of one who in sincerity bared to public gaze the deepest doubts of the human heart. That a man has walked this way before, and left the record, is an aid to us. In the hour of disillusionment we are not alone, but find ourselves in the company of pioneers of other ages. The three friends had all the answers; Job had a question that called for a new answer. It came not, but his face was toward the light.

The problem of suffering, more poignant and personal than that of the character of God, has been a source of perplexity the world over in every age. It has been widely accepted by primitive man and by traditional theologians alike as the inscrutable will of the unknowable powers of the universe. Ours not to reason why has often been accepted as the foundation of faith. More thoughtful men have concluded that it is the result of man's first disobedience (Gen. 3:1-8), thus marking an awakening of consciousness to the moral order and providing an incentive for the criticism of human activities, which, peradventure, may be the causes of prevailing ills. Jeremiah, Habakkuk, and the poem in Job all deal with this problem though they do not provide final, logical solutions.

The prose section of the book of Job (1:1-2:13; 42:7-17),[5] with dramatic art, gave an appealing turn to the old solution of suffering. Here, in a setting supplied by mythology, suffering is proclaimed as heaven's test to prove that there is disinterested goodness on the earth. The stage is set in the court of God, where Yahweh receives the homage of the sons of God and supervises the affairs of men. All is modeled on Oriental court scenes long familiar to the Jewish ancestors (I Kings 22:19-25). The drama is unfolded swiftly. Scene one introduces us to Job, a perfect and upright man, who fears God and turns away from evil (1:1-5). Scene two is laid in the courts of heaven, where the sons of God, of whom Satan, the tester, is one, come to present themselves before Yahweh. Yahweh somewhat tauntingly inquires of Satan, "Hast thou considered my servant Job, there is none like him in the earth"? (1:8). Satan in reply insinuates that Job is well paid for his integrity and loyalty (1:9-12). In scenes three and four, Job is handed over once, and a second time, to be tested to the limit. Swiftly all the dread experiences of life, loss of property, of servants, of children (1:13-22), followed by the scourge of an inescapable, loathsome disease and the cynical despair of his wife (2:7-9) overwhelm the victim of the cynical experiment. But "In all this did not Job sin with his lips"

[5] It seems probable that this prose is the beginning and the end of a brochure, written about 500 B.C., which made use of a well-known folk tale as a basis for the discussion of this problem. The dialogue between Job and his friends has been displaced by the present poem, if this theory is correct. See footnote 3, this chapter.

(2:10), which to the author was the final proof of purity. He had stood the test. The prose dialogue that followed is gone forever, but its tone is reasonably certain. The friends, the comforters, were the orthodox theologians of the day; Job, the victim, under the pressure of facts, must have been the dissenter, the innovator. After the dialogue came the conclusion. Job, having stood all the tests, was accepted of Yahweh, restored to health, and blessed with double the sheep and camels, oxen and asses that he had in the beginning (42:10–17).

The author of the prose, in the beginning, like Plato in the *Republic,* placed the ultimate cause of all human experience in the heavens, beyond the ken and the control of man. Thus the acts of God were not to be questioned. But the last scene is nothing less than revolutionary in its conclusion. This man of Uz, apparently not a Jew, amid overwhelming disaster had proved to be master over the tragic incidents of human experience, and in his integrity, towering like a mountain peak, unshaken and unsullied, he stood justified in the court of heaven. He had inner resources by which he had withstood the furious assaults of the powers of evil. Man had faced the Eternal, and was justified.

More significant still, the three friends, the defenders of the teaching of the schools, had not spoken the thing that was right (42:7, 8). Orthodoxy was discredited in the supreme court. But Job, who aware of the sinister facts of life had dared to exercise his intelligence and dispute the current theories, was approved by Yahweh. This man, owing to his integrity, his reverence, and his critical mental attitudes, became a priest for those who had spoken the thing that was not right, and to Yahweh he was "my servant" (42:7, 8). It is true that the author fell back on the old idea of rewards and punishments (42:10–16), but the man accepted of Yahweh was superior to such bribes, and his reasoning faculties had not been beclouded by these inherited doctrines. The fathers had not uttered the last word on the problem of suffering, and the assumed decrees of the court of heaven were not final.

The four Servant Songs, Isaiah 42:1–4; 49:1–6; 50:4–9; and 52:13–53:12, have a new and profoundly religious interpretation of the enigma of suffering. While probably not based specifically on the life of Jeremiah, these songs were at least influenced by tragedies of a similar nature in which the best of Jewry were engulfed. Written during the early years of the Persian ascendancy, between 540 and 500 B.C., they were imbedded in Isaiah 40–55, with which they have much in common. Linguistic features are much the same, and the ethical monotheism of Deutero-Isaiah, which underlies the songs, had added intensity to the moral issues involved in the exile.

But there are essential differences between these poems and the body of the book. The songs are poetic gems of fine quality, while the rest of the booklet, though jubilant, is rather prosy, and ofttimes repetitiously wearisome. The theme of chapters 40–55 is that Yahweh, who alone is God, had exiled his people as a punishment for their sin, and now that they had received double for their transgressions, he is about to deliver them by the hand of Cyrus, his anointed (Isa. 45:1–6). But the Servant Songs move in a different thought world. In them the purpose of the exile is declared to have been to redeem Israel, and to bring the light to the Gentiles.[6] Thus whether written by the author of Deutero-Isaiah, which seems unlikely, or by a contemporary, these poems make their own distinct contribution to the problem of suffering.

As part of the reaction against the Deuteronomic theology they widened the ancient tribal principle, my brother's keeper, to include the Gentile world. Captive Israel, broken, despised, and outcast, had something essential to the culture of Babylon the great. Their God was the righteous, the living, the only true God, hence on them lay the responsibility of teaching. This was the meaning of their suffering; not for their sins, but for the sake of others; it was vicarious. Thus out of the night came songs of greatest cheer and the profoundest faith. The detailed study of each song shows how clearly the author understood the solace of service, the primary place of the teacher, and the surpassing values in the moral and religious heritage of his people.

The term "servant," that binds these four poems together, had a long and rich history. Earlier it had been used to describe Abraham (Gen. 26:24), Moses (Num. 12:7), David (I Kings 11:13, 32), and Nebuchadnezzar (Jer. 25:9; 27:6). About this time it was used for Zerubbabel (Hag. 2:23), and for the nation as a whole (Jer. 30:10; 46:27, 28; Ezek. 28:25; 37:25). In Deutero-Isaiah [7] it is never used for an individual but always for the remnant of the nation in exile. My servant is Jacob or Israel (41:8; 44:2, 21; 45:4; 48:3, 20), and shares in the captivity (41:9; 42:22; 45:4, 5; 48:20). Also the servant is blind and deaf, which prevents any exegete from applying it literally to any individual (42:19, 20). Added to this, the verbs used, especially in 52:13–53:12, are in the perfect, which is ample evidence that they were messages to an audience living in the sixth century B.C. Thus *my servant* was the remnant in exile, or better, for the phrase is not always precise, that group of zealous Jews who were the Israel within Israel, or the church within the church. It is evident that the songs all grew out of a well-known historical situation, and greatly encouraged a nucleus in captivity by the thought that their life in a foreign land played a significant role in the world plan of their God.

The first song, 42:1–4, has often been read simply as a direct prediction to

[6] Kaufman Köhler draws attention to the fact that Jewish and Christian scholars alike recognize Israel, the martyr nation, as the suffering messiah sent forth to be the savior to the nations (*Jewish Theology*, 367–377). C. C. Torrey interprets Isaiah 40–66 as a literary unit on the theme: Israel is the servant and her hope and mission are to save the world; a message written about 400 B.C. (*The Second Isaiah*).

[7] A careful study of the twenty cases in which "servant" is used in Deutero-Isaiah shows conclusively that the term always personifies the community (G. C. Workman, *The Servant of Jehovah*, 96–162).

Christ. It is meaningful. A servant, chosen and delighted in by God; bringing justice to the nations; quiet, no crying or shouting; tenderhearted, so that the damaged flute is not destroyed; patient, and confident in the midst of shattered hopes—all such descriptions easily lend themselves to the character of Jesus. However, all these virtues and graces in some measure apply to all good men, and to groups everywhere. Moreover, the poem is so integrated in Jewish history and in the text that indubitably it was originally a song of comfort for the exiles in Babylonia. They were personified as "my servant," and as such, quietly and patiently were called on to set justice in the earth. As teachers of right, not as warriors, they would prevail, was the conviction of the author.

The second song, 49:1-6, developed the idea of the first. The servant is Israel, who from the beginning had been ordained, not only to restore Jacob, which was too light a task for a servant, but also to teach the nations and to carry salvation to the end of the earth. Thus would Yahweh, himself, be glorified in his servant. This was no small-state idea. It was a glimpse of a world mission, the only logical objective of a people who believed that their God was the Creator of all men and that religion was primarily ethical. Such a challenge to devotion has often awakened dormant energies to great achievement in conquest, exploration, and service.

The third song, 50:4-9, leads us still more deeply into the thought of the writer. The servant still is the teacher, and three ideas are emphasized. First, by listening attentively to the voice of Yahweh, the servant is taught daily, and thus is able to comfort the weary. How the voice comes is not stated; but every morning as the need arises Yahweh rouses him and grants him a vision which, though vague, is full of assurance. Somehow guidance is to be granted for the needs of the day. Second, he patiently suffers the taunts and scoffing of those who refuse to share his convictions. Ideas alien to one's inheritance, or at variance with personal interests, usually arouse suspicion or hostility; while patient persistence in a worthy program is like the leaven that ultimately leavens the whole lump. The third fact, one that is constant in all four poems, is the sublime confidence in the ultimate success of the teaching mission. Only the long view of history confirms this optimism. Prophets and dreamers are ever scorned, and ideas may lie dormant for centuries, yet the day of harvest is sure. Slowly, very slowly, the deserts are being transformed, thorns and briars are being eliminated, and the waste places are blossoming as the rose. Amid adversaries, the teaching of the prophets has a growing place in world history.

The last poem, 52:13-53:12, the best known of all, while differing in metrical form from the others is closely linked with them by phrase and ideal. "My servant" here, however, is the title under which the pious remnant among the captives is personified. This small group of men, kindred in spirit and experience with Jeremiah, caught the vision that sacrifice and service were the essential factors in life and religion. Stripped of property, power, and prestige, and separated from the homeland and temple, they had learned that they had inner resources more rewarding than the accretions from without, and that the sacrifice acceptable to Yahweh was the vicarious, living witness to a righteous and merciful God amid the nations. This insight carried with it the responsibility of living up to the conviction and of witnessing to the Gentiles. This was a world mission in practical idealism, and a redeemed humanity was the goal.

Thus vicarious sacrifice, participation in living, not substitution, is set forth as the inner meaning of suffering. Such an interpretation lit up the dark horizon of the faithful, who in a far land were pondering the apparent inequities of divine justice. Life, in reality, lay far beneath the appearance of things, and was part of the ongoing stream that was ever expanding in the interest of the deeper things of man and God. Each was like the grain of wheat that by losing its life saved it.

Every phase of this song fits into the experience of the inner circle of the faithful. They were uprooted, rejected, sorrowful and sick, avoided, beaten, scourged, unable to obtain justice, outcast, despised even by their own kin, for whose transgressions they were suffering; and yet, the servant, by means of these very sufferings, brought healing to others, and by the same sufferings he himself would be exalted and would finally triumph.

A strange philosophy of life, yet strangely realistic. It is this principle that operates throughout the biological world, from the lowest to the highest, for the better adjustment of the species. Complacency and self-interest pave the way to defeat; suffering that leads to a ministry to others has been a power for good for millennia; and in it lies the hope for peace on earth, good will to men. It would have been strange if the Christian Church had not interpreted the cross of Jesus in this context. It is fortunate when men, everywhere, learn that apart from personal participation therein there is no salvation.

The singer and his disciples had attained a view of life that triumphed over personal tragedy and rose above the ruins of national hope. Their outlook was no longer provincial, and their standard of values lay not where moth and rust do corrupt, nor where thieves break through and steal. Their energies were enlisted in the human enterprise of bearing aloft a light to the Gentiles, and proclaiming deliverance to the uttermost ends of the earth (49:6). Their religion emphasized character rather than ceremony, and was kindly and unobtrusive, patient in suffering, but quietly persistent in the mission of teaching. They rejoiced that in giving the cup of cold water to the thirsty in a far land, they were the servants of the one and only true God. These men of the spirit not only had the personal conviction that they were fulfilling destiny, but to all who have come after them they have left a priceless heritage in thought and conduct.

Wisdom, always highly prized in the Near East, took on many and varied forms of expression: the riddle, the question, the parable, the proverb, the essay, and the treatise. Basically it is sound judgment. It is the native gift by which knotty problems are axiomatically solved, the facts beneath the camouflage are detected, and the essential values in life are distinguished from the incidentals. It is the distinctive mark of the wise, those men of reflection and good judgment, who are the acknowledged guides in days of chaos and confusion.

The wise men among the Jews were acquainted with the Torah,[8] and the temple rites, but showed little interest in the pageants, while they emphasized the place of teaching. They knew the prophets, and accepted the permanent or universal elements, while they placed little emphasis on the local and the temporary. They were akin to the liberals in outlook and spirit, though they had a permanent interest in the organization of schools. They had contacts with Greek culture, which some rejected and others accepted, but most of them stopped short of the conclusions of the cynic, or the atheist.

The chief works of the wise that have been preserved are Proverbs, Job, the Song of Songs, Ecclesiastes, Ben Sirach, and the Wisdom of Solomon. Though parts of these may find their sources far back in Hebrew life and thought, in their present form they all come from the Persian and Greek periods, and, as they were contemporary with the priestly ascendancy, they relieve Jewish thought from any charge of narrowness. If the priests, faced by the catastrophe of a disintegrating nation, turned toward legalism and isolationism, the wise men, reacting against the extremes of the former and finding an ally in Greek culture, sought the solution of the problems in the broader, freer, and more genuinely human approach.

The wisdom literature is all monotheistic. The existence of God, the Creator of the universe and the Ruler of men, is never questioned by a good Semite. This assumption inhibited a good Jew from indulging in metaphysical speculation, and combined with his national disabilities to make him a pragmatist. His practical common sense, which he exercised in the solution of his social and economic problems, might have been discussed here, but is carried over to chapter XIII, where it is equally appropriate.

That the Jew was capable of abstract thought, if unhampered by presuppositions, is evident from a number of specifically intellectual contributions to religious thought. Four remarkable interpretations of wisdom, the residuum of diverse types of theology, have come down to us from these ancient days. They are Ben Sirach 24:1-34; Proverbs 8:1-9:6; Job 28:1-37, and the Wisdom of Solomon 7:1-8:36. In their present form these date from 300 to shortly after 100 B.C., and are the result of the disturbing impact of Persian and Greek culture on Judaism. These four are well-polished literary monuments of long

---

[8] An informing illustration of the broad interests of the scholar, in which ideas quite antagonistic were united, is found in Ben Sirach 39:1-35, which should be read along with 38:24-34. Here the scribe was well versed in the Torah, and in all the wisdom of the ancients. He could easily qualify as a wise man, or as a priest.

and bitter conflicts that reveal the vitality and adaptability, as well as the intellectual qualities, of Judaism.

Ben Sirach, or Ecclesiasticus 24:1–34 (cf. 1:4–26), written about 180 B.C., came out of a background of more than two hundred years of devotion to the law.[9] With colorful phrase and an imagination that closed its eyes to the lowly origin of law and augmented the values of scribal ideals beyond that dictated by modesty, it declared that the law came forth from the mouth of the Most High, and rested in Jacob, and had her inheritance in Israel. The law was thus made equivalent to the wisdom of the Almighty. This was priestly orthodoxy in its most arrogant form. No doubt this was agreeably convincing to those long absorbed in the niceties of the cult, but in fact it was provincial rather than divine, and stultifying rather than creative. It was an apologetic, deadly in its implications, for the *status quo*. Yet its influence has been far-reaching. The theory hold by Calvin that everything pertaining to the perfect rules of a good life, the Lord has so comprehended in his law, that there remains nothing for man to add to that summary, was shaped in the same mold.

The second study, Proverbs 8:1–9:6 (cf. 3:19, 20; 4:1–8; 1:2–23), is part of a discourse the material of which may have been compiled from various sources some time before 200 B.C.[10] Here the teacher is the moving spirit, and to him wisdom is vastly more inclusive than the Torah. He adjures youth to avoid that which is evil and to cling to that which is good. Emphasis is laid on the way of righteousness and the paths of justice. Knowledge and understanding always belong to the individual and are essential to sound judgment. Wisdom is ethical and is individualistic, and, being found in the very nature of things, it is universal. She is everywhere, at the caravan crossroads, in the city gates, in the public square, in the courts of kings, and beyond all in the schools. She is in the stream of social life, and is in light that may be found in all quarters. Moreover, wisdom is eternal, the companion of God from before the foundation of the earth, but she has special delight with the children of men.

In this essay, and throughout Proverbs 1–9, wisdom shows no sympathy with the priestly ideal, and ranges far beyond the glorification of the law in Ben Sirach 24:1–34. It does not express another phase of the same idea, but is antagonistic to every central proposition in the Torah as generally interpreted by the priests. The conceptions of evil, salvation, law, the dignity of man, and the chosen people in the one are mutually exclusive to those in the other. Here we find the axioms of the pre-exilic prophets, under Greek influence, flowering out into an educational system which was essentially individualistic, ethical, and universal. To the writer this was the fear of Yahweh,.

---

[9] The foundations of legalism were as old as Israel herself. The lawbook of the reform of Josiah (Deut. 4:6–8; 29:20, 21, 28), and that of Ezra (Ezra 7:25) only formulated and intensified the function of custom in human life (G. F. Moore, *Judaism*, I, 10–23).

[10] T. K. Cheyne, *Jewish Religious Life after the Exile*, 126–215.

or better still the true religion.[11] The former, that is, Ben Sirach, was a representative of the high church, while Proverbs 8:1–9:6 would be classified by many as pagan or profane or universalist. In actual history these two have always been reluctant to walk together.

The third interpretation, a choice poem, Job 28:1–27, but scarcely an integral part of the book of Job, differs from both of the above. It draws a sharp contrast between the range of man's understanding and that of God. Man refines gold, smelts copper, digs for gems, and in finding, seeing, and doing things is far superior to the swift, keen bird, the proud beast, and the fierce lion. He has learned many of the secrets of nature, and has brought to light things that were hidden (28:1–11). But the abode of wisdom—God alone has searched it out and established it. He alone knows the hidden mysteries (28:12–27).

Here wisdom is neither the Torah nor that universal knowledge that may be found by all who seek. As with the agnostic in Proverbs 31:1–4, it lies beyond the reach of man. This conclusion is a reaction against the intellectual movements that prevailed during the Greek period. Certain temperaments, fearing that free inquiry might undermine the inherited pattern of life, were ready to decry reason because its methods were experimental and its conclusions were subject to correction. To many good people this pronouncement has been a great consolation; but it is the shelter of fear, not the venture of faith, a sign of weakness, not the evidence of strength.

The fourth selection, Wisdom of Solomon 7:1–8:31, written early in the first century B.C., of all these is the most philosophic. It was definitely influenced by Greek language and thought, and in turn was freely used by more than one early Christian writer. Wisdom is here personified as a master workman (7:22; 13:1), seated on a throne beside the God of the fathers (9:4), and is the medium by which God has made everything (7:22, 24; 8:1). She is described as the only-begotten, the clear effulgence of the glory of the Almighty, an effulgence from everlasting light, an unspotted mirror of the working of God, and an image of his goodness (7:22, 25, 26). The similarities between this and Hebrews 1:2, 3; John 1:1, 3, 4, 14; and IV Maccabees are apparent. They at least belong to the same literary and intellectual world. Further, in this essay wisdom was thought of as the efficient cause of all human understanding, activity, and goodness. She made men prophets, and friends with God; taught soberness and understanding, righteousness and courage; made princes wise, and was accessible to all (7:15–21; 8:7; 6:12–15). Kinship with her brought immortality (8:17), and she reached from one end of the earth to the other, ordering all things graciously (7:24; 8:1; 12:18;

11 In Proverbs 1:7, 29; 2:5; 9:10, the phrase usually translated "fear of Yahweh" has been more accurately rendered "reverence of Yahweh," by Moffatt, and "your fear" in Job 4:6; 22:4, has been correctly translated "your religion." It is quite clear from the contexts in Proverbs that reverence of Yahweh is equivalent to the true religion.

15:1). In universality and in ethical emphasis this is in agreement with Proverbs, chapter 8, and is the acme of Hebrew thought.

Beyond this, however, we are ushered into the Greek world, where the *logos* was the creative principle, the intermediary between the High God, who was spirit, and the crass, wicked world, that was material. Many of the terms here used, descriptive of wisdom, are those that were in common use by the Stoics for *logos*. Wisdom was characterized as manifold, freely moving, unspotted, distinct, unharmed, loving what is good, keen, unhindered, penetrating through all spirits, quick of understanding, pure, most subtle; more mobile than any motion, she pervadeth, and penetrateth all things by reason of her pureness (7:22–24). Here the Jew had adopted terms from Greek philosophy, and was paving the way for the later Christian interpretation of Jesus as the *logos*. For those with metaphysical interests this gave intellectual satisfactions, and easily became the dogma of early Christianity.

In wisdom literature as a whole, but especially in these four dissertations, we clearly see certain definite trends in Jewish religious thought during the Greek period. In pre-exilic days, while priest and prophet faced each other in stormy conflict, probably both would have agreed that speculative wisdom was secular and had little place in religion. The denunciation by the prophet, "Woe to those who are wise in their own eyes, and prudent in their own sight" (Isa. 5:21), would have been loudly applauded by the average priest.

But history is always teaching those who listen. Thrown out of his narrow hillside seclusion into the wide world, the Jew had to associate with Babylonian and Egyptian, Persian, Greek, and Roman. Some became reactionary, intensified their provincialism, and froze the structure of their religion and gloried in their orthodoxy, to them the essential to their election. But under the pervasive influence of Greek life and thought, others learned from what they saw and heard. The priest beautified and enriched the ritual by additions in music and psalmody. The rabbis interpreted the Torah, so as to support the messages of the prophets and the reflections of the wise. The teacher opened the door into a thought world in which Hebrew convictions and ideals were sorely challenged, yet mellowed and expanded. The customs, literature, religion, and philosophy of the Greeks aroused the ire of many but appealed to the more thoughtful and made a lasting contribution to the strength of Judaism. Ultimately the law was not only translated into Greek, but Jewish interpreters read into their Scriptures, as they desired, all the teachings of Greek philosophy. Jewish religion, while boasting its peculiar inheritance, and for the most part remaining loyal to its essential traditions, not only read its sacred books in an alien tongue but accepted ideas and ideals that had been nurtured in the Greek schools. Again, as so often in earlier days, the Jew was able to adapt himself to his environment, profit from the universal teacher, and grow in knowledge and in stature in the things of mind and heart.

Chapter XII

THE RELIGION OF THE STATE-CHURCH.

550-400 B.C.

IN THE post-exilic period, the development of religious thought and practice in Israel was greatly diversified. Never unitedly and consistently moving in a straight line, but split up into conflicting units, antagonistic schools of thought usually expressed themselves with extreme vigor.

The priests, owing to their culture, organization, and intense zeal, easily became the leaders in Judaism. The book of Deuteronomy had been the product of an alliance of priest and prophet, constrained to unite under the persecutions of the pro-Assyrian Manasseh. Jeremiah in his later years had denounced the reform as an altogether superficial remedy for the sins of the nation (Jer. 8:8, 11). On the other hand, from the beginning it must have been quite unacceptable to many of the priesthood. It had been a compromise accomplished under duress. Many practices long observed by the faithful had been omitted, and principles underlying their ritual had been nullified. Many of the more rigid ritualists must have whispered that they had been sold out by the appeasers, and when relieved from political pressure they were assured that their day of grace had come.

For more than a century following the fall of the city (586 B.C.), all Jewry was engulfed in world catastrophe. Assyria had crashed (604 B.C.). Babylonia had risen in splendor, only to go out in total eclipse within a lifetime (539 B.C.). Jerusalem had been razed to the ground, and her people had been scattered to the four winds of heaven. Persia, gifted in organization and wise in ruling subject people, had entered the field of world empire. The impact of such upheavals had wrought far-reaching changes in the outlook and the hopes of the various divisions of Judaism.

The priests, eager for the welfare of their people, were pondering the lessons of national history. To them it was clear that the eighth-century prophets had doomed but had not liberated the nation. Further, by the death of Josiah on the battlefield, and by the fall of the city that followed so close on the heels of the reformation, they were convinced that the covenant of Deuteronomy had been altogether inadequate. The new covenant of Jeremiah, and the redemptive ideal of the servant songs must have seemed utopian futilities to those who knew the perverse ways of the human heart, and who thought in terms of rites and ceremonies. A few decades later, when the Haggai-Zechariah-Zerubbabel dream of a kingdom (Hag. 2:2–23; Zech. 4:6–10) ended in a total blackout (516 B.C.), to them it was an added proof that insistence on Jewish political independence was nothing short of suicidal, and that if Israel was to be saved the responsibility lay with them. That nothing should be added to or taken away from the law of Deuteronomy (Deut. 12:32) clearly had been nullified by history, and the will of Yahweh seemed to call for a priestly program for the redemption of his people.

Whether actually warranted by the logic of history or not, for centuries the priests toiled with the problems of reconstruction, rethought and reworked the finest in Israel's early customs, adapted what seemed worthy from Babylonia and Persia, and, guided by the hopes and ideals of their ancestors, formulated rites and ceremonies they deemed essential for the preservation of the community. The residuum of their wisdom is now found in their editorial contribution to the Hexateuch, and in three legal codes. These are Holiness Code (Lev. 17–26, H. C., which has also later priestly additions), the temple vision in Ezekiel (chaps. 40–48), both of which possibly were concluded before 500 B.C., and the Priest Code [1] nearing completion by 400 B.C. and now found scattered throughout the Hexateuch. Large sections belonging to P. are Leviticus 1:1–16:34; 27:1–34; Exodus 25:1–31:18; 35:1–40:38. Each of these codes is, in itself, composite, but though they were compiled on dates widely separated, and in places far apart, each one is in general agreement with well-recognized priestly principles.

In reading through these three priestly programs [2] we at once find ourselves in an atmosphere altogether strange to that of the prophets. It is like passing from the intellectual and moral warmth of the chapel to the maze of the High Mass in the cathedral. Everything is strange. Indeed we have to learn a new language; even old words have an entirely new meaning, and the very pattern of thought is the antithesis to that of the prophets. Words like justice, righteousness, and repentance, the stock in trade of the prophets, have all but disappeared (cf. Lev. 19:9–18, 33–36) and in their place we find the altar (100 times), the tabernacle (106 times), the sin offering and the guilt offering (126 times), the oblation (78 times), the fire offering, the mercy

---

[1] The material of P. is easily separated from the earlier codes, and from the J. and E. narratives, on linguistic and ideological grounds. Complete details may be found in any trustworthy commentary or Bible dictionary. Hastings' *Dictionary of the Bible,* either the one-volume or the five-volume set, or *Encyclopaedia Biblica* gives full information. Commentaries such as the *International Critical Commentary, Century Bible Commentary,* and *Cambridge Bible Commentary* provide detailed analyses of the documents and the codes. Helpful introductions are A. T. Chapman, *Introduction to the Pentateuch;* R. H. Pfeiffer, *Introduction to the O. T.;* S. R. Driver, *Introduction to the Literature of the O. T.*

[2] For a study of the priestly ideas it is helpful to have at hand the material segregated in its probable chronological order, within its historical framework. A convenient volume is that of C. F. Kent, *Israel's Laws and Legal Precedents,* in the "Student's Old Testament" series.

seat, and the atonement.[3] The *congregation* has displaced the nation, and the priest and his acolytes meet us at every turn. In place of repentance we catch a fleeting glimpse of *confession* (Lev. 5:5; 16:21; Num. 5:7), which originated as a magical, purificatory rite,[4] and is as far removed from the prophetic idea as penance is from penitence. Uncleanness or pollution had neither sanitary nor ethical implications, but was the result of spirit or demon possession, and was charged with grave danger similar to our idea of a miasma or electricity.[5] Hence cleansing was a ceremonial act accomplished by rites of water, fire, odors, or blood carried out with technical skill by qualified priests.[6] It follows that holiness and holy, as used in P. derived their meaning from ritual,[7] and not from the social concept of religion. The new vocabulary and new forms all belong to the hierarchy, and are the bearers of a sweet savor to Yahweh. But we have passed from the presence of the prophets, and have entered the courts of the courteous, well-groomed, soft-spoken servants of God, where we hear the call, "Be ye holy, for I am holy." If we miss the appeal for social righteousness, we cannot fail to hear the call to worship the Lord, our God in the beauty of holiness. With this background we can now form an estimate of the more definite values in each of the above codes.

Holiness Code (Lev. 17–26), came first in order of time, (*ca.* 550 B.C.). It is a collection of ceremonial practices, some of which were pre-Mosaic (possibly Azazel in Lev. 16:8, 20–22), others of recent origin, while all were assumed to be the words of Yahweh to Moses (Lev. 18:3, 24; 19:2; 20:22, 24; 23:10; 25:2; 26:46). The editor by phraseology and ideals shows an acquaintance with Deuteronomy, and may have lived in Babylonia.[8]

Incorporated in it is a section on social justice that parallels the best in the prophets. Justice for all (19:35, 36), equity for rich and poor alike (19:15), prompt payment of daily wages (19:13), the good-neighbor policy toward the resident alien, and the call to love your neighbor as yourself (19:18, 33, 34), approximates the emphasis found in the New Testament (Lev. 19:9–18, 33–37). But while the code thus pays tribute to the prophets, justice, kindness, and chastity are strangely mingled with cult practices as though both

[3] Carpenter and Battersby, *The Composition of the Hexateuch,* give a summary of the peculiar vocabulary, 249, 408–425.

[4] T. G. Pinches, "Confession," *ERE,* III, 825, 826. A. E. Suffrin, *ibid.,* 830.

[5] The general principle has been carefully stated by R. R. Marett in *The Threshold of Religion,* 1–32; and an interpretation of the Biblical material is found in A. C. Knudson, *The Religious Teaching of the Old Testament,* 137–153.

[6] W. R. Smith, *Rel. Sem.* (3), 556–559, and L. R. Farnell, *The Evolution of Religion,* 88–163, are general studies on this topic. The Biblical aspect of the theme is presented by A. W. F. Blunt in *HBD* (one vol.), "Clean and Unclean"; also by G. A. Simcox in *Ency. Bibl.,* same subject.

[7] Holiness as expressed by the Hebrew root QDSH means separateness, and to be holy was to be separated due to strangeness, or danger, or mystery. See W. R. Smith, *Rel. Sem.* (3), 140–159, 288–303, Note B, 446–454.

[8] Supported by R. H. Pfeiffer, *Introduction to the O. T.,* 248–250. A. R. S. Kennedy dates it earlier and places its origin in Palestine ("Leviticus," *Century Bible,* 25–28).

were on the same level. No difference in value is recognized between loving your neighbor as yourself and wearing garments of unmixed material (19:18, 19). Adultery and sowing two kinds of seed in the same field are equally reprehensible (19:19, 20), and the crossbreeding of animals was a sin, because "I am Yahweh" (19:19). The fact is, the emphasis has shifted from the rights of man to the demands of Yahweh, and we are on the way to the priestly doctrine that calls for unquestioned obedience on the ground not of right but of might.

Holiness, on the part of God, was thus thought of as that separation from the common and unclean that in its very nature was supercharged with danger and death; on the part of man, it was attained or maintained by observing the established taboos, and by the correct performance of prescribed ceremonies. Thus were the dangers due to contact with Deity averted. This is made clear by the fact that a wide range of taboos was strictly commanded under penalty of death (26:14-39; cf. 26:3-13). These taboos include idolatrous practices (18:21-30; 19:4, 31; 20:1-5), wearing garments of mixed stuff and sowing mixed grain in the same field (19:19), eating first fruits (19:23-25), eating with the blood (17:10-14; 19:26), eating torn flesh (17:15), eating meat not sacrificially slain (17:3-7),[9] and various monstrous sex irregularities (18:6-23; 20:13, 16, 18).

Further, it was affirmed that the strict observance of these taboos would make the land holy (25:2-7, 18-22; 26:34, 35), make the altars holy (19:30; 20:3; 21:12, 23), make the people holy (19:2, 30, 31; 20:7, 26), and make the priests holy (21:1-15; 22:3-9). Then Yahweh, whose name would be holy (19:12; 21:6; 22:2, 32), would send the rain in its season, the land would yield its increase, and peace, prosperity, and victory over the enemies would be the portion of the people (26:3-13), and Yahweh himself would walk among them and establish his covenant with them (26:9, 42-45). Thus sin, no longer regarded as a violation of social relations, but as uncleanness, was now cleansed by ablutions (17:15, 16; 22:6), and by offerings and sacrifices of various types, first fruits, and meal offerings (23:10-13), peace offerings (22:18b-25, 27-32), freewill offerings (22:18, 21, 23; 23:38), and burnt offerings (16:3, 24; 17:8; 23:18, 37).

This code is a simple manual of cult requirements, a new arrangement of old material, apparently intended for the guidance of the pious layman. It is splendidly objective, and differs from Deuteronomy in that it is definitely sacerdotal. It makes its appeal, not to inherent values, but to the authority of tradition, going back to a pre-Mosaic covenant with Abraham, Isaac, and Jacob (26:42), and resting on the external appeal, I am Yahweh your God. Those who were fearful of private judgment, and eager for a *Thus saith the Lord,* must have found this brochure a happy solution to their problems and

---

[9] This is a reversion to type, insisting on the early practice (cf. I Sam. 14:32-35), and is a direct attack on the law in Deuteronomy 12:15, 16, which was an innovation.

a sedative to their anxieties. While in no sense a complete manual, it was the expression of a definite religious movement, and provided the framework that later generations of priests filled in and expanded to meet the needs of the worshipers.

Holiness Code had neither been complete nor final, and others, stimulated by the needs of the day, were at work on plans for the new era. The temple vision in Ezekiel 40–48, the product of long reflection, was the work of a kindred spirit to the author of H.C., though he was interested in the broader outlines of reconstruction. The unknown author was acquainted with Babylonian culture, and had some knowledge of her forms of worship and her temple architecture. The date of the composition is uncertain. It may have followed rather than preceded the rebuilding of the second temple in 516 B.C. That heroic achievement, reported in Haggai, and Zechariah 1 to 8, was rebellion against Persia, and Zerubbabel, though proclaimed the signet ring on the finger of Yahweh (Hag. 2:2–4, 20–23; Zech. 3:8; 4:6–9; 6:12), was a betrayer of his trust and a traitor to his sovereign. While no record tells us what happened, we know that the insurrection did not succeed, and in all probability the blind struggle for self-rule, so native to the Jew, had been quelled by the execution of the guilty. The prophets, in the name of Yahweh, had prophesied falsely, and Yahweh had not deigned to interfere on their behalf. It may have been the failure of Zerubbabel that led to the demotion of the prince in this vision of the new state (Ezek. 46:2, 8, 12–18).

The plan of reconstruction is well ordered.[10] The twelve tribes are to be rearranged territorially, each according to its importance, in the mind of the author, on an eight-and-one-third-mile strip, which ran from the Jordan Valley to the Mediterranean (48:1–7, 23–28). Seven of these tribal strips lay to the north, and five to the south of a similar strip, called the sacred tract, which was bounded by Judah on the north and by Benjamin on the south (48:8–22).

This sacred tract, eight and one-third miles wide, and running from the Jordan to the Mediterranean, was all set aside for religious purposes. In the middle of it, though not precisely located, lay an eight-and-one-third-mile square, east of which to the Jordan, and west of it to the Mediterranean, the territory was assigned to the prince, whose chief function was to provide certain offerings for the temple service (48:21, 22; 45:7, 8, 17).

The central square in the sacred tract was subdivided into three parts, each running east and west the eight and one-third miles of the sacred tract. The northern one, eight and one-third miles by three and two-thirds miles, was to be occupied by the Levites, who were to be the servants of the priests (48:13). The third division, lying to the south alongside Benjamin, was eight and one-third miles by one and one-third miles. In the middle of this lay the

10 The details of the program are summarized by the writer in "Ezekiel," *American Commentary*, xviii–xx, xlix–lii, 148–178.

city, a square of one and one-third miles, built on the top of the mountain
(43:12), with an encircling boulevard 146 feet wide, all enclosed in walls,
pierced by twelve gates, one for each of the tribes (48:30–34). The remaining spaces in this strip, three and one-half miles east and three and one-half
miles west of this city square, were to be occupied by villages for workmen
who came from each tribe to the city, and for community tillage (48:18, 19).
Thus with ample provision made for the needs of the citizens, for their comfort and their protection, with its broad boulevard, its high walls, and its
lofty site, we have the prototype of the new Jerusalem, let down out of heaven
(Rev. 21:2).

But our chief interest lies in the middle strip, again eight and one-third
by three and two-thirds miles, in the central square. This was the priestly
possession (48:9, 10), and in the middle of it, probably directly north of the
city, stood the temple. The whole temple area was surrounded by a high wall
(40:5, 6), and was thus completely separated, by both the wall and the priestly
occupants of the land, from all that was secular or profane, so that Israel
might never again defile "my holy name" by the dead bodies of her kings
and the harlotries of her people, by "placing their thresholds against my
threshold with only a wall between me and them" (43:7–9, as against the
Solomonic temple, I Kings 6:1–10; 7:7–13).

The whole temple area was on a terrace, seven steps up (40:6, 22), and
could be entered only through three carefully guarded gates, in each of which
were six qualified officials (40:10). Inside the temple wall all the way round
ran a mosaic pavement, which led to a second terrace, reached by eight
steps (40:21, 31, 37), and again protected by guardhouses, duplicates of
those at the first entrance (40:32–34). This provided a double check against
anything that might defile gaining entrance to the area on which the house
itself stood. So insistent was the demand against defilement that, under the
influence of experiences in exile, all foreigners were to be rigidly excluded
from participation in any of the religious ceremonies (44:7–9, which is more
rigid than Deut. 23:7).

The altar stood immediately in the center of this inner area, and rose in
four stages, each narrower than the one supporting it, to the altar hearth,
which was twenty-one feet above the level (43:13–27; 40:47).[11]

The house of Yahweh was situated directly west of the altar, on a terrace
that was gained by ten steps (43:7; 40:49, LXX). Within it was the holy
place (41:2–4), and behind that was the holy of holies, the place where
Yahweh dwelt (41:4).

Not only was the structure of the temple worked out in great detail, but
the religious appointments and rites were treated with equal care. The whole
priestly organization was in the process of development. Two new types

---

[11] This is in marked contrast with the early altar, which must not be approached by steps Exod.
20:24, and apparently has been influenced by the seven-storied ziggurats of Babylonia.

of sacrifice, the sin offering (44:27, 29; 45:17, 19, 23) and the guilt offering (44:29; 46:20), were added to the earlier practice. Arrangements were made so that twice annually atonement should be offered to cleanse the sanctuary (45:18, 20). Though these never seem to have been observed, they probably prepared the way for the annual day of the atonement, which was of still later origin (Lev. 16:15–19). The chief festivals, the Passover (45:21–25) and tabernacles (45:25), were now to be observed in the first and the seventh months, and thus, no longer controlled by the fluctuations of agricultural life, they assumed historical significance. The Sabbath, likewise, grew in importance, as it was one of the few functions that could be observed in exile, and it was officially made a day of rest (46:1–11). The priests, the sons of Zadok, because they had kept the charge of the sanctuary, were elevated in rank (40:45, 46; 44:15, 16; 48:11), while the priests, the Levites, who had gone astray were reduced to menial service (40:46; 44:15; 48:11). Here again there is an advance from Deuteronomy, where priest and Levite are co-ordinate terms (Deut. 17:9, 18; 24:8; 27:29; 31:9), and a preparation for the later division of the priesthood into twenty-four courses (I Chron. 23:1–26:32). In this reconstruction, now that the kingship was but a bad memory, the prince was provided with an estate and made an ecclesiastical figurehead (45:7, 8, 17). As in the Holiness Code, the distinction between clean and unclean was vital (44:23–27), and the one thing deemed essential was the cleansed ritual, performed by a cleansed priesthood, in a cleansed house, before a cleansed altar, for a cleansed people worshiping a holy God.

All earlier programs for saving the nation, the ethical teaching of the prophets, the compromise of Deuteronomy, the new heart of Jeremiah, the vicarious suffering of the Servant, all, for one reason or another, seemed to have been discredited by history. Amid the disillusionment the author of Ezekiel 40–48 was convinced that he knew the real solution for national deliverance, viz., the state-church. With something of an apocalyptic outlook, and building on Hebrew and Babylonian priestly practices, he provided his people with the temple vision.

The vision must have been appealing. It accepted the current interpretation that evil was uncleanness, and through infection was peculiarly dangerous.[12] A clear-cut line was drawn between clean and unclean, sacred and secular, the world of God and the world of man. It was a dualism in religion. Further, that the nation might prosper in the favor of Deity, an order of worship consisting of cleansings, ablutions, deodorants, and prophylactics was provided to neutralize the infections and thus be acceptable to a holy rather than a righteous God. This program of worship, sponsored by com-

---

12 The care taken to guard against this infection is seen in the arrangement made for the isolation of priestly garments (42:13, 14), and the provision for kitchens for boiling the sacred meal for the people (46:21–24). See writer's "Ezekiel," *American Commentary*, 168, 169.

petent and devout leaders, challenged the senses by its objectivity, and by its order and beauty satisfied the esthetic demands of the multitude. The stately guards at the entrances, the gorgeous priestly ceremonies, the lofty altar visible from all quarters, and the temple, resplendent in its glory, elevated on a terraced mountain—these were a perpetual symbol and pledge of the presence of Yahweh himself in the inner sanctuary. All was a guarantee of that security so greatly desired by the timid majority in a world of bewildering uncertainty. Religion, now largely separated from socioeconomic activities, and concerned chiefly with relations in the spirit world, was placed under the direction of good men, specially trained for this task. Unlike the program of the prophets it interfered but little with either pleasure or business, and relieved the worshiper of any serious personal responsibility. It was an idealistic and inspiring project for the salvation of Israel. Opening with supernatural authentication (40:2-4), and closing with the assurance that Yahweh is there (48:35), it must have been accepted by not a few as the summation of true religion. But it was only a blueprint, and human nature frequently refuses to adjust to theories, while history has a way of disregarding reason. The tribes never took seriously the proposed territorial adjustments, and no effort ever was made to change the site of the Holy City. Indeed the rabbis long hesitated before admitting it, with stated limitations, into the canon.[13] Nevertheless it served a purpose. Its interpretation of religion was in sharp antithesis to that of the prophets, and in many ways it contributed to the later priestly program.

During the century following the temple vision in Ezekiel 40–48 world history moved apace. Persia was now master of all western Asia, ruled Egypt for a time, and in 515 B.C. aggressively set foot in Europe. Greece, during this period, not only proved her mettle on the battlefield but in literature, art, and philosophy took her place at the head of world culture.

The Jews, scattered abroad among the nations, in the meantime, had kept the lines of intercommunication open, and many of them could forget neither Jerusalem nor the religion of their fathers. Following the insurrection of Zerubbabel in 519–516 B.C. and its consequences, the Nehemiah-Ezra episodes of 444, 432, and 398 B.C.[14] were the next important known events in their history (Neh. 1:1–5; 2:6–15; 6:15; 7:1–4; 13:4–31). In his effort to provide a measure of security for the Jews in Jerusalem, Nehemiah in 444 B.C. was openly thwarted by alien elements. But he rebuilt the walls (Neh. 6:15), set up the

---

[13] See writer's "Ezekiel," *American Commentary*, vi.

[14] That the activity recorded under the name of Ezra followed the work of Nehemiah is gaining general assent. A brief presentation of the reasons is found in the writer's *Life and Literature of the O.T.*, 259, 260. R. H. Pfeiffer, *Introduction to the O.T.*, suggests that the story describing Ezra coming from Babylonia in 458 with the law of God in his hand hardly contains an element of truth (p. 256).

gates, and appointed officers and guards (7:1-4). Eleven years later he returned to the city, and closed all shops on the Sabbath, made the Jews swear to stop marrying the women of Ashdod, Ammon, and Moab, cleansed the temple of all foreign elements, and reorganized the priesthood, the offerings, and the temple treasury (Neh. 13:15-31). The crisis was reached when, if tradition be correct, Ezra the scribe put an old law (Exod. 34:15, 16; Deut. 7:1-4) into operation, and in a newly organized divorce court annulled 113 mixed marriages, and thus cleansed priests, Levites, singers, porters, and all Israel of wives of alien birth (Ezra 10:5-44).

The conclusion that what was essentially the Priest Code was in possession of the priests in Jerusalem in the time of Ezra (*ca.* 398 B.C.), is reasonably certain, though our records show evidence of much editorial activity and are lacking in convincing data (Neh. 7:73-8:18). It was a sizable roll, that for public reading and interpretation of a part of it required seven days from early morning to midday (Neh. 8:3, 8, 18). Like Holiness Code, some of its regulations were ancient, even predating Moses,[15] others showed Babylonian,[16] even Persian influence,[17] while at least one regulation, the tax of one-third of a shekel for the service of the house of God (Neh. 10:32), never mentioned earlier but in later legislation increased to one-half shekel (Exod. 30:13), was of recent origin.

The Mosaic covenant, though now radically altered, was at least considered germinal to the completed code. Parts of the law are spoken of as written by the finger of God (Exod. 31:18); others are said to have been written by Moses at the dictation of Yahweh (Exod. 34:27-32). Important institutions, even literary productions of late and unknown origin, were accepted by tradition as having been shown to Moses in the mount (Exod. 25:9, 40; 26:30). Though not a complete or a systematic compendium of accepted priestly practices, all was carefully edited, brought up to date, and dedicated to, or officially ascribed to, Moses (Neh. 8:1). Thus the priestly school made Moses, who in his own day belonged to a desert civilization and had ever faced stout opposition in both civil and religious affairs, responsible for the innumerable details of a highly complex system of rites and ceremonies that were meaningful only in a temple-centered civilization in the Persian period.

[15] Such features as the test of adultery (Num. 5:11-31), the red heifer and the water of impurity (Num. 19:1-22), the Nazarites' vow (Num. 6:2-21), the lamp in the temple (Exod. 27:21, cf. I Sam. 3:3), and the Urim and Thummim (Exod. 28:30; Lev. 8:8; I Sam. 28:6) all represent primitive practices that in all probability originated in early days.

[16] The sin offering and the guilt offering, first appearing in Ezekiel 40-48, came in under the influence of Babylonia, while the exile contributed to an emphasis on circumcision, the Sabbath, and the law. See T. H. Robinson and W. O. Oesterley, *History of Israel*, II, 134-137.

[17] Palestine by this time had been under Persian rule for more than a century, and her influence on Jewish culture had been very significant. The acts of Cyrus, Darius, Xerxes, Artaxerxes I and II, the well-organized system of government, the high type of religious thought, could not have failed to leave their impress on the priestly laws and ideals, though it would be folly to attempt to record in detail the results of such contacts. See S. A. Cook, *CAH*, VI, 167-180; L. R. Farnell, *Evolution of Religion*, 97-106, 115, 124, 127-132.

Tradition gained a measure of authority [18] for its rites by transforming a free man of the desert into a sacrosanct, ecclesiastical figurehead. He had become as a god to Pharaoh (Exod. 7:1) and talked with Yahweh as with a friend (Exod. 33:11). Aaron and the children of Israel were afraid of him as rays of light (horns) shot forth from his face (Exod. 34:29–35). Thus did tradition honor him, making him worthy to be the lawgiver. This glorification of the law continued, and two centuries later it was the hidden wisdom that came forth from the mouth of the Most High, and dwelt in Jacob (B. Sir. 24:1–34).

The priests of those days, however, were not so naïve as to believe that all lawgiving had ceased eight centuries earlier. The phrase "the glory of Yahweh," found twenty times in Ezekiel, was adopted by them as a symbol of, or the reflection of, the invisible God, who was perpetually present with his people.[19] In the priestly records the glory of Yahweh left his earthly home on Sinai (Exod. 24:18) and took up his abode over, on, or at the door of the tabernacle in order to meet with and guide the children of Israel (Exod. 40:34; Lev. 9:6, 23; Num. 14:10; 16:19, 42; 20:6). By means of this manifestation it was believed that Yahweh communed with, and communicated with, his people in the morning and evening fire offerings (Exod. 29:41–46), and on the day of atonement (Exod. 25:22). Provision was thus made that changes deemed necessary by the priesthood should have divine sanctions.[20] The Torah thus became a bond of union to the Jews scattered abroad throughout the Gentile world, and at the same time a definite bulwark against liberalism, individualism, and license. It was a comprehensive body of law, with ample provision for needed change, and as mediated by the priesthood was accepted as the will of God to his people Israel.[21]

The *holiness* of the people of Israel, so widely scattered among the nations but united in religion, was the urgent objective of the Torah. This holiness

---

[18] The types of religious authority found among various peoples is discussed by J. Wach in *Sociology of Religion*, 330–374; for priestly authority see 360–368, 385–389.

[19] It is true that the written law was considered authoritative, static in form, and final in principle, but it is equally true that the guiding spirit of Yahweh, by means of the Shekinah (source of glory), Memra (Word), or Bath-Qol (daughter of the voice), operating through his servants, was ever in the midst of his people.

[20] Changes were inevitable under changing social, economic, and political conditions. The age for Levitical service is twenty years and up in Ezra 3:8 and I Chron. 23:24–27; but it is from the age of twenty-five to fifty in Num. 8:24; and it was again changed to from thirty to fifty in Num. 4:3. The varying regulations governing the sabbatical year (Exod. 23:10, 11; 21:3, 4; Deut. 15:1–3, 12, 13; 31:10–18; Lev. 25:1–55; 27:18–25), and the cancellation of all these regulations later by Hillel clearly indicate the fact that law is always subject to revision.

[21] The Torah received an increasingly comprehensive application. The law at first was the P. Code; but it soon came to include the complete Pentateuch, which in its present form is the work of priestly editors. The rabbis, as exponents of orthodox Judaism, came to consider the Pentateuch as the only book of revelation, every letter of which emanated directly from God; both the Mosaic law and its rabbinical interpretation were from God to Moses on Mount Sinai (K. Köhler, *Jewish Theology*, 6, 45, 46; W. O. E. Oesterley, *The Synagogue*, 51).

could be attained only through the holy rites, prescribed in the holy book, performed at holy shrines, during holy seasons, by holy men; and then in a holy land, the holy people would enjoy the presence and the protection of the holy God. Holiness in the P. Code, even more rigidly than in H.C. or Ezekiel 40–48, was equated with ritual cleanness, while evil or sin was limited to ritual uncleanness.[22]

The Priest Code, the culmination of a long history, was in reality a compendium of theology, which though a vast complex of detailed regulations centered around a simple principle. It begins and ends with God, the Holy One. He is held to be the beginning and the end of all things, the Creator of the universe and the Ruler of men; and the chief end of man is to be holy as he is holy, which can be attained only by holy rites.

Monotheism is emphasized. Yahweh has become the God of heaven (Neh. 1:5; 2:4; Ezra 1:2; 5:11, 12; 6:9, 10), El Shaddai, the Almighty (Gen. 17:1; 28:3; 35:11; 48:3; Exod. 6:3), the great, the mighty, and the terrible God (Neh. 9:32; 4:14; 1:5), the God of the spirits of all flesh (Num. 16:22; 27:16). This, no doubt, was the influence of ethical monotheism, which had reached its extreme statement in "I form the light, and create darkness; I make peace, and create evil; I am Yahweh, that doeth all these things" (Isa. 45:7); but it had other, no less important roots. Genetically it was related to animism, which believed that spirits inhabited everything, visible and invisible, and were responsible for the weal and woe, the cleanness and the uncleanness, of humanity.

But it is important to note that while a spirit hierarchy lay at hand, and later was accepted by the Apocalypticists, in the Priest Code the angels never appear as intermediaries. God is not now thought of as a potter molding men out of clay; he speaks and man, male and female, appears (Gen. 1:26–28); no longer does he walk in the garden in the cool of the evening, casually talking with the human pair (Gen. 3:9–21); while his invisible presence abides with his people forever (Exod. 29:41–46; 25:22), yet he is so adequately isolated from the world of nature and of men, in which spirits with their contaminating influences are at work, that none save the high priest, and he only once a year, during a cloud-covered audience, dares pronounce the holy name. Yahweh thus became, so far as possible, the absolute Other.

A holy people is the insistent demand of a holy God. That this holiness is

---

[22] It is recognized that ritual holiness was purely external, and was transferable to persons and things, to times and places, according to their relation to Deity (K. Köhler, *Jewish Theology*, 104). In fact the entire temple in all its details as given in the Mishnah is based on the sacerdotal view of holiness (K. Köhler, "Holiness," *Jewish Encyclopaedia*). This, the priestly idea of holiness, was in sharpest contrast with that of the prophets, which was primarily ethical righteousness. The two concepts, at root, were mutually exclusive, and the antagonisms were carried down through history. The Sadducean priesthood laid the stress on external sanctity; while the Hassidim made inner holiness (morality) more and more the aim of life. Nevertheless the priests, though never changing their fundamental emphasis, did not neglect ethical righteousness, though, to quote Montefiore, "it was not, if one may say so, upon their agenda paper." See S. A. Cook, *CAH*, VI, 194.

ritualistic and not ethical is quite apparent when we note the various causes of uncleanness. To touch any unclean thing,[23] animate or inanimate, or in any way to have contact with mildewed garments (Lev. 13:47–51), moldy walls (Lev. 14:34–57), various skin eruptions (Lev. 13:2–46), running sores (Lev. 15:2–12), sexual emissions (Lev. 15:16–27), and childbirth (Lev. 12:1–8) was to be unclean. To touch any dead body, or under some circumstances to be even in its proximity, was to be polluted [24] (Lev. 5:2–6; 7:21; Num. 19:11–14). Further, contact with any of these things that were declared unclean rendered such things as clothing, beds, seats, vessels (Lev. 11:32–38), ground (Num. 35:33, 34), buildings, offerings, altars, and the mercy seat, as well as individuals and the community, unclean. To taste the flesh of a long list of animals that had been laid under an official taboo was to be polluted (Lev. 11:4–38). Unwitting sins, which like all the above could have no ethical significance, likewise caused uncleanness for which atonement had to be made (Lev. 4:2, 22, 27; 5:15, 18; 22:14; Num. 15:24–31). In this list of unwitting sins must be placed the gathering of sticks on the Sabbath day (Num. 15:32–36). The guilty party had offended the spirit of the Sabbath, which must be appeased by his death by stoning, so that the land might not be defiled either by his presence or by his blood (Num. 35:34).

The sanctity of the people, thus, called for the strict observance of all taboos, in addition to which it required perfect and perpetual cleansing provided to meet every possible source of contamination. Not only must all the needs of secular life, the land, the houses, the clothes, the food, the incidents of birth, disease, and death, but everything related to worship, vessels, garments, sacrifices, altars, and officers must undergo the most exacting purification. Nothing unclean could, without danger, enter the presence of Yahweh. No detail of the ceremonies, which were prescribed in minutiae, could be omitted with impunity. A glimpse at some of the more important rites required of the priesthood assures us of the impressive solemnity that accompanied all the religious acts.

The Jewish priesthood was required to be holy, as well as competent. For long centuries they had been the givers of oracles, the supervisors of altars and offerings, and the promoters of public worship. With the fall of the kingdom they became the chief leaders in Israel, and by the time of Ezra they had reached a new height in service and power. Aaron and his sons had been proved worthy (Num. 16:18–24, 35, 41–50; 18:1–7), and had been granted the covenant of an everlasting priesthood (Num. 25:6–13).

The Levites of all grades had been slowly gaining power, and probably had

23 As in our earlier studies, uncleanness is in no way related to dirtiness, as we think of it; it is the result of the presence of evil spirits. See L. R. Farnell, *Evolution of Religion*, 103–106.

24 Pollution by contact with the dead body is one of the most universal of primitive beliefs. Many primitives, especially those in tropical climates, are stricken with terror by the presence of a corpse. See M. Jastrow, *Religion of Babylonia and Assyria*, 602–605; L. R. Farnell, *Evolution of Religion*, 68–70; W. R. Smith, *Rel. Sem.* (3), 404–407, 427–437; J. G. Fraser, *Golden Bough*, I, 322; III, 397–401.

long since formed a guild, which was loosely the equivalent of a tribe. In earliest days, the first-born, like the first fruits, were considered to belong to Yahweh (Exod. 22:29; 13:20). Thus the patriarch was the legitimate priest at every local sanctuary. Following tribal custom, Jephthah, a Gileadite (Judg. 11:30, 31), Manoah, a Danite (Judg. 13:16–18), Samuel, an Ephraimite (I Sam. 1:1; 2:18), Micah, a Judahite (Judg. 17:7, 11), the sons of David and of Solomon (II Sam. 8:18; I Kings 8:22, 55) all acted as priests before Yahweh. Priestly theory of later days easily substituted the guild or tribe for the first-born, and thus by birth as well as by long service the Levites belonged to Yahweh (Num. 3:11–13; 8:16, 17), and genealogists then, so far as possible, provided the Levites with an undefiled pedigree (Exod. 6:14–20). But though thus approved by history and by the family tree, before even the menial offices could be performed, the Levites must be cleansed in body and in spirit from all taint of evil by elaborate purificatory rites. Thus purified from all that would contaminate, and separated from the people, they were conditioned to serve before Yahweh (Num. 8:5–22).

The priests on whom devolved the finer features of the worship had to undergo a more severe prophylaxis (Exod. 29:1–35). The dread of infection that might be transmitted to the offerings by the priest, and hence bring destruction to the people, was strangely real (Num. 8:5–22; Exod. 29:1–35). If this animistic philosophy and the supposed efficacy of the ceremonies do not greatly impress us, the care given to the details, owing to the dread, cannot escape us.

However, it is the consecration of the high priest,[25] the chief among his brethren (Lev. 21:10), that stands out as the most impressive of such ceremonies. As head of the Jewish community, he was heir to the kingship (B. Sir. 50:1–20), and as one duly anointed with oil, he was honored by the title messiah priest (Lev. 4:3, 5, 16). His initiation occupied seven days, during which period the rites of initiation, purification, consecration (Exod. 28:41; 29:7, 8; 30:30; 40:13–15; Num. 27:21), and investment with the insignia of office, all meaningful with religious symbolism, and to the multitude freighted with magic, were performed with meticulous care.

His official costumes, of which there were two types, were both appropriate in design and significant in meaning (Exod. 28:2–5; Lev. 8:7–9). That worn as he performed his usual priestly function was ornate and colorful. Above the under garment worn by all priests was the holy garment of linen—blue, and purple, and scarlet, embroidered with gold—and a skirt hung with golden bells and pomegranates. Over this was the breastplate, and the ephod with the Urim and Thummim, and he was girt about with an embroidered girdle. On his head was a miter, or turban, while a golden diadem inscribed with holiness

---

[25] The term "high priest" is of late origin (Num. 35:25, 28) probably first introduced about 411 B.C. (J. Morgenstern, *AJSL*, Oct., 1938, 360–377). The initiatory rites indicated below evidently were the culmination of a long history.

to Yahweh was on his forehead (Exod. 28:6–43). Thus attired he was the expression of the power and the glory of the priesthood, and represented the will of God in the world of men.

But when, as the representative of the congregation, specially consecrated so that no taint of uncleanness lingered (Lev. 4:3, 5; 6:22) and dressed in coat, breeches, girdle, and miter, all of pure linen, the special garb for the occasion (Lev. 16:4), once a year he entered the inner sanctuary, he was the petitioner for the people of God before the mercy seat. Well might they sing of one such: How glorious was he when the people gathered round him. At his coming forth out of the sanctuary; as the morning star in the midst of a cloud; as the moon at the full; As the shining forth upon the temple of the Most High; as the rainbow giving light in the clouds of glory (B. Sir. 50:5–7, cf. 8–12).

The means by which this so greatly desired holiness could be secured reveals the genius of the Jewish priesthood. Holy rites, in which water, odors, fire, blood, signs, and words were the cleansing agents for every known type of impurity, were presented in the Torah. From morning till night, from the turning of the year to the end thereof, all things great and small must be cleansed from, or shielded from, pollution by washings, oblations, or sacrifices supervised by the priests. These ceremonial requirements, detailed and technical, to many moderns smack of magic; yet, in a world dominated by an animistic philosophy, they were not void of psychical values; nor are they or their equivalents entirely absent from the Christianity of today.[26] Only a few of the media believed by the Jewish hierarchy to be effective for cleansing can here be considered.

Holy water, that is, water for the removal of impurity, was the most approved means of restoring holiness to a tent, a vessel, or a person that by any chance had come into contact with a dead body, a bone of the dead, or a grave (Lev. 5:2–6; 21:1–11; Num. 6:9–12; 9:6–11).[27] This, one of the most primitive purifying compounds, was prepared by burning the red cow, flesh, blood, and dung, throwing cedar wood, hyssop wood, and scarlet thread on the burning mass, and then treating the ash with fresh water (Num. 19:5, 7, 9, 17). Sprinkling this nauseating mixture on all that had been contaminated by the dead was the assured means of cleansing (Num. 19:1–26; 31:21–24). Holy water of a second type, prepared from the ashes of cedar wood, hyssop, and scarlet thread, soaked with the blood of a clean bird, that had been killed over an earthen vessel, over running water (Lev. 14:1–7, 49–57), was required for various types of leprosy, skin corruptions, moldy garments, and mildewed house walls. For many cases of supposedly milder ritual contamination, not for clean-

[26] A sympathetic study of the origin, significance, and value of the ritual of purification is made by L. R. Farnell, *The Evolution of Religion*, 88–162, esp. 89, 90, 111–113.

[27] More detailed information is found in G. B. Gray, *ICC*, Numbers 241–247; M. Jastrow, *Religion of Babylonia and Assyria*, 597, 602, 603; G. A. Simcox, "Clean and Unclean," *Ency. Bibl.*

liness, washing in fresh or running water was prescribed (Lev. 11:40; 13:6, 34, 55, 58; 14:8, 9, 47; 15:5–27; Num. 19:7, 8, 19, 21). The desired results no doubt were sometimes attained, even though the media of cleansing may not have been clearly understood.

Incense, that was most holy (Lev. 2:3) in the Priest Code, became a constituent part of many of the ceremonies. Properly compounded (Exod. 30:34–37),[28] it was to be burned every evening and morning, perpetually, as a sweet savor to Yahweh, on the altar of incense that stood before the veil in front of the mercy seat (Exod. 30:1–6). Further, frankincense, a sweet, resinous gum, was required with the meal offering, and was burned on the great altar, a memorial, a sweet savor to Yahweh (Lev. 2:1, 2, 15, 16; 6:15). Also, pure frankincense was to be put on each row of the twelve cakes of showbread, so that when at the end of the week the bread was removed, it might be a memorial, an offering made by fire to Yahweh on behalf of the children of Israel, an everlasting covenant (Lev. 24:7, 8, P.). But most important of all, it was an essential part of the ritual of the day of the atonement. The sweet incense, beaten small, was placed on the coals, following the early custom, when the chief priest entered within the veil, so that the cloud of incense might cover the mercy seat (Lev. 16:12, 13).

The use of fragrant odors was very widespread in primitive religions,[29] and still plays a role in the higher civilizations. In general such fumigations were believed to have magical properties that were effective in staying the powers of evil spirits (cf. Tob. 6:1–7; 8:1–3; Wisd. of Sol. 18:21; Bar. 6:43). It is probable that, though incense was used in early days in Canaan, Israel was slow to accept it as part of their rites. We have no indisputable evidence of its recognized use before the postexilic period.[30] Priestly tradition, however, had no doubt as to both its antiquity and its value. To this end our records preserved one dramatic incident. Yahweh, angered because the congregation murmured against Moses and Aaron, sent a deadly plague upon the assembly. Aaron, at the command of Moses, waving the censer with the holy incense before him, marched out to meet the dread terror. The scene is spectacular. In front of Aaron, the cloud of burning incense and the oncoming plague met; and lo! 14,700 dead bodies lay in front of the cloud of incense, while behind it all were alive (Num. 16:41–50, P.). No doubt plagues, at times, decimated the tribes; no doubt all such came to an end; no doubt the priests used all the means at their disposal to stay them. Nor is it to be doubted that tradition was more interested in the conclusion than in the evidence. Moreover, to the majority of the worshipers such a vivid story was ample confirmation of the divine power in holy incense.

[28] The compound from time to time must have been subject to change. In the days of Josephus thirteen different ingredients were used, making it a very different compound from that prescribed in the Scripture (Jos. *Wars*, V, v, 5).

[29] J. A. MacCulloch, *ERE*, VII, 200–205.

[30] For a full discussion of the use of incense in the Bible see G. F. Moore, *Ency. Bibl.*, II, 2166–2168.

Blood sprinkling, so common in primitive religion,[31] also occupied a prominent place in the purifying rites of Judaism. It was used particularly in connection with the postexilic sin offering for ritual uncleanness.[32] Hence blood must be dashed on the horns of the altar (Lev. 4:7, 18, 25, 30, 34) and around its base (Lev. 1:5, 11, 15; 3:2, 8, 13; 5:9), sprinkled before the veil of the sanctuary (Lev. 4:6, 17), before the holy place, upon the mercy seat (Lev. 16:14-19), and on the garments of the priest (Lev. 8:30), rubbed on the ear, the thumb, and the great toe of the priest and his sons (Lev. 8:22-24), and sprinkled on the doorposts and lintels of the private dwellings on the occasion of the Passover (Exod. 12:7, 13, 22).

The fat of the animal sacrificed for the sin offering and the peace offering was considered of equal, if not greater, importance with the blood. For human consumption the fat was the choice part of the animal (I Sam. 9:23, 24), and to Yahweh it was the food of the offering made by fire, a sweet savor to Yahweh, to make an atonement (Lev. 1:8, 9; 3:3-16; 4:9, 10, 19, 26, 31, 35; 8:25-29; 17:6).

The fire offerings,[33] in which the animal sacrificed was partially or entirely consumed by fire on the altar, in the Priest Code, were to be made simply on the ground that such was the command of Yahweh. The origin of each type lay so far back in history that the original significance and the various changes in meaning of each are not beyond question.[34] But all are agreed that the burnt offering had in P. an essential place in the most important religious rites of the community. Further, it seems clear that in this offering a variety of ideas such as fellowship, purification, propitiation, and expiation, each the product of history, has each left its influence on the ritual that gained final approval of the priests.[35]

The burnt offering, then, with all the ideals and hopes expressed in the final

[31] Many primitive people believed that blood was the essential principle of life, and was intimately related to the spirit of the animal or man, and as such it was exceedingly potent. For a brief discussion see H. W. Robinson, "Blood," *ERE*, II, 715-719. Not only was it a primary source of impurity, and dangerous when misused (Deut. 12:18, 23-25; 15:23); but, on the principle that like cures like, when properly employed it was considered a purifying agent (L. R. Farnell, *The Evolution of Religion*, 94-96).

[32] J. M. P. Smith, *Biblical World*, March, 1908, 207.

[33] Three different terms, each with its own history and distinctive meaning, are used for these most important parts of the ritual. Fire offering is a general term used more than sixty times; burnt offering, that which goes up (in smoke), is the most frequent; while whole burnt offering is usually a descriptive synonym for number 2.

[34] Such uncertainty is due, at least in part, to the fact that the Priest Code is in itself a composite of earlier ritual approved and interpreted by the priests of the fifth century B.C. Our Biblical material has thus often lost the marks of origin in this process of adoption. Some are convinced that the burnt offering developed out of the earlier animal sacrifice in which the tribe and the deity entered into *communion in the social meal*. See W. R. Smith, "Sacrifice," *Ency. Britannica*, 9th ed., or *Rel. Sem.* (3), chap. VI. Others hold that the earliest idea was that it was a *gift* to deity. This has been supported by a careful study of all the material in the O.T. by G. B. Gray, *Sacrifice in the O.T.*, 1-61. A. R. S. Kennedy, "Sacrifice and Offering," *HBD* (one vol.), presents in brief form the idea of the social meal.

[35] G. B. Gray, *Sacrifice in the O.T.*, 9-13, 32, 33, 41-51, 67-81.

ritual, was the central feature in the continual evening and morning holocaust of a lamb (Num. 28:3–8; Exod. 29:38–42), also day after day throughout the "set" festivals [36] (Num. 29:1–6, 12–39; 28:16–25), and on the day of the atonement (Num. 28:7–11; Lev. 16:5–11). In all cases it was accompanied by the meal offering and drink offering; that is, it was a full meal, meat, fine flour with beaten oil, sublimated by fire into a sweet odor for Yahweh, while strong drink was poured on the ground as his drink offering, and acknowledged to be "food for my offerings made by fire" (Num. 28:2–8, 23, 24; Lev. 3:11, 16; 21:6, 8, 17).

The day of the atonement, to which no reference is found in pre-exilic literature, was the culmination of the priestly system. The set feasts, especially that of booths, were joyous occasions; the continual burnt offering, a reminder to the Jewish community the world over that daily they were united in an acceptable worship before Yahweh, was a subtle bond of fellowship. But the day of the atonement was a milestone toward which great expectancy and high emotion were directed, and from which resolution and strength were derived by the Jewish communities.

Out of the wealth of suggestive material in the atonement ritual three significant features, that merge into one idea, claim our attention.[37] First is the fact that this day was to be a "sabbath of solemn rest," a day "on which they should afflict their souls, and do no manner of work" (Lev. 16:29–31; 19:30; 23:27–32).[38] Thereby the Jews, irrespective of distance from the sanctuary,

[36] New regulations for the "set festivals" (Lev. 23:2, 4, 37) had been worked out in considerable detail by the priests. The Passover, earlier a springtime festival of the shepherds, in Ezekiel 45:21–25, must be observed on penalty of death (Num. 9:7–13) on the fourteenth day of the first month, and continued with elaborate ceremonies for seven days, as a memorial of the deliverance from Egypt (Lev. 23:5–8; Exod. 12:14–20; Num. 28:16–25, all P.). The feast of weeks, or Pentecost, now as in H.C., dated fifty days after the Passover, still preserves its agricultural features, but being of little importance in this period is held for only one day (Num. 28:26, 27; cf. Lev. 23:15–21). Still later it was made to commemorate the giving of the law on Sinai (Exod. 19:1, 2a). See I. Benzinger, "Pentecost." *Ency. Bibl.*, III. The feast of booths, or tabernacles, has now lost all traces of husbandry, and the booths are to bring to mind the wilderness experiences (Neh. 8:14–18). It is to be observed on the fifteenth of Tishri (October), and to the seven days of the earlier period (Deut. 16:13–15: I Kings 6:65) has an added day, in which the dedication of the altar is celebrated (Num. 29:35; Lev. 23:36, P.; II Chron. 7:8, 9). Of all the festivals this was the most joyous, and at a later period a ninth day was added, called the joy of the law. See I. Benzinger, "Tabernacles," *Ency. Bibl.* Thus it was that the original fertility festivals were slowly but surely lifted from the lower to the higher areas of thought and practice.

[37] For a statement of the ritual followed on the day of the atonement, see H. Danby, *The Mishna, a Translation*, 162–172; I. Benzinger and T. K. Cheyne, "Atonement, day of," *Ency. Bibl.*

[38] The absolute prohibition of work on the Sabbath day was a gradual development that reached its climax in post-Biblical days. The command to observe the Sabbath day, to keep it holy, has come down to us through two different interpreters (Exod. 20:8–11, and Deut. 5:12–16). In Jewish history, the year 432 B.C., when Nehemiah faced the need for drastic reform, marks a definite point in the growing severity of Sabbath observance (Neh. 13:15–22). Jeremiah 17:20–27 reads much like the work of a late priestly editor. The excesses to which Sabbath regulations finally went, and the casuistry therein involved are suggested by E. Schürer, *The Jewish People in the Time of Jesus Christ*, sec. div., II, 96–105. That the Sabbath is a peculiarly Jewish institution is emphasized by G. F. Moore, *Judaism*, II, 21–39.

were participants in the ceremonies and the benefits of the day of the atone-ment. It brought to their minds that they were one people, with a glorious history, united in invisible bonds and enjoying the protection of sacred rites accepted by the wonder-working God of their fathers.

The second feature to be noted is the transfer of the uncleanness of all the people of Israel, by means of ritual, to the goat dedicated to Azazel, the wilder-ness demon (Lev. 16:2–28). The preliminaries to the final act portrayed objec-tively the ritual cleansing of the people. The high priest, divested of his glori-ous apparel, now, as representative of the people, put on a white tunic and a plain linen girdle (Lev. 16:4), thereby symbolizing the purity of those who may enter the presence of the Holy One. A bullock was then slain as a sin offering for himself and the priesthood, the blood of which was collected in a bowl (Lev. 16:11–14). He then took a censer full of coals from the altar be-fore Yahweh, and casting incense on it covered the mercy seat as with a cloud, a sign to the observing throng that he, as their representative, was divinely protected (Lev. 16:12, 13, 2). Returning to the court, he took the bowl of blood, re-entered the holy of holies, and sprinkled the front of the mercy seat seven times (Lev. 16:14). Next a goat was slain as a sin offering, an atonement for the house and for the holy of holies (Lev. 16:15). The high priest then took the blood of the goat *within the veil,* and sprinkled it seven times on the mercy seat, and before the mercy seat, to make an atonement for the holy of holies, because of the uncleanness of the children of Israel (Lev. 16:15, 16). By carefully ordered ceremonies, that have not all been recorded, by the sprin-kling of the blood of the bullock and of the goat, atonement was made for all suspected uncleanness of places, people, and priests (Lev. 16:18, 19). Then the high priest took the scapegoat, laid both hands on its head, confessed over him all the iniquities of the children of Israel, and by formulas and gesture transferred them to the victim,[39] that was then sent away to the wilderness for Azazel (Lev. 16:20–22). Cleansing was thus made doubly sure. Such a cere-mony, so objective, so symbolic, so mysterious, scrupulously carried out in the holy place by the sacred men in Israel, to the multitude must have been satis-fying, even exhilarating. The sins of Israel had been removed afar; now they might enjoy the fullness of the presence of Yahweh.

The third crucial moment came at the conclusion of the day, and culminated in the evidence that Yahweh looked with favor on them, which was followed

---

39 The transference of uncleanness, guilt, punishment, disease, or even the spirit of a person by means of magic seems to have been a widespread practice among primitive people. In addition to this strange illustration, the same principle is found in Leviticus 4:15, 24; 14:7; and Zechariah 5: 5–11, where wickedness, personified as a woman, is sealed up in a barrel and magically transported to Shinar. Such a conception may underlie some early Christian theories. A vivid scene has been described by W. B. Seabrook, who witnessed the priestly rite in which the spirit of a girl who was to be sacrificed was transferred into the goat that actually became her substitute (*Magic Island,* 61–69). See L. R. Farnell, *Evolution of Religion,* 116.

by the priestly benediction.[40] If, when the high priest, clad in white linen garments as the representative of the congregation, entered the holy of holies, uncleanness existed anywhere, it was believed he would surely die (Lev. 16:2, 13); if he reappeared before the people it was the sign that they had been accepted by Yahweh.

This was the awesome hour of the year, fraught with anxiety and expectancy. The high priest, when accepted by Yahweh, retired from the holy of holies to the holy place where he put off his white linen garments, bathed, and then attired himself as the representative of Yahweh in his glorious apparel (cf. p. 175). Thus robed in beautiful vestments rich in religious symbolism, breastplate, ephod with Urim and Thummim, the miter with the inscription "Holiness to Yahweh," he reappeared before the waiting throng, the visible assurance of the favor of Yahweh. Following the usual priestly burnt offering for himself and the congregation, he then pronounced the Aaronic benediction: "Jehovah bless thee, and keep thee; Jehovah make his face to shine upon thee, and be gracious unto thee; Jehovah lift up his countenance upon thee, and give thee peace" (Num. 6:24–26). To the devout multitude, ever eager for the protection of the most high God and trustfully accepting the guidance of the priest, this was the day of days, a holy day. All the accounts of yesteryear were canceled; all uncleanness had been cleansed; and the spirits of wickedness had been driven out of the land. A new year, without a stain, had begun. Religion to them, if not an adventure, was a sacrament.

Israel became the *holy* people by means of cleansing rites, carefully performed; and the priestly teaching assured them that by the will of the covenant God of Israel they were the *chosen* people (Deut. 4:37; 7:6; 10:15; Exod. 6:4–8; Ezek. 34:11–16, 25–30). This idea of election, which was rooted in primitive tribalism, had been enlarged and intensified by the frustrations of history. Between 586 and 400 B.C., under necessity, the priest had taken over the power of the prince, and religion had learned the language of statecraft. The experience of the centuries seemed to indicate that the hope of Israel lay not in an empire like that of Persia, which was secular, nor in a kingdom like that of David, which had fallen, but in a theocracy (Ezek. 20:33–35), in which the *congregation,* guided by an efficient priesthood, should observe to do the will of Yahweh, as expressed in the Torah (Exod. 19:6; 29:43–46; Num. 27:21).

That Israel and Yahweh formed an indissoluble unit, was held to be axiomatic. To the postexilic priesthood Yahweh had no competent worshipers

---

[40] Many details that may have been significant to ancients, such as ablutions of garments and persons, the burning of skins, flesh, entrails, and blood without the camp (Lev. 16:24–28), are of no great interest to us, and owing to constant changes in the ritual cannot with certainty be reconstructed. All discussion of such is here omitted.

apart from Israel; and apart from Yahweh Israel had no future. The teaching of the prophets that Yahweh could do without Israel (Amos 9:7, 8a),
and that apart from social righteousness Israel would be destroyed from off
the face of the earth, was preposterous to the priest. That the existence of
the nation depended on justice, kindness, and humility seemed to have been
refuted by all history; and by laying the emphasis on human activity it
seemed to rob the Almighty of the honor and the glory that was due his
holy name. Hence the priestly conclusion was that Israel's God, having
cleansed the land (Lev. 25:4–7, 10b–12), would establish his people thereon
forever (Lev. 25:23; Gen. 12:7; 35:10–12; 48:3, 4, P.), by an everlasting
covenant (Gen. 9:16; 17:7, 13, 19; Exod. 6:4, 6, 7), "not for your sakes, . . .
but for my holy name" (Ezek. 36:21–25; 20:9, 14, 22; 39:7; Exod. 32:11–14).

This everlasting covenant contained a number of new and radical features.
Fashioned by priestly thinking, it was unalterably unilateral. The Sinaitic
covenant, in which Yahweh and the people each had mutual responsibilities,
had failed, apparently owing to human frailty. The "new" covenant of Jeremiah was too subjective and too individualistic to suit ecclesiasts. So now, "I
have established *my* covenant" is the announcement of the Most High (Gen.
6:18; 17:7, 8, 19, 21; 28:4; 35:10–13). The monotheism of Deutero-Isaiah had
paved the way (Isa. 43:10–13; 45:5, 7, 22), and to the priest Yahweh enthroned
above the cherubim was absolute. He alone was the author of the covenant,
the guarantor of a numerous offspring (Gen. 17:19; 26:6; 35:11), and the
only power that could insure ultimate triumph. This was the revelation of
his glory (Ezek. 36:21–24; Gen. 9:8–17; 17:1–8). Man had grievously failed;
now Yahweh graciously came to the rescue.

Further, the covenant was no longer thought of as originating in the days
of Moses; even before the dawn of nationhood the Almighty had established
it with Abraham and with his seed throughout their generations (Gen. 17:1–
21; Exod. 6:2–8; Neh. 9:7, 8). But it was given a still greater antiquity and
a wider scope, for it was claimed to have been established with Noah, and
his seed after him, and with every living creature, before the time of the
flood (Gen. 6:18; 9:8–17). By implication the everlasting covenant was in
the plan of the eternal God from before the foundation of the world.

It was racial as well as ancient. Circumcision, the outward sign, and an unspotted lineage were the required evidences of racial purity. The former, an
ancient rite practiced in Egypt, probably long before the time of Abraham,[41]
had been observed in but a halfhearted way in early Israel (cf. Exod. 4:25, 26;
Josh. 5:2, 3). But now under priestly rule, that in exile had turned a common

---

41 Circumcision originated at a very early period in human history, when it probably was an
initiatory rite into the status of manhood. The use of flint knives (Josh. 5:2, 3) and the widely
separated areas where it has been practiced prove its antiquity. Its diffusion suggests that Egypt,
where the operation is portrayed on a Karnak temple of the fourteenth century B.C., was its first
cultural center, if not its birthplace (Herodotus, II, 36, 37, 104; A. MacAlister, "Circumcision,"
HBD (five vols.).

rite into a religious symbol, it became the badge of Judaism (Gen. 17:10–14; Exod. 12:48, 49; Lev. 12:3, all P.).

The latter, an accredited genealogy, created greater, though not insuperable, difficulties. Among the treasures in the priestly archives it is evident that not a few "family trees" had been preserved. Tradition, also, was able to add its quota, though the accuracy of such could not always be proved. Beyond these, fertile imagination, then as now, could easily discover the names needed to secure a place among the elect.[42] To meet this as well as other demands, the scribes, guided by their theological convictions, edited and rewrote, as best they could, Hebrew history.[43] From creation down to Abraham genealogical tables, which drew largely from Babylonian sources, provided in Noah and his son Shem worthy ancestors for Israel. The twelve tribes, that had long achieved a place in national tradition (Gen. 29:32–30:24; 35:18, J., E.), now that many were scattered abroad among the nations, if they were not to be largely lost to Israel were in need of credentials. Such were gathered from various sources and preserved by writers of the P. school in Genesis and Chronicles (Gen. 27:46–28:9; 35:23–27; I Chron. 2:1–8:40). But as the whole theological fabric was built on the ritual cleansing performed by the priest, much depended on the competency and validity of the hierarchy. Thus particular care was taken to trace the Aaronic priesthood back to Levi, the son of Jacob, the son of Isaac, the son of Abraham (Exod. 6:20, 23, 26; 10:4; I Chron. 6:1–3). Zadok, Abiathar, Ahimelech, and others, of rather uncertain origin, were skillfully grafted into the "Levitical tree," though Eli, the one-time honored priest at Shiloh, is completely ignored. While there is no evidence in pre-exilic literature of a hereditary hierarchy ministering throughout the land, the genealogies finally preserved by the Chronicler (I Chron. 6:1–30; 23:1–23; 24:1–26:32) no doubt rejoiced all concerned in this role of honor. These lists, with others of like type, provided the ultimate court of appeal to those in authority, the bond of unity between widely dispersed groups, and the credentials of membership in the elect nation.[44]

[42] No doubt those interested in these genealogies were competent men who had much valuable traditional material at hand. No question of their sincerity is raised; yet their definite objective was to establish the consanguinity of those, especially the leaders, of their own generation. No doubt sometimes their material, and hence their conclusions, would rest on a slight foundation. This has been judiciously expressed by President Finkelstein when he intimates that the difficulties of tracing ancestry back over seven or eight hundred years, and the ease with which those who could pay for it could obtain priestly status, is quite evident (*The Pharisees*, II, 511–515).

[43] Their reinterpretation of the early history, with genealogical lists, is found largely in Genesis 1:1–2:4a; 5:1–28; 6:9–22; 9:1–7; 10:1–7; 11:10–27, 30–32; 28:1–9; 35:23–27; Exodus 6:1–7:13, in part; 12:1–20; Numbers, chaps. 1–10, 15, 17–19; Joshua, chaps. 9–15. Later history has been completely rewritten in I and II Chronicles and Ezra-Nehemiah.

[44] The theory of a "pure race," while not without transient psychological values, faced two difficulties. First, in Judaism it was postexilic, and was in striking contrast to the practice of the pre-exilic leaders. David's grandmother was a Moabitess (Ruth 4:18–22). Moses had two wives, one Midianite (Exod. 2:21), the other an Egyptian (Num. 12:1). Joseph married an Egyptian priestess,

Sabbath observance took on a new meaning. An old lunar festival among the nomads, it had become a day of rest to the weary farmer in Canaan. In captivity, surrounded by an alien civilization where the Sabbath played a somewhat uncertain role in ritual, the exiles, because of language and interests, congregated together and naturally the Sabbath became central in their social and religious life. Gradually precise regulations for the good of the community were adopted. To preserve Jewish culture and identity, amid the seductions of prosperity in a foreign land, was the aim; and the Sabbath, with its restrictions and emphases, became a tower of strength to Jewish piety (Exod. 31:14, 17; cf. I Macc. 2:32–38).

The Torah,[45] in large part the finished product of postexilic days, was the chief treasure of Judaism, and a knowledge of it became an ideal for every loyal Jew. Assigned as it was to the Mosaic and pre-Mosaic periods, faith, not unduly hampered by the disturbing realities of history, was able to rebuild an empire. Political aspects had given way before the priestly, and morality, so central in prophetic teaching, occupied small space. The sum total of passages in P. that might claim an ethical interpretation are rather dubious witnesses. Two laws of the trespass offering call for the restitution of one and one-fifth the value of that which he hath done amiss, from anyone who has committed a trespass. But the specified trespass, in one case, is in holy things (Lev. 5:14–17), and in the other is against Yahweh (Lev. 6:1–7). These both indicate that priestly interests, and not righteousness, are involved. Five other passages have to do with the following: a primitive test for adultery (Num. 5:11–31), preserving the family inheritance within the tribe (Num. 27:8–11; 36:1–12), protection of a man involved accidentally in manslaughter (Num. 35:9; 39), and sparing the lives of virgins, captured in war, as concubines of the soldiers (Num. 31:15–18). None of these reflects even the pale shadow of the demands of the prophets for human rights. Ritual and more ritual became the engrossing theme of the priest, and the study of the law was the all-consuming passion. The rites of purification, their efficacy and meaning, the will of God ever speaking in the sacred scroll—these, the heart of the Torah, captured mind and heart of the sons of Aaron.

---

who was the mother of Ephraim and Manasseh (Gen. 41:45, 50–52), and the wives and concubines of Jacob were all Aramaean (Gen. 29:21–30; 30:3, 9). The fact seems to be that the Jew had among his ancestors not only Hebrews but Amorites and Aramaeans, Horites and Hittites, Philistines and Egyptians (Deut. 26:3; Ezek. 16:3, 45). But further, all claims of pure race, implying a consanguineous unit, are without any basis in fact. See H. J. Seligmann, *Race against Man*, for a brief summary, 17–65. The Jews, like all other groups, formed a definite cultural unit, and in the P. Code there is crystallized the deep-seated, universal antiforeign sentiment, which failed to distinguish between race and culture. See J. M. P. Smith, "The Chosen People," *AJSL*, 1929, 73–82, in which the prophetic emphasis of the divine mission is elaborated.

45 Torah is used for the Pentateuch as a whole, and at a later period included post-Biblical interpretations as well. The priests, some time after 400 B.C., combined P. Code with the earlier documents, J., E., C. C., Deut., H. C., and edited it all into a reasonably consistent whole, our Pentateuch (G. F. Moore, *Judaism*, I, 263–280).

A homeland for Israel was an essential part of the priestly program. The Holy Land, in which, unmolested by foreign tyrant, they could dwell in peace and order their lives according to the law, was the ultimate goal of this state-church. This, the land of Palestine, they claimed to be theirs by the right of purchase (Gen. 23:17–20), by the right of sepulcher of the dead (Gen. 23:19; 25:9, 10; 49:30–32; 52:12), most sacred among primitive tribes, by the right of ancient promise to Abraham (Gen. 17:8, 21) and to Jacob (Gen. 35:9–15; 48:4), and by the right of allotment made by men appointed by Moses at the command of Yahweh (Num. 34:16–27; completed in Josh. 13:15–14:5; 15:1–13, 20–62; 16:4–8; 17:8–10; 18:11–20).

As P. rested the claim to possession of the land, ultimately, on the divine decree, it is not surprising that Israel's entrance into and seizure of the land is pictured as without a struggle. Apparently after the boundaries had been announced by Moses (Num. 34:1–12), and tribal boundary judges had been appointed by him (Num. 34:16–27), the congregation crossed the river Jordan (Num. 21:1; Josh. 4:15–17, 19) and observed the Passover at Gilgal (Josh. 5:10–12) as though all life were a religious festival and the products of Canaan, like the manna, had been sent from heaven specifically for them (Josh. 5:11, 12). That we have in this the P. story of the invasion of the land essentially complete need not be questioned.[46] All had been arranged for and expedited by Yahweh himself.

While, on the face of it, this claim to the land is a late fiction, with no firmer foundation than the accumulation of naïve assumptions, and is in violent contradiction to the actual process of settlement, nevertheless it must have been gratifying to those who, like the author of Ezekiel 40–48, sought to escape from the disheartening annals of national disaster. It shifted the center of appeal from the hardships of past and present distress to the world of the imponderables, from the weakness of man to the power of God.

This completes the picture of the ideals of the priesthood in the fourth century B.C. It was a challenging yet comforting religion. Man's highest responsibilities were toward the Almighty; and a competent priesthood, divinely guided, had prescribed the cleansing rites for all human needs. Ritual stood as the sum total of the requirements of Yahweh.[47] Problems of a religious nature were thus all settled, and profitable business activities were not unduly inhibited. To many this was the acme of perfection. The well-ordered ceremonies

[46] The usual interpretation is that part of the P. story has been lost. But this is unlikely as the priestly school were the final editors of the book. See R. H. Pfeiffer, *Introduction to the O.T.*, 306–310.

[47] The Priest Code is concerned solely with ritual, by means of which man is brought into a happy relation with God. That social ethics might be a means of salvation would have been as distasteful to them as to Calvin and Barth at a later date. Ethics, or man's relation to man, was cared for by the law of the land. Later generations of priests, however, syncretized morals and cultus, thus integrating the teaching of the prophets with that of the priests. This union was the result of long centuries of struggle and compromise, rather than the initial attitude of the priests who were responsible for the state-church. See G. F. Moore, *Judaism*, II, 3–10, 79–88, 93.

satisfied the demand of the senses. Eye and ear rejoiced in the beauty and the harmony expressed in the worship. Mind and heart were aglow with the memories, the ideals, and the hopes fostered by the priestly narratives; and the devout were captured by the faith that they were the elect people, chosen by the Creator from before the foundation of the world.

It was the vision splendid, imposing in outline, attractive in detail, that stood cathedral-like on the rock of the covenant of the Almighty. To worship Yahweh in the beauty of holiness, that was the aim and the glory of the law. As conservers of values, providing a hedge around the hapless Jew, the law and the priest proved their worth through the long dark centuries following the days of Ezra.[48] Religion again was a creative force in Israel, and awakened responses and provided satisfactions. Yahweh was their king, the priests were his ministers, and Judaism was a religion—the religion of the state-church.

[48] As from the time of the Persian conquest on the Jews had no political existence, their self-preservation depended on the perpetuation of their national religion. This called for their separation from the nations. The requirements of the law made this necessary (G. H. Moore, *Judaism*, I, 21).

Chapter XIII

◄◄◄◄◄◄◄◄◄◄◄◄◄◄◄◄❈►►►►►►►►►►►►►►►►►

THE RELIGION OF MANKIND. 500-100 B.C.

A CONSIDERABLE literature expresses an attitude toward various phases of life that may be termed the everyday religion of the common man, or better still, the religion of mankind. Coming chiefly from the late period, when Jews at home and abroad were occupied with commerce, and were everywhere in contact with the Greco-Roman culture, we are not surprised to find a trend toward the profane or secular, a disregard for racial cleavages and peculiar Jewish enthusiasms, and even the rejection, by some, of widely accepted Jewish claims and practices. Yet while it reflects the attitudes of the man in the street, or the cosmopolitan, it is fundamentally Hebraic. At the same time, most of it found a response in the mind and heart of men, Jew and Gentile alike, irrespective of specific religious affiliations. Two general themes, homely virtues and the brotherhood of man, gather up the chief contribution of this varied and somewhat nondescript literature.

Homely wisdom is found throughout Proverbs 10:1–31:31, which consists of booklets collected between 600 and 200 B.C., and in Ben Sirach, which was completed by 180 B.C. These compendiums are occupied with human interests, and deal largely with commercial and social relations.

The Jew in business is an important figure in these pages. While, as in all epigrammatic literature, phrases that express half-truths, that clash each with the other, may be found side by side, in general, to the wise man in business there is ascribed a shrewdness that has been brought to a cutting edge in the markets of the world. His ancestors had always been able to safeguard their material interests, and had credited Yahweh with aiding and abetting their efforts, even when they were not entirely beyond reproach. Now in the great trading centers, as he had to face all comers, necessity made him alert to his own economic needs. The wise man in Proverbs and Ben Sirach, on the score of business, was prudent, discreet, alert, shrewd, keen, and crafty. He could drive a hard bargain with his friend, and when he traded with the alien, at best it was diamond cut diamond. He was in business for profit, not for health. The fool, on the other hand, was the simple, credulous, sluggish-minded, stupid, empty-headed individual who in the hurly-burly of barter succumbed to the sharper. Energy, aggressiveness, and discrimination were essentials in business, and prosperity was the sign of the favor of Yahweh.

It was the old orthodoxy of materialism taking its place in world commerce. Nevertheless this utilitarianism was moderated by the teaching of the prophets. Virtues such as honesty, justice, truth, kindness, and humility in word and act are emphasized in every varying and memorable phrase. But as the meaning of all such words is always flexible, individuals and groups no doubt fitted them into the general practices in their own activities. Thus it was that religion and shrewd business became agreeable yokefellows, in no way recognizing the deeper problem of Job.

The Jew, in the sphere of the home and the family, always so central in Hebrew life, in these collections of homely wisdom appears to great advantage. Loyalties and virtues are constantly praised, while disobedience and wickedness are sternly denounced. Wisdom establishes the home, but folly, now laid at the door of foreign influence, is a reproach (Prov. 13:1; 15:5; 19:13, 26). Home restraints, happy relationships, and moral responsibilities are constantly approved. The wise son listens to reproof, respects his father, and honors his mother (Prov. 15:20; 10:1; 23:22), while the discerning father wisely instructs his son and leaves an inheritance that endures to his children's children (Prov. 13:22). The homely virtues of patience, calmness, kindness, wisdom, and reserve in speech are magnified, so, while the wicked are overthrown, the house of the righteous shall stand (Prov. 12:7).

An important, if not chief, place in the family is ascribed to the wife and mother. This is significant, as in the Hebrew world woman was considered a chattel, under the authority of her father or husband, and in theory she was held responsible for man's first disobedience. Yet in history, by reason of personal gifts, as in the case of Deborah, Abigail, Athaliah, Huldah, and others, she attained great influence. Now, however, amid chaotic sex relations she is celebrated for her true worth. As a worthy woman she "buildeth her house" (Prov. 14:1; 18:22; 19:14), and as a wise woman she is "a crown to her husband" (Prov. 12:4; 15:20). In a fine acrostic poem, which is a classic description of the ideal wife-mother, she is extolled in realistic terms that are most laudatory (Prov. 31:10–30). Such a home brings honor to any people, and provides religion with a more tangible quality than that resulting from mass movements under prophetic eloquence, or from the gorgeous spectacle of temple ceremonies.

Two other pictures, that of the adulteress and that of true love, complete the contribution to this ideal of life. The denunciation of the strange woman, whose house is on the way to Sheol, is one of the most scathing in all literature (Prov. 7:5–27). Palestine, lying on the highway of commerce and of armies, was always notorious for loose sex relations. But never were these influences at work more openly and more seductively than under Roman rule. The games, the gymnasia, and the social customs all contributed to accentuate the social vices. Never was there poured out on the adulterous woman and her ways more pungent scorn than in this essay. Here the chastity of the desert and the finest idealism of Israel's leaders united to assail in unadorned language the corrupting influences that threatened the home, the nation, and the religion of Judaism.

Religion that exalted the home and womanhood must go still farther. A wedding song (Psalm 45), and a collection of more than a score of love lyrics (Song of Songs), to the perplexity of scholars and the chagrin of the pious, have been included in the canon. Interpreters long struggled, by devious methods, to fit these into the inherited theological strait jacket. Psalm 45 was accepted as celebrating the marriage of Solomon with Pharaoh's daughter (I Kings 3:1), and the Song of Songs was treated as a drama in which the Shulamite preferred her rustic lover to the great king; then by the magic of allegory these were transmuted into a spiritual message signifying the marriage of God and his people. But though this gave the appearance of sanctity to what seemed profane, and was so approved that Rabbi Akiba thought the whole world was not worthy of such importance as the day on which the Song of Songs was given to Israel (Moore, *Judaism*, I, 243), yet so great were the uncertainties of its meaning and values that the reading of the Song of Songs was prohibited to all under thirty years of age. Toward the end of the eighteenth century the poet Herder noted that these songs were similar to the erotic poetry of the Near East, and therefore should be interpreted historically (*Vom Geiste der Ebräischen Poesie,* 1783). But it was not until 1873, when J. G. Wetzstein, Prussian consul at Damascus, published a number of Syrian love songs used during the customary festival of the "bridal week," when bride and groom were feted as queen and king, that this theory was taken seriously. But the framework of the festivities, and a comparison with the modern songs, forms such a complete background for and parallel to the ancient Hebrew poems that most scholars have frankly accepted these songs [1] as an anthology of love lyrics. The charms of the bride, the strength of the groom, and the felicities of love, when made to minister to human welfare and social integrity, are well within the realm of the religious.

Thus the idea of religion has been expanded to include the widest ranges of human experience. The conduct of business, the daily task of the housewife, and the unselfish devotion of love, while a far remove from the smoking altar, the intoned formulas of the priest, and the flaming word of the prophet, are no less essential to the fullness of human life, and peradventure not less pleasing to Deity. These ancient love songs, expressive and exuberant, but chaste withal, celebrate in romantic speech the undying loyalty of husband and wife. Social virtue in the home is as profoundly religious as is the prophetic message of social justice in the market place. As the Hebrew Bible is en-

---

[1] The history of the interpretation of this collection can be found in brief form in "Song of Songs," *HBD* (five vols.), IV, by J. W. Rothstein, or in "Canticles," *Ency. Bibl.,* I, by T. K. Cheyne.

riched by the inclusion of Proverbs and the Song of Songs, so has religion gained by the straightforward historical interpretation.

The book of Ecclesiastes—the Preacher—came out of the same social environment as the above, and is a reflection on the way of life which is akin to Stoicism. The author of the first edition [2] frankly faced the paradoxical facts of life, and concluded from personal experience and observation that all life was weariness, a sore travail, vanity, and a striving after wind (Eccles. 1:8, 14). There was neither profit nor progress in the struggle for riches or pleasure, for family or wisdom, for piety or heroism (1:13; 12:1; 6:8; 7:23; 8:10, 14; 3:1–8; 8:6–8). Hence one should not take much account of the days of his life (5:19); but as life was inescapable, it was the part of wisdom to quietly perform the tasks of the day (2:11, 17, 20, 22, 24; 3:12, 13, 22; 5:7, 8, 17–19; 8:15; 9:7–10; 10:16–20). Finding the absolute good nowhere, this pessimist counseled to make the best out of bad conditions by being moderate in all things.

Men like the author of Ecclesiastes and Agur belonged to the skeptics of the day. They were living in a period of transition, and were able to glance far back over the pages of history. The dogmas and the pieties of the past were greatly discounted by the facts of history. Great enthusiasms and mass movements that had led to national reforms had come and gone, but lasting values were hard to find. The passionate call of the prophets for social righteousness had neither profited the poor nor saved the nation. The priestly pageantry, the splendor of the temple, and the sacred symbol of Deity, so carefully guarded in the darkened chamber, had contributed little, if anything, of worth beyond the momentary satisfaction of the participants. Life was drab; all issues were uncertain, and high tensions were exhausting. To perform the duty of the hour, to live calmly and confidently, that was best. Shun undue enthusiasms and leave the issues to God, to whom they belong. Such was the religion of this Jewish scholar, who had studied the conflicts, the propaganda, and the fortunes of his people. It was basic religion, as realistic, but by no means so pessimistic or pagan, as the Rubaiyat of Omar Khayyám. In the candor of expression, the transparent honesty, and the unfaltering search for unshakable truth, such thinkers must have been a steadying power to many who were disturbed by the conflicting claims and programs of partisan religious groups. Probably the man in the street held these few pages in higher favor than did the priest.

These booklets, Proverbs, Song of Songs, and Ecclesiastes, though assigned to a subordinate place, were admitted to the canon probably in large measure

---

2 The present booklet long caused difficulty by the different attitudes and contradictory statements within its pages. It is probable that the original was the work of a pessimist. To this an editor added Eccles. 4:5; 5:3, 7a; 7:1a, 3, 5–9, 11, 12, 19; 8:1; 9:17, 18; 10:1–3, 8–14a, 15, 18, 19; 14:9–12, which is of the same tone as wisdom literature. Still later another editor tried to make it more acceptable by adding 2:26; 3:17; 7:18b, 26b, 29; 8:2b, 3a, 6a, 11–13; 11:9b; 12:1a, 13, 14 (5:1–7?) (A. H. McNeile, *Ecclesiastes;* G. A. Barton, "Ecclesiastes," in *ICC*).

owing to the activities of the scribes. These editors and teachers by their additions and interpretations made what was ordinarily thought of as secular literature partially acceptable to the orthodox. They "improved" the original texts by *wise* and *pious* marginal phrases or insertions which later were incorporated into the body of the text, as in the case of Ecclesiastes. Proverbs 31:10–31 was given a religious status by changing the Hebrew in verse 31 from an intelligent woman, which is still found in the Septuagint, to a "woman who feareth Yahweh"; and in Proverbs 7, between verses 1 and 2 is inserted in the Septuagint, "My son, fear the Lord, and thou shalt be strong, and beside him fear no other," which adds a religious motive against the snares of the wicked woman. Likewise the use of the allegorical method of interpretation concealed the real nature and meaning of the Song of Songs and secured for it a limited use in the service of religion.

Thus, largely under the pressure of Greek culture, social ethics enlarged her borders, and to justice and righteousness were added the Stoic ideals of courage, patience, moderation, and self-control. Also there began to appear an appreciation for the beautiful as seen in the human form divine (Song of Songs), and for the glories of nature (Psalm 19:1–6), which for some is a sure channel of communion with the Eternal Spirit.[3] Thus, gradually, as the result of long cultural contacts, the wider range of human activities and thought relating to business, the schools of philosophy, the home, and the affairs of the world were being consecrated to religion as definitely as the altar and the incense had been. As the Jew was thrust out from his native hills he became a man of the world and learned that religion and life were inseparable; thus did some Jews worship the God of their fathers.

The universal brotherhood of man was not the bond or the slogan of any organized movement within Judaism, but was an idea expressed by unnamed individuals and apparently approved by important groups that were not under too great ecclesiastical restraints. Men who moved among the nations of the world, exercising native discernment, realized that deep down at heart all men were akin.

It was to the credit of the law and the priesthood that following the collapse of national ambitions Judaism maintained her existence and identity. Yet, while under the accepted ideology of covenant, race, and the worship of Yahweh, the only God, Israel faced the world with a degree of unity, within her ranks were dissensions and even marked hostilities. For some the law was only a means to an end; to not a few it became an end in itself; while to others it was an annoyance, if not anathema.

A liberal movement with a broadly human emphasis, that has been preserved in a number of anonymous messages, raised a protest against various features of the law with its rigid regimentation, its sacerdotalism, and its

[3] L. Finkelstein, *The Religion of Democracy*, 10–19.

narrow world outlook. Liberalism at heart was in every way the antithesis of the principles of the lawbook, with its endless and petty rites, administered and interpreted by an army of priestlings, purporting to be final and to have been dictated by the Almighty to his servant Moses, with whom he spake face to face. This, to all the free sons of the desert who had learned from Amos, Isaiah, and Jeremiah, was puerile and pagan, a misinterpretation of Hebrew history and religion. It put magic above morals [4] and confined the living God within the temple, under the care of officialdom. It may have provided a splendid spectacle, but to many the religion of a book was that neither of the fathers nor of Yahweh.

A further aggravation to many lay in the fact that, as in Ezekiel 48:1–35, piety was measured by proximity to the temple in Jerusalem, and residence in the Holy Land was the desired and ultimate goal of the Jewish people (Gen. 17:8, 21; 23:17–20; 28:4; 33:12; 48:4; Num. 27:12–23, et al.). On two counts this was a reversion to type. The idea that the activity of Deity was limited to his own soil had been discounted from the time of Amos on; and that goodness was rewarded by possessions had been challenged by Jeremiah and exploded by the captivity. To the most thoughtful in Jewry such teaching was of the earth earthy. Still further, while such a paper-program might arouse considerable enthusiasm among local Palestinians and priestly neophytes (Isa. 60:4–22; 62:1–12), it placed the Diaspora, many of whom were comfortably settled abroad, at considerable disadvantage religiously.

Even more distressing than these difficulties was the racial theory that the Jews were a covenant people of pure Semitic stock, chosen from before the foundation of the world by the good pleasure of a Deity whose will must not be questioned. Within this were two principles each with the gravest consequences. First came the demand for separation from the Gentiles, that like a sword entered the everyday life of all the people, high and low; and second was the theological theory that the God whom they worshiped was a respecter of persons. The priestly religion was thus made to rest on the might of God, not on the rights of man. Thus there were arrayed, more or less vociferously, against the advocates of the law groups that might be characterized as anti-legalists, anti-sacerdotalists, anti-materialists, anti-racialists, and anti-Deists. Disturbing elements railed, plotted, and fought against the new order, and out of the travail of the centuries slowly emerged new problems, new parties, and new and better programs. Such is the pattern of life.

The racial problem, which, then as now, was more poignant and clear cut than theological theory, most quickly stirred up violent opposition; and the liberal protest against all phases of legalism is here seen most convincingly. The anti-Gentile decree of the divorce court credited to Ezra (Ezra 10:1–44)

---

[4] Not only had cultus originated in the belief that each of its rites possessed magical efficacy, but it never quite escaped the marks of its birth, and easily became haughtily arrogant (S. A. Cook, CAH, VI, 193–199).

at once aroused hostility, and the repercussions must have been even more violent than those preserved in our reports.

Hitherto opposition to alien marriages had been of individual (Gen. 27:46) rather than community interest, and regulative measures had never seriously interfered with private happiness. (Deuteronomy 7:3 seems to be the earliest legislation against such. Exodus 34:15 is editorial.) Many peasant dwellings in every village bore the evidence of Philistine or Edomite, Egyptian, Hittite, or Canaanite ancestry, and such families were proud of their forebears. Abraham and Joseph, Moses and Gideon, David and Solomon had hallowed such unions, so why should priests and Levites be ashamed of their foreign wives (Ezra 10:18–24), or why should the grandson of the high priest turn the daughter of Sanballat, the Horonite, out of house and home (Neh. 2:10; 13:28)? Only those obsessed by the theory that all the sufferings of Israel were due to false worship introduced by foreigners, and that nothing short of absolute isolation from all such elements could save Judaism, could whole-heartedly have supported the drastic enforcement of this law. Moreover, only at a late date, after the priests had built up their supporting genealogical lists, and had canonized the law under the aegis of Moses, could the support of this theory have been accepted as a proof of piety.

This separatist program, that by 400 B.C. had gained considerable momentum, marked the opening of a struggle that down to the present day has never ceased to torment Israel. Many local leaders in and around Jerusalem revolted against the measures introduced by the newly arrived authorities from Persia. These commands from Yahweh in the new lawbook, and the decisions of the commission on divorce, were the inhuman innovations of outsiders (Ezra 10:1–44; Neh. 13:23–30). The welfare of children, wife, and home was personal and essential. Thus, in spite of pressure, after a long and bitter struggle the Samaritan group remained faithful to the home rather than submit to a theory that ignored Hebrew history and violated the most sacred of human institutions.

The Samaritans, however, did not give up their hold on what they believed to be their rights and privileges in Jerusalem in any pacific spirit. They carried the warfare to the extreme limits. When able they drove their opponents from their lands and sold them into slavery (Jos. *Ant.*, XII, iv, 1). On occasion they murdered some of them (Jos. *Ant.*, XX, vi, 1–3) and even desecrated the temple with their dead bodies (Jos. *Ant.*, XVIII, ii, 2). It was a deadly clash between two widely divergent ideals. The narrow, racial ecclesiast, claiming divine authority, was ruthlessly intolerant; and the democratic, more considerate kinsman, when attacked fought fire with fire. Both sides displayed a fury that reveals not only the murky passions of the human heart but also the native heroism that is ever ready to give its life for an ideal. Strange to say, the Samaritans, who began their separate existence as the defenders of liberty, in the course of time became the most exclusive and bigoted of all religious groups.

But even among those who remained within the fold of Judaism not all were convinced of the divine origin of this divorce decree. Historical knowledge and religious theory made common cause with the Samaritan dissenters. Israel's formative experiences had been broad and human. Their history began at Sinai in an intertribal union. Entering Canaan, Rahab was but a symbol of the spirit and the attitude of many of the inhabitants of the land (Josh. 2:1–7; 9:3–8). In the days of the kingdom Hittites, Philistines, and Phoenicians were in places of leadership and honor in the army, in commerce, and in architecture. In the Assyrian period the prophets (763–700 B.C.) with one accord insisted that the primary criterion in religion was social justice, which by its very nature was unlimited by race, or creed, or clime. Amos was even more explicit and declared that the Ethiopian, the Philistine, the Syrian, and the Israelite were all alike to Yahweh, and the sinful people would be destroyed from off the face of the earth (Amos 9:7, 8a). The exile in Babylonia added its quota to the enlarging vision. Babylonian life had a material splendor never dreamed of by the Palestinian, and was rich in architecture, in art, in literature, in religious ritual, and in great personalities. Nebuchadnezzar was the servant of Yahweh, and later Cyrus was the Lord's anointed. It was out of life's experiences that the material and the background of religious theory were furnished. Mono-humanism, in fact, pointed the way to monotheism.

With such an inheritance, the radicals of 400 B.C. were neither idle nor silent. The booklets of Ruth and Jonah, both utilizing ancient Hebrew stories, were written in this period, apparently as campaign documents against the unfounded interpretation of the chosen people. That Ruth the Moabitess was the ancestress of David was an unanswerable argument against racial discrimination. It was a definite challenge to the new rule, that Moabites and their descendants were to be banned forever from the assembly of God (Neh. 13:1–3, 23). While Jonah, possibly with an eye to the mission of Israel to be a light to the Gentiles (Isa. 49:5), by its final question, *Should not I have regard for Nineveh, . . . wherein are 120,000 children, and also many cattle?* (Jonah 4:11) ignored all lines of cleavage of race or creed as definitely as did the story of the good Samaritan, which at a later period was a barbed shaft against racial prejudice.

Similarly, when Malachi declared that there were Gentiles the world over whose worship was acceptable to Yahweh (Mal. 1:10–14), the author, though primarily interested in local worship and in his own people, had an outreach that was in sympathy with the liberalism of the day.[5] Isaiah 56:1–8, belonging

---

[5] There is good reason to interpret this passage as above suggested (S. R. Driver, "Minor Prophets," *Cent. B.,* II, 304–306; J. M. P. Smith, "Malachi," *ICC,* 30–33; C. C. Torrey, *The Second Isaiah,* 65; J. Morgenstern, *JBL,* March, 1945, 29–31).

to a later period,[6] is nothing short of a denial of the priestly right to seclude Deity behind Jewish barricades. The temple is a house of prayer for *all people,* and the foreigner and the eunuch may minister there to Yahweh. For this the requirements, to keep justice and righteousness, to observe the Sabbath, and to hold fast the covenant, were ethical with a minimum of ritual. The same universal outlook is found in the statement that in the restoration of Israel, "Some of them [Gentiles] also will I take for priests and for Levites, saith Yahweh" (Isa. 66:21).[7]

An even more iconoclastic attack on the hierarchy is preserved in Isaiah 66:1-5. "Heaven is my throne" (66:1), and sacrifice, oblation, and incense are an abomination to Yahweh (66:3), whose delight is in the humble and contrite heart, and in those who "tremble at my word" (66:2). This, which is reminiscent of the attitude of Jeremiah, implies that no temple, no holy of holies, no priesthood is needed for the worship of the living and the true God. It is no wonder that these anti-ritualists, who abhorred the rites of the temple and sought access to the Almighty without the aid of the learned scribe, were hated and cast out by those who were in authority (66:5).

But the most daring statement of all, one of those beacon lights in religion that shines high above the shoals of personal prejudice and class interest, is chronicled in Isaiah 19:24, 25. In that day *Israel shall be third* with Egypt and Assyria, a blessing in the midst of the earth; "for that Yahweh of hosts hath blessed them, saying, Blessed be Egypt my people, and Assyria the work of my hands, and Israel my inheritance."

These phrases, paragraphs, and booklets, often so edited and interpreted as to dull their edge, were the rankest heresy to those who believed themselves to be the exclusive guardians of the oracles of Israel. Hatreds that often were at white heat were a commonplace, and the conflict between the lovers of the Jewish law and the lovers of humanity raged throughout the generations. The sharp antagonism in late Old Testament literature between the righteous and the wicked, which we so often vest with ethical qualities, in all probability was due to the strife between religious parties within Judaism itself. The righteous were the lovers of the law, those rabbis who delighted in reflection on the written word, and rejoiced in the painstaking observance of all the ritual (Ps. 19:7-14; 119:1-176). The wicked, or the sinners, on the other hand, those who were so vigorously condemned (Ps. 1:1-6),[8] were the rebels. These, in the spirit of Jeremiah, rejected the assumptions of the pious, whose interests were limited to race and ritual. Like Jeremiah, for the time being they were denounced and condemned, but in the long run such voices

---

[6] C. C. Torrey considers Isaiah chaps. 34, 35, 40-66 a well co-ordinated unit which teaches that the chief mission of dispersed Israel is to bring salvation to the world, when Jew and Gentile together will worship Yahweh on Mount Zion, each in its own capacity (*The Second Isaiah,* 53-67, 71-76, 409-414).

[7] G. F. Moore, *Judaism,* II, 373, 374.

[8] R. Kittel, *Die Psalmen,* 1-7.

found response in many quarters. The ethical prophets were their forerunners. International history was their tutor. Because of their ideals and their world-wide contacts they had learned that a good Greek was better than a bad Jew, and this conviction was on the highway to a world religion and world peace.

The movement was vital but, like democracy, it was too fluid and had too little interest in machine politics to prevail against the hierarchy. Neverthe-less, the validity of its principles, supported as they were by tradition, history, and human values, must have been fully recognized by many of the leaders. The spirit of liberalism tempered the attitude of those who collected and edited the Pentateuch. They preserved in it secular regulations (Exod. 21:1–23:9), the very human stories of the J. and E. documents, the social ethics of Deuteronomy and Leviticus 19:9–20, 33–36. All these, though not peculiarly priestly, were part of the warp and woof of Israel's religious heritage. Further, they provided a world outlook in the creation story (Gen. 1:1–2:4a) and implied the brotherhood of all men in the covenant with Noah (Gen. 9:1–17), though, like all priestly activity, the ultimate objective was narrowly Jewish.

Beyond that, the message of universal brotherhood found so warm a re-sponse within Judaism that those who from 621 B.C. to 119 A.D. were responsible for the final form of the canon let its voice be heard in all three divisions, the law, the prophets, and the writings. Nor was any festival or temple service complete without its quota of Psalms, the hymnbook of the second temple; and no rabbi could neglect the prophets, that always occupied a place in every synagogue service. These two, religious experience and social ethics, took the edge off the more formal features of the cultus and the Torah, and created an atmosphere of kindly human interest that no member of the congregation could escape.[9]

Nevertheless, though the liberal and the legal groups influenced each other, and at times went far toward co-ordination, the gulf between the two was never permanently bridged. In method, emphasis, objectives, and spirit the two walked apart. For many it could never be *both . . . and;* it was ultimately *either . . . or.* The law to the orthodox Jew was the holy of holy of Scripture, and within that the precise rules, the cleansing rites, and the mercy seat formed the norm to which all else must conform. The liberal or cosmopolitan group

[9] The happy interweaving of righteous acts and ritual requirements is admirably expressed in the characterization of the priest, the keeper of the law, in Ben Sirach 35:1–20. K. Köhler draws attention to the fact that during the Maccabean period the Pharisees interpreted the Torah in the spirit of prophetic ethics, thus forming a synthesis (*Jewish Theology*, 101–111). Also L. Finkel-stein, in a fine personal testimony, holds that the Torah is the climax of the whole prophetic teach-ing (*The Pharisees*, II, 461–463). These glowing testimonies reflect personal character that is of a high order. They also imply, if they do not explicitly state, an interpretation of Scripture which is based on the untenable assumption that the written word, from all periods and in all parts, was in complete agreement (see chap. i, p. 3). On this theory all the divergent religious ideas of the Hebrews were supplementary to each other, and all converged on the duty and the destiny of Israel. Thus the universal brotherhood of man and his equality before God as part of Scripture is ignored.

worshiped a God who dwelt in the home and in the human heart as surely as in temple or cathedral built by human hands, and who accepted the Moabite as gladly as the Jew. Acquainted with the peoples of many nations, they believed that men everywhere had access to the Eternal, and that the Almighty showed his mercy to the Assyrian as well as to the Israelite.

Without question, those keeping the law found therein a supreme satisfaction and a joyous delight. But in no less measure did those of broader sympathies, without pride of ancestry or benefit of priesthood, attain a fullness of life, perform a lasting service to humanity, and enjoy the presence of the God and Father of all mankind. While these two walked apart, yet each in its own way contributed to the enrichment of religious experience and knowledge. Each ministered to a group largely conditioned by temperament and training to respond to its message. Each as a critic of the other was a restraining influence limiting undesirable extremes, sometimes even converting its opponents. Orthodoxy persistently harked back to those forms and ideas long established by tradition, to the faith of the fathers. Primarily it was authoritarian; God *has said* in his Torah. Liberalism appealed to the worth and dignity of man, to a faith in the moral order of the universe. Primarily it was democratic; God *is saying* in human experience. It was experimental, ever learning, growing, trying to think God's thoughts after him. It was universal, exploring the needs and expressing the aspirations of mankind.

Chapter XIV

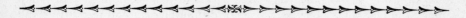

THE RELIGION OF SUPERNATURALISM.

350 B.C.–A.D. 135

ESSIANISM, in its origin, can be traced under varying forms back to the beginnings of Israel's history, or if you wish, even back to that universal hope that springs eternal within the human breast.[1] The covenant in the wilderness had in it the seeds of nationalism, which in the hour of disaster sought relief in the more specific, though less realistic, Messianism, which in turn passed over into the eschatological hope.

Saul was called the Messiah of Yahweh (I Sam. 24:6, 10; 26:9, 11, 16; II Sam. 1:14; 19:21) as he was the anointed deliverer of his people; and David, the most creative leader of the nation, established a dynasty that lasted for four centuries and was celebrated in two passages that at least have the Messianic spirit. Both of these, in the present text of Samuel (II Sam. 7:8-17, and 7:18-29), have been edited, and they were re-edited with definite theological changes by the Chronicler (I Chron. 17:11-14, and 17:16-27). What seems to have been the original form of these early poems is tender and wistful, basing all the hope for the future on the goodness and the greatness of God.[2] Yahweh is a father to the dynasty. Each ruler is his son, chastened when in error but never forsaken, and thus the dynasty is to be established forever.

When in 586 B.C. Jerusalem was destroyed and the people were carried into captivity, in spite of the disaster, and though not a few of David's descendants had been unworthy, many Jews clung tenaciously to the old order and planned and dreamed of a new and greater empire. This was their tradition, and to them tradition was the final voice of God. Hananiah's prediction that the temple vessels would be returned within two years (Jer. 28:1-4) gladdened many hearts, and a little later eager eyes turned hopefully to Jeconiah, the captive king, as the restorer of the kingdom (Ezek. 17:22-24; 21:27). But with the passing of the years this phase of the hope slowly faded from the picture (II Kings 25:27-29).

[1] The antiquity of the idea, and the various forms it has assumed through the ages, are discussed by A. R. Gordon, *The Ancestral Hope of the Ages;* K. Köhler, *Jewish Theology*, 378-391; A. C. Knudson, *Religious Teaching of the O.T.*, 351-364, 371-377. Messianism in its narrowest sense finds its basis in the future hope of almost all humanity (W. Bousset, *Die Religion des Judentums im späthellenistischen Zeitalter*, 255-261; S. J. Case, *The Millennial Hope*, 1-47).

[2] The meaning, values, and date of these important sections are discussed in the writer's "Samuel," *American Commentary on the O.T.*, 128-133.

From 586 to 540 B.C. the years were dark and tedious, both in Judea and among the Diaspora. They were years of disillusionment and reconstruction. But when in 539 B.C. Cyrus the conqueror appeared before the walls of Babylon, songs of comfort were again on the lips of the Dispersed, and this world conqueror was hailed as the Messiah of God (Isa. 44:28–45:4). Under the Persian rule all exiles were granted the privilege of repatriation, but most of the Jews living abroad were content to remain in what was the land of their birth and the center of their business. Small groups of religious enthusiasts from time to time found their way back to the bare hills of the fatherland.

In Jerusalem a native prince, Sheshbazzar, appointed governor by Persia, set about repairing the fortunes of Israel. The ruins were great; the people were few and dispirited. Nothing is known about his accomplishments, nor how he passed off the stage; but by 520 B.C. Zerubbabel, a prince of the house of David (I Chron. 3:19), was the ruler in Jerusalem, under the authority of Persia. The time surely was ripe to regain the longed-for freedom. When Darius I seized the throne of Persia in 522 B.C., the great empires so recently conquered by Cyrus with one accord revolted, and nine usurpers in various capitals of the ancient world challenged the authority of the untried princeling. The overthrow of Darius and the collapse of Persian world empire seemed a mathematical certainty. Moreover for seventy years prophetic oracles had been assuring the captives that Yahweh would restore them to the homeland, and that Jerusalem would be rebuilt in splendor (Zech. 1:12; Jer. 25:12–14; 27:7–11; 28:2–11).

By August of the year 520 B.C. the program for rebuilding the temple, which would become the center of Jewish national life and would assure the presence of Yahweh in the midst of his people, was brought out into the open. Haggai, the prophet, was the foremost and most pronounced promoter of the venture (Hag. 1:1–2:23). Zechariah, who may have been a priest (Neh. 12:16), was a close associate in the project (Zech. 1:1–8:23, written from November 520 to December 518 B.C.). To rebuild the temple to install Joshua as high priest, and to make Zerubbabel the independent, princely ruler was the task. It was a heroic undertaking.

Confidence rose to the highest pitch, inspired by the leadership and sustained by the conviction that it was "not by might, nor by power, but by my Spirit, saith Yahweh" (Zech. 4:6). The people set to work with a will. Joshua and Zerubbabel accepted the responsibilities. Zerubbabel was believed to be the *branch* of Messianic promise (Zech. 3:8; 6:12; cf. Jer. 23:5) and the *signet ring* on the finger of the Most High (Hag. 2:23; cf. Jer. 22:24). He had laid the foundation of the temple; his hands would also finish it (Zech. 4:9). The temple, in the face of great difficulties, was completed (Hag. 2:9, 18; Zech. 4:7–9; Ezra 3:8, 10; 5:1, 2). A crown of gold was sent by the captives in Babylon for Zerubbabel (Zech. 6:10–14),[3] and a service of dedication of the temple and coronation of the prince was planned (Zech. 3:8; 4:7–10; 6:12, 13).

This movement was primarily religious, and in the strictest sense of the word Messianic.[4] The temple was central, and Joshua the high priest was co-partner with Zerubbabel, the Sprout, or Branch, who was of the house of David. In Jewish history there was no time when some of the most definite Messianic oracles fitted the situation more perfectly than now. Such well-known expressions of national hope or Messianism as those found in Jeremiah 23:5, 6 and Isaiah 9:5–7; 11:1–5 may well have had Zerubbabel in mind as the Branch or the Sprout of the house of David, under whom the kingdom would be established forever.[5] This was the day of liberation, when each would re-joice under his own vine and fig tree (Zech. 3:10), and when Jerusalem would be impregnably walled round about by the Almighty, as a fire (Zech. 2:3–5; 8:4–8), while Yahweh of hosts himself would be with them (Zech. 8:23).

This ardent hope, that like a beacon light had given courage and direction to the little community, in some unrecorded way was completely quenched. The program was treachery against the great king; and the curtain on the drama of Jewish history was rung down for some seventy years (516–444 B.C.). This long silence is in itself a revelation. Zerubbabel, whether removed by Persia in 518 B.C.[6] as a traitor or not, disappeared from history without a trace. The promised kingdom was a house of cards, a fantastic dream that vanished before the angry breath of Persia. The joy of that day was eclipsed by sorrow. The Messiah of God, the hope of Israel, was a broken reed that pierced the hand that leaned on it. Again, God was not in the storm, nor in the earthquake. He was not with his people after the manner of their expectation.

The high venture had failed in its main objective; yet it had inherent values. It had awakened the slumbering energies of many, and had left a memorial of devotion to all later generations. Beyond that, such exploded dreams are an

[3] The Hebrew text of Zechariah 6:10–14 is evidently corrupt. The plural form *crowns* in verse 11, in the Syriac and Targums is rendered by the singular, which seems to be correct. Also 11b, in which the crowns are set on the head of Joshua, is strange. In 3:5 Joshua was to wear, as was natural, the priestly headdress, a clean turban, while the crown naturally belonged to the prince. It is possible that 11b is a scribal addition, the omission of which leaves the implication that Zerub-babel was crowned. Or it may be that originally the name Zerubbabel stood in place of Joshua. For complete critical discussion see H. G. Mitchell, "Haggai, Zechariah," *ICC*, 183–190.

[4] T. K. Cheyne, *Jewish Religion after the Exile*, 14, 15.

[5] These three passages, which do not belong to their present context, have much in common with the hope so vivid to Haggai and Zechariah. Such oracles usually refer to a definite historical person belonging to the period of the writer. But they are always in part idealistic, thus making it easy to apply them to leaders in later generations; but to do so is beyond the rights of exegesis. G. R. Berry considered the figure in these poems to be literary rather than historical (*JBL*, 1926, 232–237). Their idealism no doubt furnished a preparation to later eschatology.

[6] The date of the removal of Zerubbabel from the governorship is uncertain. The probability is it was some time before 516 B.C. J. Morgenstern is convinced that it occurred toward the end of 520 B.C. (*AJSL*, 1938, 191).

integral part of human history, and they mark all the pathways of life. The story of our laboratories is one long tale of failure, gladdened only here and there by success. Like climbing the Himalaya peaks, success is achieved only by stern endeavor and keen observation, by retracing steps, by feeling the way through fog and storm cloud, by perpetual reconstruction in the light of accumulating facts. Thus are the frontiers of truth pushed back, and the ignorance of yesterday gives way to the knowledge of tomorrow. Such is the highway of revelation. Shattered hopes prove to be the road signs, signalizing danger, detour, or dead stop. This general fact is amply confirmed by the Zerubbabel episode. It required some seventy years for Jewish thinkers to reconstruct their hope, but like the "Boston Tea Party," it left an indelible impression on all later history.

Many saw in this the handwriting on the wall, that nationalism was not the will of God, and wholeheartedly turned to religion as the chief satisfaction of life. Thus did the priest and the teacher adjust to history. Others, of different temperament and wider outlook, faced life as it was, and concluded with Ecclesiastes that the quiet acceptance of things as they are is best; or decided, in the spirit of much of Proverbs and Ben Sirach, that alert, shrewd, driving business methods, without too much sentimentality, in the long run paid largest dividends. Still others, of a more emotional and less independent type, sporadically turned to the heavens for the fulfillment of their dreams. A few late oracles expect that Yahweh will establish the dynasty of David by his own power (Jer. 33:14-26, late and not in the Septuagint; 31:2-6, 16-22; Ezek. 34:23-25), or better still that he himself will be king (Zech. 14:9, 16, 17) and will rule over all nations (Ps. Sol. 17:36; 18:6, 8; Ps. 2:2). But while, at times, this dying hope flashed out anew with the turning of a page in history, and lingered on in poetic expression,[7] on the whole it merged into the more spectacular and less hampered movement of Apocalypticism. Many of the forlorn and the distracted reveled in release from all human endeavor, and in an abandon to the supernatural.

Apocalypticism, the heir to the hope and the spirit of Messianism, slowly emerged from the ruins of nationalism. With the downfall of Zerubbabel, Judaism, though shocked, was by no means defeated. The Palestinian peasants, "the people of the land," had been the most eager participants in the re-establishment of the kingdom. But many priests in Babylon, wise men at home and abroad, the adherents of liberalism everywhere, though interested probably formed no close alliance with the movement. By its failure each of these groups ultimately gained strength. Within a century we have the priest with the

---

[7] Many passages, early and late, torn out of their contexts and out of history, have been used to support the idea that the kingdom of God will be established by supernatural power on the earth with Jerusalem as its center. History for more than two thousand years has proved all such interpreters deluded, blind leaders of the blind.

Torah, and shortly thereafter the fully organized hierarchy (I Chron. 23:1–26: 32), at the head of which stood the Aaronic priesthood, the chief of whom at times was called the Messiah (Lev. 4:3, 5, 16; 6:22; Ps. 84:9). The wise men developed their schools and dedicated themselves to the propagation of practical wisdom; while many with broad cultural contacts lost interest in the forms of Judaism and became tolerant of Persian, Greek, and Roman ways of life.

But a considerable number of Jews, chiefly among the lower classes who had suffered greatly, found all of these inadequate. The priesthood was a closed corporation; the Torah was too elaborate and too technical; the sages were coldly intellectual and humanistic, and liberalism to them was a compromise with paganism. Even reliance on a prince of the house of David seemed a futility as kings from Saul to Zerubbabel had been a disappointment. Staking so much on a man had always been disastrous, hence Yahweh alone was competent for the deliverance of Israel. Here a thwarted Messianism, by proclaiming Yahweh the king of Israel (Isa. 17:22; 35:2–6; Mic. 2:13; 4:7; Zeph. 3: 15–17; Jer. 46:15, 18; 51:57; Zech. 14:9–17; Ezek. 34:1–10, 11–16, 23, 24), had pointed the way to a heavenly kingdom. This peasant group was passionate, narrow-minded, and deeply religious. Out of lost causes flaming convictions had been forged. They were confident their rights had been violated, and certain that the God of their fathers would crush their enemies and establish them in his kingdom. This was their Messianic hope. Such people, uncritical and unstable, easily roused to heroic action, closely akin to the Essenes,[8] formed the chief element in the apocalyptic movement.

The apocalyptists [9] in large measure drew their inspiration and their thought forms from far back in national history. In spirit they were closely related to the court prophets (I Kings 22:6, 10–12), later called the false prophets (Jer. 8:10; 23:17) whose chief function was to intensify the tribal interests, thereby keeping up the morale of the nation (cf. Exod. 15:21; Judg. 5:23, 31; Num. 22:6, 40–23:4; Jer. 27:14, 15; 28:3, 4, 11). Nahum, who cursed Nineveh (2:3–3:9), and Obadiah, who poured his vengeance on Edom, belong to this school. But the most soul-searing of such ancient hymns of hate is Psalm 137:9 where in a frenzy of savagery a singer hissed, "Happy shall he be who taketh and dasheth thy little ones against the rock."

Literature of this type sorely lacked the ethical convictions of the great prophets (Amos 1:3–10, 13–15; 2:6–16; 9:7, 8a; Isa. 10:12–15) and the sages, in which the outlook was universal. These writers under the urge for freedom, coupled with the hatred of alien rule and a chauvinistic theology, were in-

---

[8] See K. Köhler, *Jewish Theology*, 378–391, where he discusses the Messianic hope.

[9] Apocalypse, literally the uncovering, that is, revealing that which is hidden, in one sense or another is a world-wide phenomenon. Oracles, dreams, and visions, by which the mysteries of the future were revealed to prophet or priest, have played a large part in the religious practices of most primitive people. The particular form this took in Jewish apocalypticism is found only partially developed among others.

dignant because their tribe could not sit astride the highway of commerce and do as they pleased amid a world civilization. In postexilic days it became a popular sport to sing and write woes against far-distant or long-vanquished nations, and in time many of these curses were attached to the authentic works of earlier prophets. These later oracles [10] are vague, unhistorical, armchair dreams, comforting to the vengeful. In phrase and spirit they paved the way for later outbursts of an even more lurid nature. The scene was slowly shifting from social ethics to the racial demands of a pressure group, from reality to fantasy, from the wearying human struggle to the irresistible power of the wonder-working God.

Apocalypticism, also, took over as symbols two features of early Hebrew ideology, the battle of Armageddon and the Day of Yahweh. The former, Mount Megiddo, comparable to Waterloo in European history, was the strategic battleground in the Esdraelon Valley, where a thousand years earlier Egyptians and Hittites had met in decisive conflict. Now it was taken as a symbol for an assumed last battle in human history, in which the armies of the nations would be gathered against the elect, and Yahweh, entering the fray with the hosts of heaven, would wipe out all the enemies of Israel.

The Day of Yahweh, an old mythological idea that can be traced to Babylonia,[11] had been part of the common speech from the days of the early settlement in Canaan. It was akin to the widespread primitive idea that in the hour of need, the god of the tribe would reveal himself in power for the deliverance of his people. It is no surprise that such was the common, even universal, belief in Israel during the early centuries of her history. Indeed it has been rare for any group at any time, even in modern religion, to lack the conviction that the chief task of its god is the promotion of its welfare.

But Amos and his contemporaries declared that owing to social iniquities the Day of Yahweh for Israel would be darkness and desolation (Amos 1:2; 2:6, 8; 3:9, 12; 5:10, 13; 6:1, 8; Isa. 2:12, 19; also Jer. 4:5, 8, 13, 19, 26, 29, 31; 5:15–17; 6:15–17; 22–26). Zephaniah immortalized this principle when he proclaimed the Day of Yahweh to be a day of wrath and anguish, of gloom and darkness, of cloud and thick cloud; men fleeing, blood flowing, and flesh rotting because of the idolatry, arrogance, indifference, and injustice of Judah (Zeph. 1:7–18).

These three, the spirit of the court prophets, the battle of Armageddon, and the Day of Yahweh, each idealized by tradition and fused in one, were made the vehicle of various and sometimes contradictory messages, all in agreement in assuring Israel that Yahweh of hosts himself was immediately going to

[10] Much of Isaiah 13:1–19:17; Jeremiah 46:1–51:58; Ezekiel 25:1–32:32, and parts of Isaiah 56: 1–66:24, belong to this category. See R. H. Pfeiffer, *Introduction to the O.T.*, 506–510.

[11] In Babylonia it was the day when deity would reveal himself, and would destroy all enemies (G. Hölscher, *Die Ursprung der jüdischen Eschatologie*, 13). For its significance in Hebrew thought see J. M. P. Smith, "The Day of Yahweh," *AJTh*, 1901.

appear to overthrow the nations and establish the empire of his chosen people on Mount Zion.

Gradually, under the pressure of history, this type of thought developed its own form of literary expression, which was calculated from both form and content to make a wide appeal. The book of Joel, written about 350 B.C., stands midway between the historical and the visionary. The locust plague, as here described, does not exceed reality [12] and is often read as such. But it is called the Day of Yahweh (Joel 1:15; 2:1, 10–12, 16), is equated with Armageddon (3:1–3, 9–17), and is the preparation for the outpouring of the Spirit of Yahweh (2:28–32).[13] Here the operation of the Spirit, as in the cases of Samson (Judg. 13:25; 14:6, 19; 15:15) and Saul (I Sam. 10:6, 10), is a manifestation in the physical and psychological areas (Joel 2:28–32, cf. 3:14–17), and is divorced from ethical ideals as completely as Joel 3:16 reverses the judgment of Amos 1:2. It was V Day for Israel, and the preparation, the process, and the culmination all belonged to Yahweh. The source of triumph had shifted from justice and human effort to the wonder-working power of Yahweh alone.

A little later, but early in the Greek period, a poem now imbedded in Isaiah 24–27, a more complete expression of apocalypticism, was composed (Isa. 24:1–23; 25:6–8; 26:20–27:1, 12, 13).[14]

During the following century this distorted view of human history was accelerated by the buffetings received by the Jewish people. The Seleucid-Ptolemaic (Syria and Egypt) wars between 321 and 280 B.C., in which Palestine changed hands no less than eight times, made the land one continuous Armageddon grinding the occupants between the upper and the lower millstones. From 280 to 198 B.C. the Ptolemies (Egypt) ruled, with but brief interludes; but Palestine, always the frontier of the land of Egypt, was garrisoned by Greek soldiers, and more than once the Jews suffered enslavement by the overlord.[15] When in 198 B.C. the Seleucids (Syria) conquered the country, for a few brief years conditions were happier, but under Antiochus IV, 175-164 B.C., they became intolerable. When, as a last resort to make the Jew profit by the culture of the Greeks, the headstrong monarch prohibited Sabbath observance, circumcision, and possession of copies of the law, required all the Jews to eat swine's flesh, and erected an altar to Zeus in the Jerusalem temple on

---

[12] A swarm of locusts will strip every leaf off any tree, and destroy the last vestige of green in a field within a few hours. See S. Kraus, ZDPV, 1927, 244–249; PEQ, 1931, 111.

[13] Clear distinctions should be made as to the meaning of Spirit and Spirit of God as found in different writings. In the pre-prophetic literature it is used for the display of abnormal physical gifts, or ecstasy, or other unusual activities. In the prophets, though rarely used, it always has moral or intellectual connotation. Deuteronomy and Jeremiah, owing to the popular, unethical usage, never use it. In apocalyptic literature as here (Joel 2:28–32) it is used as a manifestation of power; in part a reversion to type.

[14] For a detailed study of the critical background and the significance of this poem see G. B. Gray, "Isaiah," ICC, I, 397–408.

[15] The history is briefly summarized in the writer's O.T. Life and Literature, 282, 283.

which he offered swine's flesh, on December 15, 168 B.C. (I Macc. 1:41–64), indignities had reached the climax.

Worse than this, if possible, was the fact that a greedy and treacherous priesthood for more than three-quarters of a century, from Onias II, 246, to Menelaus, 172 B.C., by shameless racketeering had prospered greatly at the expense of the tortured people. After four hundred years of hoping, planning, striving in the face of disaster after disaster, and with a century in which agony was piled on agony, that ended in the great humiliation, the desecration of the temple of Yahweh, we are not surprised that all hope of gaining their end by human effort was exhausted.

The Jewish apocalyptic literature, some twenty pamphlets written between 170 B.C. and A.D. 200, was the theological response to this dark despair.[16]

The characteristic features of all of this literature, Daniel included, may be briefly summarized. All of it was published anonymously, and most of it was pseudepigraphic. Each writer ascribed his message to someone such as Enoch, the Twelve, Moses, Daniel, Elijah, Isaiah, Baruch, Jeremiah who because of tradition, "walking with God," "ascending into heaven in a cloud," or "communing with Yahweh on the mountain top," seemed an appropriate medium for a new revelation. While this use of names would today be reprehensible, it was neither uncommon nor considered unworthy two thousand years ago. In the days before there were copyright laws,[17] and ideas were not considered private property, the disciple often sought in this way to honor his master. A highly honored name would also add some weight to the message, and at the same time conceal the identity of the author, who might easily be charged with high treason.

Symbolism, in which beasts, figures, numbers, and catchwords took the

[16] The following is a list of this literature in what is approximately its chronological order. While only the book of Daniel was admitted into the canon of the Old Testament, and only Revelation gained acceptance with the Christians, all of it is of great value, even essential, for the understanding of the theological background of the New Testament. A careful reading of it enables us to judge more accurately of the temporary values of books such as Daniel and Revelation, and at the same time is likely to cure the wild theorizing of modern apocalyptists. It was a strange, superheated, visionary philosophy that can have no place in the thinking of today. Ethiopic Enoch, i–xxxvi, by or before 170 B.C.; Daniel, 168 B.C.; Ethiopic Enoch, lxxxiii–xc, by 161 B.C., Sibylline Oracles, Proem and iii, 97–818, after 150 B.C.; XII Patriarchs, in part before 100 B.C.; Ethiopic Enoch, xci–civ, by 95 B.C.; Ethiopic Enoch, xxxvii–lxx, by 64 B.C.; Psalms of Solomon, between 70 and 40 B.C.; Sibylline Oracles, iii, 1–62, by 31 B.C.; II Maccabees, before 1 B.C.; Book of Jubilees, by A.D. 10; Assumption of Moses, by A.D. 29; Slavonic Enoch, by A.D. 50; IV Maccabees, by A.D. 70; Apocalypse of Baruch, at least five independent sections, completed by A.D. 100; Apocalypse of Isaiah, by A.D. 100; IV Ezra, also composite, before and after A.D. 70; Revelation, after A.D. 100; and later Sibylline Oracles, not earlier than the end of the third century A.D. The most complete studies of this literature in which the whole field is covered are those of R. H. Charles in *A Critical History of the Doctrine of the Future Life*, see pp. 162–305; *Ency. Bibl.*, Vol. 1, 213–250; *HBD*, I, 109, 110. The texts of most of these, with critical commentaries, are found in the two volumes of Apocrypha and Pseudepigrapha, edited by R. H. Charles.

[17] The copyright law was first introduced in England in the reign of Queen Anne (G. H. Putnam, *Copy-right Laws*).

place of plain speech, was us██ ████ █asons of safety as well as vividness. Each booklet, a meaningless myster███ █he general public and to state authorities, when decoded became to the in█████ a blueprint of coming events.

Prediction of things to come was thus a prominent feature of each of these programs. A sketch of history, put into the mouth of the selected author in the form of prediction, was made the introduction and the basis of the revelation that the end was at hand. Eschatology, that is, "last things," was thus always an integral part of apocalypticism. For two and a half centuries these distraught enthusiasts struggled with the problem of the time of the end. When the first, second, and third date was proved to be wrong someone with later inside information usually appeared and with enviable resourcefulness presented another, final chart (cf. Dan. 12:11; 8:14; 12:12, 13) of the long-awaited day of redemption. Shepherds, beasts, days, weeks, half-weeks, years, and numbers were sufficiently ambiguous to be reinterpreted over and over again whenever a new *key* was found, so that the futile process has continued to the present among certain esoteric groups.[18]

Pessimism as to the natural world order was an underlying presupposition of all this literature. The fullness of the whole earth was not the glory of Yahweh, as it had been to the great prophet (Isa. 6:3), but, to use late phrases, this present evil world was under the prince of the powers of the air (Eph. 2:2), who was also called the prince of this world (Asc. Isa. 10; John 12:31; 14:30; cf. Matt. 13:38, 39). The monotheism of Deutero-Isaiah, that made Yahweh primarily responsible for evil, presented grave difficulties to many Jewish thinkers. Dualism, in which the ancient Semitic idea of a spirit world (see I Kings 22:9–22; Job 1:6–12; 2:1–6; Deut. 33:2, 3) had been organized and developed, partly under Persian influence, seemed more acceptable to

[18] An illustration of how fatal to Biblical knowledge such methods may be is seen in the history of the interpretations of the seventy years of Jeremiah 29:10. In 593 B.C. the prophet indicated his conviction that the return of the exiles would not be in the immediate future, but would be beyond seventy years, that is, the lifetime of the then generation. This seems clear from the context in which the exiles are counseled to establish permanent settlements in Babylonia (Jer. 29:1–7), and in a parallel passage in which the duration of the captivity is equated with the reign of Nebuchadnezzar, his son, and his son's son (Jer. 27:7). But this general statement has attracted through the ages those who were more interested in clairvoyancy than in morals. In 519 B.C., Zechariah cried out, "How long wilt thou not have mercy on Jerusalem, . . . against which thou hast had indignation these seventy years?" (Zech. 1:12). In 306 B.C. the author of the Epistle of Jeremy was convinced that seventy years was a symbol for seven generations, and equaled seven by forty, that is, 280 years; thus the return would be in 313 B.C. In 170 B.C. the writer of Enoch knew the seventy years stood for 70 shepherds, or rulers, and by manipulating history proved that the last days had come (Enoch 89:59–90:19). In 168–167 B.C. Daniel found the key. The seventy years were week-years; and seven by seventy gave 490 years (Dan. 7:25; 9:12, 24, 25–27), and left only a time, and a time and a half time. The full end was determined. In A.D. 116 IV Ezra came to the rescue of disappointed eschatologists with a new key. The seventy years and the four kingdoms of Daniel were symbols of kings and wings, and now at last the end lay just ahead (IV Ezra 12:11–32). Thus throughout the generations, by ignoring the context of Scripture, fanciful programs of the future were constructed on most precarious foundations. Jeremiah, like all the great prophets, was a realist, a preacher of justice who called to repentance, rather than a predictor of events yet to come, couched in unintelligible symbols. See S. A. Cook, *The O.T.; a Reinterpretation*, 108, 172.

many.[19] Thus, it was believed that t[...] world was divided into two great antagonistic armies. One was und[...] chief variously named Beliar (XII Patriarchs, Test. Levi, iii, 3; xviii, [...]; xix, 1; Test, Jude, xxv, 1), Asmodeus (Tob. 3:8, 17; 6:14, 15, 16; 8:3), Semjaza (En. 6:2; 69:2) the great dragon (Rev. 12:13; 13:2), the devil (Test. Napht., viii, 4; Wisd. of Sol. 2:24; Rev. 20:2). The other, under good spirits such as Gabriel, Michael, Raphael, and Phanuel (En. 40:9, 10; 71:8, 9; Dan. 10:13, 20, 21; 12:1; Tob. 12:15), had Yahweh himself as the commander. The former, enemies of the children of men, ruled in large measure over this world; while the latter, though specially interested in the destiny of the Jews, had its seat in the heavens. The perpetual tragedy of Judaism was thus explained by the theory that all the kingdoms of the world, and the glory of them, were under the rule of the devil (see Matt. 4:8, 9).[20]

Optimism as to the immediate future, owing to the direct and miraculous intervention of God on behalf of his people, was the counterpart of pessimism as to the natural world order. After the failure of the plot of Zerubbabel many turned to Yahweh as the only source of deliverance, and celebrated him as the King of Israel who would rule on Mount Zion (Zeph. 3:15; Jer. 46:18; 48:15; Isa. 24:21–23; Zech. 14:9–11, 16, 17). Under repeated disappointments the apocalyptists turned everything over to Yahweh, who could and would overthrow the nations, destroy the earth by fire, and create new heavens and a new earth as the abode of his chosen people. Such, with a great variety of detail, were the main features of the feverish dreams of these single-minded torchbearers of hope. Their freedom thwarted by the nations, and the observance of their religious customs prohibited on pain of death, they had taken refuge from the world of things as they were in the promised land of the God whom they worshiped. It was a glad new world, a world of joy and beauty secure from fiend and foe, the very dream of which released deep-seated energies that were exhilarating and creative.

The book of Daniel,[21] of which the sections 2:31–45; 7:1–11:45; 12:1–13 constitute the most thorough apocalypse in the Old Testament, can be under-

[19] K. Köhler, "Demonology," *JE*, IV, 519. See also G. A. Barton, *ERE*, IV, 598–601.

[20] Many rabbis, who considered this theory of the origin of evil shallow and inadequate, held that in man there was the evil impulse, the *yeser ha-ra'*, which was the root of all evil. The individual was thus held responsible for his own sin. See F. H. Porter, *Biblical and Semitic Studies of members of the Yale Faculty*. For a Biblical basis for this theory note Gen. 6:5; 8:21; Deut. 31:21; I Chron. 28:9; 29:18. See also Test. Asher 1:2–6; 8:19; Test. Benj. 6:4; Pirke Aboth 37; 148; II Esdras 4:30–32; G. F. Moore, *Judaism*, I, 474–496; Oesterley and Box, *Religion and Worship in the Synagogue*, 229–252.

[21] In the book of Daniel there are two distinct elements; one the apocalyptic as indicated above, the other a number of legends, each of which probably had a long history and may even have been in written form before they were incorporated in the present book. That the book was not completed earlier than 168–167 B.C. is supported by the definite historical references. See J. A. Montgomery, "Daniel," *ICC;* S. R. Driver, "Daniel," *Camb. B.;* R. H. Charles, "Daniel," *Cent. B.;* K. Köhler *JQR*, 1920–1921, 145–150.

stood only in this background. This revelation, probably more than any other, was of vital influence to many who lived during the trying experiences beginning in 170 B.C. It was a call to resist to the death the tyranny of Antiochus Epiphanes in affairs of culture, race, and religion. It was crisis theology, and for many of the loyal it was the final word of Deity. Its clearly etched symbolism, the stone cut out of the mountain without hands (Dan. 2:31–35), the ancient of days sitting on his throne (7:9—11), one like unto the son of man, descending on the clouds of heaven to rule over all peoples, nations, and languages (7:13, 14), the saints of the Most High established as an everlasting kingdom (7:27)—these caught the imagination of the populace when ordinary language and correct logic would have fallen on deaf ears.

National pride had been aroused by the menace of Greek culture; old ideals, deep-rooted in racial history, were taking on new life, and now passionate hatreds flamed up at the sacrilegious edict and the revolting practices of Antiochus (I Macc. 1:20–46). Daniel, and similar pamphlets, appealed to self-preservation and revenge, the most primitive instincts, and in the name of God assured the people of a glorious triumph. Some Quisling Jews cravenly acquiesced in the foreign policy (I Macc. 1:52; 2:23; 7:5–9, 21–24, 33), but for many the perils of revolt were blacked out by the emotional appeal of the hour. The defense of the faith became of supreme importance. Apocalyptic literature, though rejecting history, was at once a product of the past and a determining factor in the future. Theory took on life and, relying on the power of the supernatural, incited open rebellion against the powers of this world.

The explosion came in 168 B.C. when at Modin Mattathias, a priest and ruler, not only refused to obey the order of the king's officer to offer unlawful sacrifice on the altar built for idols, but when an obsequious Jew stepped forward to perform the royal behest struck him down, slew the king's officer, and with his five sons, the Maccabees, raised the standard of revolt against Syria (I Macc. 2:1–28). The slaughter of a group of Jews who would not violate the Sabbath regulations even to save their own lives (I Macc. 2:20–38), the later decision to disregard the law rather than die (I Macc. 2:39–41), the enlistment of many who were lovers of the law and hated the Greeks, and the massacre of others who refused to join the revolt (I Macc. 2:42–44), the smashing of pagan altars, the circumcision by force of certain Jewish children (I Macc. 2:45, 46), and the rescuing of the law from the hands of the Gentiles (I Macc. 2:48)—such drastic actions cleansed the loyalists from apostates and halfhearted followers, and prepared the way for the almost unbelievable Maccabean victories over the trained armies of Syria (I Macc. 3:1–4:35). Religious zeal has rarely been so speedily rewarded. On the twenty-fifth of December, 165 B.C. regular worship in the temple was restored, high walls with strong stone towers were built around Mount Zion (I Macc. 4:36–

61), and by 163 b.c. the Jews were granted freedom in religion by Syria (I Macc. 7:10–16).

These victories and the zeal for the law that joyously accepted death rather than defilement (I Macc. 2:50–64; II Macc. 6:18–31; 7:1–42; 14:37-46) are lasting testimony to the latent resources of mankind and the powers that are ready for release under great inspiration. This apocalyptic theory that transferred the major interest from earth to heaven, and had shifted confidence from the ordinary to the cataclysmic, had contributed to the achievement of the impossible. As earlier the law, by its disciplines, had saved Judaism, so now, by its intense otherworldliness and its glorious vision of a new earth and a new heaven, though somewhat fantastic (Isa. 65:17, 25; 66:22; En. 45:5; 58:3; 62:16; cf. Rev. 21:1–22:5), the faith of the apocalyptists preserved it from eclipse under the Seleucid persecution.

But beyond this local, and temporary, gain these fervid propagandists opened up definite areas of thought that became important in later theology. The tantalizing problem of the moral order of the universe, always under consideration, was solved by the assurance that in the "next world" all men would be equitably rewarded or punished by a righteous God. The judgment, the great white throne, resurrection from the dead, individual immortality, hell and heaven all came to varied and complex expression in these writings. The vague popular expressions found ready to hand by eschatology readily took on definite forms that, at least to the individual writer, satisfied the ethical demands.

The judge, the judgment, and the judgment throne belonging to everyday life had long claimed as final authority the sanction of the invisible power that lay behind and beyond the incidents of local history. The battle of Armageddon and the Day of Yahweh furnished the basis for an infinite variety of details for the activities of the supreme Judge of all nations as he brought this evil world to an end and introduced the new era (Joel 1:15; 2:1; Isa. 61:8; Dan. 2:44; 7:22).

Sheol, the grave (literally "the hollowed-out place") in the popular mind was the place in which were gathered all the dead, "who know not anything, neither have they any reward" (Eccles. 9:3–6). It was the "land of darkness, yea of deep darkness, without any order" (Job 10:21, 22), where existence was bloodless, listless, semiconscious, and where there were no social or moral distinctions (Job 3:13–19; 7:9, 10; 14:1–12, 21; 17:13–16; 21:26; B. Sir. 14:16; 17:22, 27; 22:11; 46:19). Yet on occasion a noted prophet might be roused from the general stupor to declare the destiny of the nation (I Sam. 28:19). Also in the postexilic days it seemed appropriate that the king of Babylon should be thrust into the hindermost part of the pit, and that those who had suffered so grievously at his hand should exult at his humiliation (Isa. 14:4–20; Ezek. 32:23). This, a natural response to hatred for the foreign tyrant, may be considered one of the earliest glimpses of hell. Later still it was conceived that further distinctions between the evil and the good were needed. In 170 B.C. Ethiopic Enoch provided four hollow places, three of which were deep and dark, and one was bright with a fountain of water in its midst, in which all the spirits of the dead were to be gathered and life's inequalities were to be somewhat balanced before the day of resurrection. It is noteworthy that for the godless and lawless there is to be no resurrection (Eth. En. 22:2–13). From this it is but a step to the seven heavens (Slavonic En. chaps. 3–21; Test. Levi, 2:7–3:3; Greek Apoc. Bar., chaps. 2–10), and to the seven circles of hell so vividly developed by Dante. The local valley of Hinnom, that is, Gehenna, where the city refuse was perpetually burning (Isa. 66:24; Dan. 12:2; Eth. En. 27:1, 2), and volcanic fires (Deut. 32:22; Eth. En. 10:13; 18:11; En. 90:20–25) were drawn on to illustrate the intensity of suffering that great sinners should undergo. By this process, the ethical judgment of the prophets, so inoperative in this workaday world, was transferred to the world beyond the grave.

The resurrection and individual immortality now emerged in Jewish theology as an essential part of this ethical reconstruction. In pre-exilic days the social emphasis of the prophets, the prohibition of all cult practices related to necromancy, and the national interest in solidarity all had united to prevent any development of the idea. In these later days, however, at least two passages in the Hebrew Scriptures confidently assert this belief. "Thy dead shall live, my dead bodies shall arise" (Isa. 26:19) glories in the confidence of the physical resurrection and the individual immortality of Israelites. The second passage, which reads, "Many of them that sleep in the earth shall awake, some to everlasting life, some to shame and everlasting contempt" (Dan. 12:2), limits the resurrection to *many,* and draws a sharp distinction between the good and the evil, apparently in Israel. Beyond these a few verses such as Psalms 49:15; 73:24, 25; and Job 19:25–27, though our English translations lack the support of the original text, are sometimes accepted as supporting personal immortality.[22] But while our Old Testament material is so scant, and in the abundant extra-Biblical literature there is no unified system of thought, nevertheless there was indisputably in many quarters an overwhelming expectancy that in the immediate future the new age would be ushered in, and that all the saints, living and dead, would enter into the glory of the kingdom of God. To suggest that this was an ecstasy to the initiated is to put it mildly. To escape from the weariness of life and the miseries under foreign tyranny to the unalloyed joys of the world beyond and the patronage of the infinite Majesty was to be transported from hades to heaven. This was the religion of many of the chosen people to the nth degree of emotional certitude. The Maccabean victories, the martyrs, and the saints are lasting testimony to the influence of these conceptions.

[22] This problem is carefully discussed by A. C. Knudson, *Religious Teaching of the O.T.*, 382–404.

The moral issues that had directed thought to the world beyond also contributed to the problem of the nature and the sovereignty of God. Exilic theology had attained one of the great insights of mankind in the declaration of ethical monotheism, "I form the light, and create darkness; I make peace and create evil" (Isa. 45:7). But this dictum involved the morality of Deity. How could a good God be the author of evil? Slowly, in order to save the character of Deity, a dualism developed, in which God and the Devil were assigned different spheres of influence. In late Hebrew Satan, the tester, is granted limited powers on the earth (Zech. 3:1, 2; Job 1:6–12; 2:1–7; I Chron. 21:1; cf. II Sam. 24:1; Eth. En. 54:6); while the Lord of spirits, though temporarily frustrated by evil men and evil spirits (Eth. En. chaps. 6, 7; 40:7, 10; 53:5; 54:5, 6) was supreme. The kingdom of God is variously represented by various writers. To some it is to be a thousand years on earth; to others it will be on a new earth; and to still others it will be in the heavens where, surrounded by archangels, angels of light, the righteous perpetually praise the Lord of life (Eth. En. 39:1–41:2).[23] But the high objective toward which all was swiftly moving was the ultimate triumph of the Lord of glory over all the powers of evil (Eth. En. 38:3, 5, 6; 45:5, 6; 54:5, 6; 56:1–3; 62:11, 12; 64:1, 2; cf. Rev. 20:2, 3, 10).

Apocalypticism not only aided in the Jewish struggle for freedom in religion, but, though somewhat abnormal, it was deeply rooted in Jewish faith. Its insistent demand for a hereafter, that would compensate for the injustices of this life, was but an extension of the ethical emphasis of the prophets. Its hope for a kingdom, established in peace and power in the new era, was but the ripe fruitage of early tribal consciousness, intensified by the Sinaitic covenant, enlarged by the kingdom conquests, and transformed into the chosen people by the priesthood and Messianism. The Lord of glory, a transcendent Deity, revealed not in common experiences in nature or in society, but in tremendous cataclysms, and in the program of the Great Glory unfolded to those long dead (En. 14:15–24)—this was the Yahweh of Sinaitic traditions, and of the holy of holies of the priesthood, now clothed in flowing fire and transported to the lofty, crystal throne in the heavens (En. 14:18).

This movement, so colorful and so otherworldly, has been characterized as one of the great revolutions in human thinking.[24] Yet, while its impact has never ceased throughout the centuries, at best most of that which was peculiar to apocalypticism was temporary, and quite subsidiary to the main current of Judaism. Many of the conservative Jews, as well as those who were kindly

---

23 The multiple, and often mutually exclusive, programs that were proposed are in agreement only in the most general features. Particulars can be followed only in the careful presentation of individual apocalypses. Summaries are found in R. H. Charles, *A Critical History of the Doctrine of the Future Life,* and F. C. Burkitt, *Jewish and Christian Apocalypses.*

24 J. T. Shotwell, *The History of History,* I, 325–335. For all who believed, life beyond the grave became a keenly conscious, highly ethical reality.

disposed toward Greek culture, were quite untouched either by its heroics or by its philosophy.[25] The Hassidim, the probable founders of the Pharisees, who in the Maccabean crisis had joined the rebellion, after 163 B.C., when freedom of worship had been granted, gradually separated themselves from militant Messianism (I Macc. 7:13, 14).[26] The priesthood was never carried away with it, and the sages could have had little sympathy with its enthusiasms.

Further, when the glamour of the vision and the mists of battle are cleared away it is evident that the main conclusions of this type of theology rest on foundations of sand. The theory that the earth is flat, that the abode of the dead is in chambers deep within it, that it will ultimately be destroyed in a cataclysm of fire, that the heavens lie in seven stages one above the other over the earth, though reasonable to sense perception, all have no basis in fact. Its theory of history completely ignored the facts of origin, the growth of ideas, the development of institutions, the significance of human relations, and denied that in the structure of society and in history there was a power making for righteousness. Such a negation of social values and the worth of human personality would seem to be essentially irreligious. One might say, religion cannot escape history. The question of morals was shelved, but not solved. Not only were the apocalyptists antisocial, but in shifting the problem of justice over into the next world they only by-passed the hard facts of life. To thus take refuge in a "revelation" that can in no way be tested gives no evidence of intellectual or moral stamina. Nor are the theological conclusions any more convincing. An escape from reality to supernaturalism, and to a universe in which God and the Devil are left to fight it out, is little less than fantastic. Pardonable, indeed laudable, 2,500 years ago in Persia, or 2,000 years ago in Palestine, as an experiment in thinking, it is passing strange that thoughtful people today should accept it as a valid interpretation of the order of the universe. Great as was the ministry of apocalypticism, the passing centuries have provided a better understanding of man, of society, and of God.

Prophet and priest, sage and psalmist, reformer and apocalyptist each followed a way of life that, to its own sect, gave comfort, strength, and joy; and each left a heritage of experience, warnings, and guideposts valuable for all who came after. No group, even the most backward, failed to add a modicum to the sum total of the understanding of man and God. Nor did any order, however pontifical, speak the final word of the Eternal Spirit to the heart and mind of man. In every age, and in every school of thought, there were restless spirits who, dissatisfied with the ignorance, the unsocial conduct, the political practices, the lack of reverence, or the existing ways of worship, were

[25] S. Schechter, *Aspects of Rabbinic Theology*, 5.
[26] L. Finkelstein, *The Pharisees*, II, 592–595, 608–620.

ever eagerly scanning the horizon for the daystar from on high. These all had witness borne to them through their faith that some better thing lay ahead. This Messianic consciousness of the Jew, a defiant confidence that disregarded all national tragedies, is a sure cornerstone on which religion can build the noblest of its cathedrals.

Chapter XV

❮❮❮❮❮❮❮❮❮❮❮❮❮❮❮❮❮❮❮❮❮❮＊❯❯❯❯❯❯❯❯❯❯❯❯❯❯❯❯❯❯❯

THE RELIGION OF JUDAISM. 400 B.C.–A.D. 135

The far-reaching reforms introduced in 400 B.C. by the charter of the state-church (chap. xii) were no more than stabilized when vast international upheavals took place that not only changed the currents of world history, but affected, specifically, the life and the outlook of the people of Israel. Persia's national glory was eclipsed by the battle of Issus in 333 B.C., and during the next ten years the world was in one of its great convulsions. Alexander of Macedon, a disciple of Aristotle, led his armies in triumph down to Egypt, then to far-off India, and planted Greek colonies throughout the then known world (332–323 B.C.). For a century and a half (323–175 B.C.) the rulers of Egypt and Syria settled down to a cat-and-dog game over the borderland of Palestine. Then Rome came on the scene. By the battle of Magnesia in 190 B.C. she put an end to the conflicts in Asia Minor. By 168 B.C. Egypt was her vassal and she was dictating the policies of the Syrian rulers. When in 146 B.C. she had destroyed Carthage, her hands were freed for tasks in the north and east. In 63 B.C., wearied of local intrigues and revolts, she took Palestine under her jurisdiction and, with reverence for law and order, established the *Pax Romana*.

In this large background our interest must be limited to those events that had a definite bearing in shaping and giving direction to the religion of the Jews. They were a small people, caught in the vortex of world forces that would not be denied; yet they were no less powerful than the Caesars, and had a culture as penetrating and as potent for human welfare as that of the Greeks. For convenience we shall sketch Jewish reactions under the impact of the realignment of world powers as follows: Judaism in the homeland, under Greek, Egyptian, and Syrian rulers, from 332 to 175 B.C.; during the Maccabean revolt and the Second Jewish Commonwealth, from 175 to 63 B.C.; under the Roman rule, from 63 B.C. to A.D. 135; and among the nations from 400 B.C. to A.D. 135.

Judaism in the homeland from the closing years of the Persian period down to the Maccabean revolt, amid the distractions of warfare, was constantly in turmoil. In 365 B.C. Judea apparently became involved in the widespread insurrections against Artaxerxes II (404–361 B.C.) that continued into the reign of Artaxerxes III (361–338 B.C.), and around 350 B.C. many Jews were deported

233

to Hyrcania and to Babylonia.[1] At about the same time internal affairs were even more distressing. Johanan, the incoming legal high priest, within the temple precincts slew Jason his younger brother, who had intrigued for the sacred office. Bagoas, the commander of the local Persian forces, and a friend of Jason, marched to Jerusalem, entered the temple, thereby defiling it, and imposed a tax of fifty shekels on the treasury for every lamb offered in the daily sacrifice.[2] Corruption among the priesthood, fratricide, blood spilled in the temple, an alien within the sacred place, and a heavy tribute that continued for seven years were humiliating, oppressive, and sacrilegious.

Then came Alexander, the conqueror, the city builder, the herald of Greek culture. He was gladly received, so much so that tradition, as usual, reported the event in terms of the supernatural.[3] The Jews were granted freedom of worship, the privilege of following their own customs, and the local administration of their provinces,[4] while they paid the same land tax that had been required by Persia.[5] This new regime was spectacular, expansive, even revolutionary, and though the Samaritans rebelled and suffered, in Judea great hopes were raised.

But the Macedonian genius, dying in 323 B.C., left no successor, and his five generals, dividing up the empire among themselves, then turned and fought for wider boundaries. Palestine, lying between Egypt and Syria, was desolated by the armies of both sides. Eight times, at least, between 323 and 301 B.C. the land passed from one to the other, and thus the country was demoralized by the uncertainties that followed the wake of the armies. In 320 B.C. Ptolemy of Egypt took Jerusalem on the Sabbath day without any resistance,[6] and carried off to Alexandria many captives from Jerusalem, Judea, and Samaria. In 312 B.C. Ptolemy had to retreat from Palestine before Antigonus of Syria, and in doing so applied the scorched-earth policy to Acco, Samaria, Joppa, Gaza, and many other cities. He also took Jewish captives to recruit his military garrisons and to add to the growing population of Jews in Alexandria. In this catastrophe Jerusalem suffered, and it is believed that many of the Jewish aristocracy, including priestly families, left for Alexandria where living was more ample and dangers were fewer.[7] The despoiled cities of Palestine were then repopulated by foreigners from Macedonia and elsewhere. From 301 B.C. for twenty-three years Syria struggled to rule Palestine, which had been granted her by treaty after the battle of Ipsus, 301 B.C., but the forces of

---

[1] While this captivity is questioned by Margolis and Marx, *History of the Jewish People*, 127, it is accepted as probable by most. See C. G. Montefiore, *Hib. Lec's.*, 360, 361; Graetz, *History of the Jews*, I, 417; G. A. Smith, *Jerusalem*, II, 359; *Diod. Sic.*, XVI, 40, 4; 45, 6.

[2] Jos. *Ant.*, XI, VII, I. Graetz, *Hist. Jews*, I, 409, 410.

[3] Jos. *Ant.*, XI, VIII, 5.

[4] Graetz, *Hist. Jews*, I, 415–419.

[5] *Ibid.*, 413.

[6] Jos. *Ant.*, XII, I, I. This caused the Jews to revise the law of the Sabbath (Margolis and Marx, *Hist. Jew. People*, 198).

[7] Jos. *C. Ap.*, I, 22. Montefiore, *Hib. Lec's.*, 363, 364. Graetz, *Hist. Jews*, I, 417, 418.

Egypt ultimately prevailed in 280 B.C. From then until 198 B.C., though not without contention, the Ptolemies were the masters of Palestine. But in 198 B.C., by the battle of Banias, Antiochus III of Syria (224–187 B.C.), to the great joy of Jerusalem, became master of the country.[8]

Thus it was that for two hundred years preceding the Maccabean revolt (168 B.C.) the external forces at play on the life of Palestine were disturbing, if not disintegrating. The march of armies, the forced captivities, the destruction of cities, the infiltration of aliens of many types, the recurring financial penalties, the flight of the well-to-do, the growth of strange, new city life, and the change of rulers, these compelled the Jew continually to reorganize his thought and his practice. Not only had the Sabbath law to be revised, but the social, economic, and political phases of life were always under tension and in a state of transition. Socially the Jew grew accustomed to the alien, and to the Greek city life. Here was a new thing under the sun [9]—the gymnasia for sport, the social club, the drama and the theater, the schools of philosophy, the emphasis on joy and beauty, and the thrill of corporate city life. These captured many of the youth, and threatened the very life of Judaism. The economic opportunities provided by the widely scattered Jewish colonies, and the astonishing increase and importance of city life, rapidly changed the Jew from a farmer and a herdsman into a middleman, a merchant, and a banker, while under the fluctuating political changes not a few of the sons of Jacob proved to be adept in gaining private or religious ends for personal profit.

Unhappy as Judea may have been under the constant irritation of external forces, her condition due to the reactions of her leaders was no less deplorable. Joseph, the taxgatherer [10] (230–208 B.C.), son of Tobiah and nephew of Onias II the high priest, through cunning gained the appointment of taxgatherer over all Phoenicia and Palestine from Ptolemy III (247–222 B.C.), and Ptolemy IV (222–205 B.C.). For twenty-two years, supported by Egyptian soldiers, he collected an exorbitant tribute, even at the sword's point. Objectors to his demands were slain and their properties confiscated, when it suited his purpose, as at Beth Shan and Gaza. Thus for himself and the priesthood, who were his friends and aids, were amassed immense fortunes. Hyrcanus, his youngest and favorite son, on his death in 208 B.C., by the authority of Egypt took over his office and continued his activities. Like his father he was capable, a master of court intrigue, greedy of gain, a lover of power, a devotee of Bacchanalian festivities, and a partisan of Egypt. With him stood many of the aristocratic priesthood who had profited by his father's regime, and those who preferred the refinements of Greek culture to the austerities of the Jewish law. He and his friends continued to wax fat at the expense of the people until after the bat-

[8] Jos. *Ant.,* XII, III, 3.

[9] Ed. Bevan, *Jerusalem under the High-Priests,* 18–20, 31–43. R. W. Moss, "Alexander, the Great," *ERE,* I.

[10] Jos. *Ant.,* XII, IV, 1–6; Bevan, *Jerusalem under the High-Priests,* 45–47; S. Zeitlin, *History of the Second Jewish Commonwealth,* 45–48; Graetz, *Hist. Jews,* I, 423–427.

tle of Banias in 198 B.C., when Antiochus III of Syria took over the control of all Palestine. Hyrcanus, the pro-Egyptian, fled to Arak el-Amir in Transjordania, where he collected tribute from whom he could, depositing his treasure for safekeeping in the temple in Jerusalem (II Macc. 3:11–13). Like his father, and those of the priesthood who by their greed had become wealthy through the toil and suffering of their brethren, he was a stench in the nostrils of the common people.[11] For more than thirty years within the priestly circle cunning, cupidity, and treachery had held sway. Life was considered cheap, and high office had been defiled by men whose family pedigree and devotion to the claims of the temple had been beyond dispute.

But the opposition to this regime was vigorous throughout the land. The people who suffered economic hardship under the taxgatherers, the orthodox Jews who were incensed against the invasion of Grecian culture, high-minded high priests like Onias II and his son Simon II were united in common cause against the tyrants, and against Egypt. Syria was their only hope and to her they looked for deliverance. Many gave what aid they could to Antiochus III both before and after the battle of Banias, and rejoiced greatly in victory and in the new privileges granted them by the new sovereign.[12]

The situation as sketched above presents a dark, almost a desperate, picture. Yet the Jew, buffeted by the crosscurrents of adversity, had a heritage not easily uprooted. Slaughter, captivity, desolation, and suffering, the penalties exacted for rebellion, always loomed up as a possibility due to local insistence for special privilege. But so long as the annual tribute was paid and the peace was maintained, the Jewish communities suffered few inconveniences under any foreign government. As a result of the shifting of population and the changes of rulers, there were always modifications of privileges, and even changes of boundary lines, but on the whole the villages and the cities were able to develop and sustain their own type of life under foreign rule.[13]

Judea, always central in the hopes and plans of the Jew, was dominated by Jerusalem. Here, within straitened boundaries, surrounded by hated aliens, and ruled over by foreigners, she developed her inner resources, at times made gains through proselytizing,[14] and strengthened the barriers against unkindly intrusion. The temple, the home of the priest and the symbol of religion, the one thing for which Judea was famous throughout the world,[15] dominated Jerusalem. By its ancient origin and rich symbolism (I Kings 6:1–36), its preservation from the ravages of Sennacherib (Isa. 10:24–34), the affirmation of its

---

11 Graetz has summarized the activities of Joseph in *Hist. Jews,* I, 423–430. He favored Grecian culture in its gayest, even in its depraved, forms. He went so far as to introduce the Bacchanalian dance into the Jerusalem festivals.

12 S. Zeitlin, *Sec. Com.,* 12–16.

13 Margolis and Marx, *Hist. Jew. People,* 131.

14 It has been suggested that between 516 and 490 B.C. considerable proselytizing was carried on in the country (J. Morgenstern, *JBL,* March, 1945, 15–27).

15 C. G. Montefiore, *Hib. Lec's.,* 387; *Diod. Sic.,* XVI, 39.

divine status by Deuteronomy (Deut. 12:11; 16:11–16), and not least by the temple tax of Nehemiah (Neh. 13:8–14) and the later canonization of the law (Neh. 10:33–11:2), it became a beacon light for Jewry the world over.

The temple, however, was but the monument to the devotion and the vision of the priesthood. They were its guardians and ministering servants, but far beyond that they had been the architects of its beauty, the creators of its ideals, and they were the trustees of its perpetual service and its destiny. From the days of the exile the priest and the teacher became the acknowledged rulers of the land. The priests had produced the book, and in turn they became its chief beneficiaries. This gave them a lease of life, with new and growing responsibilities, as interpreters and teachers.

The scribes, a school of experts, gradually came into being owing to the complexities of the lawbook of Ezra, and the need of co-ordinating its requirements with those of earlier codes.[16] They were men of priestly training and mentality, familiar with the traditions (II Chron. 13:22; 24:7) and at first largely, if not exclusively, of the priestly order. But before the Maccabean period they had become a professional class (B. Sir. 38:24–29) who devoted their energies to the understanding and the propagation of the Torah (II Chron. 15:3; 17:7–9; 19:8–11). As such they were ranked in importance with the masters of temple ritual.[17] By their enlightened devotion to their tasks (B. Sir. 42:4–8), they acted as a stabilizing force in a storm-tossed world, in itself no small contribution to human welfare.

As scholars they edited or rewrote the national history from the creation down to their occupation of Canaan, guided by the priestly formulas that the law was the final and perfect revelation of the will of God, and that Israel was his elect people. To them we are indebted for the editorial work in the Pentateuch in which the fathers are idealized so that they might be the unsullied ancestors of the nation. The shady acts of the patriarchs, as recorded in J. and E. were either omitted or toned down. Abraham's falsehood to Pharaoh, Jacob's trickery with Laban, Rachel's theft of the teraphim, Judah's episode with Tamar, and other similar features find no echo in the editorial work of the P. school, while acts considered praiseworthy are often highly colored.

Further, their philosophy of history, which was the antithesis of that of the eighth-century prophets, and also diverged widely from that of the Deuteronomic school, seemed to them beyond dispute. In the new law, the Priest Code, as in H.C. (Holiness Code), no distinction was recognized between social wrongdoing and the incorrect performance of the minutiae of the cult. The Creator and the Lawgiver was the God of Israel, the King of the universe, and obedience to all his requirements was the only basis for his favor. This philosophy seemed more comprehensive, more logical, and more divine than those of earlier days; so the disciples of the law went to work with a will. Evidence

---

16 G. A. Smith, *Jerusalem*, II, 364–366.
17 G. F. Moore, *Judaism*, I, 37–47, 287, 308, 309.

that seemed to support this conclusion was abundant in both the written and the oral material in the possession of the priests. Traditions of the experiences in the wilderness that confirmed the necessity of attending to the most minute details of the ritual were numerous. Incense that had not the proper ingredients was not acceptable to Yahweh, and Nadab and Abihu were consumed by fire (Lev. 10:1–3). The failure of the priests to eat the flesh of the sin offering in the place of the sanctuary brought down the wrath of Moses on their heads (Lev. 10:16–18). The man who blasphemed the Name and cursed must suffer death by stoning at the hands of the congregation (Lev. 24:10–14, 23). The Sabbath day must be observed as a day of rest. Even God himself was subject to the law, and rested on the seventh day from all his work which he had made (Gen. 2:2). Even the manna did not fall on the Sabbath day for it was a solemn rest, a holy Sabbath to Yahweh (Exod. 16:23), and the man found gathering sticks on the Sabbath must be punished by death (Num. 15:32–36).

Moreover the will of God must be obeyed without question or the direst consequences may follow. The congregation murmured against their authentic leaders, and but for the quick action of Moses the plague from Yahweh would have destroyed them (Num. 16:41–45). The ten spies brought back an evil report, and they died by the plague before Yahweh (Num. 14:36, 37), and the people bore their iniquity forty years in the wilderness (Num. 14:34, 35). Not only did the assembly perish because they believed not Yahweh (Num. 20:9–13) but also Moses and Aaron, because they rebelled at Meribah, were denied the joy of reaching the desired goal (Num. 20:24; 27:14). That failure to observe the jot and tittle of the law, or a hesitant response to the will of Yahweh brought plague, defeat, and death to the guilty, was proved to the satisfaction of all believers.

The scribes, disciples of the priestly theology, carefully edited the earlier histories of J. and E. and the law codes D. (Deuteronomy) and H.C. (Holiness Code), incorporating the new law code P. (Priest Code) in an appropriate background with the needed historical notes. Thus was completed the enlarged, revised, and modernized edition of Israel's history and law, our present Hexateuch. It was an achievement of great devotion and conspicuous merit. Tales otherwise discordant, sketchy incidents and diverse laws, were thereby co-ordinated in a framework that provided at least a semblance of unity. More than that, from the opening phrase of the majestic, orderly creation story in Genesis (Gen. 1:1–2:4a) until Joshua sets up the stones of witness in Shechem (Josh. 24:1–28, E.), it is ever the Omnipotent who speaks. Land and sea, sun and moon, all life large and small came into being at the word of him who gave his law to the nation. The scribe has so interwoven throughout the Hexateuch his conviction that Israel's history and Israel's laws were the chief works of the Almighty, the focal point of all creation, that an unearthly splendor gilds the page, lifting all above the commonplace. True, it is an idealization, or a religious interpretation of the facts, but facts without idealization have but little vitality. We might call the whole work a theological treatise, so ordered as to inspire the strictest obedience to all the rites and ceremonies in the book.

The Chronicler, probably a Levite, a century or more after the time of the Ezra movement, or between 300 and 250 B.C., completed his ecclesiastical history of Judah, our present I and II Chronicles, Ezra, and Nehemiah.[18] In these, in the light of priestly theory, he rewrote the history of Judah [19] from its national beginnings down to his own day, and recorded the organization of the Levitical hierarchy, as he knew it, with the needed documentary evidence of legitimacy. These four books were a telling apologetic for Judaism of the third century B.C., and a bulwark against the encroachments of alien, especially Grecian, elements of culture and religion.

The preceding hundred years had brought great changes in the fortunes of Judah. Persia had passed from the scene. The Greek overlordship, with the Syrian-Egyptian conflict for dominion in Palestine, with Jewish leaders lined up on each side, was in process. The Samaritans about 332 B.C. had built their own temple on Mount Gerizim,[20] and, possessing a copy of the Pentateuch, the law of Moses, after a long and bitter struggle had finally separated from Judah and Jerusalem. Hellenic culture, with its appeal to the sensuous and the beautiful, in which liberty and luxury verged on licentiousness,[21] was penetrating every hamlet throughout the land. Not less important than any of these influences were the Jewish colonies, living apart in great centers in Babylonia, in Alexandria, and elsewhere, where they were learning the ways of the nations, and in turn were subtly casting a spell over the very thinking of the people at home. Critical changes such as these had been playing on the life in Jerusalem for more than a century, and the priests and the teachers had been quite alert to the needs. The work of the Chronicler marks their achievement in institutionalizing their religion.[22]

18 Problems connected with the authorship of these books are discussed by Pfeiffer, *Introduction to the O.T.*, 801–812, 830–838; E. L. Curtis, "Chronicles" in *ICC*, 1–26. S. R. Driver, *LOT*, "Chronicles, Ezra, Nehemiah." Albright, *JBL*, 1921, 104–124, considers Ezra the author of Chronicles and Ezra, about 400–350 B.C.

19 So far as the theories of the author were concerned the North, that is, Ephraim or Samaria, did not come into the picture. In his own day Samaria was apostate, and throughout all history had been schismatic. In fact its religion was pagan and its ancestry was Gentile.

20 Details of the struggle between the Jews and the Samaritans are far from certain. There had always been contention between the North and the South, with ever recurring reconciliations and revolts. In 408 B.C. the Jewish colony at Elephantine appealed first to the Jews, then to the Samaritans to aid them in gaining permission to rebuild their temple that had been destroyed. This dual appeal indicates that at that time no religious schism had been completed between the two groups (A. Cowley, *Aramaic Papyri of the Fifth Century B.C.*, 110). Jos. *Ant.*, XI, VII, 2; XI, VIII, 2–4; XII, V, 5; XIII, III, 4, though somewhat highly colored, places the building of the Samaritan temple shortly after the invasion of Alexander, which probably is correct.

21 Graetz, *Hist. Jews*, I, 426–430.

22 This is only one line of activity that was carried on during this period. Parallel to it, sometimes antagonistic to it, at other times complementary or supplementary to it, went much of the wisdom literature, Jonah, Ruth, Canticles, Ecclesiasticus, translation of the Pentateuch into Greek. See chap. XIII.

Theological theory rather than the facts of history guided the author as he rewrote the history of the kings of Judah. Failures that had been recorded by earlier writers were ignored, while achievements and virtues were made to reflect the splendors of national hopes.[23] Disasters were accounted for by the failure to observe the requirements of the law. The mother of Rehoboam was an alien by birth, and her son failed (II Chron. 12:13, 14). Joash had set up false worship, and he died a horrible death (II Chron. 24:18, 23–25). Uzziah offered incense in the temple, therefore he became a leper (II Chron. 26:16–21). Manasseh, the pro-Assyrian, in late life repented and confessed his sin; thus was explained his long reign of fifty-two years (II Chron. 38:10–20). Judah was blessed in measure as she punctiliously kept the prescribed rites of the temple (II Chron. 16:8, 9; 28:9–15; 29:4–11, 20–36), but when the king, the priests, and the people polluted the house of Yahweh by their abominations, then in his wrath Yahweh sent the Chaldean who slew their young men, destroyed the temple, and took king and princes to Babylon (II Chron. 36:11–21).

Ancestors of the approved strain, always the pride of a tribe or a nation, became of supreme importance in the religion of priestly Judaism. In the conflict with alien forces ancestry became an essential passport to privilege and high society. That all Jews were the legitimate sons of Jacob, that all priests had an unspotted paternity back to Aaron, and that all the temple servants were sons of Levi according to the flesh was the ideal for the holy nation. That a school of experts arose in answer to the demand, men trained in research and skilled in discovering the required data,[24] is quite evident from a glimpse at I Chronicles 1:1–9:21, and similar lists.

The Aaronic priesthood in the time of the Chronicler was organized into twenty-four courses, sixteen from the house of Eleazar and eight from that of Ithamar, whose line had been discredited by Solomon (I Kings 2:27), all of which were duly certified in the presence of the king (I Chron. 24:1–6). This orderly disposition of authority and duties, which continued down until the destruction of the temple, was the conclusion of a long history. A few hints of its growth are found in earlier writings. Twenty-two courses are mentioned in Nehemiah 12:1–7, 12–21, and twenty-one are named in Nehemiah 10:2–31; but only fourteen of these are the same in both. Going back to the time of Zerub-

---

[23] To read the history of David in I Sam. 17:1–I Kings 2:9, and then turn to the portraiture in I Chron. 11:1–29:30, is to pass from a flesh-and-blood hero to an impeccable head of the religious state, largely the product of tradition.

[24] The genealogical lists can be treated neither too lightly nor too seriously. They were the product of immense labor, and are of great value. Apparently they had both written and oral material behind their present form. But like all such they are not infallible. The desire for a properly attested ancestry must have been urgent for many. Experts would be well paid, and the payee would be well satisfied. For judgments of the value of such lists see E. L. Curtis, "Chronicles," *ICC*, 16, 17; F. Brown, "Chronicles," *HBD* (five vols.); S. R. Driver, "Chronicles," *Ency. Bibl.;* Pfeiffer, *Introduction to the O.T.*, 800.

babel, reference is made to four priestly clans (Ezra 2:36–39; 10:18–22), and a little later it seems that two more were added (Ezra 8:2).

The organization of the Levites likewise was the result of long and tedious activity. In early days in Canaan, when the little nation was feeling its way, there were many shrines, and each as it grew in importance had its local priest. The son of Micah (Judg. 17:5), a wandering Levite from Judah (Judg. 17:9–13), prisoners of war who like the Gibeonites had been made hewers of wood and drawers of water for the house of God (Josh. 9:23), or Ephraimites like Samuel (I Sam. 1:1–3), they or their descendants must sometimes have risen to positions of influence in the ritual functions of Yahwism. As the complexity of ritual kept pace with the importance of the temple and the growing civilization, division of labor became desirable. Thus it is that in this period we meet Nethinim (Neh. 11:3; 7:46), porters (I Chron. 9:21, 22, 24–27), doorkeepers (I Chron. 26:1–19), overseers, and treasurers (I Chron. 9:19, 28–32; 23:4; 26:20–32), all belonging to the lower grades, servants of the house of Yahweh (I Chron. 23:28–32). In earlier records the porters and singers are distinct from, and of a lower order than, the Levites (Ezra 2:40, 41; Neh. 7:44), while the Nethinim are an ill-defined group. But by the time our author completed his book, porters, Nethinim, and singers had been raised to the dignity of Levites (I Chron. 6:16–48; 15:16; 26:1–19). Loyal servants, long identified with worship, when competent deserve to be promoted. To be grafted into the tribe of Levi [25] would be the most natural and the most desired reward for efficient service. This, whether the result of pressure group tactics or not, was the public declaration of the indispensable values in the minutiae of worship. No part of the cultus, not even the dirtiest, was degrading; and no servant in the temple was a menial. By exalting the lowest, they had honored the highest and magnified the Most High. Each member of the vast temple retinue, an army 38,000 strong (I Chron. 23:1–6), in fitting garb and with the utmost precision performed his specific task, gladly and with proud dignity as unto the Lord.

Music, both vocal and instrumental, had been highly developed and incorporated in the temple worship before the time of the Chronicler. He reports twenty-four courses or guilds of musicians, 288 in all, all belonging to the Levitical order, who had been set apart and trained in prophesying with harps, psalteries, and cymbals, and in singing unto Yahweh (I Chron. 25:1–31; 15:16–24).

This was a radical departure from the original service in the temple, and gave a new and healthier tone to religion. In the first temple the priest and the sacrifices were supreme, and while calls, responses, and benedictions marked

---

[25] The Hebrew use of terms such as father, son, mother, daughter, and tribe, is much wider than that usual to Western theologians. For a well balanced study of this question see S. A. Cook, "Genealogies," *Ency. Bibl.*, II.

the changing phases of the routine, music certainly was at a minimum.[26] The destruction of the temple in 586 B.C. and the exile induced changes that proved to be revolutionary. Lacking a central sanctuary, Jews, at home as well as those in captivity, developed compensations. Music, song, and dance, prayer, and praise had always in crucial moments been the spontaneous expression of joy, hope, and desire (Gen. 12:8; 26:25; Exod. 15:21; 34:9; I Kings 8:12–14). Many such easily became formulas that were enlarged by the religious routine of the seasonal festivals. It is quite possible that the same process was encouraged at some of the chief shrines, as Bethel and Dan.[27] The influence of neighboring nations, as Babylon, Egypt, Syria, and Greece,[28] where hymnody and drama had long formed part of the worship of the gods, may well have aided in establishing the songs of Zion in the temple in Jerusalem. By the time the second temple was built two generations had learned the values of responses, prayer, and praise in worship, and a return to pre-exilic practices would have been impossible.

The course of this development cannot be traced, nor can the liturgical order at any given period be stated with certainty. But that by 250 B.C. there was in connection with the temple worship a well ordered musical service, vocal and instrumental combined, is a reasonable assumption. The choruses were well trained, and Psalms were familiar to the Chronicler (I Chron. 16:8–36; II Chron. 6:41, 42; see B. Sir. 50:16–18, the description of a service at a little later time). It is quite possible that by the opening of the Maccabean period a different Psalm was recited at the morning service, one for each day of the week,[29] as follows: Pss. 24, 48, 82, 94, 81, 93, 92. The use and the composition of Psalms grew rapidly from this time on, and played an important part in the religion of those in Jerusalem and also among the Dispersion. The temple service, thereby, was greatly enriched. Some of the cruder aspects of the cultus were veiled by the presence of the chorus; and by the repetition of the liturgy, the whole assembly was stirred by new and noble ideals, the work of the teacher rather

[26] Two facts of a general nature make this clear. The temple of Solomon was the house of Israel's God (II Sam. 7:2, 5–7), and all its appointments are of a sacerdotal nature. See Benzinger and Box, "Temple, Temple-Service," *Ency. Bibl.,* IV. Further, few of the Psalms were written before the exile, and still fewer were appropriate to such worship (W. R. Smith and T. K. Cheyne, "Psalms," *Ency. Bibl.,* III; Pfeiffer, *Introduction to the O.T.,* 619–644; C. A. Briggs, "The Book of Psalms," *ICC,* lvii–xcii).

[27] J. P. Peters has drawn attention to this possibility, suggesting that a collection of Psalms (Pss. 42–49) may have originated at Dan, and another booklet (Pss. 50, 73–83) may have been collected at Bethel (*The Psalms as Liturgies,* 59–65, 273–291, 298–337). This is suggestive, but not a certainty.

[28] For the hymnology of Egypt, see Breasted, *Development of Religion and Thought in Ancient Egypt,* 13–17, 93–98, 121, 124, 310–315; J. Baikie, *The Amarna Age,* 338–341, and *ERE,* VII, 38–40. For Babylonia, see M. Jastrow, *The Religion of Babylonia and Assyria,* 247, 248, 300–310; T. G. Pinches, *ERE,* VII, 1–3. For Greek and Roman, T. W. Allen, *ERE,* VII, 40–42. The Syrian hymnology, especially that of Ugarit, as revealed in recently discovered tablets, is in process of interpretation.

[29] This is a conclusion based on what is known of the service in the Herodian temple, and later (I. Abrahams and S. Singer, *The Authorized Daily Prayer Book,* 9th ed., xcv–xcvi, 168).

than the priest. Joyous confidence in the goodness and mercy of the Lord strengthened all, and amid the seductions of alien cultures helped to keep alive the flame of Judaism.

The scribe, Jesus ben Sirach, has helped to complete the picture of Judaism in the pre-Maccabean period. The book of Ben Sirach, or Ecclesiasticus,[30] was written in Hebrew about 180 B.C. and translated by the author's grandson in 132 B.C. into Greek, from which our Authorized Version translation was made.

The author, like the compilers of Proverbs, was interested in homely wisdom, and emphasizes honesty in business and good sense in social relations. He was a scholar, a lover of wisdom (B. Sir. 1:1-20, 26-30; 4:11-23; 14:20-15: 10; 24:1-34; 39:1-11; 51:13-30), and in a sort of comprehensive way equates wisdom with the Jewish Torah (24:1-8; 45:1-22).[31] As a representative of the finest Jewish culture of the period he shared the prevailing idea of the history and the destiny of his own people. They were the first among the nations (36: 1-17), and were like the first-born among the nations (36:12); as the inheritance of Yahweh (17:17; 24:12), their days would be innumerable (37:25). Their religion, the fear of Yahweh, was his stay and confidence (1:18-21; 19: 20-23), for the temple in Zion was the abode of the Most High (36:13, 14, 17).

Moreover, he was a teacher of the law, a friend of the scribes, and no doubt qualified as one himself (38:24-39:11). By his teaching and writing he aided in stemming the excesses of cosmopolitan culture (9:2-9; 11:21-12:7; 41:17-24; 42:12-14), as well as in exalting Judaism. But it was the priest, the son of Aaron, who to him was the Lord's anointed. His eulogy on Simon, the great priest (50:1-21), 226-198 B.C., is the work of a poet who celebrated his ideal in the loftiest language. An admirer of stately ritual in which fine raiment, gesture, and fitting word were rich with mystic meaning, his enthusiasm was unbounded when on the day of the atonement the high priest came from the sanctuary, amid the exultation of the throng, and pronounced on them the blessing of the Most High (50:16-21). He revered the sacred office for what it signified, and the climax of his joy was reached when that office was adorned by a man who had won the affection and esteem of all.

He was a Jew, even an orthodox Jew, and yet he was not immune to the intellectual atmosphere of the day. His booklet is the medium of some of the finer features of Hellenism. Moderation in all things is to be practiced (3:21-24; 13:1-26; 31:1-31); and beauty, music, wine, and the joys of life are not to be despised (7:13; 32:3-6; 39:14, 15; 45:25). But his philosophy is even more significant. The Torah, to him, has subtly expanded so as to include the Greek idea of wisdom, and has reached out to embrace the laws of nature (32:24-33:3;

---

[30] For full information as to date, various texts, and a translation, see R. H. Charles, *Apocrypha and Pseudepigrapha*, I, 268–517. Editorial additions of considerable importance found their way into the Greek text. For references we follow the AV, as revised in 1894.

[31] Chapter XI above.

35:1–11). Hebrew law is here the incarnation of a cosmic principle,[32] and Israel is the center of all and the heir of all the ages. He even goes so far as to speak of God as the *All* (43:27; cf. 1:1–26, 27; 36:1–17). Such phrases and ideas but suggest the debt of the final addition of the book to Greek life and thought. The author was a Jew but he had learned the language of the Greeks, and was trying on the toga of the philosopher. It was an attractive apologetic to the thoughtful, both Jew and Greek, throughout the ancient world.

At the close of the period Judaism was thoroughly furnished, and had a glorious heritage. A people with an ancient and honorable history, the people of God, they had a law, detailed and comprehensive to meet all needs; teachers who were learned and competent; a priesthood with ample wealth, thanks to the activities of the taxgatherers,[33] and with unchallenged integrity, thanks to the character of Simon, the Just; a temple, established on a rock, and pleasing to the eye; and a God, the God of their fathers, who for a thousand years had been their help and stay, and their abiding presence. Such a heritage, granted to few if any people, was the measure and the symbol of Judaism.

The Second Commonwealth, 141–63 B.C., was a triumphant moment in the history of Judaism. It was equal in duration to that of the united kingdom of David and Solomon (1013–933 B.C.), and though it attained the old boundary lines for only a few years, in achievement it was equally spectacular. The immediate cause of the revolt leading to freedom was the edict of Antiochus IV (175–164 B.C.), but that was only the final act in a long tragedy in which pent-up aspirations had kept alive deep, undying resentments. In 933 B.C. Judea had lost the richer and larger part of the domain of David owing to the insolent stupidity of Rehoboam. In 722 B.C. she became a vassal to Assyria, and in 608 passed under the yoke of Egypt, only to become a pawn to Babylonia four years later, and then in 597 and 586 to be desolated and dragged into captivity by the conqueror. In 538 B.C. she became the chattel of Persia, and in 332 Alexander received her homage. Then in 301 Ptolemy took her over, and in 198 she became the spoil of Syria. While ambitions were thus thwarted by the realities of history, she had throughout the centuries been building dream castles of empire, that had ministered to her ego and rendered her growingly rebellious with her lot.

Added to these indignities, the influx of the foreigners and the culture of the Greeks, so different from her own and so hateful to her orthodox leaders, had now for more than a century and a half been invading every phase of her life. From 301 to 198 B.C. Greek culture had been mediated through Egypt, and was rather innocuous, as it was somewhat philosophic, with strong ascetic tenden-

---

[32] Ed. Bevan, *Jerusalem under the High-Priests*, 50–68, elaborates this fact.

[33] By 175 B.C. the Jewish people were indulging in happy memories of the wealth and the luxury of the sons of Tobias, not in the way they had accumulated it (Ed. Bevan, *Jerusalem under the High-Priests*, 44, 45).

cies. Also the economic opportunities of Alexandria and Cyrene that attracted many of the enterprising Jews naturally kindly disposed them to the hand that fed them. The translation of the Hebrew Scriptures into Greek was a real boon to Judaism [34] in Palestine as well as in Egypt; and not a few orthodox Jews, like Ben Sirach, were quite willing to press the spirit of Judaism into Greek molds without the loss of their faith. The sore spot had been the work of Joseph, who had introduced the Bacchanalian orgies into the festivals in Jerusalem, and with his son Hyrcanus had grecianized priestly society.

But when in 198 B.C., by the battle of Banias, Palestine became a part of the Syrian empire, Hellenism of a new and more appealing type soon threatened the very existence of Judaism. Palestine in every way belongs to Syria rather than to Egypt, and Syrian contacts with Greece were much closer than were those of Egypt. Hence a culture more definitely Grecian now entered Palestine, building on foundations already partially established. The emphasis on physical beauty, the pleasures of social life, the charms of light literature, the schools of philosophy, and the ideal of city life now came into full play. Antiochus III of Syria (222–187 B.C.) was staunchly pro-Grecian, but the privileges he granted the Jews in 198 B.C., freedom from taxes for three years, religious liberty, and local self-government (Jos. *Ant.*, XII, III, 4) must have won many to the ways of the new monarch. Hence gymnasia, the hippodrome, and the theater were soon introduced in many cities, and a youth movement for beauty, health, and freedom met with a quick response.

During the reign of Antiochus IV (175–164 B.C.) events moved rapidly to a climax. Liberty became license among the masses, and opportunity for personal gain corrupted the leaders. The slimy trail of Joseph soon became the pattern for the rulers. Jason, Greek for Joshua, swindled his brother Onias III out of the high priesthood by reckless bribery, gained Athenian citizenship for the Jews of Jerusalem, built a gymnasium in Jerusalem, and let loose in the city a flood of customs that were shocking and illegal to the loyal Jews (II Macc. 4: 7–22). Menelaus, of the priestly family, in turn bought up the priesthood in 171 B.C., sacked the temple treasury, and when accused bought up the court and assassinated the witnesses. On his acquittal he took Antiochus IV into the holy of holiness and permitted the removal of the temple treasures (II Macc. 4:23–43). Lysimmachus, his brother, who was in charge of the temple, because he constantly violated his trust was slain beside the treasury (II Macc. 4:39–42). In 169 B.C. Jason returned to the city with a thousand soldiers to regain his lost power. Without mercy he butchered his Jewish opponents, but at the approach of a Syrian army fled for safety, while the Syrians put many Jews to death on the Sabbath day (II Macc. 5:5–10). Such godless degeneracy on the part of

---

[34] This translation was begun probably about 250 B.C. for the use of Alexandrian Jews to whom the Hebrew had become a dead language. Josephus states that some opposed it, and that at least one by touching upon it had become demented (Jos. *Ant.*, XII, II, 14); but he also asserts that the leaders approved of it, and requested that it should not be altered (Jos. *Ant.*, XII, II, 13).

rulers, and the flaunting of Greek customs and symbols, combined to raise the emotional tensions of the decent Jew to the boiling point. Antiochus IV was equally irritated that so petty a folk should hold so tenaciously to their uncouth practices. As they would keep the peace neither between themselves nor with the empire, he determined to wipe out their religion. Thus in 168 B.C. he proscribed circumcision, Sabbath observance, and the possession of a copy of the Scriptures, ordered the use of pork, and defiled the temple.

That spark touched off the powder magazine. When at Modin an obsequious Jew made ready to sacrifice a hog on the local altar, Mattathias, a priest, outraged, struck down the apostate. Led by his sons, the loyal in Judah [35] rose in their fury and gave their lives for freedom in religion. Under skillful leadership they blasted the veteran armies of Syria out of the country. The temple was cleansed and the worship of Yahweh restored in 165 B.C. In 164 Antiochus V is said to have confirmed the privileges of worship in a letter to the Gerousia in Jerusalem (II Macc. 11:28–33), and a year later Lysias the Syrian general confirmed the peace with the nation. In 161 B.C. Menelaus, the breaker of the law, was hurled to his death from a high tower (II Macc. 13:33), and Alcimus, a priest of legitimate descent, became high priest [36] (II Macc. 14:3; I Macc. 8:21–25; 9:1) under the influence of Bacchides the Syrian general. In the annals of history, the victory of the Maccabees is a lasting monument to the supremacy of the spirit over the flesh.

Judaism again stood at the parting of the ways. The great crisis was over, and now each group felt it could follow its religious convictions, or fight for private interests, without regard for the general welfare. The Hassidim, who had no interest in politics, when freedom of worship had been guaranteed believing that a high priest of the seed of Aaron would do them no harm, withdrew from all participation in further aggression [37] (I Macc. 7:13–16). Judas, the Maccabean leader, however, either suspicious of Alcimus (I Macc. 7:21–25; II Macc. 14:14–25) or encouraged by his victories, insisted on continuing the war for political independence. Also within Judaism was the pro-Syrian party loyal to the king, ready to adapt themselves to changing customs and to acknowledge the authority of the ruling power even in affairs of religion. It is probable that these constituted the majority of the nation.

Syria sent Bacchides, Nicanor, and Bacchides a second time, with armies, into Palestine in order to keep peace in the rebellious city. Alcimus no sooner had authority than he slew sixty of the Hassidim leaders (I Macc. 7:16–20), and Bacchides supplemented this with a great slaughter (I Macc. 7:18–20). Nicanor soon arrived with a large army and drove Judas to the hills (I Macc. 7:26–50), but lost his life, and Bacchides had to return to the battlefield.

---

35 Within Jewry the old and the new were at war. Pro-Hellenist had little sympathy with the old-fashioned religion. Jews in Syrian garrisons became executioners for Antiochus IV (J. Wellhausen, *History of Israel and Judah,* 145), and at home there were divided interests. It was a religious war.

36 S. Zeitlin, *Sec. Com.,* 33–38.

37 S. Zeitlin, *Sec. Com.,* 37, 38.

Judas in 161 B.C., finding himself far outnumbered, is reported to have sent an embassy to Rome [38] to establish a confederacy with that rising power (I Macc. 8:17–32). But no immediate help came from his ally, and he virtually became an outlaw. In desperation he plundered caravans, burned villages, and boasted of butcheries of the godless, the traitors to the covenant, the apostates who were in power (I Macc. 9:1–14:22; II Macc. 12:15–13:21). The story, in its sickening inhumanity, is a match for anything in later annals. It was the fury of a frustrated patriotism, intensified by religious fanaticism, that easily leads to the betrayal of humanity. Defeated but unsubdued, forsaken by most of his army, with a pitiful remnant dedicated to political independence or death, he who had been the savior of Israel insisted on giving battle to an overpowering Syrian army at Eleasa, near Beth-horon, in 161 B.C. Zeal, heroism, and faith were not enough. The army was utterly routed. Judas was slain, and his mantle was laid on the shoulder of his younger, more diplomatic brother, Jonathan (I Macc. 9:7–31).

Jonathan, who was no less gifted or determined than Judas, after years of desperate and unceasing struggle in camp and court, with the consent of Syria became high priest in 153 B.C.; and a year later Syria, wearied by the persistence of the Jews and the distracting raids of a guerrilla army that would not yield and could not be destroyed, confirmed the independence of Judah (I Macc. 10:22–45). Rome renewed the league with Jonathan in 143 B.C. (I Macc. 12:1–23), and again with Simon, his brother and successor, in 139 B.C., when the friendship and the confederacy were confirmed on tablets of brass (I Macc. 14:16–24). In the meantime, in 141 B.C., Simon had broken the yoke of the heathen, crushed the apostates, cleansed the city and the citadel from pollution, and had been acknowledged the high priest, and captain, the leader of the Jews (I Macc. 13:41–53; 14:27–49). The long-hoped-for kingdom had been achieved.

The Second Jewish Commonwealth, 141–63 B.C., the fruit of Maccabean heroism and martyrdom, beginning so auspiciously under Simon the high priest and prince (I Macc. 14:14–15, 27–49), will surely long continue a model of peace and prosperity. But alas! Self-rule doubled responsibilities and opportunities but did not change human nature. The Jew, who could not live quietly under Egypt and Syria, could not live in peace and harmony with his own kin. Simon and two of his sons, invited to a banquet by Ptolemy, his son-in-law who lived in Dok, near Jericho, were murdered in cold blood, and his wife soon after also was slain [39] (I Macc. 16:11–18; Jos. *Ant.*, XIII, VII, 4).

John Hyrcanus, an older son, intercepted the murderer, seized the power, and ruled with a strong hand from 135 to 104 B.C., extending the kingdom to the old Solomonic boundaries (Jos. *Ant.*, XIII, chaps. 8 to 10). Thoroughly

---

[38] While this story comes from partisan sources, in which perspective may have been lost by enthusiasm for a racial hero, it is possible that this tradition rests on fact (R. H. Charles, *Apocrypha and Pseudepigrapha*, I, 93).

[39] Graetz, *Hist. Jews*, I, 522–531; II, 1–83.

devoted to the faith of his fathers, he destroyed the temple of the Samaritans in 128 B.C. (Jos. *Ant.,* XIII, IX, 1; II Macc. 6:1) and forced circumcision on the Idumeans.[40] Aristobulus, his son, ruled for one year, and though he imprisoned his mother and three brothers and was responsible for the murder of his favorite brother, he was serviceable to the Jews as he forced the conquered tribes of Iturea and South Lebanon to be circumcised.[41]

Alexander Jannaeus (103–76 B.C.), who during his reign was supported chiefly by the Sadducees, roused the deadly enmity of the Pharisees.[42] As priest at the feast of tabernacles in 95 B.C. he made light of some technicality of the water libation and was pelted with citrons by the angry mob. He slew six thousand of them for this indignity.[43] Then ensued a struggle with the Pharisees that continued over six years, as to his right to violate a technicality of the law. Tradition reports that he slew fifty thousand Pharisees and then, weary of the fruitless struggle, called for peace. The Pharisees refused, suggested that he kill himself, and then appealed to Syria for aid (Jos. *Ant.,* XIII, XIII, 5). Syria sent an army and combined with the Pharisee forces defeated him; then some six thousand Jews betrayed their ally and joined forces with Jannaeus, who won the final battle. He then meted out his wrath to his old-time enemies. Eight hundred of their ringleaders were crucified, and while writhing on their crosses saw the throats of their wives and children being cut, a memorable lesson to all generations.[44] Three years later on his deathbed he counseled Salome Alexandra, his wife and successor, to make peace with the obdurate Pharisees.

The tide of Judaism at last had turned. Salome, though sympathetic with Grecian culture,[45] granted large authority to her brother, Simon ben Shetach, who was a scholar and an ardent Pharisee. He reorganized the council of state, or Gerousia, filling vacancies with Pharisees, who had become the experts in

40 The history of the times of John Hyrcanus and his achievements are briefly presented in Margolis and Marx, *Hist. Jew. People,* 151–163; Ed. Bevan, *CAH,* IX, 397–406; J. S. Riggs. *History of the Jews,* 97–118.

41 Jos. *Ant.,* XIII, XI, 1–3; G. F. Moore, *Judaism,* I, 336; Graetz, *Hist. Jews,* II, 36–38.

42 The Pharisees probably emerged from the Hassidim during the Maccabean struggle, as they are first mentioned during the time of Jonathan (G. F. Moore, *History of Religions,* II, 53). They were separatists, or dissenters, as the name implies (S. Zeitlin, *Sec. Com.,* 42–56), and in the days of John Hyrcanus had formed a voluntary religious community within Judaism (Ed. Bevan, *CAH,* IX. 406–417; W. Fairweather, *Background of the Gospels,* 140–146). The body of them belonged to the common people, as distinguished from the priests, and the Sadducees, and were lovers of the law. As such they had among them many scholars, and they accepted the oral law as well as that which was written. For critical discussion see L. Finkelstein, "The Pharisees," *Harv. Th. Rev.,* July, 1929, 188–261; *The Pharisees,* two vols. The Sadducees, from Zaddok, were the aristocratic landowners, and the allies of the priests. They were the conservatives and refused to accept the oral law and a belief in the physical resurrection. The cleavage between them and the Pharisees was economic, social, political, and religious.

43 Jos. *Ant.,* XIII, XIII, 5. Margolis and Marx, *Hist. Jew. People,* 155.

44 Jos. *Ant.,* XIII, XIV, 2. Margolis and Marx, *Hist. Jew. People,* 156, 157.

45 The fact that she had coins struck in Greek, with her name Queen Alexandra, at least indicates a tendency that way (Graetz, *Hist. Jews,* II, 48). For an idyllic picture of this queen see Graetz, pp. 47–61.

the law. He brought Tabbai Judah, a noted scholar, from Alexandria to aid in the administration. According to report they held rigidly to the strictest, literal interpretation of the Torah. Many Sadducees were condemned to death as their interpretations were too liberal. Tradition reports that eighty women of Askelon were crucified for witchcraft, and that Simon's own son went to death on a technical blunder.[46] Because their theology implied man was made for the law, their devotion to the jot and tittle was praiseworthy, though sadly moronic.

Reaction set in on the death of the queen in 67 B.C. Aristobulus, the younger but more vigorous son, supported by the Sadducees attacked and defeated Hyrcanus, who had been made high priest. Then Antipater,[47] the Idumean, the father of Herod the Great, came to the support of Hyrcanus. Both sides appealed ultimately to Pompey of Rome, and in 63 B.C. Jerusalem, that would not submit peacefully, was besieged and captured by the Roman soldiers. It is said twelve thousand were slaughtered, among whom were the priests, whose throats were cut as they ministered at the altar. Only thus did the minorities, and the religious belligerents, find peace under the protection of Rome (Jos. *Ant.,* XIV, chaps. 2–4).

But this, a glimpse into the horrors that accompanied the lust for power, and the pogroms that resulted from the clash of religious ideas, is not the whole story. Changes were taking place that were determining for all time the basic principles of Judaism.

The economic life had definitely changed. During the century Jewry had completed the transition from agricultural to city life. At 200 B.C., thanks to the taxgatherers, the priests, who were the rulers, were wealthy aristocrats while the mass of the people were peasant farmers or were making a slow adjustment to city life. At home and abroad by 63 B.C. they were largely city dwellers, living by trade rather than by the sweat of their brow. Owing to the captivities, the migrations, and the change to city life, wealth was widely distributed and the son of the peasant had often moved up in the social register. Naturally the new wealth, and the changed way of life, reacted on the social, intellectual, and religious trends of the day.

Cultural ideas that were too pervasive to be held at bay, either by force of arms or by pontifical edict, had made themselves felt. Love for the beautiful in nature, in art, in architecture, in music, and in literature [48] had been fostered by the Greek invaders, and now was a commonplace in most Palestinian centers.

[46] Graetz, *Hist. Jews,* II, 53–55.

[47] Jos. *Ant.,* XIV, I, 1–4; XIV, II, 1, 2.

[48] In architecture the military fortresses, the gymnasia and the hippodrome, the colonnaded palaces fashioned after the Greeks, and above all the mausoleum at Modin, a memorial to Mattathias, testify to foreign influence. Likewise in art the coinage and the memorial tablets pay tribute to the same influences (Graetz, *Hist. Jews,* II, 13–15). In literature and religion Psalm 19:1–7, and Job 39:1–30 show the same tendency.

The organization of Jewish community life, the very framework of Judaism, during this period had undergone the most profound changes. Submission to Persia, adjustments to Egypt and Syria, and interrelations with the Dispersion had been leaven at work in the body politic. But it was the Commonwealth, in which the genius of the people was put to the test, that modified the spirit, the characteristics, and the functions of the governing body of the nation.

The elders of the tribes, the cabinets of the kings, and the various courts of justice, as suggested by the reform of Deuteronomy (Deut. 17:8–10; 19:16–19), the divorce court of Ezra (Ezra 10:14–16; Neh. 10:13–35), and the high court of Jehoshaphat (II Chron. 19:8–11) had met the needs for centuries, and each contributed to the evolution of what now became a new instrument of government.[49] The Great Assembly, or Sanhedrin, which tradition linked up with the council of the elders (Num. 11:16, P.), is now generally accepted as a priestly telescoping of the actual history. The Gerousia, later usually called the Sanhedrin (Jos. *Ant.,* XIV, ix, 4), is first mentioned in a letter from Antiochus III to Ptolemy of Egypt, shortly after 198 B.C. (Jos. *Ant.,* XII, III, 3), which is indisputable evidence that for some considerable time it had been a recognized institution. It was a self-perpetuating body of seventy or seventy-one members, with jurisdiction, without the power of death, over most civil and criminal cases, and in religion was virtually the supreme court in Judaism.[50] Its membership as suggested by scattered references came from Levites, priests, and heads of families of Israel (Ezra 10:16; II Chron. 19:8), that is, of priests and their friends the aristocratic Sadducees. The high priest, by virtue of his office, was head of the body, and exerted great if not absolute power in the appointment of members. As was meet, this chief council met regularly in the precincts of the temple in the Holy City. In the pre-Maccabean days it was decidedly ecclesiastical, autocratic, and imperialistic.

The Sanhedrin, by the beginning of the Roman period in 63 B.C., had significantly changed both in the composition of its membership and in its functions. Its ecclesiastical tone had given place to a layman's movement. The priesthood during the days of the taxgatherers, by their greed, their inhumanity, and their pro-Hellenic sympathies, had lost the confidence of the common people. This distrust deepened when many of the priesthood and the aristocracy were willing to wink at, or even support, the infamous decree of Antiochus IV in 168 B.C. The revolt of the Maccabees was supported to the death by the Hassidim, from whom emerged the Pharisees. This new body, because of their principles and their personal courage, soon came to play an important

---

49 Important articles on the origin and development of the chief council, or sanhedrin of the Jews are: I. Abrahams, "Sanhedrin," *ERE,* XI. I. Benzinger, "Government," *Ency. Bibl.,* II. W. Bacher, "Sanhedrin," *HBD* (five vols.). E. Schürer, *HJP,* II, 1, 163–195. S. Zeitlin, *JQR,* Oct., 1945, 109–140; Jan., 1946, 303–316.

50 Numbers, functions, and authority naturally varied with time and place, and changing relations with the rulers (G. A. Smith, *Jerusalem,* I, 419, 420; E. Schürer, *HJP,* II, 1, 174–184).

role in the thought of the nation. They were devoted to religion but had no interest in politics. They were enthusiasts for the law, and strongly opposed to Hellenism. They believed in the resurrection from the dead, which appealed to popular imagination but was rejected by the Sadducees, and they were mild eschatologists, as against the Apocalyptists. They were scribes, scholars, teachers of the law, not sacerdotalists. Though individuals of all ranks made common cause with them, they at first came from the poorer and the middle class, as opposed to the aristocracy. They were a new democracy united in loyalty to the Torah as understood by enlightened intelligence.

The function of the Sanhedrin, though as always occupied with civil and religious affairs,[51] was undergoing change. Its scope had broadened and its objectives had moved into new spheres. The complex of new laws introduced about 400 B.C. by the scribe made intelligent interpretation and comparison with earlier laws imperative. Experts in the religious requirements of the law, rather than technicians in ritual, were in demand. Schools for the study of the law grew up at home and abroad, and the synagogue, a needed institution among the Dispersion, soon found its way to Jerusalem, even into the temple. Thus the teacher of the law rose to a position of great prominence.

Further, these teachers of the law, the scribes, most of whom belonged to the Pharisees, aware of the difficulties of interpretation and the needs of adjustment to the inexorable pressures of history, accepted the unwritten law,[52] that is, the judgments of earlier teachers, as valid alongside the written law. The Pharisee by adopting this principle provided for reinterpretation of the law as wisdom dictated. The door was left open for growth in religion amid a changing environment. By way of illustration the Pharisee was able to accept the idea of resurrection from the dead, though on that question the law is silent. Further, when the temple was destroyed Judaism was able to keep alive without benefit of priest or altar.

The experiences of the wars of the Maccabees and of eighty years of self-rule brought into sharp focus the personal antagonisms and the incompatible ideologies within Judaism herself. But by the time the strong hand of Rome stayed this fratricidal strife, religion, as above indicated, had made substantial gains. Even more important than these were the teachers, Pharisees chiefly, both at home and abroad, of whom it could justly be said: Israelites indeed in whom there is no guile.

[51] An important contribution to the history of the Sanhedrin has recently been made by Dr. S. Zeitlin of Dropsie College. Making a critical study of all the relevant material he concludes that there was a *Synedrion* under the high priest that had charge of all civil affairs in Judea, but under the Second Commonwealth this council had no jurisdiction over religion. To meet the need the *Beth Din*, or *Sanhedrin*, was established (Zeitlin, "The Political Synedrion and the Religious Sanhedrin," *JQR*, Oct., 1945, 109–140; criticism and reply in *JQR*, 303–316). Whichever theory be proved correct, the fact remains that during this period there was a definite change in the functions of the judicial institution or institutions.

[52] The first record of the Halakot, or the decision of an individual teacher, is in the Hasmonean period (S. Zeitlin, *Sec. Com.*, 40).

Pax Romana,[53] one of the great boons in the ancient warring world, was ushered in for Judea in 63 B.C. Aristobulus II, his son Alexander, his family, leading supporters, and thousands of his followers were carried captive to Rome (Jos. *Ant.,* XIV, IV, 5). The nation was now confined within its own bounds (Jos. *Ant.,* XIV, IV, 4); the temple was cleansed; the daily sacrifice was restored; Hyrcanus, the high priest, was made ethnarch of Judea under supervision of the Roman governor of Syria; and Jerusalem was garrisoned by Roman soldiers. Peace and order seemed to be securely established, and all was quiet, if restless, throughout the land for five years.

Then in 57 B.C. Alexander, the son of Aristobulus, who had escaped from the captive train on its way to Rome, reached Judea, sought the throne, was joined by the nobles, and raised an army of 10,000 foot soldiers, and 1,500 horse. He was quickly suppressed; Hyrcanus was stripped of all civil power; Jewish territory was split up into five districts, each governed by a Jewish council directly responsible to the Roman governor of Syria; and all affairs in the city were to be settled under the advisement of Antipater (Jos. *Ant.,* XIV, V, 2-4; XIV, VI, 1-4). Three more insurrections took place between 56 and 52 B.C. Aristobulus escaped from Rome and led a revolt in which five thousand Jews were slain (Jos. *Ant.,* XIV, VI, 1). The following year Alexander led twenty thousand men to their death at Mount Tabor (Jos. *Ant.,* XIV, VI, 2-4). In 52 B.C. Crassus, the Roman general, enraged by these tribal rebellions, pillaged and desecrated the temple. To this Jews of all classes replied by joining the rebels, who were crushed at Tarichaea, on the shores of Galilee, where some thirty thousand were taken into captivity (Jos. *Ant.,* XIV, VII, 1, 3).

These were years of destiny, and Rome was on the threshold of world empire.[54] Crassus died in 52 B.C., and at Pharsalia in 48 B.C. Caesar defeated Pompey and then followed him to Egypt where, aided by Alexandrian Jews who had been rallied to his side by Antipater and Hyrcanus, he completely defeated his enemy. In gratitude Caesar reunited in one the five districts of Judea, granted the Jews freedom from military taxes and service, guaranteed freedom in religion, and centered the jurisdiction of all Jewish affairs in Jerusalem with Antipater as prime minister to Hyrcanus, the high priest (Jos. *Ant.,* XIV, X, 1, 8, 20). In 44 B.C. Caesar was assassinated; Antipater was poisoned; and Herod, his son, the governor of Galilee, took over the control of Judea. But all the world was in uproar and riot. Nowhere were intrigue and violence more at home than in Palestine. Antigonus, son of Aristobulus, in defiance of Herod became king and high priest in Jerusalem. Supported by the Sanhedrin and the nobility, he called to his aid the Parthian army that already was in Syria. Herod, far outnumbered, fled to Alexandria, then to Rome, where Antony

---

[53] The basis of this was not the conquest of arms so much as the conquest of culture; and thus Rome romanized all the Western world. Those islets of culture that refused to adapt themselves to the culture and the customs of the Empire naturally were always disturbing elements. See H. Last, "Race and Culture," *CAH*, X, 425-429.

[54] E. Schürer, *HJP*, I, 1, 375-385.

in 40 B.C. proclaimed him king of the Jews but gave him no aid. A masterful man, he returned to Palestine, landing at Tyre. Joined by old supporters he regained Galilee, and struggled grimly on. He held Bethel in 38 B.C. and in 37 B.C. laid siege to Jerusalem. At last a Roman army joined him. The walls of the city were breached, and for fifteen days barbarian and Jew slaughtered the Jewish defenders from street to street up to the court of the temple, which Herod personally preserved from pollution. Antigonus surrendered and begged for mercy, but, sent to Antony in Antioch, he was beheaded. Forty-five of the chief leaders were executed while the rest of the army was annihilated in an orgy of blood. Thus ended the last semblance of Jewish independence, and Herod the Great [55] (37-4 B.C.) became king of the Jews by the grace of imperial Rome. He was not a Jewish king, for Jewish blood was not in his veins. His ancestors had been forceably circumcised, and though he had taken a daughter of the Hasmoneans to wife, he was still the Idumean slave. Yet Graetz, one of his keenest critics, admits that his reign contrasted favorably with that which followed. It might be added it was not quite so disastrous to Judaism as that of some of his predecessors who were legitimate priest-kings.

Relevant as the history from 37 B.C. down to 73 or to A.D. 135 is to the religion of Judaism, it lies beyond the scope of this work. The general appraisal of the spirit and the developments within Judaism can be appreciated in the background already studied. This century but repeated the history of earlier periods with ever deepening horrors.

Roman rule on the whole was wise, considerate, and generous. It promoted prosperity within all parts of the Empire, but nowhere more so than in Palestine. Freedom of religion, self-government in local affairs, and strict regard for national ideals within the Empire was the rule rather than the exception. From Herod's effort to prevent any possible pollution to the great temple by having none but Levites, expert in all kinds of work, employed in its construction (Jos. *Ant.*, XV, xi, 2, 6), down to the long detour planned for the army by Vitellius, in its march against the Arabs, so that not even the shadow of the flag on which was the figure of the emperor might fall on the sacred soil (Jos. *Ant.*, XVIII, v, 3), Rome and her officers were usually ready not to offend Jewish sensitiveness.

Roman authorities, however, both in the councils at home and among their representatives abroad, were human, and some were impatient, arrogant, frivolous, or vengeful. Herod the Great had executed a robber chief without consulting the Sanhedrin. He made a Babylonian Jew high priest, and had placed a golden eagle, the glory of Rome and the shame of Israel, over the entrance door of the temple (Jos. *Ant.*, XVII, vi, 2-4). Pilate brought an

---

[55] The history of the period of Herod the Great, so important for the understanding of both Judaism and Christianity, may be found in the following: Jos. *Ant.*, XIV, l-XVII, viii, 3. E. Schürer, *HJP*, I, i, 383–416. Graetz, *Hist. Jews*, II, 77–117. A. Momigliano, *CAH*, XI, 316–339. Margolis and Marx, *Hist. Jew. People*, 164–176. J. S. Riggs, *History of the Jewish People*, 164–231.

army with their banners, on which were the effigies of the emperor, into the city by night, and he had votive shields, without images, in his private palace (Jos. *Ant.,* XVIII, III, 1). Caligula (A.D. 37–41) ordered an image of himself to be prepared and set up in the temple (Jos. *Ant.,* XVIII, VIII, 2). A stupid Roman soldier made an unseemly gesture near the temple altar (Jos. *Ant.,* XX, V, 2), and another one tore up a roll of the law (Jos. *Ant.,* XX, V, 3). These and similar indignities led to protestations, riot, and bloodshed. The Jewish leaders preferred death to acquiescence in such violations of their law (Jos. *Ant.,* XVIII, III, 1; XVIII, VIII, 3).

Many Jewish leaders were noted for their sound judgment, their unselfish interests, their broad outlook, and a correct appreciation of the place and function of the Roman Empire in the world order. But there were others, probably the majority, whose vision never passed the borders of Judea, and who thought in terms of politics rather than religion. Still others to whom Judea meant nothing more than their own private interests, or their own religious sect, were found throughout all the land, but especially in Galilee. Blinded by bigotry, under the guise of religion they capitalized their tribal hatreds. Josephus speaks of them as robbers, impostors, deceivers, false prophets, who delude the multitudes and fill every city with impiety (Jos. *Ant.,* XX, VIII, 5; Jos. *Wars,* IV, VII, 2). In one thing only would all the Jews agree: They were all humiliated to have to live under an alien government. Beyond that they were split up into numerous warring factions.

The strife within Judaism was as fierce and fatal as was the struggle with Rome. While both were deadly, both contributed to a residuum of life and thought which was being conditioned to fulfill its mission in the world without benefit of land, or city, or temple. In this process group after group, in one way or another, was sloughed off, while the main body continued its struggle with environment. The Samaritans (*ca.* 300 B.C.), were the first to be cut off from the main branch, as a protest against the inroads made by alien blood and foreign customs in Israel's religion. National independence and political interests, as indispensable to Judaism, were repudiated by many in 161 B.C. The Pharisees, a heroic little band, at this time registered their conviction that the objective of religion was neither political nor national. The Essenes,[56] probably an offshoot of the Hassidim, emphasized justice and simplicity of life, despised riches, were scattered throughout the villages, and held all things in common. They were strict in Sabbath observance, insisted on purity of blood, and emphasized celibacy. They believed in immortality of the soul but not of the body, and had no political interests. Though they made a notable contribution to the spirit of Judaism, the victims of their

---

[56] The Essenes are known to us chiefly through Jos. *Ant.,* XVIII, 1, 5; Jos. *Wars,* II, VIII, 2–13. See Ed. Bevan, *CAH,* IX, 423–427; M. S. Enslin, *Christian Beginnings,* for Essenes, 120–125, and John the Baptist, 149–153. Graetz states the Essenes were the first to raise the cry, "The Messiah is coming, and the kingdom of heaven is at hand" (*Hist. Jews,* II, 145–147).

own principles they died a natural death. Apocalyptic visionaries and patrons of supernaturalism at times led the multitudes astray (Jos. *Ant.,* XVII, x, 4-10), but few Jewish leaders so lost their perspective that they abandoned the realities of social and political existence. The Sadducees,[57] who were aristocrats, and their friends the priests, were supporters of the established order, and with the passing of the state and the church both ceased to function as independent units.

The Nazarenes,[58] though of little consequence in the tumult of their early days, deserve a notice because of origin, principles, and later development. They came out of Galilee, a center of political unrest and violence. Like the Essenes they were unworldly, simple in their manner of life and speech, with a tendency toward community life. With no Jewish national interests they were taught to render to Caesar the things that were Caesar's. Like the Pharisees they accepted the Scriptures—the canon, not the oral tradition—emphasized the golden rule, were given to prayer, almsgiving, and good works, and believed in the physical resurrection. But unlike them they belonged to the common people, and associated with publicans and sinners. They were not scholars deeply versed in the law, but like the prophets they called for righteousness, mercy, and goodness among men. They were kindly disposed toward the unfortunate, even should they be Samaritans, and when Saul of the Dispersion joined their ranks, they became active in proselytizing. With broad human sympathies they refused to be hedged in by the petty regulations of the law, and without racial interests or political ambitions they were apostates to the Pharisees. They had much in common with Apocalyptists, and were devoted to the teaching and the person of Jesus of Nazareth. They were Jews, but they had little in common with Sadducees or priests, and soon departed from the unorganized simplicities of the Essenes. They lacked the erudition, the religious egotism, and the national ambitions of many Pharisees, but they were aggressive, and too virile to be confined in any single pattern of the past. Some time during the siege of the city, to the benefit of all concerned, it is believed, the Christians migrated to Pella in Transjordania. Thus relieved of a child that could no longer develop its own life within the confines of its father's house, Judaism was left to face its destiny within the walls of the doomed city.

The process of elimination, however, was not yet complete. Judaism had still self-destroying antagonisms of thought and action within herself. Never were warring factions within a nation more furious than during the last months of the siege of the Holy City. Toward the end of the fourth year of

57 E. Schürer, *HJP,* II, ii, 29–46. S. Zeitlin, *Sec. Com.,* 41–56, a study of Sadducees, Pharisees, and Essenes.

58 Origins and historical background are discussed by Margolis and Marx, *Hist. Jew. People,* 181–183; Graetz, *Hist. Jews,* II, 141–171; E. Schürer, *HJP,* I, ii, 143–149; M. S. Enslin, *Christian Beginnings,* 154–168.

the conflict,[59] John of Gischala, the leader of the Galilean rebels,[60] the left wing of the Pharisees supported by the Sicarii,[61] and the impetuous youth set up an anti-Roman government within the city and proceeded with thoroughness to liquidate all suspects. The wiser leaders at last united against this violence, only to be overwhelmed when John enticed an Idumean rabble to join him. The city became a slaughterhouse as Jew butchered Jew, while the Roman army under Titus mercilessly closed in for the kill. The city fell in A.D. 70. The inhabitants were slain, or enslaved for the galleys or the gladiatorial arena, or to grace the triumphal entry of Titus into Rome, with John and Simon bar Giora. But many of the patriots fought on in caves in Jerusalem, then for three years in Masada, where in A.D. 73. 960 of them committed mass suicide. Nor was this the end.

During the following generation Jewish revolts that were of a somewhat serious nature broke out in Egypt, Cyrene, Cyprus, and Babylonia. The Jewish temple in Heliopolis was destroyed, and in many places privileges were withdrawn from the Jews. In Judea in A.D. 132 a ban was placed on circumcision, and plans were made to build a temple to Jupiter in Jerusalem. Bar Cochba, probably accepted by Rabbi Akiba as the Messiah (Num. 24:17), led an uprising, but in A.D. 135 it was completely crushed. Jerusalem was made a Roman colony, a temple to Jupiter Capitolinus was built on Mount Zion, and Jews were prohibited on pain of death from entering the city. Rome had conquered.

But Judaism, what of it? In the hot fires of revolution she had been purged

---

[59] The conflict began in 66 A.D. in Galilee, where the Jewish army was led by Josephus, the historian who belonged to the Pharisees. His army was soon scattered, and he was captured. John of Gischala then took over, and continued the struggle for four years. Slowly the insurgents were driven from fastness and fortress until in 68 A.D. they took refuge in Jerusalem. The Roman army encamped round about the city gradually drew the lines tighter, let plague, despair, and dissension play their part, and finally brought up the engines of war, broke down the walls, and ended the misery. Details are found in Jos. Wars, II, 14–IX, 2; E. Schürer, HJP, I, II, 207–255; Momigliano, CAH, X, 859–865; Margolis and Marx, Hist. Jew. People, 196–204.

[60] Galilee, with a very mixed population and almost inaccessible hiding places, had long been the center of lawlessness, in which highway robbery and religious fanaticism easily joined hands. Herod the Great in 45 B.C. put down a robber band—or a patriot party—decapitating Hezekiah the leader and a number of others. Judah, son of Hezekiah, is credited with organizing a patriot party in the name of religion, and leading an unsuccessful revolt (Margolis and Marx, 179, 180). In the present uprising Eleazar, a descendant of Judah, supported John of Gischala throughout, and was with him in the final collapse. Graetz is of the opinion that the policy and the action of these revolters would have been approved by the school of Shammai, but not by the Hillelites. The slogan of the patriots was, "Yahweh alone is king, and any infringement of the law is apostasy" (Graetz, Hist. Jews, II, 276–283; Margolis and Marx, Hist. Jew. People, 179, 181, 191, 193, 199, 205).

[61] The Sicarii were so called because they carried a short dagger (sica) concealed in their cloaks, and at festivals or in crowds silently struck down Roman officials and their Jewish satellites, even counting among their victims Jonathan the high priest (Jos. Wars, II, XIII, 2; II, XIII, 6; Graetz, Hist. Jews, II, 233–239). They have been called the scum of the earth, and the cause of all the disaster that had overtaken the land; but in a forthright way they were obeying the law in Deuteronomy 12:2; 13:1–18; 28:1–14.

of the dross. The Sicarii and the war party had been slain, scattered, and discredited. But a remnant remained. Rabbi ben Zakkai, a leader of the peace party, some months before the fall of Jerusalem had retired to Jamnia, where he established his school in A.D. 70. Akiba in A.D. 135, after the defeat of Bar Cochba, with a group of rabbis met at Lydda and addressed themselves anew, in the light of history, to the interpretation of the law. The significance of these movements will be taken up later. In the meantime, in order to gain an understanding of the religion of the Jews we turn to the Dispersion, apart from which there would be no Judaism.

The Jew among the nations was a Jew no less than his brother who remained behind in Jerusalem. Yet his interests and his sympathies were different. The Dispersion was one of the most amazing phenomena in world history. Under the rule of Babylonia, Persia, Greece, Egypt, Syria, and Rome, from 597 B.C. to A.D. 70, as the result of successive deportations, military drafts, colonial settlements, and voluntary migrations, Jewish communities had been established in more than 300 cities, reaching from Media to Spain, and from mid-Europe to Assuan in Egypt, and numbered between four and seven million, while those at home did not exceed 250,000.[62] In Egypt, with Alexandria as the center, where they numbered a million, and in South Babylonia,[63] which until the time of Titus lay outside the Roman dominion, they formed colonies that were practically independent, and vied with Jerusalem in influence.

The Jewish colony, irrespective of origin, size, or location, by its very nature kept itself separate from the Gentile world. Speech, foods, interests, and religious principles, which were so interwoven in the very fabric of their lives, made a gulf between them and their neighbors over which no good Jew ever passed. Circumcision usually, and food taboos always, interfered with their social relations (Dan. 1:7). Sabbath observance, in which from sundown to next sundown no work was done, but the whole day was devoted to religious activities, not only interfered with business relations but proclaimed to all that they were a peculiar people. To so limit one's business and so exalt religion was unheard of in the pagan world.

Moreover, they had a sacred law teaching that there was no God save Yahweh, and that all others were false, the work of men's hands. Because of this strange monotheism, they refused to pay due homage to the gods

---

62 Evidence has been tabulated showing that Jewish communities were in at least 336 cities. The estimate of the total population is a general judgment based on a wide range of fact (J. Juster, *Les Juifs dans l'empire Romain*, I, 179–212; E. Schürer, *HJP*, II, ii, 219–242). For the Dispersion as treated in the O.T. see A. Causse, *Les Dispersés d'Israël*. Philo states there were at least a million in Egypt; *Against Flaccus* VI.

63 The community in South Babylonia was almost exclusively Jewish, called the land the land of Israel, and considered itself superior to that in Jerusalem (Graetz, *Hist. Jews*, II, 502–530).

of the country in which they lived. This was no slight matter; it was atheism, and for this indignity the gods might, indeed often did, punish the entire community. Further, this view of the local gods prevented them from engaging in most social affairs, games, and festivals,[64] as all in one way or another were under the patronage of the gods.

This separateness was further intensified as the Jews frequently claimed and gained privileges not granted to the natives and only rarely to other settlers. As the more than three hundred Jewish colonies were a nation within the Empire, under any government, they had powerful friends in the great centers always ready to insist that special privileges be granted to the members of their race wherever situated[65] (Jos. *Ant.*, XI, viii, 5; XII, iii, i). Such favors may have been the reward for service rendered or the result of political expediency, but they scarcely endeared the alien to the native citizen.[66]

Isolated as they were from their neighbors, and firmly established in their own principles, the Dispersion nevertheless were learning from the nations. Wherever they were, climate, landscape, business, politics, and religion were strange; but they were observant, and quickly proved their genius for adjustment. Many of them became traders, middlemen, and bankers,[67] gained considerable wealth, and thus attained a new economic level. This in itself was revolutionary. It provided a more abundant food supply, that increased the stamina and stimulus for new adventures, that opened up new social and intellectual horizons. Not a few turned to intellectual pursuits and succeeded as teachers, scholars, artists, scientists, and lawyers.[68] Some of those drafted into the army became competent and trusted military leaders (Jos. *C. Ap.*, II, 5), while others learned the ways of society, graced the court circles, and became the confidants of kings (Neh. 1:11-2:1).

Wherever they were they became familiar with the language, the customs, and the philosophy of the peoples, and through succeeding generations their responses, though slow, were far-reaching. Many in Babylonia learned the folklore, mythology, and priestly practices of their masters and passed them on to Judaism. Under Persian rule homage was paid to the priests of Zoroaster,[69] and the doctrine of dualism was accepted to the satisfaction of some late Jewish writers. That Greek language and philosophy captured many

64 E. Schürer, *HJP*, II, 1, 23, 24, 32. Ed. Bevan, *The Legacy of Israel*, 29–67.

65 Freedom from military service, when desired, from military taxes, and other imposts, the privilege of self-government, freedom of religion, and, no less important, the decree of Julius Caesar making Judaism a legal religion (J. Juster, *Les Juifs dans l'empire Romain*, I, 213–245, 358–365, 409–413; E. Schürer, *HJP*, II, ii, 244, 245, 253–263).

66 E. Schürer, *HJP*, II, ii, 273–275.

67 The story of the wealth of the Jewish colony in South Central Babylonia is graphically portrayed in Graetz, *Hist. Jews*, II, 502–530. The activities of Joseph the taxgatherer and Hyrcanus his son are illustrative.

68 J. Juster, *Les Juifs dans l'empire Romain*, II, 297–326. The names of Philo, Zeno, and Josephus are known throughout the world.

69 Graetz, *Hist. Jews*, II, 524–526.

of the Jewish faith is beyond question.[70] The honored place given the Septuagint; the work of Philo, who found Moses to be a Greek philosopher, but the greatest and the best; and the numerous Jewish booklets, such as the Wisdom of Solomon, that were expositions of Greek thought—all such are testimony that many Jews adjusted their ancestral ideas most remarkably to the intellectual formulas of their day.

The Dispersion was thus in the process of forming a new pattern of organization. While centrifugal forces were at work producing diversity, the centripetal pull of a common heritage and a common center (Jerusalem) was operating to bind all together in a vital unity. In these tensions the corporate life of each community, which in a measure was thrown on its own inner resources, became a contributing factor to growing Judaism. This development of the inner life of the individual community can be here suggested only as it bears somewhat directly on religion.

The religious inheritance of the Dispersion was by no means meager. In addition to circumcision and the food taboos, the old religious festivals could and would be observed by most of those in the far land. Passover, that opened with the mystic meal [71] (Exod. 12:1–14), united them in imagination with the founders of the nation, who had escaped from the Egyptian servitude. Pentecost lasted but one day (two in some places), but no work was done and it was a holy convocation, when in spirit the lonely Jew was united with an innumerable fellowship throughout the whole world. Tabernacles, when for seven days all lived in booths, brought to memory the assurances of the Sinaitic covenant. These festivals were all joyous occasions, and it is probable that at an early date Psalms 113–118, 120–134 were used at the festival of tabernacles [72] in jubilant thanksgiving for the overflowing goodness of Yahweh to his people during the year.

The Sabbath, however, was the great day for all members of the Dispersion. Religious festivals were primitive and commonplace, but a day devoted to rest, fellowship, and worship was novel. Like the synagogue, it had developed during the days of the Babylonian captivity in response to the pressing needs of the exiles. The standardization of the worship was gradual, but must have approximated its final form by the beginning of the Christian era.

Every Sabbath evening, at the sound of the shofar, all work stopped.[73] There was no harvesting, no trading, no traveling until after sundown on the Sabbath (Saturday evening). All went home for the evening meal, which was a religious function. The mother, who was the queen of the home, after

[70] Fr. Cumont, *CAH*, XI, 639–649. G. A. Jülicher, "Hellenism," *Ency. Bibl.* E. Hatch, *The Influence of Greek Ideas and Usages on the Christian Church.* M. S. Enslin, *Christian Beginnings,* 78–98. A. Causse, *Du Groupe ethnique à la communauté religieuse,* 318–325.

[71] G. F. Moore, *Judaism,* II, 40–48; III, 174.

[72] Abrahams and Singer, *Prayer Book,* 109–122, 137–142, cxx–cxxxiv, cxlv–cxlviii.

[73] Nehemiah 13:16, 19; 10:31; Exodus 35:2; Genesis 2:3. *Tractate Shabbath,* translated by W. O. E. Oesterley, lists thirty-nine prohibitions. See also Jubilees 2:26–35; 50:6–13.

the first blast of the shofar had lit the candle, a symbol of joy, and pronounced a benediction.[74] She then placed the repast on the table, and, when all arrayed in their best apparel were seated, the father recited in Hebrew the authorized grace over the bread, and then over the wine. No matter how humble the home the meal was a memorable ritual, and the home, the entrance of which was always protected by the mezuzah,[75] had become a domestic sanctuary.

The synagogue service,[76] similar to that arranged for the home, provided for the development of a vigorous and intelligent religious life. Before the destruction of Jerusalem, among the four to seven million Jews of the Dispersion there were more than a thousand synagogues, each a center and symbol of the aspiration and the resourcefulness of the Jewish community. Numerically they were important, but their attitude and spirit far outweighed their numbers. The local synagogue had control over civil affairs, and directed the programs of worship and education. Important as the civil functions of the synagogue were in the disciplines of democracy and the development of trained leadership,[77] our interest lies in the fields of worship and education.

Evening worship, which often followed the evening meal, as it had no relation to any temple service was more or less voluntary. Morning worship, which was synchronized with, and duplicated or imitated so far as possible, the temple ritual, was profoundly impressive and was shared in by every devout Jew. They could not offer sacrifices save by proxy, but all could offer the bullocks of their lips (Hos. 14:2) as acceptable substitutes. While there was always some flexibility in the order of the service, it is agreed that even before the fall of the city a general pattern that expressed the genius of Judaism was in general use.[78] The following outline is an approximation to the program of morning worship in the synagogues at the beginning of our era: Opening with a Psalm [79] or a prayer of thanksgiving, the *Shema' Yisrael,* which may be called

---

[74] An appropriate and beautiful benediction (Abrahams and Singer, *Prayer Book,* cxviii, cxix. *Tractate Shabbath,* xi.

[75] The mezuzah, a roll on which was written in Hebrew the *Shema' Yisrael* (Deut. 6:4–9; 11:13–21; Num. 15:37–41), enclosed in a metal or glass case and fastened on top of the doorframe or to the right-hand doorpost. It was a reminder of the importance of instruction in the home; but it often became a charm equivalent to blood sprinkled on the doorpost.

[76] Synagogue has two meanings. It means the building used by the community for its gatherings, which were chiefly religious. It was provided with a reading desk and an ark, in which were kept the sacred rolls. In a sense it was a substitute for the temple. It is also the term for the community organization. It was the product of the Dispersion, and its origin and functions are suggested in the following: I. J. Peritz, "Synagogue," *Ency. Bibl.* Margolis and Marx, *Hist. Jew. People,* 208–211. K. Köhler, *Origins of the Synagogue and the Church,* 14–17. E. Schürer, *HJP,* II, II, 243–256. G. F. Moore, *Judaism,* I, 284–306; II, 12–15.

[77] C. G. Montefiore, *Hib. Lec's.,* 389.

[78] E. Schürer, *HJP,* II, II, 75–88. G. H. Box, *ERE,* XII, 595a. H. Loewe, *ERE,* XII, 806b.

[79] The Psalms formed so important a part in the synagogue worship that it seems likely that many of them owe their origin directly to this service (R. T. Herford, *The Pharisees,* 96–103; R. H. Pfeiffer, *Introduction to the O.T.,* 620–630; W. O. E. Oesterley, *The Psalms in the Jewish Church,* 142–147). Forty-seven of the Psalms now found in books four and five (90–106; 107–150) are in the Jewish Prayer Book edited by Abrahams and Singer.

the Jewish creed, was then recited. After a benediction, the eighteen benedictions or part of them were repeated. Then came the reading of the prescribed section of the law [80] by those appointed, then the prophetic section was read, on which there might be a homily, if any member or visitor present were deemed competent. In this way from three to six people, apart from the chief officials, often took part. Blessing by the head, praises by the assembly, and the pronouncement of the Aaronic blessing (Num. 6:24–26) completed the worship.

Certain features are noteworthy. Contrary to what might be expected among the Dispersion it was a joyous hour of worship, which opened and closed with praise, thanksgiving, and benediction. The joy of the Lord was their strength (Neh. 9:8–10). Further, all the service, as well as the worshipers (Dan. 6:10; Tob. 3:11–13), was oriented toward the temple, and historically and emotionally all was linked up with idealized ancestral achievement. Throughout all there was a marked emphasis on ideas. The creed (Deut. 6:4–9, et al.) was always in the forefront, and the scroll of the law, so carefully guarded in the ark and so reverently spread out on the reading desk, was the visible sign of that which was eternal. Thus it was that in the synagogue worship and teaching were inseparable yokefellows.

Education in religion was but an extension of the synagogue worship among the Dispersion. The memorization of the Shema' Yisrael, which was considered the crystallization of the law, and the eighteen benedictions, many of which were in daily use, was a fundamental requirement. In these the three cardinal points of Judaism, monotheism, the Torah, a revealed religion, and Israel, the chosen people, were central.

To teach the law was an obligation as old as Deuteronomy (Deut. 6:7; 11:9), and the new lawbook of 400 B.C. enlarged the responsibilities. Long before the end of the period, the teaching profession, which was open to anyone, layman or Levite, who had an accurate knowledge of the law, was, though unpaid,[81] one of the most honored in the nation.[82] Most communities had established elementary schools for the instruction of the youth in the fundamentals of Judaism before the beginning of the Christian era. So thoroughgoing was this program that as early as 100 B.C. in Jerusalem, at least, this elementary education was compulsory for all boys between the ages of six and sixteen, while it was optional for girls.[83] So consistently was this policy carried out that Jose-

[80] The Pentateuch was so divided that it would be read in the synagogues in three years, and the portion read on important Sabbaths synchronized with the special features in the temple service. The Prophets were also so arranged that the reading for the day was appropriate to the reading from the law, and to the practice in the temple.

[81] As the law was sacred the teacher should not take hire for interpreting it. He should gain his livelihood by some trade. But sometimes he was paid for teaching secular subjects (Margolis and Marx, Hist. Jew. People, 210; E. Schürer, HJP, II, 1, 317).

[82] G. F. Moore, Judaism, I, 316, 322. E. Schürer, HJP, II, 1, 323–326.

[83] G. F. Moore, Judaism, I, 316–326; III, 104.

phus could boast, "For our people, if anyone do but ask any of them about our laws, he will more readily tell them all, than he will tell his own name" (*C. Ap.,* II, 19).

Talmudic schools for advanced study, which included the oral law, flourished under famous teachers in great centers such as Nisibis, Nehardea, Babylon, Alexandria, Rome, Jerusalem, and then Jamnia and Tiberias. These were oases of learning in which the law, written and oral, was memorized, and discussed in its manifold implications as a way of life.[84] From such centers there spread to the far distant communities zeal for the law and reverence for scholarship, so that the study of the law was believed to be a foretaste of immortal life.[85] Sharp conflicts in interpretation, however, between schools situated amid dissimilar cultures, or even between members of the same school, were not uncommon. But with patience, the wisdom of neighboring teachers, or the counsel of the Sanhedrin in the Holy City, that always assumed a degree of patriarchal responsibility, dissensions were usually resolved or moderated, while essentials of the law gained in clarity and emphasis.

Even the Sanhedrin and the scholars in Jerusalem were never all of one mind in interpreting the law. From about 150 B.C. to A.D. 70 tradition reports that in this central seat of Jewish learning there were *five pairs* [86] of teachers, or scribes, that is, there were two schools of thought fundamentally opposed to each other. Both were named after renowned leaders who had been active during the last half of the first century B.C., Shammai,[87] who was severely legalistic, and Hillel, who was guided by human interests. In the "war of the schools" controversies on 316 questions are recorded, and some of them were never settled. However, elementary schools in every synagogue throughout the Roman Empire, and the Talmudic schools in the great world capitals, with students seriously at work studying and teaching the divine law of the one and only God, not only united Judaism in a vital organism,[88] but made such an impression on the Gentile world that proselytes by the thousands sought to become sons of the law. Even after the disasters of 70 and A.D. 135 high and low flocked to Judaism [89] until prohibited by Rome. This amazing movement, which usually brought hardship to the convert, was the highest tribute to the

---

[84] G. F. Moore, *Judaism,* I, 102–107. E. Schürer, *HJP,* II, 1, 330–339. R. T. Herford, *The Pharisees,* 53–87; 108–114.

[85] L. Finkelstein, *The Religion of Democracy,* 12.

[86] The five pairs, or five yokes, are named in Pirke Aboth 1:4–18. E. Schürer, *HJP,* II, 1, 351–365.

[87] Shammai, see J. Abelson, "Shammai," *ERE,* XI; Hillel, E. G. Hirsch, "Hillel," *ERE,* VI; E. Schürer, *HJP,* II, 1, 351–379.

[88] The integrating power of ideas and worship is emphasized by J. Wach, *Sociology of Religion,* 33–44.

[89] Among the most notable proselytes were Izates, Prince of Adiabene, and Helen his mother; Fulvia, the wife of a Roman senator; Flavius Clemens, nephew of Domitian; Aquilla, a wealthy nobleman from Pontus. For an early missionary movement see J. Morgenstern, *JBL,* March, 1945, 15–37. For history of the later movements, Margolis and Marx, *Hist. Jew. People,* 207, 289, 290; E. Schürer, *HJP,* II, II, 303–327; Graetz, *Hist. Jews,* II, 215–219, 383–392, 433, 562.

inherent worth of Judaism, as represented by the teacher rather than by the priest. The influence on Judaism of this influx cannot be estimated. But that it affected the blood stream is certain; and strict though new converts may have been, not all of their inherited ideas could have been uprooted. Thus to both the racial and the religious structure of Judaism the proselytes in all probability made some worth-while contribution.

The destruction of the temple in A.D. 70 was a tragic blow to the aspirations of world-wide Jewry. To the Dispersion it was a calamity. The city of their dreams was wiped out. Their hope of visiting the temple and on the day of the atonement gazing on the high priest when in his glory he came from the holy place, and hearing his benediction over all Israel had vanished in the wake of the terrors of war. But they were not altogether desolate. They still had the school and the synagogue, the Sabbath worship, circumcision, the Torah, the growing hope of the world to come, and theirs was the one and only God. Dreams had passed, realities remained; and in their long years away from the city they had learned to worship without the aid of priest or temple.

To the Jew at home, who lived through the mad horrors and saw the priest slain at the altar, the temple burned and wrecked, the golden altar of incense, the golden candlestick, and the book of the law carried as trophies of war to Rome, it must have seemed the collapse of Judaism, the end of religion. But even here not all was lost. There was a scroll that was more meaningful than the altar, a spirit that could outlive the temple, and a small band of men who rose above the ruins to fashion a more lasting way of worship than that of Solomon or of Herod.

Rabbi Johanan ben Zakkai,[90] even before the fall of the city, because he had no political interests was permitted by Titus to leave Jerusalem and set up a school at Jamnia. Here he remained as head of the school probably from 70 to 90 A.D., to be succeeded by Gamaliel II (A.D. 90–110),[91] who was followed by Akiba (A.D. 110–135).[92] This school, when all seemed lost, gave direction to Judaism and in no small measure determined her destiny. Four developments, each of crucial importance to the future of religion, were completed during this period. Ben Zakkai probably contributed to each one of these, but the school as a whole was responsible for the final achievements.

Ben Zakkai himself founded in Jamnia the Beth-Din [93] or the Court of Justice, which, without legal authority but by common consent, was soon

---

90 Ben Zakkai belonged to the school of Hillel, and to the peace party, so that it was the part of wisdom to escape from the city when the nationalist party was hunting down the less belligerent Jews (Margolis and Marx, Hist. Jew. People, 205, 206; E. Schürer, HJP, II, 1, 365–367; Graetz, Hist. Jews, II, 323–333).

91 Margolis and Marx, Hist. Jew. People, 206–208. Graetz, Hist. Jews, II, 334–350, 363, 364.

92 Akiba became an extreme nationalist, proclaiming Bar Choziba the Messiah (Bar Cochba, Num. 24:17) (E. N. Adler, "Akiba," ERE, I; Margolis and Marx, Hist. Jew. People, 213–215; Graetz, Hist. Jews, II, 350–359, 381, 408–410; H. Loewe, ERE, VII, 594).

93 E. Schürer, HJP, I, II, 273–277. Graetz, Hist. Jews, II, 325, 360.

acknowledged the chief Jewish judiciary in the homeland, and in large measure by those among the nations.[94] This council provided for the ordination of teachers, that is, rabbis, and for the succession of its presiding officers. Thus an authoritative Jewish council was set up outside the Holy City. This was a step toward liberating Judaism from the soil of Palestine[95] and preparing it for the future.

A second forward step was taken when the disciples of both Shammai and Hillel were united in one school.[96] The law was thus settled by weight of argument in conference; and co-operation began to take the place of partisan action. Final decisions, when reached, were by majority vote, or by the Bath-Qol,[97] the voice from heaven. A revealing illustration of the spirit of the court is worth pondering. It is said that after a certain problem had been debated in the school for three and a half years the Bath-Qol was heard saying, "The teaching of both schools is the word of the living God, but in practice the Halakhah of Hillel is to be followed."[98] This union of the schools, and the patient review of problems with a growing awareness of the pertinent facts, integrated the diverse parties in Judaism into a working, religious democracy.

Further, it was officially decided that the oral law was valid alongside the written law. Ben Zakkai is reported to have gathered together these oral decisions and to have laid down rules for interpretation, but to Akiba belongs the glory of having codified them and developed the allegorical method of interpretation so that it was put beyond doubt that the oral law was in agreement with that which was written.

No less memorable was the decision of the council that met in a garret in Lydda in A.D. 135. The situation was desperate beyond words. All that the nationalists, Bar Cochba and Akiba, had fought for was lost; a Roman colony would occupy the new city Aelia Capitolina, and Jupiter would be worshiped on the old temple site. Circumcision, Sabbath observance, study and practice of the law were banned on pain of death. The council, among whom was

---

[94] This council controlled the religious calendar for the set festivals and the observance of the new moon (Graetz, *Hist. Jews,* II, 325, 360). It aided in organizing the worship, providing teachers, and settling difficult questions among the Dispersion (E. Schürer, *HJP,* I, II, 275–277). While the heads of various schools abroad ruled within their own provinces, even exercising the right of excommunication (Graetz, *Hist. Jews,* II, 337), and at times were restive (Solo Baron, *The Jewish Community,* 140–145, 150–155), yet this council was usually admitted to be the head of Judaism (Graetz, *Hist. Jews,* II, 552). After the patriarchate was abolished in A.D. 425 the headship passed from Palestine to other lands (Margolis and Marx, *Hist. Jew. People,* 230; Graetz, *Hist. Jews,* II, 612, 618).

[95] That Judaism was not necessarily bound up with the temple and the land seems to have been recognized by Ben Zakkai, and that the move to Jamnia released religion from the rite of burnt offerings and rendered it independent, is the conviction of Graetz, *Hist. Jews,* II, 324, 325.

[96] Margolis and Marx, *Hist. Jew. People,* 206.

[97] Bath-Qol, literally "daughter of the voice," that is, the divine voice (G. F. Moore, *Judaism,* I, 85). The rabbis hesitated to use the *Thus saith Yahweh* of the prophets, but still felt the need of some mystery to support their decisions.

[98] Graetz, *Hist. Jews,* II, 337. G. F. Moore, *Judaism,* I, 85.

Akiba, faced the life or the death of Judaism. Some insisted that the law was the revealed will of God, and that death was preferable to its slightest infringement. Others held that the law was given to live by, not as a means of death. The decision·was that in order to avoid death all laws save idolatry, adultery, and murder might be broken.[99] It is noteworthy that only one of these, idolatry, and that only rarely, might in any way interfere with the most drastic demands of Rome. This action of the council, composed of the most noted rabbis left in the land, though fewer than the usual seventy, was in line with earlier practice. The law had not been considered final or infallible. The Sabbath law had been changed to permit fighting in self-defense.[100] Life in such a case was rated more important than the letter of the law. The law of the release of a debt on the sabbatical year (Deut. 15:1–11) became a dead letter by the *Prosbol*[101] of Hillel in which the debt was given over to the Council of Elders, who collected it. Here self-interest outweighed both the letter and the spirit of the law. Rabbi ben Zakkai is reported to have changed or annulled nine laws, at least two of them, the test for adultery and the sin offering, because they could not be enforced.[102] The council of Lydda by adding to earlier precedents aided in establishing the principle that the law was made for man and not man for the law.

The religion of Judaism, so paradoxical and so complex, and hence so difficult to define, by A.D. 135 had been reduced to what may be considered the essentials. Three hundred years of horror, of mass murder and national suicide, by ridding her of factions that refused to assimilate, and of accretions that were detrimental, had freed her creative spirit for new undertakings.

Though the child of a thousand years, Judaism was neither the sum total of all preceding movements[103] nor the equivalent of any one of them. Indebted to all, those elements that were eliminated, as well as those that were accepted, without pressing language too far, it was a new corporate entity[104] in the field of religion. Vestigial remnants remained, and from time to time became active and were the cause of trouble, but they were not the body.

Three changes, observable in the physical world, marked the end of the old

99 Graetz, *Hist. Jews*, II, 421–427.

100 I Macc. 2:34–42. Jos. *Ant.*, XII, VI, 2; XIV, IV, 2. E. Schürer, *HJP*, I, 1, 322, 323; I, II, 234; II, II, 105.

101 Graetz, *Hist. Jews*, II, 100. E. Schürer, *HJP*, II, 1, 362.

102 Graetz, *Hist. Jews*, II, 229, 240, 326.

103 It is a popular assumption that Judaism is that creative idealism that stemmed from Abraham, was clarified by Moses, and wrought by prophets, priests, and sages into a final, homogeneous product as expressed in the Scripture and in oral tradition (K. Köhler, "Judaism," *JE;* also *Jewish Theology*, 7–18). This fails to acknowledge the errors and the imperfections that were rejected in the progress of religion.

104 That this was the beginning of a new epoch in the religious history of Israel is emphasized by R. H. Charles, *Apocrypha and Pseudepigrapha*, II, vi–xi; C. G. Montefiore, *Outlines of Liberal Judaism*, 280, 314. Others, emphasizing continuity, insist that Judaism was not essentially changed at this time (G. F. Moore, *Judaism*, I, 44; III, 17–22; F. C. Burkitt, *The Gospel History and Its Transmission*, 169–174). The difference lies in the approach.

and the beginning of the new. Jerusalem, as the motivating center of Judaism, gave way to a world-wide horizon. Not only was the Holy City no longer holy save in memory, but the center of gravity, long leaning away from Judea, was shortly transferred to that outer world. The Dispersion, in numbers and wealth, had long outweighed those in the homeland ten or twenty to one; and in scholarship, in loyalty to the law, and in character they were no whit behind residents of Palestine.[105] While a temple tax was sent by all loyal Jews to the homeland for the teachers of the law until the fourth century A.D.,[106] and by common consent the school at Tiberias was recognized as a sort of High Court until A.D. 425,[107] when the patriarchate was abolished, at the same time the Dispersion, its problems, and its interests dominated the stage. Thus the religion of Israel, as at Sinai (Exod. 33:14-16), as in Jeremiah's counsel to the captives (Jer. 29:5-7, 12-14), and as in the mission of the Servant in Deutero-Isaiah (Isa. 42:1-4; 49:5, 6), ceased to be landlocked. The people rather than the place, history rather than geography, thereby gained first consideration. This, the result of the iron heel of Rome, was an incalculable boon to Judaism.[108] Religion tied to the soil is in its very nature self-destructive;[109] and an emphasis on a *holy* [110] land is a reversion to peasant religion. History in a drastic way has proved that a Jewish center was not essential to enable the genius of Judaism to assert itself.[111]

The temple lay in ruins, and without an altar the priest had no function. The sacrificial system, so central in the state-church religion, in its most important details was prohibited by Rome. Among the Dispersion, the cultus element had long played only a secondary role, and the synagogue, the Torah, and the teacher, all functioning for generations, were able and ready to meet the emergency. By means of these, the Sabbath worship, the study of the law, in which all participated, and the prestige of the teacher, Judaism now became more democratic, more intelligent, and more vital. By means of these services, not by the cultus which was her most primitive element, did she make her chief contribution to the world. What had seemed to many a disaster in reality proved to be an opportunity.

Nation and race, likewise, went into the discard. Race, meaning a people

[105] Mention need only be made of Judah ben Tabbai, Philo of Alexandria, and Hillel of Babylon. Following A.D. 135 seven of Akiba's pupils are reported to have gone to Nisibis and Nehardea (Graetz, Hist. Jews, II, 432).

[106] E. Schürer, HJP, I, II, 272, 277; II, II, 269, 290.

[107] Margolis and Marx, Hist. Jew. People, 230. At this date the last semblance of visible national organization disappeared.

[108] Not only did the Dispersion preserve the Jewish people as a people, but it safeguarded their religion and made them a world influence. This is one of the conclusions in an important monograph by President J. Morgenstern, of Hebrew Union College, Cincinnati, Nation, People, Religion, What Are We? 29, an address delivered on Oct. 16, 1943.

[109] P. Tillich, The Interpretation of History, 67-73.

[110] K. Marti, Religion of the O.T., 200, 215-218.

[111] H. Loewe, "Judaism," ERE, VII, 608.

whose ancestry all belonged to a common stock, without mixture of alien blood, is a fiction. It is true that following Nehemiah the priests endeavored to support and make effective such a theory in Judea. But not only pre-exilic history, as indicated earlier, but the multitude of proselytes made by the Dispersion, though strictly regulated, reduced the restriction of the priests to a dead letter.[112] Judaism was cultural, not racial, and the converts and their descendants would often be numbered among the most loyal Jews.[113]

Nationalism was also crushed.[114] The annihilation of the seditionists was a warning that islets which at the sword's point insisted on contravening the policy of the government could not long exist within the Roman Empire, and that claims of religion that invaded the rights of the state could not ultimately be tolerated. Rome, protecting four million Jews throughout her broad dominions, looked on Jewish demands in Palestine as petty tribalism aggravated by religious fanaticism, and acted accordingly. Judaism, plunged into the affairs of state by her most rabid, literal-minded devotees, had overstepped her mission, and had failed. Every recrudescence of nationalism, whether under the name of religion or politics, has brought misfortune to the Jews and disaster to Judaism.[115] Religion was being taught to render unto Caesar the things that are Caesar's. Pagan Rome, in insisting on emperor worship,[116] which offended none save the monotheists, had entered the realm of conscience, and also had failed. The state was learning to render unto God the things that are God's.

Judaism, reduced as it was to extremes, had, however, lost nothing of its creative force. Monotheism, which was its very *raison d'être*,[117] had not been impaired by contact with the nations; and long years of suffering and reflection had but deepened and enriched its idea of God. Judaism, however, cannot be identified with a system of theology, for essentially it was a religion of the people, a way of life, guided by the Torah as interpreted by her teachers. That the conduct of life was its primary concern is vouched for by two witnesses:

---

112 In the time of the Second Jewish Commonwealth there was no pure Jewish race (S. Zeitlin, *Sec. Com.*, 21–30).

113 Aquilla and Helen of Adiabene are well known illustrations.

114 The idea of an independent Jewish state has been so seldom advocated that it can be said to have been almost dropped (C. W. Emmet, *ERE*, VIII, 581). At the same time modern Zionism has developed a nationalism that is independent of religion (H. Loewe, *ERE*, VII, 607). During the intervening centuries numerous Messiahs have appeared among the Jews, usually with unfortunate results (A. M. Hyamson, "Messiahs (Pseudo-)," *ERE*, VIII, 581–588).

115 A very judicious treatment of Judaism by a leading Jewish authority is found in "Judaism," *ERE*, VII, 581–609, by H. Loewe, esp. 608.

116 The institution of emperor worship is briefly discussed by A. D. Nock, in *CAH*, X, 481–503.

117 Physiological inheritance has often bulked large in Jewish thought, but her great teachers have usually recognized that the implications of monotheism transcend race and nation (C. G. Montefiore, *JQR*, XII, 177–194; H. Loewe, *ERE*, VII, 607). Two recent brochures emphasize the same conclusion: S. Zeitlin, *The Jews: Race, Nation, or Religion?* Philadelphia, Dropsie College for Hebrew and Cognate Learning, 1936, and J. Morgenstern, *Nation, People, Religion, What Are We?* Hebrew Union College, Cincinnati, Oct., 1943.

the prophetic teaching [118] of justice, mercy, and good will toward one's neighbor; and the innumerable minute regulations [119] prescribed for daily guidance. Hence the ethical principles of the prophets were co-ordinated with the rules of the lawgiver.

The Torah, comprising the law, the prophets, the writings, and the Talmud, was complex, preserving rules and decisions from all periods of history, and was inclusive, inasmuch as by allegorical interpretation the alert teacher could find Egyptian and Babylonian mythology, Greek philosophy, and Roman law implicit in Moses. Two desirable objectives were thus united. The law was believed to be a perfect and final revelation of the will of God, written in heaven from before the foundation of the world.[120] This promoted a sense of security among the people. The ebb and flow of history were incidental, but the law was eternal and their destiny was sure. The second fact is that the interpretation of the law could be progressive. By the decision of a chief rabbi or of a competent council changes could be made as needed.[121] Thus the Halakhah, that is, the rules of conduct, were elastic.

The teachers (rabbis) in the schools and their disciples in a thousand synagogues in every center throughout the Empire were the instructors in the Torah. They had long guided the Dispersion in the rules for personal and social conduct, and in an understanding of the world order. They had taught them to sing the songs of Zion in strange tongues and in strange lands, and had led them to worship, in spirit and in truth, the God who tabernacled in the hearts of good men everywhere. They had been the bearers of light to the Gentiles. Their lofty ethical ideals, their appealing philosophy, and their missionary zeal had been rewarded by many proselytes,[122] who forsook paganism for the better way. Thus Judaism, the religion of the book, and of a people scattered to the four corners of the earth but united in allegiance to the one God, was well equipped to succeed in the struggle of existence. By losing its life as a nation, it saved itself as a religion. Happy was the man whose delight was in the law of the Lord, in whose law he meditated day and night.

[118] In rabbinic teaching repentance, restitution, conciliation, and confession must always precede the sin offering (A. Büchler, *Studies in Sin and Atonement in Rabbinic Literature*).

[119] There were 613 rules of conduct largely of a ceremonial nature (D. M. Kay, *ERE*, VII, 608).

[120] K. Köhler, *Jewish Theology*, 1–6: the law was perfect and permanent. H. Loewe, *ERE*, VII, 607, 608: the law though changed was never abandoned. E. Schürer, *HJP*, II, 1, 307, 344: according to tradition it originated in heaven.

[121] H. Loewe, *ERE*, VII, 608.

[122] Judaism was a missionary religion from the early days of the exile until, under Christian influence, it was restricted by Alexander Severus (A.D. 222–225) and finally prohibited in A.D. 325 by Constantine (Margolis and Marx, *Hist. Jew. People*, 229, 291; Graetz, *Hist. Jews*, II, 433, 562–563; E. Schürer, *HJP*, II, II. 304–327).

APPENDICES

ABBREVIATIONS

Abbreviations for books of the Bible, Apocrypha, and Pseudepigrapha are those in general use. Those used for individual volumes follow the title of each as listed in the Bibliography.

Miscellaneous

A.T., AT. *Alte Testament*
AV. Authorized Version.
c. with.
C.C. Covenant Code.
cf. compare.
chap. chaps. chapter, chapters.
D. Deuteronomic Code.
E. Ephraimitic document.
ed. editor.
e.g. for example.
esp. especially.
H.C. Holiness Code.
J. Judean document.
LOT. Literature of the Old Testament.
LXX. Septuagint.
MS. MSS. Manuscript, Manuscripts.
MT. Massoretic Text (Hebrew).
O.T., OT. Old Testament.
P. Priest Code.
R.V. Revised Version (American translation).
Vol. Vols. Volume, Volumes.

Publications; Bible Dictionaries, Commentaries, Encyclopaedias, Journals, etc.

AASOR. Annual of the American School of Oriental Research.
AJArch. American Journal of Archaeology.
AJSL. American Journal of Semitic Languages.
AJTh. American Journal of Theology.
BASOR. Bulletin of the American School of Oriental Research.
Bib. Arch. The Biblical Archaeologist.
BW. The Biblical World.
CAH. Cambridge Ancient History.
Camb. B. Cambridge Bible for Schools and Colleges.
Cent. B. The Century Bible.
Ency. Bibl. Encyclopaedia Biblica.

ERE. Encyclopaedia of Religion and Ethics.
ET. Expository Times.
Expos. The Expositor.
Harv. Th. Rev. Harvard Theological Review.
HBD (one vol.). *Dictionary of the Bible, ed. Jas. Hastings. Complete in one volume.*
HBD. (five vols.). *Dictionary of the Bible, ed. Jas. Hastings. Five volumes.*
HUCA. Hebrew Union College Annual.
Ill. L. News. Illustrated London News.
ICC. International Critical Commentary.
JAOS. Journal of the American Oriental Society.
JBL. Journal of Biblical Literature.
JE. Jewish Encyclopaedia.
JEg. Arch. Journal of Egyptian Archaeology.
Jos. Ant. F. Josephus, *The Antiquities of the Jews.*
Jos. Wars. F. Josephus, *The Wars of the Jews.*
Jos. C. Ap. F. Josephus, *Contra Apionem.*
JPOS. Journal of the Palestinian Oriental Society.
JQR. Jewish Quarterly Review.
J. Rel. Journal of Religion.
JRAS. Journal of the Royal Asiatic Society.
PEQ. Palestinian Exploration Quarterly.
Rev. bib. Revue biblique.
Rev. hist. et phil. Revue d'histoire et de philosophe religieuses.
Rev. hist. des rel. Revue de l'histoire des religions.
ZAW. Zeitschrift fur die Alttestamentliche Wissenschaft.
ZDMG. Zeitschrift der Deutschen Morgenlandischen Gesselschaft.
ZDPV. Zeitschrift des Deutschen Palestine-Vereins.

SELECTED BIBLIOGRAPHY

Most of the articles and not a few of the books referred to in the body of the book, as well as innumerable stimulating contributions, to Old Testament studies, have been omitted for lack of space. A more complete list may be found in R. H. Pfeiffer, *Introduction to the Old Testament*, 849–884. Abbreviations not already listed are found after the title of the volume.

The Meaning of Religion

AUBREY, E. E.	*Present Theological Tendencies.*
BIXLER, J. S.	*Religion for Free Minds.*
BRIGHTMAN, E. S.	*A Philosophy of Religion.*
BURTT, E. A.	*Religion in an Age of Science.*
DEWEY, JOHN	*A Common Faith.*
FERM, VERGILIUS	*The First Chapters in Religious Philosophy.*
HAYDEN, A. E.	*The Quest of the Ages.*
HOPKINS, E. W.	*Origin and Evolution of Religion.*
KNUDSON, A. C.	*Present Tendencies in Religion.*
MACINTOSH, D. C.	*The Problem of Religious Knowledge.*
———.	*The Pilgrimage of Faith in a World of Modern Thought.*
MOORE, G. F.	*The Birth and Growth of Religion.*
MORGAN, L. C.	*Emergent Evolution.*
PRATT, J. B.	*Naturalism.*
RALL, H. F.	*Christianity. An Inquiry into Its Nature and Truth.*
SCHMIDT, WM. (FATHER).	*The Origin and Growth of Religion.*
WHITEHEAD, A. N.	*Religion in the Making.*
WIEMAN, H. N., AND HORTON, W. M.	*The Growth of Religion.*

Primitive Culture, in General; Anthropology and Social Origins

BOAS, FR.	*Theory of Man.*
DURKHEIM, E.	*The Elementary Forms of Religious Life.*
———.	*The Rules of Sociologic Method.*
FARNELL, L. R.	*The Evolution of Religion.*
GALLOWAY, GEO.	*Beginnings and Growth of Religion.*
LOWIE, R. H.	*Primitive Religion.*
———.	*Culture and Ethnology.*
MALINOWSKI, B.	*The Dynamics of Cultural Change.*
MARETT, R. R.	*Anthropology.*
PRATT, J. B.	*Psychology of Religious Belief.*

RADIN, P.	*Primitive Man as Philosopher*
REINACH, S.	*Cultes, mythes, et religions (CMR).*
SHOTWELL, J. T.	*The History of History.* Two vols.
TILLICH, P.	*The Interpretation of History.*
TYLOR, E. B.	*Primitive Culture.*
WACH, JOACHIM.	*Sociology of Religion.*
WESTERMARCK, E. A.	*The Origin and Development of the Moral Ideas.*

Primitive Semitic and Arabic Culture

BARTON, G. A.	*Semitic and Hamitic Origins.*
BELL, GERTRUDE	*Syria, the Desert and the Sown.*
BERTHOLET, A.	*A History of Hebrew Civilization.*
CANAAN, T.	*Aberglaube und Volksmedizin.*
CONTENAU, G.	*La Civilization Phénicienne.*
DHORME, ED.	*La Religion des Hébreux nomades.*
DOUGHTY, CHARLES M.	*Arabia Deserta.* Third edition; one vol.
HITTI, P. K.	*History of the Arabs.*
HOOKE, S. H.	*The Origins of Early Semitic Ritual.*
HURGRONJE, S.	*Mecca.*
JAMES, E. O.	*Origins of Sacrifice.*
———.	*Primitive Ritual and Belief.*
JAUSSEN, J. A.	*Coutumes des Arabes au pays Moab.*
———.	*Naplouse et son district.*
LAGRANGE, M. J.	*Etudes sur les religions Sémitiques.*
LAWRENCE, T. E.	*Seven Pillars of Wisdom.*
MALINOWSKI, B.	"Magic, Science and Religion," in *Science, Religion and Reality,* ed., J. Needham.
MARGOLIOUTH, D.	*The Relations between Arabs and Israelites Prior to the Rise of Islam.*
MONTGOMERY, J. A.	*Arabia and the Bible.*
MUSIL, A.	*Manners and Customs of the Rwala Bedouins.*
———.	*Topographical Itineraries of Exploration in Arabia and Mesopotamia.* Six vols.
PHILBY, H. ST. JOHN.	*Arabia of the Wahhabis.*
———.	*The Heart of Arabia.*
RASWAN, C.	*The Black Tents of Arabia.*
RUTTER, ELDON	*The Holy Cities of Arabia.* Two vols.
SMITH, W. R.	*Lectures on the Religion of the Semites.* Third edition; ed., S. A. Cook. *(Rel. Sem.* 3).
THOMAS, BERTRAM.	*Arabia Felix.*
VAN LENNEP, H.	*Bible Lands; Their Customs and Manners.*
WELLHAUSEN, J.	*Reste arabischen Heidentums.*

Archaeology, as Related to Religion

ALBRIGHT, W. F.	*The Archaeology of Palestine and the Bible (Arch. P. and B.).*

———.	*Archaeology and Religion of Israel* (*Arch. and Rel.*).
———.	*From the Stone Age to Christianity.*
BARTON, G. A.	*Archaeology and the Bible.* Sixth edition. (*Arch. and Bib.*)
BENZINGER, I.	*Hebräische Archaeologie.*
BURROWS, M.	*What Mean These Stones?*
CONTENAU, G.	*Manuel d'archéologie Orientale.* Three vols.
COOK, S. A.	*The Religion of Ancient Palestine in the Light of Archaeology* (*Rel. Anc. Pal.*).
COOKE, G. A.	*North Semitic Inscriptions* (*NSI*).
COWLEY, A. E.	*Aramaic Papyri of the Fifth Century B.C.*
DRIVER, S. R.	*Modern Research as Illustrating the Bible.*
GARSTANG, J.	*The Foundations of Bible History.*
———.	*The Heritage of Solomon.*
GRANT, E. (Ed.).	*The Haverford Symposium on Archaeology and the Bible.*
GRESSMANN, H. (Ed.).	*Altorientalische Texte und Bilder zum AT.* Two vols.
JEREMIAS, A.	*The O.T. in the Light of the Ancient East.* Two vols.
KNUDTZON, J. A.	*Die el-Amarna Tafeln.*
McCOWN, C. C.	*The Ladder of Progress in Palestine.*
NOWACK, W.	*Lehrbuch der hebräischen Archaeologie.* Two vols.
PRICE, I. M.	*The Monuments and the Old Testament.*
ROGERS, R. W.	*Cuneiform Parallels to the Old Testament.*
VINCENT, H.	*Canaan d'après l'exploration récente.*

Introductions to the Old Testament

BEWER, J. A.	*The Literature of the Old Testament in Its Historical Development.*
CARPENTER, J. E., AND HARFORD-BATTERSBY, G.	*The Composition of the Hexateuch.*
CHAPMAN, A. T.	*An Introduction to the Pentateuch.*
CREELMAN, H.	*An Introduction to the Old Testament.* Chronologically arranged.
DRIVER, S. R.	*Introduction to the Literature of the Old Testament.* Ninth edition (*LOT*).
EISSFELDT, O.	*Einleitung in das AT., unter Einschluss der Apokryphen und Pseudepigraphen.*
FOSDICK, H. E.	*A Guide to Understanding the Bible.*
FOWLER, H. T.	*A History of the Literature of Ancient Israel.*
MEINHOLD, J.	*Einführung in das AT. Geschichte, Literatur und Religion Israels.*
PFEIFFER, R. H.	*Introduction to the Old Testament.*
SELLIN, E.	*Introduction to the Old Testament.*
STRACK, H. L.	*Einleitung in das AT, einschliesslich Apokryphen und Pseudepigraphen.* Sixth edition.

General Background: History, Geography, and Culture

BREASTED, J. H.	*Ancient Records of Egypt.* Five vols. (*BAR*)
———.	*A History of the Ancient Egyptians* (*Anc. Eg.*).
CHILDE, V. G.	*The Most Ancient East.*
DALMAN, G.	*Arbeit und Sitte.* Five vols.
DELAPORTE, L.	*La Mesopotamie.*
ERMAN, A.	*The Literature of the Ancient Egyptians.*
GOODSPEED, G.	*A History of the Babylonians and Assyrians.*
GORDON, C. H.	*The Living Past.*
JASTROW, MORRIS, JR.	"Religion of Babylonia," *HBD* (Five vols., extra vol.).
KING, L. W.	*Legends of Babylonia and Egypt in Relation to Hebrew Tradition.*
MEYER, ED.	*Geschichte des Altertums* (*Gesch. Alt.*).
OLMSTEAD, A. T.	*History of Palestine and Syria to the Macedonian Conquest.*
ROBINSON, E.	*Biblical Researches in Palestine.* Three vols.
ROBINSON, T. H., AND OESTERLEY, W. O. E.	*History of Israel.* Two vols.
ROGERS, R. W.	*History of Babylonia and Assyria.*
SMITH, G. A.	*Historical Geography of the Holy Land* (*HGHL*).
———.	*Jerusalem.* Two vols.
SMITH, SIDNEY	*Early History of Assyria.*
SPEISER, E. A.	*Mesopotamian Origins.*
STADE, B.	*Geschichte des Volkes Israel.* Two vols. (*GVI*)
WOOLLEY, C. L.	*Excavations at Ur and the Hebrew Records.*

The Religion (and Theology) of Israel (General)

ADDIS, W. E.	*Hebrew Religion to the Establishment of Judaism.*
DUFF, ARCH.	*The Theology and Ethics of the Hebrews.*
EICHRODT, W.	*Theologie des A.T.* Two vols.
FOWLER, A. T.	*The Origin and Growth of the Hebrew Religion.*
HÖLSCHER, G.	*Geschichte der israelitischen und judaischen Religion.*
KAUTZSCH, E.	"Religion of Israel," *HBD* (Five vols., extra vol.).
KITTEL, R.	*The Religion of the People of Israel.*
LÖHR, MAX.	*A History of Religion in the Old Testament.*
MARTI, K.	*The Religion of the Old Testament.*
MOORE, G. F.	*History of Religions.* Vol. II.
OESTERLEY, W. O. E., AND ROBINSON, T. H.	*Hebrew Religion: Its Origin and Development.*
OTTLEY, R. L.	*The Religion of Israel.*
PETERS, J. P.	*The Religion of the Hebrews.*
ROBINSON, H. WHEELER.	*The Religious Ideas of the Old Testament.*
SMEND, R.	*Lehrbuch der alttestamentlichen Religionsgeschichte.*
SMITH, H. P.	*The Religion of Israel.*
STADE, B.	*Biblische Theologie des Alten Testaments.* Two vols.

Pre-exilic Period: Socio-political Developments

ALBRIGHT, W. F. The Role of the Canaanites in the History of Civilization.

————. Studies to W. S. Leland, 1942, pp. 11–50.

BARON, S. W. A Social and Religious History of the Jews. Three vols.

BERTHOLET, A. A History of Hebrew Civilization.

BLUNT, A. W. F. Israel's Social and Religious Development.

BÖHL, F. M. T. Kananäer und Hebräer.

CARPENTER, S. C. Politics and Society in the Old Testament.

CAUSSE, A. Du Groupe ethnique à la communauté religieuse.

COOK, S. A. The Old Testament; a Reinterpretation.

CROSS, E. B. The Hebrew Family.

DAY, E. The Social Life of the Hebrews.

DUSSAUD, R. Les origines cananéenes du sacrifice israélite.

FLIGHT, J. W. "The Nomadic Idea and the Ideal in the Old Testament," JBL, 1923, 158–227.

GALLING, K. Die Israelitische Staatsverfassung in ihrer vorderorientalischen Umwelt.

GRAHAM, W. C., AND MAY, H. G. Culture and Conscience.

JACOBSON, D. The Social Background of the Old Testament (SBOT).

KENNETT, R. H. Ancient Hebrew Social Life and Custom.

MACDONALD, D. B. The Hebrew Literary Genius.

MEYER, ED. Die Israeliten und ihre Nachbarstämme.

PEAKE, H., AND FLEURE, H. J. The Law and the Prophets.

PEDERSEN, J. Israel: Its Life and Culture.

SCHAEFFER, H. Social Legislation of the Primitive Semites.

Pre-exilic Religious Development

BROWN, C. R. The Story Book of the Early Hebrews.

BUDDE, K. Religion of Israel to the Exile.

DHORME, ED. La Religion des Hébreux nomades.

GRAHAM, W. C. The Prophets and Israel's Culture.

KNUDSON, A. C. The Religious Teaching of the Old Testament.

LESLIE, E. A. Old Testament Religion in the Light of its Canaanite Background.

LODS, A. Israël des origines au milieu du viii. siècle.

MANSFIELD, G. C. The Book of Yahweh.

MEEK, T. J. Hebrew Origins.

NOYES, C. The Genius of Israel.

PATON, L. B. The Early Religion of Israel.

STRACHAN, J. Hebrew Ideals.

WELCH, A. C. The Religion of Israel under the Kingdom.

WOOD, W. C. "The Religion of Canaan," JBL, 1916, pp. 1–113, 164–279.

Pre-exilic Prophets

CORNILL, C. H.	*The Prophets of Israel.*
GORDON, A. R.	*The Prophets of the Old Testament.*
HÖLSCHER, G.	*Die Propheten.*
JAMES, FLEMING	*Personalities of the Old Testament.*
KITTEL, R.	*Gestalten und Gedanken in Israel.*
KNUDSON, A. C.	*Beacon Lights of Prophecy.*
MORGENSTERN, J.	*Amos Studies.* Vol. 1.
ROBINSON, T. H.	*Prophecy and the Prophets in Ancient Israel.*
SCOTT, R. B. Y.	*The Relevance of the Prophets.*
SKINNER, J.	*Prophecy and Religion. Studies in the Life of Jeremiah.*
SMITH, G. A.	*Jeremiah.*
SMITH, J. M. P.	*The Prophet and His Problems.*
———.	*The Prophets and Their Times.* Second edition by W. A. Irwin.
SMITH, W. R.	*The Prophets of Israel.*
WATERMAN, L.	"The Ethical Clarity of the Prophets," *JBL,* Sept., 1945, pp. 297–307.

Post-exilic Period

Volumes listed under Religion of Israel (General) as a rule cover post-exilic as well as pre-exilic religion.

Priests, Ritual, and Liturgy

BAUDISSIN, W. W.	"Priests and Levites," *HBD* (Five vols.).
———.	*Studien zur Semitischen Religionsgeschichte.* Vol. 2.
BLAU, J.	"Liturgy," *JE.*
DRIVER, S. R.	"Expiation and Atonement," *ERE,* Vol. 5.
FARNELL, L. R.	*The Evolution of Religion.*
GRAY, G. B.	*Sacrifice in the Old Testament.*
GUNKEL, H.	*What Remains of the Old Testament,* pp. 69–114.
HOSCHANDER, J.	*The Priests and the Prophets.*
JAMES, E. O.	*Origins of Sacrifice.*
JAMES, FLEMING.	*Thirty Psalmists.*
KENT, C. F.	*Israel's Laws and Legal Precedents (The Student's Old Testament).*
OESTERLEY, W. O. E.	*A Fresh Approach to the Psalms.*
———.	*Sacrifice in Ancient Israel.*
PETERS, J. P.	*The Psalms as Liturgies.*
WELCH, A. C.	*Prophet and Priest in Old Israel.*
WESTPHAL, G.	*Jahwes Wohnstätten nach den Anschauungen der alten Hebräer.*
WOOD, F. H.	"Priests and Levites," *HBD* (One vol.).

Wisdom and Problem Literature

BALL, C. J.	*The Book of Job.*
BALSCHEIT, B.	*Alter und Aufkommen des Monotheismus in der israelitischen Religion.*
BLANK, S. H.	"Studies in Post-Exilic Universalism," *HUCA*, 1936 (Vol. 11), 159–191.
CHEYNE, T. K.	*Jewish Religious Life after the Exile.*
———.	*Job and Solomon.*
DAVISON, W. T.	*The Wisdom Literature of the Old Testament.*
DILLON, E. J.	*The Sceptics of the Old Testament.*
FINKELSTEIN, L.	*The Religion of Democracy.*
GORDON, A. R.	"Wisdom," *ERE*, Vol. 12.
HEMPEL, J.	*Gott und Mensch im A.T. (Zweite Auflage).*
KENNETT, R. H.	*The Servant of the Lord.*
KÖHLER, K.	"Wisdom," *JE.*
MACDONALD, D. B.	*The Hebrew Philosophic Genius.*
PEAKE, A. S.	*The Problem of Suffering.*
TOY, C. H.	"Wisdom Literature," *Ency. Bibl.*
WORKMAN, G. C.	*The Servant of Jehovah.*

Nationalism and Eschatology

BRIGGS, C. A.	*Messianic Prophecy.*
BURKITT, F. C.	*Jewish and Christian Apocalypses.*
CADBURY, H. J.	*National Ideals in the Old Testament.*
CAUSSE, A.	*L'Evolution de l'esperance Messianique.*
CHARLES, R. H.	*A Critical History of the Doctrine of the Future Life.*
———.	"Eschatology," *Ency. Bibl.*, Vol. II.
DUHM, B.	*Das kommende Reich Gottes.*
FINKELSTEIN, L.	*The Pharisees*, Vol. 2.
GORDON, A. R.	*The Ancestral Hope of the Ages.*
GRESSMANN, H.	*Die Ursprung der israelitisch-jüdischen Eschatologie.*
HÖLSCHER, G.	*Die Ursprung der jüdischen Eschatologie.*
MOORE, G. F.	*Judaism*, Vol. II, 377–395.
SCHMIDT, N.	"The Origin of Jewish Eschatology," *JBL*, 1922, 102–114.

Judaism

ABRAHAMS, I., AND SINGER, S.	*The Authorized Daily Prayer Book.* Ninth edition.
BARON, S. W.	*The Jewish Community.*
BEVAN, EDWYN.	*Jerusalem under the High-Priests.*
———.	*The Legacy of Israel.*
BOUSSET, WM.	*Die Religion des Judentums im newtestamentlicher Zeitalter.* Second edition.
BURKITT, F. C.	*The Gospel History and Its Transmission.*

Causse, A.	Les Dispersés d'Israël.
———.	Du Groupe ethnique à la communauté religieuse.
Charles, R. H.	Apocrypha and Pseudepigrapha.
Duff, Arch.	History of the Religion of Judaism.
Enslin, M. S.	Christian Beginnings.
Fairweather, Wm.	Background of the Gospels.
Finkelstein, L.	The Pharisees. Two vols.
Friedländer, M.	Synagogue und Kirche im ihren Anfangen.
Graetz, Heinrich.	History of the Jews from the Earliest Times to the Present Day. Five vols. and index (Hist. Jews).
Herford, R. Travers.	The Pharisees.
Hughes, H. M.	The Ethics of Jewish Apocryphal Literature.
Juster, J.	Les Juifs dans l'empire Romain. Two vols.
Köhler, K.	Jewish Theology.
———.	Origins of the Synagogue and the Church.
Levinthal, I. H.	Judaism; an Analysis and Interpretation.
Loewe, H.	Judaism and Christianity.
Margolis, Max L. AND Marx, Alex.	A History of the Jewish People (Hist. Jew. People).
Montefiore, C. G.	The Origin and Growth of Religion, as Illustrated by the Ancient Hebrews. Hibbert Lectures, 1892 (Hib. Lec's.).
———.	Outlines of Liberal Judaism.
Moore, G. F.	History of Religions, Vol. II.
———.	Judaism. Three vols.
Morgenstern, J.	Nation, People, Religion, What Are We?
Oesterley, W. O. E., AND Box, G. H.	Religion and Worship in the Synagogue.
Riggs, J. S.	History of the Jewish People.
Schürer, E.	A History of the Jewish People in the Time of Jesus Christ. Five vols., second revised edition (HJP).
Toy, C. H.	Judaism and Christianity.
Zeitlin, S.	The History of the Second Jewish Commonwealth (Sec. Com.).
———.	The Jews; Race, Nation, or Religion?

INDEX OF SUBJECTS

Aaron, 48, 50 (n. 31), 53, 193, 196, 238
Abiathar, 145, 202
Abigail, 22
Abimelech, 12 (n. 14), 93
Abiram, 53
Abraham, 9, 11, 12 (n. 15), 57 (n. 51), 88, 102, 139, 175
Absalom, 12 (n. 14), 94 (n. 2)
Achan, 14
Adad, 32
Adultery, 190 (n. 15)
Agriculture, 87, 88
Agnostic, 180, 209
Agur, 209
Ahab, 111
Ahaz, 102, 135
Ahikam, 55
Ahimelech, 202
Ain-Kadeish, 37
Akiba, 256, 263, 265
Alcimus, 246
Aleppo, 72
Alexander, 234, 252
Allegorical interpretation, *see* Interpretation
Almighty, 192, 201, 205, 219; *see also* God
Altar, Sinai, 52; Canaanite, 87, 117; Solomon, 102; Ahaz, 102; Manasseh, 104; Ezekiel, 187; golden, 104 (n. 31); incense, 105, 146 (n. 6), 196, 199; Zeus, 223
Amalekites, 46, 53, 66, 139
Amarna tablet, no. 51, 96
Amon, 133
Amorites, 68, 69, 73
Amos, 121, 123, 160
Anat, 75 (n. 21), 79 (n. 40)
Anathoth, 145, 146, 150
Animism, 31, 81, 192, 195; *see also* Spirits
Anointing, 11, 96; *see also* Messiah
Antigonus, 252, 253
Antiochus IV, 223
Antipater, 249
Aperu, 44
Apocalypticism, 159, 209 (n. 2), 225, 231
Apocalypses, 224, 224 (n. 16), 227, 228
Apostasy, 139

Arabs (Seminomads), 7 (n. 3), 14 (n. 21), 24–26
Arabia, 7, 8, 8 (n. 4), 5, 9 (n. 8), 10 (n. 9), 10
Aramean, 16, 72
Archaeology, 6, 8 (n. 7), 44, 81, 82
Aristobulus, 248, 249, 252
Ark, 51, 60–64, 81, 83, 87, 107, 108
Armageddon, 222, 223
Asa, 115
Asherah, 75 (n. 21), 103, 115, 141
Ashtoreth, 76 (n. 24)
Ashur, 55, 124
Asmodeus, 226
Assyria, 133, 134, 141; *see also* Worship
Astarte, 75 (n. 21), 76 (n. 24), 103; *see also* Ishtar
Athaliah, 104, 110, 115, 116
Atonement, 195, 197, 198, 199; day of, 188, 198 (n. 37)
Authority, 3, 185, 191, 191 (n. 19), 216
Azazel, 187, 199

Baal, 55, 75
Baalat, 75
Baalism, 86, 89, 101, 102; *see also* Fertility cult
Baal-peor, 37, 70
Baal of Tyre, 110
Bab edh-Dra', 37, 74
Balaam, 36
Bar Cochba, 256, 257, 265
Baruch, 144, 148, 155, 166
Bath Qol, 191 (n. 19), 264
Beard, 11, 11 (n. 11), 22
Bedouin, 8 (n. 7), 17 (n. 28)
Beliar, 226
Benediction, 200
Beni-Hassan, 43
Benjamin, 16
Beth-Din, 263, 264
Beth Shemesh, 87
Bethel, 110
Bildad, 171
Blood, 19, 38, 39, 57; blood money, 17, 18; blood revenge, 15, 16, 17, 19, 135 (n. 1); blood-spirit, 38; blood-sprinkling, 197

Bridal week, 208
Brick making, 43, 44, 44 (n. 12)
Brotherhood, 57, 206, 210–215
Bull worship, 34, 64, 110
Burial customs, 73, 74
Burning bush, 49, 52
Burnt offering, 88, 197, 198; see also Offering

Caesar, Julius, 252
Cain, offering of, 86
Calebites, 53
Calendar, Jewish, 11
Canaan, 71, 72
Canaanite, culture, 72, 73, 74; see also Religion of
Canaanite language, 81; law, 135
Captivity, 155, 158
Captives, 163
Caravan routes, 10 (n. 10)
Carmel contest, 111, 112
Chastity, 21, 135 (n. 1), 136, 208
Chemosh, 13, 32, 55, 68, 124
Cherubim, 61, 63, 63 (n. 60), 107
Chronicler, 217, 239; facts idealized, 240
Chronicles, 24
Circumcision, 49, 201; banned, 223; forced on Itureans and S. Lebanese, 243
Concubinage, 16, 18, 85, 139, 203
Confession, 184
Congregation, 184, 200
Copyright law, 224
Covenant, Noah, 201; Abraham, Isaac and Jacob, 57 (n. 51), 139, 185, 201; Sinai, 54, 57, 150; Josianic, 141, 150; racial, 201; everlasting, 196, 201; new, 164, 165, 182; universal, 214; My covenant, 201
Covenant Code, 118 (n. 10)
Creation, 106
Cult practices, 35, 36, 38, 87; see also Ritual
Cyrus, 175, 213, 218

Dan, 110
Dances, sacred, 37
Daniel, 88, 90 (n. 18); Legends of, 226 (n. 21); Apocalypse of, 226
Dathan, 53
David, 94, 175, 240 (n. 23)
Davidic dynasty, 99, 217, 219, 220
Day of Yahweh, 222, 223, 228
Deborah, 21, 83, 84, 93, 94
Decalogue, ethical 128 (n. 7), 128, 135 (n. 1); ritual, 118, 124 (n. 3)
Democracy, 3, 110, 165, 6, 215, 260, 264, 266
Democratic, 133, 168, 212
Demon worship, see Sorcery
Dervish, 27, 27 (n. 79), 113

Deuteronomy, 65; composite, 135, 136, 139, 140, 142, 149; editor, 142 (see also Scribes); reform of, 139, 141, 142; philosophy of, 140, 143
Devil, 226, 230
Diaspora, 211, 218; see also Dispersion
Dinah, 17
Dispersion, 189, 198, 234; in Alexandria, 234; education, 257, 258; religion, 259, 266; see also Diaspora
Divination, 36, 138
Divorce, 20
Divorce court, 190, 211, 212
Documents, J, 48, 82 (n. 8), 116, 117; E, 48, 134
Dreams, 130, 161
Drink offering, 198
Dualism, 225, 226, 230

Earth, 101 (n. 18); see also Land
Ecstasy, 130
Editors, see Scribes
Edom, 53
Education, 140, 207, 261, 262
Eldad and Medad, 59
Eli, 52, 202
Elihu, 171 (n. 3)
Elijah, 110–114, 149, 160; at Horeb, 112; revolution of, condemned, 127
Eliphaz, 171
Elisha, 127
Ephod, 130, 200
Ephraim, 9, 45, 61 (n. 58), 69, 71; see also Joseph
Eschatology, 225
Espionage, 139
Essenes, 254
Eunuch, 214
Evil impulse, 226 (n. 20)
Exiles, 175, 176, 218
Exodus, date, numbers and tribes, 44–48, 52
Ezekiel, 166, 167
Ezion-geber, 95
Ezra, 189, 190

Family life, 91, 207, 212
Fat, burnt offering, 197
Fear, 34, 35
Feasts, sacred, 38
Fertility cult, 34, 47, 70, 75, 87, 103, 103 (n. 27), 124, 163; see also Baalism; Goddess; Isis-Osiris; Canaanite religion; Tammuz
Festival, 39; agricultural, 75, 102, 118, 135, 137; "set" festivals, 198
Fire offering, 197; see also Offerings

Firstborn, 118
Foreigners, 116, 117, 118, 136, 187, 212; see also Gentiles; Strangers; Law of

Gad, 53, 69
Gabriel, 226
Galilee, 254, 256 (n. 60)
Gamaliel II, 263
Gedaliah, 162
Gehazi, 127
Gehenna, 229
Genealogies, 25, 202, 240, 240 (n. 24)
Gentiles, 175, 213; see also Strangers; Foreigners
Gerousia, 246, 248, 250, 251
Gibeonites, 14, 24
Gideon, 83, 86–88, 93, 94
Gilgal, 74
God, incarnated in the tribe, 12; Lord of spirits, 230; Lord of life and glory, 230, 265; Most High, 171, 191, 201, 218, 227, 241, 243; moral qualities, 130, 170, 171; Sovereign, 172, 230; wonder-worker, 222; Unknown, 33, 39, 65; Holy One, 199; Omnipotent, 238; the Absolute Other, 192; the All, 244
Goddess, 32, 74; see also Anat; Baalat; Astarte; Ishtar; Fertility cult
Goshen, 43
Greek culture, 178, 180, 181, 210; see also Hellenism
Guest privileges, 18; see also Hospitality

Habakkuk, 151, 171, 173
Habiri, 8, 10, 69, 72
Hananiah, 148, 156, 158, 159, 217
Harlot, 125 (n. 4)
Harran, 9, 72, 152
Hasmonean, 253
Hassidim, 231, 246, 250, 254
Heaven, 173, 229
Hebrew, ancestors, 10, 202 (n. 44); language, 10, 11; see also Israel
Hell, 228, 229
Hellenism, 235, 236, 239, 245, 246, 249, 250
Herem (annihilation), 16, 18
Herod the Great, 252, 253, 254
Hexateuch, 183, 238; see also Pentateuch
Hezekiah, 64, 133, 154, 155
High Places, 87, 103, 141
High Priest, consecration, 194; costumes, 194, 195
Hilkiah, 135, 136
Hillel, 256 (n. 60), 262
Hittites, 41, 42, 71
Hobab, 49, 53

Horeb-Sinai, 37, 43, 52 (n. 32), 55, 139
Horites (Hurri), 71
Holiness, 60, 184, 185, 191, 192, 193
Holiness Code, 153, 183–185
Holy of Holies, 61, 101, 107, 187, 197
Holy People, 192, 193, 200
Holy Place, 83
Holy Land, 83, 162, 164, 167, 211
Holy Water, 195, 196
Honor, 17, 22
Hophni, 47
Hosea, 121, 123, 127, 147, 160
Hospitality, 10 (n. 9), 18, 22
Huldah, 19, 135
Human rights, 121, 122, 126
Hyksos, 43, 71, 74
Hyrcanus, 235, 236, 247, 248, 252

Idolatry, 138, 139, 141, 167, 169
Immortality, 229
Imprecations, 166
Incense, 105, 146 (n. 6), 196, 199
Incubation, 90 (n. 18)
Individualism, 13, 14, 144, 162, 164, 164 (n. 17), 167, 179
Injustice, 129, 167; see also Social ethics
Inquisition, 139
Internationalism, 129, 132
Interpretation, method, 4–6; allegorical, 5, 210, 267; Deuteronomic, 140, 143; Hellenistic, 181; priestly, 183, 188, 249; progressive, 191; symbols, 225 (n. 18)
Isaiah, 121, 123, 160
Ishmael, 18, 162, 163
Ishtar, 32, 77
Isis-Osiris, 42, 47, 77
Isolation, 139, 212
Israel, 45, 51, 61 (n. 58); mixed ancestry, 45, 47, 65, 67, 70; people of Yahweh, 140, 200; My servant, 175
Ittobaal, 110

Jacob, 175
Jannaeus, Alexander, 248
Jason, 234, 245
Jeconiah, 217
Jehoiakim, 152, 155, 156
Jehoiakin, 158
Jehoshaphat, 115
Jehu, 113, 118, 120, 125
Jephthah, 12 (n. 4), 84, 90, 93, 194
Jeremiah, 61, 62; book of, 144, 145, 156; heresy trial, 154, 155; life and message, 145–148, 163–173
Jericho, 72 (n. 10), 82
Jeroboam I, 63 (n. 60), 64, 110

Jeroboam II, 120, 125
Jerusalem, 74, 95, 101; Ezekiel's vision, 186, 187; captured, 161, 162, 256; a Roman colony, 256
Jethro, 49, 52, 53
Jezebel, 110
Joash, 115
Job, 88, 151, 171, 173
Jochebed, 50, 55
Joel, 223
Johanan, high priest, 234
John of Gischala, 256
Jonah, 213
Jonadab, 49
Jonathan, 247
Joseph, the tax gatherer, 235
Joseph tribes, 52; see also Ephraim
Joshua, high priest, 218, 219
Josiah, 133, 141, 145, 146, 152; reform of, 155
Judah, 152
Judas Maccabee, 246, 247
Justice, 229; see also Social ethics

Kenites, 43, 49, 53
King, deified, 47, 97, 99; mana possessed, 97, 98; begotten of God, 97; vice-regent of Yahweh, 98; a priest, 98, 108 (n. 46)
Kingdom, 109, 162, 221, 230
Kingship, 54 (n. 39); the will of Yahweh, 93, 96, 97; discredited, 109, 123, 188
Kinship of all life, 13, 15, 32, 34, 54 (n. 39)
Korah, 53

Laban, 57 (n. 51)
Land, Yahweh's, 33, 101 (n. 18), 117, 204
Lamp, 105, 190 (n. 15)
Language, Arabic 27, 28
Law, 5, 90, 154, 210; changeable, 264, 265; pre-Mosaic, 135; home born and foreigners, 16, 116, 117; inviolable, 237, 238; in heart, 164
Law Codes, ritual decalogue, 117; Covenant Code, 118, 118 (n. 10), 120; Deuteronomy, 135, 136, 141; Holiness Code, 183–186; Priest Code, 192–200
Laymen, 18, 121; see also Religion of
Legends, Canaanite adopted by Hebrews, 48, 79, 88
Legalism, 179 (n. 9), 183, 193, 203, 211, 237, 238, 239
Leprosy, 195
Levites, 51, 51 (n. 33), 137, 152, 153, 186, 188, 193, 194, 241; see also Priest
Liberalism, 210, 211, 215
Life, 33

Light, 105
Locusts, 9

Macaah, 115
Maccabeean, revolt and victory, 227, 246
Machir, 53, 69
Magic, 35, 36, 46, 48, 50, 81, 184, 194, 195, 196, 211; magic rod, 64; fire, 112 (n. 4); mantle, 113; word, 29; curse, 29, 36, 150, 156, 222; sympathetic, 37, 75, 156, 157
Malachi, 171
Mana, 30, 31, 56
Manasseh, 45, 104, 133, 139, 142, 145, 182
Manoah, 194
Marduk, 42, 55, 107
Mattan, 116
Marriage, 12 (n. 12), 20, 82, 88, 118, 139, 190, 208; dowry, 21; Levirate, 135 (n. 1)
Masada, 256
Matriarch, 12, 12 (n. 12)
Mazzoth, 138
Meal offering, 198
Mecca, pilgrimage, 21, 46; sacred stone, 65
Medes, 151, 152
Melchizedek, 79, 101
Memra, 191 (n. 19)
Menelaus, 224, 245
Mercy seat, 61, 197
Merneptah, 43, 45
Messiah, 96, 100, 194, 217, 221, 256
Messianism, 217, 219, 232
Mezuzah, 260
Micah, the Levite of Judah, 87
Micah, 121, 155, 160, 194
Micaiah ben Imlah, 114, 149
Midianites, 43, 49, 55
Milcom, 124
Minhah, 85 (n. 11)
Miriam, 20, 53
Mizpah, 93, 162
Moab, 53
Moloch, 32, 141
Mono-humanism, 213
Monotheism, 129, 168, 169, 169 (n. 1), 174, 178, 192, 225
Moses, 15, 43, 47–53, 64, 69, 70, 102, 128 (n. 7), 137, 139 (n. 6), 175, 190, 191, 196, 238
Mountain, sacred, 65
Mythology, appropriated by Hebrews, 79, 79 (n. 40), 88, 102, 106, 116, 173

Naaman, 101 (n. 18)
Naboth, 113, 114
Nahum, 151, 152, 221

Name, a reality, 29; the Name, 238; My Name's sake, 201

Nation, elect, 164; *see also* People

Nationalism, 140, 159, 163 (n. 15), 183, 217, 219, 266, 267; anti-, 214

Nazarenes (Christian), 255

Nazarite, 89, 113; vow of, 190 (n. 15)

Nebuchadnezzar, 148, 155–158, 175; servant of Yahweh, 161, 165

Necromancy, 160

Nehemiah, 189, 190

Nethinim, 241

New moon, 11, 102

Nicanor, 246

Ninevah, 151

Obadiah, 221

Obed-Edom, 87

Offering, fire, 197; guilt, 188; sin, 188; wave, 75

Oman, 17

Omri-Ahab, 110

Onias II, 224

Oracle, 57–59, 61, 90, 130

Overseers, 241

Pashur, 148, 151

Passover, 76, 102, 138, 141, 188, 197, 198 (n. 36)

Patriarch, 117, 194

Patriarchate, 12, 14

Pentateuch, 117 (n. 8), 261 (n. 80); *see also* Hexateuch

Persia, 158, 182, 190, 190 (n. 17), 218

Personality, 28, 170; corporate, 14

Phallic, 34

Phanuel, 226

Pharaoh Necho, 152, 155

Pharisees, 231, 248, 250, 251, 254, 255; crucified, 248

Philistines, 46, 72, 93, 94

Philosophy of history, Apocalyptists, 231; seminomads, 29, 30, 120, 185; prophets, 122, 126, 237; Deuteronomist, 129, 142, 167, 237; priests, 202–205, 237; wise men, 177, 181, 209, 216

Phineas, 47

Phoenicia, 102

Phylacteries, 153

Pilate, 254

Pithom, 44, 45

Plagues, 47, 50, 102, 196

Prediction, 130, 130 (n. 10), 157–159, 175, 176, 217, 218, 225; seventy years, 158, 159, 218, 225 (n. 18)

Priests, 106, 110, 120, 124, 125, 138, 182, 188, 194, 199–205, 235, 236, 238, 249

Priest Code, 24, 183, 190, 192, 193, 202, 204, 237, 238; *see also* Levite; Zadokite

Priest-king, 101

Priesthood, 3, 153, 191; divisions of, 193, 194; Aaron and Levi, 138, 188, 202; aristocratic, and wealthy, 224, 235, 236, 249

Prophets, guilds of, 124; false, nationalists, 125, 156, 159–161; true, 159, 160, 182; writing, 132

Prosbol of Hillel, 265

Proselytes, 262

Prostitution, 125, 136; *see also* Temple women

Queen of Heaven, 105 (n. 32), 163

Qos, 32

Raameses, 44, 45

Race, 7, 20, 202, 202 (n. 44), 211, 213, 266, 267

Rahab, 213

Raid, 17

Raphael, 226

Ras Shamra, 55, 74, 79 (n. 40), 90 (n. 18)

Rechab, 49

Red heifer, 34, 190 (n. 15)

Reform of Josiah, 133, 143, 152, 154

Religion, definitions, 1–6; fratricidal, 116, 243, 247, 248, 249, 254, 256; of Apocalyptists, 221, 222, 225, 226, 231; of Canaanites, 71–79; of dispersion, 258, 259, 260; of Egypt, 42, 47, 77 (*see also* Isis-Osiris); of Judaism, 5 (n. 13), 203, 243, 244, 255, 256, 268; personal, 127, 164, 165, 263, 264; of seminomads, 39, 74, 76, 109, 110, 113

Reuben, 17, 53, 59, 83

Reul, 49

Resurrection, 228, 229

Revelation, mediated through primitive methods, 5, 90 (n. 18), 129, 130, 131, dreams, etc., 90 (n. 18); priestly methods, 62, Urim and Thummim, 162, 163; reflection, 3, 6, 129, 148, 149, 158; social experience, 118, 127, 128; history, 127, 130; 220; trial and error, 3, 33, 67, 68, 231

Ritual, result of experiment, 3, 102; pre-Mosaic, 184; pagan, 124, 125; initiatory, 13 (n. 16), 14 (n. 19); Sinai, 57; cleansing, 195; way of salvation, 182, 183, 203; rejected, 128, 214

Roman rule, 233, 247, 251–254, 257, 267

Rosh Hashana, 76

Ruth, 213

Sabbath, 11, 188, 190, 198, 203, 223, 227, 238; law revised, 235; among dispersion, 227, 260

Sacred places, 37, 65, 153; *see also* Altar

Sacrifice, meaning, 85 (n. 11); Abel's, 86; child, 90, 125, 138; human, 21, 90; repudiated, 125; vicarious, 177; virginity, 78

Sadducees, 248, 249, 250, 255

Salome Alexandra, 248

Samaria, 110, 152

Samaritans, 212, 213, 254; schism, 239, 239 (n. 20)

Samuel, 93, 194

Sanballat, 212

Sanhedrin, 250, 262

Sargon, 101 (n. 18)

Satan, 173, 230

Saul, 13, 14, 16, 17, 94, 173

Saul (Paul), 255

Scapegoat, 199

Schools, Talmudic, 251, 262, 264, 266

Scribes, students, editors and interpreters of Scripture, 4–6, 144; harmonizers, 6, 178 (n. 8); Deuteronomic, 142, 143; Hellenic, 181, 210; priestly, 183, 190, 202, 210, 214, 217, 237, 238

Scythians, 146, 151

Second Commonwealth, 244, 247, 249, 250

Seminomads, 8, 9, 10, 24–27; ideal 29, 30

Sennacherib, 133, 135

Septuagint, 144, 145 (n. 3), 210, 220, 245 (n. 34)

Seraphim, 107

Serpent worship, 34, 64, 78; brazen serpent, 64, 104, 105

Shammai, 256 (n. 60), 262

Shaphan, 135

Sheba, 94 (n. 2)

Shema' Yisrael (Jewish creed), 260, 261

Sheol, 77, 228

Shiloh, 60, 61, 87, 154

Shimei, 94 (n. 2)

Shittim, 70, 81

Showbread, 104, 105 (n. 32)

Sicarii, 254, 256, 257

Simeon, 17, 53

Simon bar Giora, 256

Simon ben Shetach, 248

Sinai, 10 (n. 10), 45; alliance of, 53, 54, 69, 70; covenant of, 94

Sin offering, 197, 199

Sins of Israel, transferred, 199, 199 (n. 39)

Sins, unwitting, 193

Singers, 241

Skepticism, 157, 171

Skeptics, 148, 151, 209

Slavery, 18, 162, 165; law of, 135 (n. 1); 136

Social ethics, 21, 116, 117, 121, 122, 126, 128, 129, 149, 154, 169, 170, 184, 207

Social vices, 115, 125 (n. 4), 136, 207

Solidarity, 13, 14, 15

Solomon, 94, 95

Song of Songs, 208

Sorcery, 19, 90, 102, 138, 160; *see also* Witchcraft

Statistics, 24, 24 (n. 70 and 71)

Spirit world, 31, 32, 34, 103, 104, 105 (n. 32); evil spirits, 19, 39, 196, 200; the Spirit, 59, 223 (n. 12)

Stoicism, 209, 210

Strangers, 16, 18, 139; *see also* Foreigners

Suffering, 173, 174, 176, 177

Suffering servant, 174–177, 213

Sun worship, 30, 103, 141

Swines flesh, 34, 223

Synagogue service, 260, 261

Sumerian, 106

Tabbai Judah, 249

Taboo, 30, 36, 135 (n. 1), 138 (n. 4), 185, 193

Tammuz worship, 76, 77 (n. 28); *see also* Fertility cult

Tax on daily sacrifice, 234

Teacher, 131, 176, 179, 268; *see also* Education

Tell en-Nasbeh, 72 (n. 10), 74 (n. 20)

Tell er-Retabeh, 44

Temple, 74 (n. 19 and 20), 87, 95, 100, 154, 214, 236, 256; Assyrian and Babylonian, 107 (n. 41); Bethel, 101 (n. 19); Ezekiel, 186, 187; of Solomon, 101–104; dedication of, 108; second, 218, 242, 243; Heliopolis, 256; desecrated, 223, 224; restored, 245; destroyed, 248, 263

Temple tax, 190, 266

Temple women, 79; *see also* Prostitution

Tent of meeting, 59

Teraphim, 58, 130

Thaumaturgy, 37

Threshold, 103, 104

Tishbite, 111 (n. 2)

Tithing, 135

Titus, 256, 263

Tophet, 156, 157

Torah, 178, 179, 181, 191, 200, 203, 221, 268; meaning of, 203 (n. 45); Hellenized, 243, 244; cosmic principle, 244; changes possible, 268; eternal and final, 268; *see also* Law

Totemism, 31, 34

Tradition, 25, 196, 202, 217

Transjordania, 69

Tribes, pre-Mosaic, 9; kin to deity, 13; unstable, 17; twelve, 57, 139 (n. 6), 186, 202; law of, 16, 200

Troy, fall of, 41

Tyrian-Baalism, 111, 112, 114, 115

Universalism, 165, 210–216; see also Brotherhood

Uriah, 166

Urim and Thummim, 58, 130, 190 (n. 15), 194, 200

Usury, 16, 136, 139

Uzziah, 120

Vices, sexual, 78, 85, 89, 125, 136, 185

Virgin, 20, 136

Virgin birth, 4 (n. 11)

Vitellius, 253

Voice, 130, 132; inner, 147, 148; see also Bath Qol

War, atrocities, 83, 115, 116; values, 84; see also Yahweh

Water, holy, 106 (n. 39); of impurity, 190 (n. 15)

Wisdom, 5, 177–181, 209 (n. 2); hidden, 180; an efficient cause, 180, 181

Witchcraft, 35, 160; see also Sorcery

Woman, 19, 20, 207; rebuked, 122; rights of, 136

Word, an entity, 29, 238; magical, 29, 165; of God, 29, 153, 160, 163, 227, 264, 265; universal, 132; destructive, 167

Worship, 137, 184, 188, 205; ancestor, 34, 64; Assyrian, 134, 141; centralized, 135, 137; heavenly bodies, 30; detailed ritual, 241

Xerxes, 63

Yahweh, the name, origin and meaning, 54, 55, 56; tribal, 49, 50, 55; God of the fathers, 51, 54, 55 (n. 42), 118, 119; nomadic, 86; characteristics, 65–67; jealous, 68, 113, 114, 118, 134; chaste, 66, 89; just, 68, 126, 128; kindly, 66, 67, 127; human, 65, 66, 83, 113; evolving, 85–92, 126, 160, 161; personal relations, 58, 67, 68, 86, 156, 165; giver of grain and rain, 112, 114; Baalism conquered and absorbed, 85, 86, 87, 110, 118, 126; oracle giver, 16, 113, 136, 195, 203; reformer, 115, 116; war god, 63, 66, 82, 83, 89, 112–116, 129; God of heaven, 63, 129, 226; king of Israel, 221, 226; creator, 107; supreme, 123, 169; arbitrary, 66, 237, 238; universal, 169 (n. 2), the Absolute Other, 192, 201; the All, 244; democratic, 165; symbols of, 64, 83; day of, 22, 223, 228

Zadok, 188, 202

Zakkai, Rabbi ben, 257, 263

Zedekiah, 157

Zephaniah, 151

Zerubbabel, 175, 218, 219

Zeus, 56 (n. 46), 63

Zionism, 13

Zoan (Tanis), 44, 45

Zophar, 171

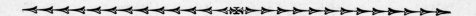

INDEX OF SCRIPTURE PASSAGES

Genesis

1:1–2:4a 215, 238
1:3 107
1:5 11
1:8 11
1:13 11
1:21 ....138 (n. 4)
1:24 ....138 (n. 4)
1:25 ....138 (n. 4)
1:26–28 192
1:27 75
1:28 19
2:2 238
2:3 ....259 (n. 73)
2:4a–4:26 117
2:5 ....112 (n. 3)
2:24 ....12 (n. 12)
3:1–24 78
3:1–8 173
3:1–5 78
3:6–8 19
3:8 11
3:9–21 192
3:24 107
4:3 ....75, 85 (n. 11)
4:5 75
4:9 14
4:10 39
4:14 49
4:16 49
4:22 49
4:26 54
5:2 75
6:1–11:9 117
6:2–4 ....32 (n. 97)
6:5 ....226 (n. 20)
6:18 201
8:22 ....226 (n. 20)
9:1–17 215
9:8–17 201
12:1–8 139
12:1–3 117
12:4–10 9
12:7 201
12:8 242

12:13–13:2 16
12:16 66
12:20 66
13:5–12 12
13:14–17 ....117, 139
14:6 71
14:14 ....12 (n. 15)
14:15 11
14:18 101
15:1–18 139
15:7 117
15:10 57
15:17 57
15:16 ....43 (n. 7)
15:18, 19 117
15:19 49
16:10 24
17:1–21 201
17:1–8 201
17:1 192
17:2 192
17:4–8 192
17:7, 8 ....201, 204
17:10–14 202
17:19 201
17:21 201
17:21 ....204, 211
18:4 11
19:2 11
19:33–38 89
20:11–16 16
20:12 ....12 (n. 12)
20:16 66
21:1–7 26
22:1–13 90
22:2 102
22:9 102
22:16–18 139
23:3 71
23:4–6 ....73 (n. 16)
23:5 71
23:9 ....73 (n. 16)
23:10 71
23:16 71
23:17–20 ....204, 211

23:18 71
23:19 204
23:20 71
24:1–10 164
24:2 34
24:5 ....12 (n. 12)
24:9 34
24:10 24
24:32 11
24:67 ....12 (n. 12)
25:9, 10 ....71, 204
25:9 ....73 (n. 16)
26:6 201
26:24 175
26:25 242
26:30 58
26:31 57
27:46–28:9 202
27:46 ....212, 15
28:3 192
28:4 ....201, 211
28:11–17 ....26, 130, 159
28:12 ....90 (n. 18)
28:13–15 130
28:17–19 65
28:18 74
29:11–14 164
29:21–30 ....203 (n. 44)
29:32–30:24 202
29:34 ....51 (n. 32)
30:3, 9 ....203 (n. 44)
30:30–43 ....16, 66
31:19 130
31:44–49 ....57 (n. 51)
32:13, 18 ....85 (n. 11)
32:22 11
32:24–32 .....90 (n. 18), 159
32:29 29
33:18–34:21 82
33:32 211
34:25–31 ....51 (n. 32)
34:31 ....125 (n. 4)
35:9–15 204
35:10–13 201
35:11 ....192, 201

35:18 202
35:23–27 202
37:5–7 159
37:5, 9 ....90 (n. 18)
37:25–36 43
37:25, 27 ....10 (n. 10),
                47 (n. 27)
37:28 ....47 (n. 27)
38:15–24 79
38:21, 22.......125 (n. 4)
39:1 ....10 (n. 10)
39:15 ....125 (n. 4)
40:5-20 159
40:8 ....90 (n. 18)
41:15–25 130
41:45 ......45, 203 (n. 44)
41:50–52 ...45, 203 (n. 44)
41:51, 52 47
42:5 43
42:6 ....47 (n. 27)
43:15 ......43, 47 (n. 27)
43:18, 25 .....47 (n. 27)
43:24 11
46:1–7 43
48:3 ....192, 201
48:4 ....201, 204, 211
48:14–22 45
49:24 106
49:29 ....71, 73 (n. 16)
49:30–32 204
49:32 71
50:24–26 63
50:30 ....73 (n. 16)
52:12 204

Exodus

1:3–10 24
1:6, 8 47
1:11 44
1:15–22 46
1:20 24
2:1 ....51 (n. 32)
2:10 50
2:15–22 49
2:15–17 45
2:15 ....47 (n. 27)
2:21 ......49, 202 (n. 44)
2:22 49
3:1 .....43 (n. 7), 45, 49, 52
3:2–12 159
3:2–5 49
3:2 ....37, 43 (n. 7), 52
3:3 ....43 (n. 7), 52
3:4 43
3:5 ....43 (n. 7)
3:6 ....43, 48

3:7, 8 ....43 (n. 7), 71
3:9–14 43
3:13–17 ......51, 54, 29
3:14 56
3:15 48
3:16–18 48
3:17 71
3:18 ....47, 76, 138
3:21, 22 66
4:2–6 64
4:2 50
4:14 45
4:18–20 49
4:24–26 ....49, 65, 43 (n. 7)
4:25, 26 201
4:27 ....47 (n. 27), 52
5:3 ....51, 138
5:7 ....44 (n. 12)
6:2–8 ....54, 201
6:3 192
6:4–8 200
6:9 48
6:11 ....43 (n. 7)
6:12 ....48, 43 (n. 7)
6:14–20 194
6:16, 18 ....43 (n. 7),
                51 (n. 32)
6:19 ..:...............47
6:20 ......43 (n. 7), 47, 51
           (n. 32), 202, 50, 55
6:23 202
6:26 11
6:27 ....43 (n. 7)
7:1 ....43, 48, 191
7:9 ....50 (n. 31), 64
7:10 48
7:12 ....50 (n. 31)
7:15 50
7:16 76
7:17 50
7:20 50
8:1–4 48
8:5 ....50 (n. 31)
8:7 ....43 (n. 7)
8:10–13 50
8:16 ....50 (n. 31)
8:18, 19 ......43 (n. 7)
9:8 48
9:11 ....43 (n. 7)
9:22 50
9:29, 33 50
10:4 202
10:12 ....48, 50
10:13 50
10:21 50
12:1–14 259

12:7 ....103, 197
12:13 ....103, 197
12:14–20 .....76, 198 (n. 56)
12:21–27 76
12:21–23 138
12:22 197
12:24 11
12:35, 36 66
12:37...24, 44, 46 (n. 21), 45
12:38 ....45, 51, 52
12:39, 42 51
12:48, 49 202
13:1, 2 90
13:4 54
13:17–22 9
13:17 ....46, 47
13:19 63
13:20 194
14:10 46
14:14–26 117
14:16 ....48, 50
14:21, 22, 26 48
15:1–18 ....66 (n. 70)
15:13 101
15:19–21 9
15:20 9
15:21..20, 51, 66 (n. 70), 83,
          94, 221, 242
16:3 ....138, 203 (n. 44)
16:23 238
16:33, 34 62
16:45 ....203 (n. 44)
17:5 50
17:6 ....50, 52
17:7 67
17:8–16 ......61 (n. 58), 66
17:8–12 50
17:10–12 46
18:5–12 52
18:5 50
18:11 ....49, 50
18:12 ....50, 58
18:15 ....43 (n. 7), 52
18:17–26 ....50, 57
18:24 52
19:1, 2a ....198 (n. 36)
19:3 51
19:6 ....119, 200
19:9–20 215
19:9 52
19:11, 12 ....51, 57
19:11b–14 56
19:14, 15 ....36, 57
19:16 ....56, 58
19:18 ....52, 56, 58
19:20 ....51, 52

19:21–24 56
19:21 51
19:23 52
19:33–36 215
20:2–17 ....128 (n. 7)
20:3, 5 91
20:6 29
20:8–11 ....198 (n. 38)
20:12 91
20:23–26 ......102, 124, 134
20:24 87
20:26 24
21:1–23:19..118 (n. 10), 135, 215
21:1–7 136
21:12–14 137
21:15 ....91 (n. 19)
21:24, 25 15
22:12 90
22:16, 17 89
22:18 ....130, 160
22:19 89
22:21, 22 90
22:25 ....90, 136
22:26 90
22:29 ....90, 194
22:31 119
23:10–19 ....124, 134
23:14–17 87
23:20–23 ....58, 67
24:1, 2 ....47, 57
24:3 68
24:6, 8 57
24:7 68
24:9, 10 ....57 (n. 47)
24:11 58
24:15 58
24:18 191
25:1–31:18 183
25:9 190
25:10 60
25:10–15 60
25:10, 11 ....191 (n. 20)
25:12 191
25:16 62
25:22 ....22, 192
25:31–40 105
25:40 190
26:30 190
27:20 105
27:21 ......105, 190 (n. 15)
28:2–5 194
28:6–43 195
28:30 ....190 (n. 15)
28:41 194
29:1–35 194

29:7, 8 194
29:38–42 198
29:41–46 ....191, 192
29:43–46 200
30:1–10 106
30:1–8 105
30:1–6 196
30:13 190
30:19 ....106, 138
30:30 194
30:34–37 196
31:14, 17 203
31:18 190
32:3–16 34
32:7–14 ....50, 65
32:12 15
32:17, 18 ....61, 58
32:30–33 50
33:7–11 ....51, 59
33:11 ....61, 58, 191
33:14–16 ....66, 67, 266
33:14 58
33:16 52
33:19 67
34:2–4 51
34:6 67
34:9 ....58, 67, 242
34:13 76
34:14–26 124
34:14–16 134
34:14 ....67, 91, 118
34:15, 16 ....118, 190
34:17 118
34:19 ....90, 118
34:20 118
34:22, 23 ....87, 118
34:25 ....89, 118
34:26 89
34:27–32 190
34:29–35 191
34:34 118
35:1–40:38 183
35:2 ....259 (n. 73)
37:1–9 ....61, 65
37:1–5 60
37:1 60
39:35 60
40:13–15 194
40:34 191

Leviticus

1:1–16:34 183
1:5 ....103, 197
1:8, 9 197
1:11 197
1:15 197

2:1, 2, 3 196
2:15, 16 196
3:2 ....104, 197
3:3–16 197
3:8 197
3:11 198
3:13 197
3:16 198
4:2 193
4:3, 5 ....195, 221
4:6, 7 197
4:9, 10 197
4:15 ....199 (n. 39)
4:16 ....194, 221
4:17, 18, 19 197
4:22 193
4:24 ....199 (n. 39)
4:25, 26 197
4:27 193
4:30, 31 197
4:34, 35 197
5:2–6 ....193, 195
5:5 184
5:9 197
5:14–17 203
5:15, 18 193
6:1–7 203
6:9 105
6:15 196
6:22 221
7:21 193
8:7–9 194
8:8 ....190 (n. 15)
8:22–24 197
8:25–29 197
8:30 197
9:6, 23 191
10:1–3 238
10:16–18 238
11:40 196
11:44 119
12:1–8 193
12:3 202
13:2–46 193
13:6 196
13:34 196
13:47–51 193
13:55, 58 196
14:1–7 195
14:7 ....199 (n. 39)
14:8, 9 196
14:32–38 193
14:34–57 193
14:47 196
14:49–57 195
15:2–12 193

15:5–27 196
15:16–27 193
15:18 36
16:2–28 199
16:2 ....108, 199, 200
16:3 185
16:4 ....195, 199
16:5–11 198
16:8 184
16:11–14 199
16:12, 13 199
16:13 200
16:14–19 197
16:14 199
16:15–19 188
16:15, 16 192
16:18, 19 199
16:20–22 ....184, 199
16:21 184
16:24–28 ....200 (n. 40)
16:24 185
16:29–31 198
17:1–26:46 ......153, 183
17:3–7 185
17:6 197
17:8 185
17:10–14 185
17:10 13
17:12, 13 39
17:15, 16 185
18:3 184
18:6–23 185
18:6–18 89
18:21–30 185
18:21 90
18:22 89
18:23 89
18:24 184
19:2 ....91 (n. 19), 184, 185
19:4 185
19:9–18 ....183, 184
19:9 75
19:12 185
19:18 ....184, 185
19:19, 20 185
19:23–25 185
19:26 ....185, 90, 130
19:30 ....185, 198
19:31 ....90, 130, 185
19:33–36 ....183, 184
20:1–5 185
20:2 90
20:3 ....90, 185
20:6 ....90, 130
20:7 185
20:9 ....91 (n. 19)

20:13, 16 185
20:17 89
20:18 185
20:22, 24 184
20:26 185
20:27 19
21:1–15 185
21:1–11 195
21:6 ....185, 198
21:8 198
21:10 194
21:12 185
21:17 198
21:23 185
22:2 185
22:3–9 185
22:6 185
22:14 193
22:18b–25 185
22:18, 21, 23 185
22:27–32 185
22:32 185
23:2, 4 ....198, (n. 36)
23:5–8 ....198 (n. 36)
23:10–13 185
23:10 184
23:15–21 ....198 (n. 36)
23:18 185
23:27–32 198
23:36 ....198 (n. 36)
23:37 ....185, 198 (n. 36)
23:38 185
24:1–4 105
24:7, 8 196
24:10–14 238
24:23 ....15, 238
25:2–7 185
25:2 184
25:4–7 201
25:10b–12 201
25:18–23 185
25:23–25 ....114 (n. 5)
25:23 201
26:3–13 185
26:9 185
26:14–39 185
26:34, 35 185
26:42–45 185
26:42 185
26:46 184
27:1–34 183

Numbers
1:45, 46 ....46 (n. 21)
3:5–10 ....51 (n. 33)
3:11–13..51 (n. 33), 90, 194

3:12 90
3:40 90
3:41, 45 ....51 (n. 33)
4:3 ....191 (n. 20)
4:5 60
5:7 184
5:11–31.....190 (n. 15), 203
6:2–11 ....190 (n. 15)
6:5 11
6:9–12 195
6:24–26 ....200, 261
7:89 ....60, 61
8:1–4 105
8:5–22 194
8:16, 17 194
8:17 90
8:24 ....191 (n. 20)
9:6–11 195
9:7–13 ....198 (n. 36)
10:29–32 ....49, 53
10:33 ....51, 60, 62, 83
10:35 ....67, 83
10:35, 36 ....51, 60, 62, 63
11:1–3 53
11:4 52
11:16 ....59, 250
11:17a 59
11:20 67
11:21 ....24, 46 (n. 21)
11:24b–30 59
12:1.....47, 53, 202 (n. 44)
12:2 53
12:6–8 ....53, 130
12:7 175
12:9 65
12:10 ....53, 65
12:11 53
12:14, 15 53
12:37 ....46 (n. 21)
12:38, 39, 42a .... 51 (n. 34)
13:8 ....61 (n. 58)
13:11, 12 66
13:28 ....46, 72 (n. 10)
13:29 71
13:30 53
13:31 46
14:2, 3, 4..........53
14:6, 7 ....61 (n. 58)
14:8, 9b.............53
14:10 191
14:11 67
14:12 65
14:14 62
14:20–23 66
14:30 ....61 (n. 58)
14:36, 37 238

14:38 ....61 (n. 58)
14:43–45 ....46, 53
15:24–31 193
15:32–36 ....193, 238
15:37–41 ......260 (n. 75)
16:1a 53
16:1b 53, 57
16:12–15 ....53, 57
16:16–24a 53
16:18–24 193
16:19 191
16:22 192
16:25 ....53, 57
16:26 57
16:27b–31 53
16:30 57
16:35 193
16:41–50 ....193, 196
16:41–45 238
16:42 191
18:1–7 193
19:1–26 195
19:1–22 ....190 (n. 15)
19:2–19 34
19:5 195
19:7 ....195, 196
19:8 196
19:9 195
19:11–14 193
19:17 195
19:19, 21 196
20:6 191
20:9–13 238
20:14–18 53
20:24 238
21:1–3 66
21:1 ....53, 204
21:2 ....16, 53
21:3 16
21:4–9 78
21:8, 9 ....34, 64, 105
21:14, 15 83
21:29 13
22:2–24 53
22:6 221
22:15 53
22:27 129
22:34 159
22:40–23:4 221
23:7–24 36
23:22 68
23:24 36
24:8 68
24:17 ....129, 256
24:22 49
25:1–5 ....9, 79, 81

25:1, 2, 3a, 3b, 4, 5 70
25:6–13 193
25:29 ....43 (n. 7)
26:50 55
26:51 ....46 (n. 21)
26:59 50
27:8–11 203
27:12–23 211
27:14 238
27:16 192
27:21 ....194, 200
28:2–8 198
28:3–8 198
28:7–11 198
28:16–25....198, 198 (n. 36)
28:23, 24 198
28:26, 27 .....198 (n. 36)
29:1–6 198
29:12–39 198
29:35 ....198 (n. 36)
31:15–18 203
31:21–24 195
32:1–5 53
32:34–38 53
33:5–37 ....52 (n. 35)
33:41–49 ....52 (n. 35)
34:1–12 204
34:16–27 204
35:9, 39 203
35:33, 34 193
36:1–12 203

Deuteronomy
1:8–4:44a 136
1:17 137
2:12 ....71, 72 (n. 10)
2:34 16
3:1–22 69
3:6 16
3:12–20 53
4:2 140
4:6–8 ....179 (n. 9)
4:9 140
4:19 ....130 (n. 9)
4:37 200
4:44b–10:22 136
5:9 14
5:12–16 ....198 (n. 38)
5:16–20 ....135 (n. 1)
5:16 91
6:4–9 ......260 (n. 75), 261
6:4 ....137, 142
6:5 ....138, 142
6:7 ....140, 261
6:8, 9 ....140, 153
6:20–23 140

7:1–4 190
7:1 139
7:2 ....85, 139, 16
7:3, 4 139
7:6 ....140, 200
7:16 139
9:10 62
10:1–6 51
10:3 60
10:4 62
10:8 60
10:15 200
10:17, 18 137
11:1 32
11:6 57
11:9 261
11:1–26:13, 28:1–69....135
11:1–17:20 135
11:13–21 ......260 (n. 75)
11:18–25 140
11:18 140
11:19 140
11:21–25 139
12:1–13 62
12:2, 3 138
12:3 76
12:5–14 137
12:5 ....135, 137
12:6 138
12:7 137
12:11 ....135, 237
12:12–14 137
12:12 ....137, 138
12:14 135
12:15, 16 137
12:17–19 137
12:18 ......137, 197 (n. 31)
12:19 138
12:21 137
12:23–25 ......197 (n. 31)
12:23 ....135 (n. 1)
12:31 90
12:32 ....141, 153, 183
13:5 139
13:6–11 139
13:10 15
13:12–18 139
14:1 ....138 (n. 4)
14:2 140
14:7, 8, 10........135 (n. 1)
14:12–17 ....135 (n. 1)
14:21 ....16, 139, 140
14:22 135
14:24–27 137
14:28 ....135, 139

14:29 139
15:3 16
15:7-11 136
15:8 136
15:12-18 ....135 (n. 1), 136
15:12-14 162
15:25 ....197 (n. 31)
16:1-17 137
16:1-8 102
16:2 135
16:3 138
16:4 138
16:5-17 137
16:5, 6 135
16:6 137
16:8, 9-11 135
16:11-16 237
16:11, 12 137
16:13-17 135
16:13-15 ......198 (n. 36)
16:18, 19 137
16:28 135
17:2-7 ....138, 139
17:5, 6 39
17:8-13 140
17:8-10 250
17:9 ....138, 188
17:14-20 142
17:18 ....138, 188
18:1-26:13, 28:1-69.....136
18:1-8 138
18:1-5 137
18:6-8 ....137, 138, 153
18:9-14.....62, 90, 138, 160
18:10, 11......19, 130 (n. 9)
18:15-19 140
19:1-18 137
19:1-13 ....135 (n. 1)
19:1-10 ....139 (n. 6)
19:16-21 139
19:16-19 250
20:7-9 137
20:14...........16, 18, 136
21:10-14....18, 85, 136, 139
21:10-13 16
21:18-21 139
21:21-23 85
22:5 ....138, 138 (n. 4)
22:9-11 ....138 (n. 4)
22:13-30 139
22:13-21 136
22:13-19 ....135 (n. 1)
22:22-30 136
23:2 136
23:3 139
23:7 ....139, 187

23:8 139
23:15, 16 ....136, 137
23:17, 18.....125 (n. 3), 136
23:18 79
23:19, 20 ....136, 139
24:1-5 136
24:8 ....138, 188
24:14, 15 136
24:16..14 (n. 20), 135 (n. 1),
                         136, 137
24:17, 18 137
24:19-22 136
24:19 75
25:1-3 137
25:5, 8 ....135 (n. 1)
25:17-19 139
26:3 ....203 (n. 44)
26:5 72
26:11, 12 137
26:17-19 ....57, 140
27:1-26 136
27:5 137
27:20-23 ....89, 136
27:26 140
27:29 188
28:1-6 140
28:1 141
28:2-14 141
28:4 136
28:7 152
28:9-13 140
28:12 ....112 (n. 3)
28:13 152
28:15-68 141
28:15-19 150
28:18 136
28:20-68 150
28:51 136
29:1-34:12 136
29:20, 21, 28......179 (n. 9)
30:11-14 140
31:9-24 135
31:9 ....60, 188
31:21 ....226 (n. 20)
31:25, 26 60
32:7 140
32:22 229
33:2-29 ....139 (n. 6)
33:2, 3 225

Joshua

1:12-18 69
2:1-12:24 ....61 (n. 58)
2:1-24 81
2:1-7 213
2:1 ....125 (n. 4)

3:3, 8 81
3:13-17 61
3:13 60
4:5 ....60, 61
4:7 83
4:9 61
4:10, 11, 16...........60
4:15-17 204
4:18 61
4:19 204
5:2, 3 ......201, 201 (n. 41)
5:10-12 204
5:13-15 83
5:15 101
6:7, 8, 11 83
6:17, 21 83
6:22, 23 85
6:26 103
7:2-8:29 82
7:24 24
7:25 ....14, 15
8:24 16
8:29 83
8:30 82
9:3-27 85
9:3-8 ....57, 213
9:3-5 82
9:11-15 57
9:24 83
10:20, 26 83
10:28 ....16, 83
10:30, 32, 35..........16
11:4 24
11:6-15 83
13:15-14:5 204
14:1, 2 130
14:6-15 53
15:1-13, 20-62 204
15:22 49
15:57 49
16:1 130
16:4-8 204
17:8-10 204
18:11-20 204
19:1-9 53
24:1-28 238
24:8, 18 71
24:32 63

Judges

1:5-7 85
1:16 ....49, 53
1:17 83
1:22-28 ....61 (n. 58)
1:25 83
2:2 85

3:12–17 ....81 (n. 1)
3:15 ....85 (n. 11)
3:16–26 82
3:17 ....85 (n. 11)
4:1–5:31 ....82, 84
4:11–17 49
4:11 49
4:17–20 19
4:17 ....12 (n. 12), 85
5:6 ....49, 84
5:7 ....21, 84
5:16 83
5:16, 17 ....93 (n. 1)
5:20 129
5:23......83, 93 (n. 1), 221
5:24–27 16
5:24 49
5:30 18
5:31 ....62, 221
6:1–5 ....81 (n. 1)
6:11–8:32 87
6:11–8:21 84
6:13 87
6:18 ....85 (n. 11)
6:20, 21 87
6:24, 26 87
6:25–27 88
6:26 ....76, 88
6:36 88
7:9–8:28 82
7:13 130
7:15–25 82
7:20............83, 88, 94
7:25 83
8:1 85
8:18, 19 85
8:21 83
8:22, 23 ....93 (n. 1)
8:29–32 ....82, 85
9:1, 2 85
9:4–6 ....12 (n. 14)
9:5 85
9:7–20 ....93 (n. 1)
9:20 ....29 (n. 89)
9:27 ....29 (n. 89), 87
9:36–40 85
9:42–49 82
9:44, 45 85
9:47–54 85
9:57 ....29 (n. 89)
10:3, 8, 9.............87
11:1–12:7 84
11:1–3 82
11:3 ....12 (n. 4)
11:24 68
11:30 194

11:31 ....90, 194
11:34 ....20, 87
11:39, 40 90
12:5, 8 ....81 (n. 1)
13:3–7 26
13:16–18 194
13:19, 23 87
13:25 223
14:1, 5 20
14:6 223
14:10 20
14:16 13
14:19.......12 (n. 12), 223
15:1, 2 ....12 (n. 12)
15:1 20
15:15 223
17:5 ....87, 241
17:6 84
17:7.........51 (n. 33), 194
17:9–13 241
17:10–13 ....51 (n. 33)
17:11 194
18:1 84
18:30 87
19:1 84
19:14 16
19:22–26 89
19:25 16
20:8–35 89
20:19–21 85
20:25–48 85
21:8–12 85
21:10–12 16
21:12–14 85
21:19–33 82
21:19–21 87
21:21 20
21:25 90

Ruth
4:8–22 ....202 (n. 44)

I Samuel
1:1–3:31 87
1:1–3 241
1:1 194
1:3–5 9
1:3 ....47, 60
1:7, 9 61
1:17 87
1:24 ....75, 87
2:7 87
2:11 60
2:13–15 61
2:17 60
2:18 194

2:22 ....125 (n. 4)
2:27, 28 ....51 (n. 33)
3:1–21 87
3:3–14 159
3:3..60, 62, 90 (n. 15, n. 18),
                        105
3:4.........90 (n. 18), 130
3:6 130
3:10.........90 (n. 18), 130
3:24 ....90 (n. 18)
4:3–5 83
4:3, 4 ....60, 61, 62
4:6–11 61
4:6 62
5:1–5 103
5:2–5 83
6:12 63
6:13, 14 87
8:1–22.......93 (n. 1), 123
8:4–9 93
8:5 97
8:19 93
8:20 ....93, 97
9:1–27 93
9:1–10:16 123
9:20 94
9:22–24 9
9:23, 24 197
9:25–27 93
10:1 ....96, 97
10:3 75
10:6.........96, 97, 98, 223
10:9–11 124
10:9 ....97, 98
10:10 223
10:17–27a.....93 (n. 1), 123
10:19–24 97
11:1–11 93
11:2 85
11:3 ....81 (n. 1)
11:5 87
11:6–11 97
11:9–11 ....81 (n. 1)
13:5 24
13:9 9
13:19–23 94
14:6 11
14:18 130
14:32–34 39
14:36, 37 130
14:40–42 130
15:2, 3 17
15:6 53
15:14–23 16
15:16 49
15:18–20 18

15:20, 22 90
15:32, 33 ....16, 85
15:33 ....83, 90
16:13 ....96, 97, 98
17:1–I Kings 2:9..240 (n. 23)
17:47 94
17:45 129
18:3, 4 ....13 (n. 16)
19:13 130
19:23 98
20:5, 6 102
20:6 ....9, 13
20:18, 24 102
20:27 13
20:29 9
20:31 123
21:2–5 87
21:5 104
21:6 ....75, 104
21:7 87
21:9 83
21:11 20
21:15–23 ....36 (n. 120)
22:2, 8 123
22:18 130
23:6, 9 130
24:6............96, 98, 217
24:10 ....98, 217
25:2, 3 22
25:13–38 22
26:9............96, 98, 217
26:11 217
26:16 ....98, 217
26:19...101, 101 (n. 18), 164
26:23 98
27:10 49
28:6,......130, 190 (n. 15)
28:7–14 19
28:7 90
28:9.........90, 130, 160
28:15 130
28:19 228
30:6 ....94 (n. 2)
30:7 130
30:14 53
30:29 49

II Samuel

1:14 ....98, 217
1:16 ....96, 98
2:29 11
3:1, 6 ....94 (n. 2)
3:36 94
5:19 130
5:21 83
5:24 129

6:11 108
6:12–19 ....61, 108
6:12 ....26, 87
6:13 87
6:14, 16 98
6:20 ....94 (n. 2)
7:2 ....242 (n. 26)
7:5–7 ....242 (n. 26)
7:6 61
7:8–17 217
7:11 13
7:14–17 100
7:14 ....97, 99
7:18–29 217
8:1–14 94
8:2, 6 ....85 (n. 11)
8:15–18 98
8:18 194
10:1–5 22
11:11 98
11:15 98
12:1–7 ....9 (n. 8)
12:7–12 ....94 (n. 2)
12:15–18 26
13:13 ....12 (n. 12)
13:37–39 ....12 (n. 14)
14:4–11 19
14:19 98
14:26 95
15:21 98
16:5–8 ....94 (n. 2)
17:13 87
19:21 217
19:22 98
20:1, 2 ....94 (n. 2)
20:4–6 98
20:16 19
21:1–6 ....14, 57, 98
21:7–9 90
24:1 230
24:12–15, 17 98
24:18 102
27:11 24

I Kings

2:26 145
2:27 ....145, 240
3:4–14 ....90 (n. 18)
3:5 130
4:2–19 ....95, 98
5:1–10:29 94
5:13–18 94
6:1–36 236
6:1–10 187
6:16 101
6:23–28 107

6:65 ....198 (n. 36)
7:1–8:9 ....102 (n. 25)
7:7–13 187
7:12 101
7:13–47 102
7:13–22 103
7:23–26 106
7:26 106
7:39b 106
7:40 105
7:48 104
7:50 101
8:4–6 62
8:4, 5 60
8:5–8 98
8:6–9 65
8:6 101
8:6, 7 ....63, 107
8:7 107
8:9 62
8:10 101
8:12b–14......101, 108, 242
8:12, 13 108
8:14 ....51 (n. 33)
8:22 ....98, 194
8:28–30 98
8:55 ....51 (n. 33), 194
8:62–66 101
9:17–19 95
9:20, 21 94
9:26–28 95
10:1–13 94
10:14–17 94
10:14, 23 95
10:28, 29 94
11:1–3 95
11:8 110
11:13 175
11:26–31 95
11:29–31 ....110, 123
11:32 175
11:40 95
12:1–15 109
12:16 109
12:28–33 110
12:28–30 106
12:28 34
12:28, 29 64
13:34 98
14:1 110
14:16 98
14:24.........79, 125 (n. 4)
14:25–28 110
14:25, 26 ....104, 115
15:12.........79, 125 (n. 4)
15:12, 13 115

15:15 115
15:18–20 113
15:26, 34 98
16:13, 16 98
16:32 113
16:34 103
17:1.........111 (n. 2), 113
17:5 113
17:14–16 113
17:21–24 113
18:1–5 111
18:2 98
18:8–12 124
18:10–12 113
18:17.....98, 111, 112 (n. 3)
18:19–24 ....112 (n. 4)
18:19 111
18:21 103
18:30–34 113
18:30 111
18:31, 36 114
18:44 ....112 (n. 3)
18:45 112
19:2 112
19:4–8 112
19:9–14 113
19:11, 12 112
19:14 112
19:15–17 ....112, 113
20:1–34 120
20:1–3 113
21:1–20 113
21:17 ....111 (n. 2)
22:6 ....111, 221
22:9–22 225
22:9 114
22:10–12 221
22:13, 14 114
22:17 114
22:19–25 ....123, 173
22:19–23 114
22:24 114
22:26–28 160
22:46.....79, 115, 125 (n. 4)

II Kings

1:1–4 113
1:8 113
1:10, 12......112 (n. 4), 113
2:1–25 127
2:2 113
2:3 ....111, 113
2:5 ....111, 113
2:7 111
2:8 ....113, 124
2:11 ....112 (n. 4)

2:12–15 124
2:13, 14 113
2:23 127
2:24 ....29, 127
3:27 80
4:1–6:22 127
4:13 13
5:6 98
5:17 ....101 (n. 18)
5:27 127
6:19 83
8:1–15 127
8:8–15 113
9:24, 27............83, 113
9:28 113
9:30–10:28 113
9:33 83
10:7, 11 83
10:13 115
10:14 ....83, 115
10:15 49
10:23–27 83
10:23 49
10:30 113
10:32, 33 120
11:1–3 116
11:4, 11 104
11:13–16 116
11:14 103
11:18 ....104, 116
12:46 116
12:9 104
13:14–21 127
13:15–19 ....90 (n. 18)
14:13, 14 104
14:26 120
15:17 101
16:3 90
16:10–19 124
16:10–18 104
16:10–16 102
16:10, 11 124
16:17 ....106 (n. 38)
17:17 90
17:21–23 98
18:4.....34, 64, 78, 104, 105
18:14–16 133
19:29–31 133
19:32–34 135
21:1–9 133
21:4, 5 104
21:6 90
21:16 133
21:18–26 145
21:19 133
21:23, 24 ....133, 139

22:1–24 136
22:3–19 135
22:4 104
22:15–20 135
23:1–3 141
23:3–25 152
23:3........103, 142, 150
23:4–20 138
23:4–14 141
23:4–12 104
23:4 124
23:5 ....124, 141
23:7 ....125 (n. 4)
23:9 ....138, 153
23:11, 12, 13.........124
23:15–20 141
23:19 125
23:20 141
23:21–23 ....102, 141
23:22 138
23:29 152
23:31–37 152
23:37 155
24:10–14 157
24:20–25:1 157
25:13, 16 ......106 (n. 38)
25:23–26 162
25:27–29 217

I Chronicles

1:1–29:30 ....240 (n. 23)
1:1–9:21 240
1:1–8:40 202
2:55 49
3:19 218
6:1–30 202
6:1–3 202
6:16–48 241
9:19, 21, 22, 24–27......241
9:28–32 241
15:16–24 241
15:16 241
16:8–36 242
17:11–14 217
17:16–27 217
21:1 230
23:1–26:32 ....188, 221
23:1–23 202
23:1–6 241
23:4 241
23:28–32 241
24:1–26:32 202
24:1–6 240
25:1–31 241
25:24–27 ....191 (n. 20)
26:1–19 241

26:20–32 241
28:5 99
28:9 ....226 (n. 20)
29:18 ....226 (n. 20)
29:20 99
29:23 99

II Chronicles
3:10–13 107
4:1–6 ....106 (n. 38)
4:1–5 106
4:5 106
4:7 105
4:10 106
6:41, 42 242
7:8, 9 ....198 (n. 36)
9:8 99
12:13, 14 240
13:11 105
13:22 237
15:3 237
16:8, 9 240
17:6–9 115
17:7–9 237
19:8–11 ....237, 250
19:8 250
19:9–11 115
20:23 115
24:7 237
24:18, 23–25 240
26:16–21 240
28:9–15 240
29:4–11 240
29:20–36 240
36:11–21 240
38:10–20 240

Ezra
1:2 192
2:36–39 241
2:40, 41 241
3:8........191 (n. 20), 218
3:10 218
5:1, 2 218
5:11, 12 192
6:9, 10 192
7:25 ....179 (n. 9)
8:2 241
10:1–44 ....211, 212
10:5–44 190
10:14–16 250
10:16 250
10:18–24 212
10:18–22 241

Nehemiah
1:1–5 189
1:5 192
1:11–2:1 258
2:1 54
2:4 192
2:6–15 189
2:10 212
4:14 192
6:15 189
7:1–4 ....189, 190
7:44 241
7:46 241
7:73–8:18 190
8:1, 3 190
8:8, 18 190
9:7, 8 201
9:8–10 261
9:32 192
10:2–31 240
10:13–35 250
10:31 ....259 (n. 73)
10:38 190
10:33–11:2 237
11:3 241
12:1–7, 12–21 240
12:16 218
13:1–3 213
13:4–31 189
13:8–14 237
13:15–22 ....198 (n. 38)
13:15–21 190
13:16, 19........259 (n. 73)
13:23–30 212
13:23 213
13:28 212

Job
1:1–2:13 173
1:1–5 173
1:6–12 ....225, 230
1:8 173
1:9–12 173
1:13–22 173
2:1–7 230
2:1–6 225
2:7–9 173
3:1–27:25 ....171 (n. 3)
3:1–26 ....172 (n. 4)
3:13–19 228
3:23 171
4:1–5:27 171
6:1–7:21 ....172 (n. 4)
7:9, 10 228
7:19, 20 171
8:1–22 171

Psalms (right column, under 9:1 etc.)
9:1–10:22 ....172 (n. 4)
9:17, 20, 21...........171
10:21, 22 228
11:1–20 171
12:1–14:22 ....172 (n. 4)
14:1–12, 21 228
15:1–15 171
15:2, 3 171
16:1–16 ....172 (n. 4)
16:18–22 172
16:18 39
17:13–16 228
18:1–21 171
19:1–29 ....172 (n. 4)
9:6–12 171
19:25–27 ....4 (n. 11)
19:25, 26 229
20:1–29 171
21:1–34 ....172 (n. 4)
21:26 228
22:1–30 171
23:1–24:25 .....172 (n. 4)
26:5–14 171
27:1–23 ....172 (n. 4)
28:1–37 178
28:1–27......171 (n. 3), 180
29:1–31:41 ....171 (n. 3)
29:1–31:40 ......172 (n. 4)
31:1–40 171
32:1–37:14 ....171 (n. 3)
38:1–42:6 ....171 (n. 3)
38:1–39:30 172
38:39–39:30 172
40:3–5 172
40:8 172
42:1–6 172
42:7–17 173
42:7, 8 174
42:10–17 174

Psalms
1:1–6 214
2:2 220
2:7 ....97, 99
19:1–6 210
19:7–14 214
24:1–10 242
24:7–10 ....54 (n. 39)
24:7, 8 63
42:1–49:20 242
45:1–17 208
47:1–8 ....54 (n. 39)
48:1–14 242
49:15 229
50:1–23 ....242 (n. 27)
68:24–26 ....54 (n. 39)

73:1–83:18 .....242 (n. 27)
73:24, 25 229
74:12–17 ....54 (n. 39)
81:1–16 242
82:1–8 242
84:9 221
89:26 97
92:1–15 242
93:1–5 242
94:1–23 242
113:1–118:29 259
119:1–176 214
120:1–134:3 259
132:2, 5 106
137:9 221
138:2 101

Proverbs
1:1–9:18 179
1:2–23 179
1:7, 29 ......180 (n. 11)
2:5 ....180 (n. 11)
3:19, 20 179
4:1–8 179
7:1, 2 210
7:5–27 207
8:1–9:6 .....178, 179, 180
9:10 ....180 (n. 11)
10:1 207
12:4, 7 207
13:1, 22 207
14:1 207
15:5, 20 207
18:22 207
19:13, 14, 26.........207
23:22 207
31:10–31 ....207, 210

Ecclesiastes
1:8, 13, 14...........209
2:11, 17, 20, 22, 24....209
3:1–8 209
3:12, 13, 22..........209
5:7, 8 209
5:17–19 209
6:8 209
7:23 209
8:6–8 209
8:10, 14, 15..........209
9:3–6 228
9:7–10 209
10:16–20 209
12:1 209

Song of Solomon
1:1–8:14 208–210

Isaiah
1:6 126
1:7–9 133
1:11–17 125
1:17 131
1:24 106
2:6 160
2:12, 19 222
3:16, 17 122
5:21 182
6:1–12a 131, 147
6:1–3 129
6:3 225
6:5 126
7:13–17 130
7:13–15 123
7:14 ....4 (n. 11)
7:18 130
7:20–25 133
7:25 162
8:6 126
8:16 132
8:19 130
9:5–7 219
9:6, 7 ....100, 123
9:13 126
9:15, 16 124
10:14–34 236
11:1–5 ....100, 219
11:1–6 123
13:1–19:17 .....222 (n. 10)
14:4–20 228
17:22 221
19:24, 25 214
22:2 11
24:1–27:13 223
24:21–23 226
25:6–8 223
26:19 229
26:20–27:1 223
27:12, 13 223
28:7 124
28:24–29 ....138 (n. 4)
30:21 131
34:1–35:10 .....214 (n. 6)
35:2–6 221
37:33–35 154
40:1–66:24 .....214 (n. 6)
40:1–4 170
40:1–55:13.....169, 174, 175
40:12–17 169
40:18–20 169
40:28 169
41:2 169
41:2, 3 170
41:8 175

41:9 175
42:1–4....174, 175, 176, 266
42:19, 20, 22..........175
43:10–13 201
44:2 175
44:6 170
44:12–20 169
44:21 175
44:26–28 170
44:28–45:4 218
44:28 169
45:1–6 175
45:4 175
45:5 201
45:7 ....192, 201
45:22 201
46:1, 2 170
46:12–47:7 170
47:4 129
47:7 170
47:13 129
48:1 175
48:2 129
48:20 175
49:1–6 ....174, 176
49:5 ....213, 266
49:6 ....177, 266
49:23 170
49:26 106
50:4–9 ....174, 176
52:13–53:12...174, 175, 176, 177
54:5 129
56:1–66:24 .....222 (n. 10)
56:1–8 213
60:4–22 211
60:16 106
61:8 228
61:15 129
62:1–12 211
65:11 ....105 (n. 32)
65:17, 25 228
66:1–5 214
66:20 101
66:21 214
66:22 228
66:24 229

Jeremiah
1:1–9:25 144
1:1 144
1:4–9 147
1:6 147
1:9..........147, 157, 160
1:11–15 146
1:11, 13 ....147, 148

1:14, 15 148
1:16 ....146 (n. 6)
1:18, 19 164
1:19 149
2:1–3 148
2:5 ....146, 147
2:6 ....146, 148
2:7 148
2:8 ....146 (n. 6)
2:11 149
2:13.........145, 146, 165
2:14 149
2:18, 20 148
2:20, 23 ....146 (n. 6)
2:23 147
2:24 ....145, 149
2:27 ....146 (n. 6)
2:28 ....146 (n. 6), 156
2:32 145
2:35 147
2:36 148
2:37 13
3:2, 3 ....146 (n. 6)
3:9 148
3:16 61
4:2 ....146 (n. 6), 165
4:3, 4 149
4:5–9 146
4:5–8...146 (n. 7), 148, 222
4:11 145
4:13.........146 (n. 7), 222
4:18 146
4:19–21 ....146 (n. 7)
4:19 222
4:20, 22 146
4:23–29 145
4:26 222
4:29 ......146 (n. 7), 222
4:31 ....166, 222
5:1–5 147
5:1, 4 146
5:2 165
5:8 ....145, 149
5:11, 12 147
5:15–17..146 (n. 7), 148, 222
5:21, 23 149
5:25–30 ....146, 148
5:25 148
5:26–30 149
5:30, 31 147
6:1–6 ....146 (n. 7)
6:7 ....147, 148
6:11 147
6:13, 14 147
6:15–17 222
6:16 149

6:18 149
6:20 ....105, 149
6:22–26 ......146 (n. 7), 222
7:1–8:9 153
7:2, 3, 4 ....154, 164
7:9, 10, 11 154
7:12–15 ......148, 154, 164
7:16 166
7:21–24 154
7:22–25 148
7:23, 24 154
7:32, 33 154
8:8–10 154
8:8.....154 (n. 12), 164, 182
8:9 165
8:10 221
8:11 182
8:14–9:1 145
8:18–22 166
8:21, 22 166
9:1, 2 166
9:11 162
10:6–8 ....145 (n. 3)
10:10 165
10:19, 20 166
10:22 162
11:1–12:16 144
11:1, 6 150
11:12 148
11:14 166
11:18, 19 150
11:20–23 150
11:20 165
11:22 148
12:1–3 150
12:1 ....147, 151
12:3 166
12:5 151
12:15 165
13:1–27 144
13:1–11 156
14:1–17:18 144
14:8, 9 165
14:11–13 166
14:14 159
14:20, 21 166
15:1 166
15:5–9 145
15:10 157
15:15 ....148, 166
15:17 165
15:18 ....165, 166
15:19, 20 164
16:14 68
17:9 165
17:10 ....164, 165

17:13 165
17:14–17 157
17:18 ....148, 166
17:22–27 ......198 (n. 38)
18:1–20:18 144
18:1–12 156
18.2 148
18:5–10 160
18:9, 10 165
18:19 148
18:20 147
18:21–23 166
19:1–13 156
19:10–15 157
20:1–6 ....148, 157
20:7–12 157
20:7 ....147, 165
20:8 165
20:11 148
20:12 ....165, 166
20:17 147
20:19 160
22:1–19 144
22:13–19 155
22:15–17 148
22:15, 16 165
22:18 77
22:24–30 148
22:24 218
23:5 ....100, 218
23:5, 6 219
23:7, 8 165
23:9–22 144
23:9 ....160, 166
23:10 ....144, 161
23:14–40 124
23:16 ....159, 161
23:17 ....161, 221
23:18–23 161
23:18 160
23:21–23 160
23:21, 22 160
23:22 161
23:23 165
23:25, 26 161
23:26–28 160
23:29 161
23:30 160
23:31, 32 161
23:32, 33 160
23:36, 39, 40 161
24:1–10 163
24:1–3 ....148, 161
25:1–14 144
25:9 ....161, 175
25:11–14 158

25:12–14 218
25:29 148
26:1–24 153
26:2 154
26:7, 8 155
26:8, 9 154
26:10, 16 155
26:12–15 155
26:17–19 155
26:22, 23 121
26:24 155
27:1–29:32 144
27:1–11 156
27:2–10 157
27:3 157
27:6 ....161, 175
27:7–11 218
27:7....158, 159, 225 (n. 18)
27:9 159
27:12 157
27:13 158
27:14, 15 221
27:18 158
28:1–17 148
28:1–4 217
28:2–11 218
28:2–4 158
28:3, 4 221
28:6, 8, 9, 10..........158
28:11 ....158, 221
28:14 158
29:1–14 163
29:1–7 ....225 (n. 18)
29:4–10 158
29:5–7 266
29:8 159
29:10...158, 159, 225 (n. 18)
29:12–14 266
29:14....145 (n. 3), 165
29:21–32 148
29:26 157
30:1–31:40 144
30:9 100
30:10 175
30:10–12 ....145 (n. 3)
31:2–6 220
31:16–22 220
31:30 164
31:31–34 ....161, 164
31:31, 33 165
31:34 164
32:6–15 162
32:11–15 162
32:16, 24, 25..........162
32:36–44 162
33:14–26 220

34:8–10 162
34:11–16 162
34:17–22 162
34:18, 19 57
35:14–26 ....145 (n. 3)
36:1–31 144
36:5 155
36:9–26 156
36:9, 10 156
36:22–25 144
36:29–31 ....148, 156
36:30 155
36:32 144
37:5–10 148
37:5 162
37:7–11 ....162 (n. 13)
37:11 162
37:13 156
38:2 156
38:3–13 162
38:17 156
39:4–13 ....145 (n. 3)
39:15–18 165
40:1–49:39 144
40:1–4 163
40:4 156
40:5, 6 163
41:1–11 162
42:1–17 156
42:7–22 163
43:1–7 163
43:10 161
44:15–19 163
44:19 ....105 (n. 32)
44:20–23 163
44:24, 25 163
45.4 165
46:1–51:58 .....222 (n. 10)
46:15, 18 221
46:18 226
46:27, 28 175
48:15 226
50:1–52:34 144
51:57 221
51:59 158
52:28–30 162
52:28–33 ....145 (n. 3)

Lamentation
4:8–10 ....161, 162

Ezekiel
1:5–25 107
1:22–25 108
2:3–5, 7 167
3:1–3 167

3:10 219
3:11 167
3:16–21 164
3:16–19 167
3:19 167
4:1, 2, 9, 11...........167
5:1–3 167
6:1–5 167
6:10–14 ....219 (n. 3)
8:1 105
8:14 77
8:23 219
10:1–22 107
11:2–6 167
11:2, 3 167
11:14–16 167
12:1–11 167
12:18–11 167
12:21–23 167
12:26–28 168
13:1–5, 17–19 167
14:1–3, 6 167
14:9 220
14:12, 13 167
14:16, 17 220
15:1–5 167
16:30–34 79
17:22–24 217
18:1–4 167
20:9, 14, 22...........201
21:1–3, 5–7, 9–11.......167
21:21 130
21:24, 25 167
21:27 217
22:1–4 167
22:23, 24 167
23:1–3, 5 167
24:1–5, 9, 10..........167
25:1–32:32 ......222 (n. 10)
28:25 175
32:10 167
32:23 224
33:7–9 167
33:10–20 164
34:1–10 221
34:1, 2 167
34:11–16 ....200, 221
34:23–25 220
34:23 ....100, 221
34:24 221
34:25–30 200
36:18 167
36:21–25 201
37:24 100
37:25 175
39:7 201

40:1–48:35....183, 186, 188, 189, 192
40:2–4 189
40:5, 6, 10............187
40:21, 22 187
40:31–34 187
40:37 187
40:45, 46 188
40:47 187
41:2–4 187
41:4 187
42:13, 14 ....188 (n. 12)
43:7–9 187
43:12 187
43:13–27 187
43:40–49 187
44:7–9 187
44:15, 16 188
44:23–27 188
44:27, 28 187
44:29 188
45:7, 8 ....186, 188
45:17 ....186, 187, 188
45:18 188
45:19 187
45:21–25....188, 198 (n. 36)
45:23 187
46:1–11 188
46:2, 8, 12–18.........186
46:20 188
46:21–24 ....188 (n. 12)
48:1–35 211
48:1–7 186
48:8–22 186
48:9, 10 187
48:11 188
48:13 186
48:18, 19 187
48:21, 22, 23–28.......186
48:30–34 187
48:34 189

Daniel
1:7 257
2:2, 25–45......90 (n. 18)
2:31–45 ....226, 227
2:38 130
2:44 228
2:47 129
4:4–27 ....90 (n. 18)
6:10 261
7:1–11:45 226
7:1 130
7:9–11 227
7:13, 14, 27..........227
7:22 228

7:25 ....225 (n. 18)
8:14 225
9:12 ....225 (n. 18)
9:24 ....101, 225 (n. 18)
9:25–27 ......225 (n. 18)
10:13, 20, 21..........226
12:1–13 226
12:2 ....226, 229
12:11, 12, 13..........225

Hosea
1:4 127
2:4 ....128 (n. 7)
2:8 127
2:10 ....112 (n. 3)
4:2 128
4:6 131
4:14.........79, 125 (n. 4)
4:29 126
5:1 121
6:5 121
6:6 125
7:3–7 123
7:4 126
8:4 123
11:1–4, 8 127
12:10 68
13:4 68
13:10, 11 123
14:2 260

Joel
1:15 228
2:1 ....223, 228
2:10–12 223
2:10 129
2:16 223
2:28–32.....223, 223 (n. 13)
2:30, 31 129
3:1–3 223
3:9–17 223
3:16 223
3:17 101

Amos
1:2 222
1:3–10 221
1:9 57
1:11 13
1:13–15 221
2:6–16 221
2:6, 8 222
2:7.........79, 125 (n. 4)
2:10 68
2:12, 13 121
3:9, 12 222

4:1–3 122
4:6, 9 126
4:13 129
5:10 ....121, 122
5:10, 13 222
5:21–25 125
5:27 129
6:1–8 ....123, 222
7:1–9 ....130, 131, 126
7:10, 11 ....121, 123
7:12 124
7:12 102
7:13 ......101 (n. 19), 102
7:14–17 130
7:14, 15 121
7:16, 17 121
8:4–10 130
8:4–6 126
8:9 129
8:10 77
9:7, 8a..68, 129, 201, 213, 221
9:8b 129

Jonah
4:11 213

Micah
1:5 126
1:7 125
2:13 221
3:5–8 124
3:5, 7 131
3:6, 7 160
3:8 ....131, 132
3:9–12 121
3:11 125
3:12 ....133, 155
4:7 221
5:12 160
6:7 90
6:8 128
7:10–17 121

Nahum
2:3–3:9 221
2:3–3:19 152

Habakkuk
2:1 158
3:17, 18 170

Zephaniah
1:7–18 222
1:9 103
1:12 ....151, 171
3:15–17 221
3:15 226

Haggai

1:1–2:23 218
2:2–23 183
2:2–4 186
2:9, 18 218
2:23 ....175, 218

Zechariah

1:1–8:23 218
1:12........218, 225 (n. 18)
2:3–5 219
2:12 101
3:1, 2 230
3:8 ....186, 218, 219
4:6–10 ....100, 183
4:6 218
4:7–10 ....218, 219
5:5–11 ....199 (n. 39)
6:10–14 219
6:12 ....186, 218
6:12, 15 219
8:3–5 100
8:48 219
10:2 130
12:10 77
14:9–17 221
14:9–11, 16, 17........226

Malachi

1:8 171
1:10–14 213

Apochrypha and Pseudepigrapha

Tobit

3:8, 17 226
3:11–13 261
6:1–7 196
6:15–16 226
8:1–3 196
8:3 226
12:15 226

Wisdom of Solomon

2:24 78
6:12–15 180
7:1–8:36 178
7:1–8:31 180
7:15–21 180
7:22–24 181
7:22–26 180
8:1, 7, 17 180
9:4 180
12:18 180

13:1 180
15:1 181
18:21 196

Psalms of Solomon

17:36 220
18:6, 8 220

Ben Sirach (Ecclesiasticus)

1:1–26, 27 224
1:1–20 243
1:4–26 179
1:18–21 243
1:26–30 243
3:21–24 243
4:11–23 243
7:13 243
9:2–9 243
11:21–12:7 243
13:1–26 243
14:16 228
14:20–15:10 243
17:17 243
17:22, 27 228
19:20–23 243
22:11 228
24:1–34 ....5, 178, 179, 191, 243
24:1–8 243
24:12 243
31:1–31 243
32:3–6 243
32:24–33:3 243
35:1–20 ....215 (n. 9)
35:1–11 244
36:1–17 ....243, 244
36:12 243
37:25 243
38:24–39:11 243
38:24–44 ....178 (n. 8)
38:24–29 237
39:1–35 ....178 (n. 8)
39:1–11, 14, 15........243
41:17–24 243
42:4–8 237
42:12–14 243
43:27 244
45:1–22, 25 243
46:19 228
50:1–21 243
50:1–20 194
50:5–7, 8–12 195
50:16–21 243
50:16–18 242
51:13–30 243

Baruch and Epistle of Jeremy

6:43........196, 225 (n. 18)

I Maccabees

1:20–46 227
1:21, 22 106
1:21 105
1:41–64 224
1:52 227
2:1–28 227
2:2–38 227
2:23 227
2:32–38 203
2:39–41, 42–44 227
2:45, 46, 48 227
2:50–64 228
3:1–4:35 227
4:36–61 227
4:49 105
4:50 106
7:5–9 227
7:10–16 228
7:13–16 246
7:13, 14 231
7:16–20 246
7:18–20 246
7:21–25 246
7:21–24, 33 227
7:26–50 246
8:17–32 247
8:21–25 246
9:1–14:22 247
9:1 246
9:7–31 247
10:22–45 247
12:1–23 247
13:41–53 247
14:3 246
14:14–25 246
14:14, 15 247
14:16–24 247
14:27–49 247
16:11–18 247

II Maccabees

1:18–36 105
1:19–36 ....112 (n. 4)
3:11–13 236
4:7–22 245
4:39–42 245
5:5–10 245
6:1 248
6:18–31 228
7:1–42 228
11:28–33 246

12:15–13:21 246
13:33 246
14:36–46 228

IV Maccabees

IV 180

Enoch

6:2 226
14:18 230
40:9, 10 226
45:5 228
58:3 228
62:16 228
69:2 226
71:8, 9 226
89:59–90:19 .... 225 (n. 18)
90:20–25 225

Enoch (Ethiopic)

6:1–7:6 230
10:13 229
14:15–24 230
18:11 229
22:2–13 229
27:1, 2 229
38:3, 5, 6 230
39:1–41:2 230
40:7, 10 230
45:5, 6 230
53:5 230

54:5, 6 230
56:1–3 230
62:11, 12 230
64:1, 2 230

Jubilees

2:26–31 .... 259 (n. 73)
50:6–13 .... 259 (n. 73)

Testaments of XII Patriarchs

Jude

25:1 226

Benjamin

6:4 ....226 (n. 20)

Asher

1:2–6, 8:19 .....226 (n. 20)

Levi

2:7–3:3 229
3:3, 18:12 226
19:1 226

New Testament
Matthew

4:8, 9 226
13:38, 39 225

John

1:1, 3, 4, 14...........180
8:7 15
12:31 225
13:2–10 11
14:30 225

Acts

15:8 59

Romans

1:18–20 165

Ephesians

2:2 226

Philippians

4:7 11

Hebrews

1:2, 3 180

Revelation

11:19 62
12:13 226
13:2 226
20:2, 3, 10 230
21:1–22:5 226
21:2 187
21:2, 18, 21 100